The Berkshire Hills & Pioneer Valley of Western Massachusetts

The Berkshire Hills
& Pioneer Valley
of Western
Massachusetts

Christina Tree & William Davis

*Principal photography
by the authors and Kim Grant*

The Countryman Press ✳ Woodstock, Vermont

SECOND EDITION

DEDICATION

To our family: Liam, Topher, Tim, Yuko, Aki, and Taiga

We welcome your comments and suggestions. Please contact Explorer's Guide Editor, The Countryman Press, P.O. Box 748, Woodstock, VT 05091, or e-mail countrymanpress@wwnorton.com.

ISSN: 1547-2205
ISBN: 978-0-88150-773-7

Cover and interior design by Bodenweber Design
Composition by PerfecType, Nashville, TN
Cover photograph of the Bridge of Flowers in Shelburne Falls, MA, by Matthew Cavanaugh courtesy of the Shelburne Falls Area Business Association, www.shelburnefalls.com.

Maps by Mapping Specialists Ltd., Madison, WI, © The Countryman Press

Published by The Countryman Press, P.O. Box 748, Woodstock, Vermont 05091

Distributed by W. W. Norton & Company, Inc., 500 Fifth Avenue, New York, NY 10110

Printed in the United States of America

10 9 8 7 6 5 4 3 2 1

EXPLORE WITH US!

Welcome to the Berkshire Hills and Pioneer Valley of Western Massachusetts. In writing this guide, we have been increasingly selective in making recommendations based on years of conscientious research and personal experience. What makes us unique is that we describe the state by locally defined regions, giving you Western Massachusetts's communities, not simply its most popular destinations. With this guide you'll feel confident to venture beyond the tourist towns, along roads less traveled, to places of special hospitality and charm.

WHAT'S WHERE

In the beginning of the book you'll find an alphabetical listing of special highlights, with important information and advice on everything from antiques to weather reports.

LODGING

Prices: Please don't hold us or the respective innkeepers responsible for the rates listed as of press time in 2007. Some changes are inevitable. Massachusetts has a statewide 5.7 percent lodging and meals tax. Communities also have the option of levying an additional local tax of up to 4 percent, and most resort towns opt for the full amount.

Smoking: Massachusetts enforces a statewide ban on smoking in restaurants, bars, and nightclubs.

RESTAURANTS

Note the distinction between *Dining Out* and *Eating Out*. By their nature, restaurants listed in the *Eating Out* group are generally inexpensive.

KEY TO SYMBOLS

- ⚭ The wedding-rings symbol appears beside facilities that frequently serve as venues for weddings and civil unions.
- ♞ The special-value symbol appears next to lodgings and restaurants that combine high quality and moderate prices.
- ✎ The kids-alert symbol appears next to lodgings, restaurants, activities, and shops of special appeal to youngsters.
- 🐾 The dog-paw symbol appears next to lodgings that accept pets (usually with a reservation and deposit) as of press time.
- ♿ The wheelchair symbol appears next to lodging, restaurants, and attractions that are partially or fully handicapped-accessible.

We would appreciate your comments and corrections about places you visit or know well in the state. Please use the card enclosed in this book, or e-mail us directly: ctree@traveltree.net or bill@davistravels.com.

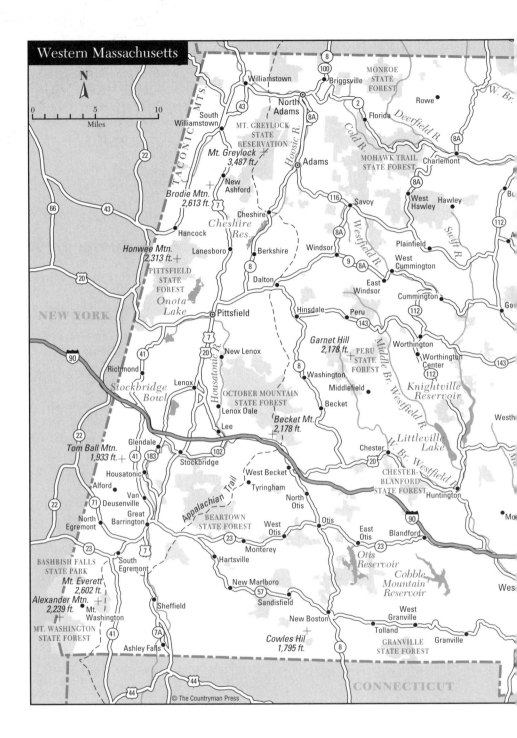

Western Massachusetts

N

0   5   10
Miles

Williamstown

Briggsville

MONROE
STATE
FOREST

Rowe

North
Adams

South
Williamstown

Florida

Deerfield R.

W. Br.

MT. GREYLOCK
STATE
RESERVATION

Adams

MOHAWK TRAIL
STATE FOREST

Charlemont

Mt. Greylock
3,487 ft.

Savoy

West
Hawley

Hawley

Bu

New
Ashford

Brodie Mtn.
2,613 ft.

Cheshire

Cheshire
Res.

Plainfield

Swift R.

Hancock

Honwee Mtn.
2,313 ft.

Lanesboro

Berkshire

Windsor

West
Cummington

PITTSFIELD
STATE
FOREST

Dalton

East
Windsor

Cummington

Go

Onota
Lake

Pittsfield

Hinsdale

Peru

NEW YORK

New Lenox

Garnet Hill
2,178 ft.

PERU
STATE
FOREST

Worthington

Worthington
Center

Richmond

Lenox

Washington

Middlefield

Knightville
Reservoir

Westh

Stockbridge
Bowl

Housatonic R.

OCTOBER MOUNTAIN
STATE FOREST

Becket

Lenox Dale

Lee

Becket Mt.
2,178 ft.

Littleville
Lake

Tom Ball Mtn.
1,933 ft.

Glendale

Chester

W. Br. Westfield R.

Stockbridge

West Becket

CHESTER-
BLANFORD
STATE FOREST

Housatonic

Tyringham

Huntington

Alford

Van
Deusenville

North
Otis

North
Egremont

Great
Barrington

BEARTOWN
STATE FOREST

West
Otis

Otis

East
Otis

Blandford

Monterey

Otis
Reservoir

BASHBISH FALLS
STATE PARK

South
Egremont

Hartsville

Cobble
Mountain
Reservoir

Wes

Mt. Everett
2,602 ft.

Alexander Mtn.
2,239 ft.

New Marlboro

Sandisfield

West
Granville

Mt.
Washington

Sheffield

New Boston

Tolland

Granville

MT. WASHINGTON
STATE FOREST

Ashley Falls

Cowles Hil
1,795 ft.

GRANVILLE
STATE FOREST

CONNECTICUT

© The Countryman Press

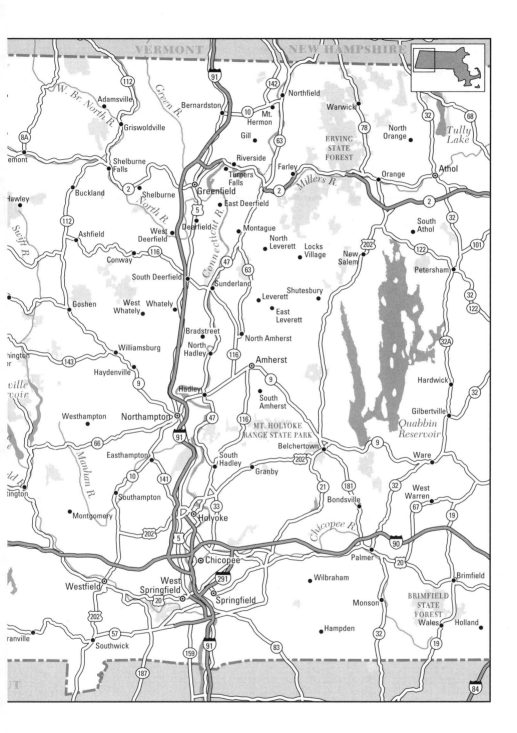

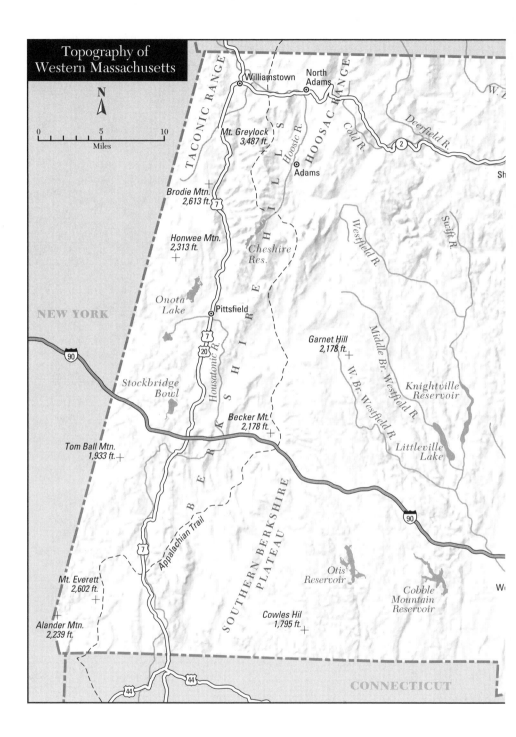

Topography of
Western Massachusetts

N

0   5   10
Miles

TACONIC RANGE

Williamstown   North Adams

Mt. Greylock
3,487 ft.

HOOSAC HILLS

Hoosic R.

HOOSAC RANGE

Cold R.

Deerfield R.

W. Z

2

Sh

Brodie Mtn.
2,613 ft.   7

Adams

Honwee Mtn.
2,313 ft.

Cheshire
Res.

Westfield R.

Swift R.

Onota
Lake   Pittsfield

NEW YORK

90

7

20

Housatonic R.

Garnet Hill
2,178 ft.

Middle Br. Westfield R.

W. Br. Westfield R.

Knightville
Reservoir

Stockbridge
Bowl

BERKSHIRE

Littleville
Lake

Becker Mt.
2,178 ft.

Tom Ball Mtn.
1,933 ft.

Appalachian Trail

90

SOUTHERN BERKSHIRE PLATEAU

Otis
Reservoir

Cobble
Mountain
Reservoir

W

Mt. Everett
2,602 ft.

7

Cowles Hil
1,795 ft.

Alander Mtn.
2,239 ft.

44   44

CONNECTICUT

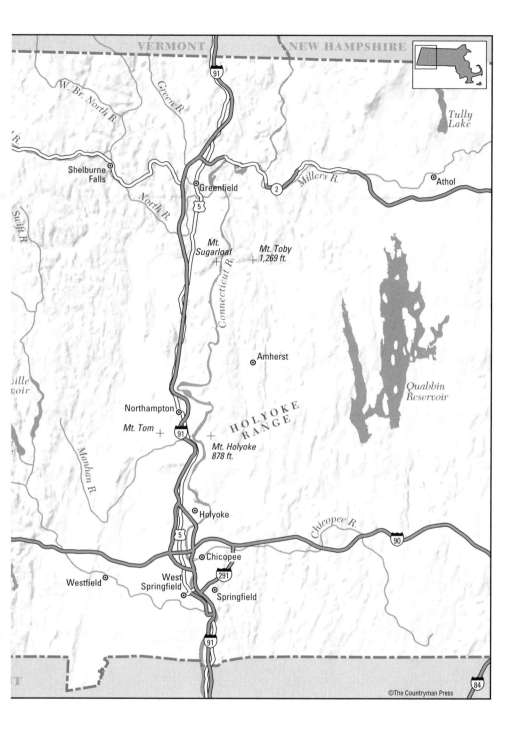

CONTENTS

INTRODUCTION

Too often when we begin to enthuse about Western Massachusetts, we watch eyes glaze over, but when we mention "the Berkshires" people listen up. We talk about the "Pioneer Valley," however, and even Berkshire residents are puzzled. We rave about the "Hilltowns" and they are really confused. By bundling these three neighboring, variously known, and very different—but all culturally rich and scenic—areas into one book, we hope to suggest what an altogether amazing region Western Massachusetts is.

We make the case that "Culture in the Country"—a slogan coined for Berkshire County—applies to all Western Massachusetts. Berkshire County is indeed the setting for internationally famous summer music, theater, and dance festivals, and the Pioneer Valley is home to a dozen colleges, an equal number of outstanding museums, and numerous concerts and performances, adding up to far more year-round "culture" within a small radius than can be found in many major cities.

The semantics of what's where in Western Massachusetts is, admittedly, confusing and unrelated to topography. Berkshire County posts WELCOME TO THE BERKSHIRES signs at its borders, while in fact the Berkshire Hills roll eastward, in places almost to the Connecticut River Valley—which of course needs a name other than *Connecticut*, because this is Massachusetts. Suggestions have included Asparagus Valley, Happy Valley, King Philip's Realm, and Knowledge Corridor, but *Pioneer Valley* is what's stuck since the 1940s. It refers to the 17th-century arrival of English colonists a century before they settled the flanking hills.

Politically the Pioneer Valley encompasses three counties—Franklin, Hampshire, and Hampden—that extend far into those hills. Physically the east–west Holyoke Range divides the Valley itself into the Springfield area to the south and the more rural Upper Valley to the north, and the Upper Valley in turn divides into the Five-College Area (with Amherst and Northampton as its dual hubs) and the Deerfield/Greenfield Area in the narrowest, northernmost end of the Valley. Technically part of the Pioneer Valley, the Hilltowns are salted through the roll of hills between Berkshire County and the Connecticut River Valley. They are the state's highest and most remote towns, with the kind of white-clapboard villages, orchards, sugarbushes, and farmscapes generally associated with Vermont.

Our definition of Western Massachusetts stops east of the Quabbin Reservoir and measures, based on the way the roads run, little more than 50 miles from east to west and less than 70 miles north to south. Divided as this small area is, however, by hills and mind-sets, it seems larger.

In 1910 Jacob's Ladder (the hilly stretch of Rt. 20 east of Becket) was graded so that motorcars could access south Berkshire County from the east. In 1914 the more dramatic Mohawk Trail (Rt. 2 between Greenfield and North Adams), including a dramatic stretch over the higher Hoosac Range, was engineered and promoted as the country's first scenic auto route. Today both roads have been backroaded by the Massachusetts Turnpike (I-90), as the river roads have been by north–south I-91 along the Connecticut. It's all about scenic roads once you're here.

Lodging includes the state's most elegant and expensive inns, resorts, and spas, and its most reasonably priced and rural B&Bs. Dining runs the same gamut— from exquisite gourmet to farm snack bars at which everything is home grown as well as baked. With the exception of its most famous towns and attractions, little in this region is obvious. Few signs point the way to waterfalls and mountain summits, to bike trails, or even to world-class museums.

More so than other parts of New England, Western Massachusetts resembles European landscapes in the sense that the centuries have stamped it, leaving few corners untouched in a variety of ways, yet preserving things both natural and human-made that deserve to be preserved. It's a landscape that generously rewards those who explore it.

Kim Grant

When the predecessor of this book, *Massachusetts: An Explorer's Guide*, was initially published, it was the first complete 20th-century guide to the state. This book has, however, been researched repeatedly from scratch. We have visited and otherwise checked out almost every place to stay we list and driven thousands of miles, much of it over unpaved roads. To our amazement this book is actually almost as large as the original guide to the entire state, which included Boston and Cape Cod. Read on and you will see why.

Chris would like to thank, first and foremost, Ann Hamilton of Franklin County and Art Schwenger of Shelburne Falls for their unfailing support, and Bill Schweikert for his many suggestions and corrections. In the Berkshires, Ann Claffie of the Berkshire Visitors Bureau, Rod Bunt of North Adams, and Joy Lyon and Claudia Leibert of Great Barrington were

Kim Grant

particularly helpful. Heartfelt thanks also go to Harry Dodson of Ashfield, Arnold Westwood of West Cummington, Carol Angus, John Koull, and Joan Temkin of Amherst, Katherine Schiff of Northampton, Judy Loebel of Hadley, Sandy Ward of Holyoke, and Ruth Bass of Richmond. Thanks, too, to Clint Richmond for his help with the Mohawk Trail.

Bill would like to thank Cherie McBride of the Greater Springfield Convention and Visitors Bureau and Shannon McNulty of the Lenox Chamber of Commerce.

Thanks, too, to the many others who helped us along the way; to Jennifer Thompson at The Countryman Press, who has helped us illustrate this book with the many images and maps that make all the difference; and to our speedy and competent copy editor Laura Jorstad for keeping us precise and grammatical. We appreciate your comments and welcome your suggestions for the next edition of this guide. Feel free to contact us directly: ctree@traveltree.net or bill@davistravels.com.

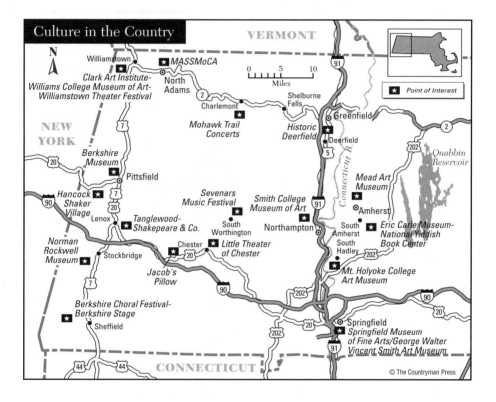

Culture in the Country

N

VERMONT

Williamstown ★ MASSMoCA

Clark Art Institute-
Williams College Museum of Art-
Williamstown Theater Festival

North
Adams

0   5   10
Miles

Shelburne
Falls

NEW
YORK

Charlemont

Mohawk Trail
Concerts

Historic
Deerfield

Greenfield

Deerfield

Quabbin
Reservoir

Berkshire
Museum

Pittsfield

Sevenars
Music Festival

Smith College
Museum of Art

Mead Art
Museum

Amherst

Hancock
Shaker
Village

Lenox

Tanglewood-
Shakepeare & Co.

South
Worthington

Northampton

South
Amherst

Eric Carle Museum-
National Yiddish
Book Center

Norman
Rockwell
Museum

Stockbridge

Chester ★ Little Theater
of Chester

South
Hadley

Jacob's
Pillow

Mt. Holyoke College
Art Museum

Berkshire Choral Festival-
Berkshire Stage

Sheffield

Springfield

Springfield Museum
of Fine Arts/George Walter
Vincent Smith Art Museum

CONNECTICUT

★ Point of Interest

© The Countryman Press

WHAT'S WHERE IN WESTERN MASSACHUSETTS

AGRICULTURAL FAIRS (www.mafa
.org). The Berkshire Agricultural Society, incorporated February 15, 1811,
was this country's first such society,
and Elkanah Watson, its founder, is
recognized as "the father of American
fairs." The first was held in Pittsfield
in 1814. By 1818 the state's agricultural societies included Northampton,
which still holds its annual Three
County Fair on Labor Day weekend.
The Franklin County Fair at the
Greenfield Fairgrounds is usually the
following weekend. It's also worth
checking out the colorful old-fashioned fairs in small towns that feature
pulling contests (by oxen, draft horses,
and trucks), plenty of livestock, and
live music. The Littleville Fair in
Chester and the Middlefield Fair are
early in August, and the Cummington
and Blandford Fairs are in late
August.

The **Eastern States Exposition**
(www.thebige.com), held mid- to late
September in West Springfield, is in a
class by itself, a six-state event with
thousands of animals competing for
prizes along with a midway, conces-
sion stands, big-name entertainment,
and the Avenue of States with a pavilion for each New England state.
Check the web site for a year-round

Kim Grant

calendar of events at the fairgrounds.

Up-to-date lists of fairs are available from the **Massachusetts Agricultural Fairs Association**
(781-834-6629; www.mafa.org) and
from the **Massachusetts Department of Food and Agriculture**
(617-626-1720; www.mass.gov/agr).

AIRPORTS Contact the **Massachusetts Aeronautics Commission**
(617-973-8881; www.massaeronautics
.org) in Boston for a database about
the state's airports, big and small.
Bradley International Airport
(888-624-1533; www.bradleyairport
.com) in Windsor Locks, Connecticut,
is the region's major airport, served by
16 major airlines with connecting

flights to just about anywhere you want to go. With its new, centralized terminal and easy highway access (I-91, exit 40), it's one of New England's more visitor-friendly gateways. **Albany International Airport** (518-242-2200; www.albanyairport.com) is served by 10 carriers and is handy to much of Berkshire County.

AMTRAK (800-USA-RAIL; www.amtrak.com). On its way from New York to Burlington, Vermont, the **Vermonter** stops in Springfield and Amherst. Springfield is also a stop on some Boston-bound trails, and the **Lakeshore Limited** stops in Pittsfield en route to Chicago. There is frequent service from New York to Albany. *Note:* Canny Berkshire residents take reasonably priced Metro-North (www.mta.info) from Grand Central Station to Wassaic Station, New York; on July through Labor Day weekends a connecting bus drops passengers in Great Barrington.

AMUSEMENT PARKS While all the state's other amusement parks (all founded in the late 19th century by trolley companies as an inducement to ride the cars out to the end of the line) have bitten the dust, Riverside Park in Agawam is now **Six Flags New England** (www.sixflags.com), the region's largest theme and water park, home to "Superman Ride of Steel."

    Animals Forest Park in Springfield (www.forestparkzoo.org) and the much smaller **Christenson Zoo** (native deer, peacocks, pheasants, and raccoons) in Northampton's Look Memorial Park are the area's only formal zoos. Check out our farm listings in each chapter for many more friendly animals to visit. At **Flayvors**

of Cook Farm in Hadley you can see the cows that supply your ice cream. **McCray Farm** in South Hadley has both ice cream and an extensive barnyard meagerie. **Ioka Valley Farm** in Hancock features a Halloween-time maze as well as pigs, sheep, goats, calves, and rabbits. The most exotic collection of animals in Western Massachusetts is probably at **Tregellys Fiber Farm** (www.tregellysfibers.com) in Hawley, where animals include unusual heritage breeds such as Galloway cattle, yaks and camels, llamas, and Bactrian (two-humped) camels from Mongolia, not to mention peacocks and an assortment of birds.

ANTIQUARIAN BOOKSELLERS For a descriptive listing of local dealers, check out the web site of the **Massachusetts and Rhode Island Antiquarian Booksellers** (MARIAB; www.mariab.org) or pick up their booklet guide at one of the shops. Western Massachusetts is studded with antiquarian bookstores; you'll find them listed in each chapter. Many, like the **Bookmill** in Montague (www.montaguebookmill.com) and **Meetinghouse Books** in South Deerfield (www.meetinghousebooks.com), are destinations in their own right.

ANTIQUES Berkshire County represents a major antiques center; the **Berkshire County Antiques Dealers Association** (www.berkshireantiquesandart.com) publishes a pamphlet listing most of the shops, which we describe individually in each chapter under *Selective Shopping*. Sheffield alone has two dozen galleries, while at the **Buggy Whip Antiques Market** (www.buggywhipantiques.com) multiple dealers fill two floors of a vast old buggy whip

factory. In the Pioneer Valley, Northampton has its share of antiques shops, and auctions are frequent in the Deerfield/Greenfield Area.

APPALACHIAN TRAIL The AT runs 87.7 miles through the Berkshires, beginning near Sages Ravine in Mount Everett State Reservation in the town of Mount Washington in the very southwestern corner of Massachusetts. It leads up over Mount Race and Mount Everett, then turns east through Sheffield and continues on up by Benedict Pond in Beartown State Forest; heads through Tyringham and on up through October Mountain State Forest; proceeds through Dalton and Cheshire, and on up along the eastern flank of Mount Greylock to the summit. Then it's down to Rt. 2 in North Adams and on up through Clarksburg State Forest to the Vermont state line. Access points, with and without parking, are far more frequent here than along the AT in northern New England, and many stretches are spectacularly beautiful.

APPLES Contact the **Massachusetts Department of Food and Agriculture** (617-626-1720; www.mass.gov/agr/massgrown) for the *Pick-Your-*

Own guide. The Berkshire Hilltowns represent one of the state's prime orchard areas. For apple wine lovers, **West County Winery** (413-424-348; www.westcountycider.com) distributes throughout the East. Anything you want to know about apples can be found through the **New England Apple Association** (www.apples-ne .com), headquartered in Hatfield. The first Saturday in November is Cider Day (www.ciderday.com) in Franklin County. It's the start of a weekend of apple- and cider-oriented events, including cider tastings and open houses at local orchards.

AREA CODE 413 applies to all of Western Massachusetts.

ART MUSEUMS Within Western Massachusetts, an area little more than 50 miles wide and less than 70 miles long, are found several major art museums and as many smaller museums with world-class art pieces in their collections. The most famous is

FUMÉE D'AMBRE GRIS (SMOKE OF AMBER-GRIS) BY JOHN SINGER SARGENT (1880)
Sterling and Francine Clark Art Institute, Williamstown, MA

the **Sterling and Francine Clark Art Institute** (www.clarkart.edu) in Williamstown, drawing art lovers from throughout the world to see its French impressionists and 19th-century American artists. Just around the corner is the **Williams College Museum of Art** (www.wcma.org), with its wealth of works by Maurice Prendergast and other choice American pieces donated by alumni. These museums in turn are complemented by **MASS MoCA** (**Massachusetts Museum of Contemporary Art**; www.masmoca .org), which opened in 1999 and is billed as one of the world's largest contemporary art centers. Continue west along the Mohawk Trail and down to Deerfield, site of **Historic Deerfield** (www.historic-deerfield .org) with its many portraits and decorative art pieces, then zip down I-91 to Northampton, where the recently expanded **Smith College Museum of Art** (www.smith.edu/artmuseum) showcases a superb collection of primarily 19th- and early-20th-century art as well as major contemporary exhibits. Drive east 9 miles to Amherst to see the **Mead Art Museum** (www .amherst.edu/mead) with its well-rounded permanent collection, much of it again contributed by alumni. In another corner of Amherst the **Eric Carle Museum of Picture Book Art** (www.picturebookart.org) shows work by the world's top children's book illustrators, recognizing this as an art form in its own right. The neighboring **National Yiddish Book Center** (www.yiddishbookcenter.org) also frequently hosts art exhibits worth stopping for.

A short drive south on the scenic Notch Rd. (Rt. 116) over the Holyoke Range to South Hadley takes you to the **Mount Holyoke College Art Museum** (www.mtholyoke.edu/go/ artmuseum), one of the country's oldest collegiate art collections, ranging from ancient Asian and Egyptian works through 19th-century landscapes and contemporary pieces. Another short ride to I-91 and into Springfield brings you to the **Quadrangle** (www.springfieldmuseums.org) of museums. This includes the **Museum of Fine Arts**—18th-century portraits and 20th-century works, complemented by decorative arts— and the **George Walter Vincent Smith Art Museum**, with an outstanding collection of Japanese armor and cloisonné. For an overview of museums in the Valley see www .museums10.org.

Hop on the Mass Pike (I-90) and in less than an hour you are back in Berkshire County at the **Norman Rockwell Museum** (www.nrm.org) in West Stockbridge, exhibiting not only works by its eminent namesake illustrator but also changing exhibits by other noted illustrators. Finally, north on Rt. 7 in Pittsfield are the **Berkshire Museum** (www.berkshire museum.org), a fine regional museum with a respectable collection of American paintings, and nearby **Hancock Shaker Village** (www.hancockshaker village.org), which displays distinctive Shaker spirit paintings as well as furnishings.

Obviously no one should try to complete this marathon circuit in a day, but it could easily make up a 2- to 5-day tour given the scenery, shopping, lodging, and dining. Art lovers will also find quality galleries along the way (listed in each chapter under *Selective Shopping*).

BALLOONING Both **Pioneer Valley Balloons** (www.pioneervalleyballoons

.com) in Northampton and **Worthington Hot Air Ballooning** (413-238-5514) in Worthington offer hot-air balloon flights year-round, weather permitting.

BASKETBALL The Naismith Memorial Basketball Hall of Fame (www.hoophall.com) in Springfield celebrates Dr. James Naismith's invention of basketball at a local YMCA college in 1891. The present $45 million Hall of Fame museum is Springfield's pride, its most visible landmark (it's shaped like a giant basketball and illuminated in different colors at night), and its biggest tourist attraction. A combination history museum, shrine, computer game arcade, and gymnasium—there's nothing else quite like it.

BED & BREAKFASTS A B&B used to be just a private home in which guests paid to stay and to breakfast. The definition has broadened in recent years to include farms and fairly elaborate and formal lodging places that resemble inns but do not serve dinner. Happily, B&Bs are now widely scattered

Kim Grant

throughout the state and remain reasonably priced, especially in less touristed areas. Many are run by long-time residents who are knowledgeable about the surrounding area and delighted to orient their guests. Our lodging focus here is on B&Bs. In the process of updating this book, we visited every B&B we could find. **We do not charge for listings in this book and include only those that we would like to stay in ourselves.**

BICYCLING We have noted rentals and outstanding bike routes in most sections. The 10-mile **Norwottuck Rail Trail** between Northampton and Amherst is a popular bike path; it's possible to come from New York City to Amherst on Amtrak's Vermonter and pedal off to a B&B in either town. A new trail, the 11-mile **Ashuwillticook Rail Trail** (www.berkshirebikepath.org), connects Adams and Cheshire paralleling Rt. 8 but hugging the shores of Berkshire Pond and Cheshire Reservoir. The **Franklin County Bike Trail** is making slow progress. The bridge across the mouth of the Millers River has been opened to cyclists, permitting a nice ride from Northfield Mountain down under the French King Bridge. The 4-mile **Canalside Rail Trail** running south from the discovery center in Turners Falls is nearing completion.

A glossy *Massachusetts Bicycle Guide* pamphlet available from the Massachusetts Office of Travel and Tourism (800-227-MASS; www.mass-vacation.com) lists state forests with bicycle facilities. Cyclists find the *Rubel Western Massachusetts Bicycle and Road Map* (www.bikemaps.com) indispensable. At this writing a *Berkshire Bike Touring* map—a free version of the county's section of the

Christina Tree

BICYCLISTS ATOP MOUNT HOLYOKE

Hampden. In Berkshire County the major wildlife sanctuaries are **Pleasant Valley** (413-637-0320) and **Canoe Meadows**, both in Lenox. In addition, numerous smaller sanctuaries are scattered through this area and described within individual chapters.

Hawk-watchers, we should add, converge on the Connecticut Valley in September, watching these birds ride the thermal highs; favorite lookout spots are Mount Tom and Mount Holyoke. The most famous birds in Western Massachusetts are, however, probably the nesting eagles in Barton Cove. TV cameras are trained on the nest and can be viewed at the discovery center in Turners Falls. *Birding Western Massachusetts* (New England Cartographics) by Robert Tougias describes more than two dozen birding sites.

Rubel map—is available from the Berkshire Visitors Bureau (www.berkshires.org). *Bicycling the Pioneer Valley…and Beyond* by Marion Gorham (New England Cartographics) is also recommended.

Serious mountain bikers should check out River Road south from Chesterfield Gorge to the Knightville Dam (see "Hampshire Hilltowns"). Many state forests offer trails beloved by mountain bikers. Check out the Department of Conservation and Recreation web site (www.mass.gov/dcr), as well as the Massachusetts Bicycle Coalition site (www.massbike.org).

BIRDING The **Massachusetts Audubon Society** (781-259-9500; www.massaudubon.org), founded in 1896 to discourage the use of wild bird plumage as hat decorations, also pioneered the idea of wildlife sanctuaries. Mass Audubon maintains two staffed sanctuaries in the Pioneer Valley— **Arcadia Nature Center** (413-584-3009) on the Oxbow of the Connecticut River in Easthampton/Northampton, and **Laughing Brook Education Center** (413-655-8034) in

BOAT EXCURSIONS Seasonal cruises of the Connecticut in the Five-College Area are offered aboard the *Lady Bea* in South Hadley (413-315-6342) and in the Greenfield area on the *Quinnetukut II* (800-859-2960), based at Northfield Mountain.

BOAT LAUNCHES Sites are detailed at **Massachusetts Office of Fishing and Boating Access** (www.mass.gov/dfwele/pab). Also see *Boating* and *Fishing* entries in each chapter.

BUTTERFLIES Magic Wings (www.magicwings.com) in South Deerfield is a flowery, lush, year-round oasis filled with thousands of butterflies.

BUS SERVICE Bonanza Bus (800-556-3815; www.bonanza.com) runs from New York City to Sheffield, South Egremont, Great Barrington, Lee, Lenox, and Pittsfield, with connections to Williamstown. **Peter Pan Bus–Trailways** (800-343-9999; www .peterpanbus.com) connects Boston with Springfield, Holyoke, South Hadley, Northampton, Amherst, Deerfield, and Greenfield and with Lee, Lenox, and Pittsfield. From Albany, Bonanza and **Greyhound** (www.greyhound.com) both offer service to Pittsfield.

CAMPING The **Department of Conservation and Recreation** details information about camping in state forests in a *Camping* brochure as well as listing sites in its map and on its web site (www.mass.gov/dcr). Campsites can be reserved through **www .reserveamerica.com** (877-422-6762). Site occupancy is limited to four people or one family, and to 14 days. Rates vary with the park or site; many parks also offer log cabins.

Check out the **Beartown State Forest** in Monterey (413-528-0904); **DAR State Forest** in Goshen (413-268-7098); **Mohawk Trail State Forest** in Charlemont (413-339-5504); **Mount Greylock State Reservation** in Lanesborough (413-499-4262; www .mass.gov/dcr); **October Mountain State Forest** in Lee (413-243-1778); **Pittsfield State Forest** (413-442-8992); **Savoy Mountain State Forest** in Savoy (413-664-9567); **Tolland State Forest** in East Otis (413-269-6002); and **Windsor State Forest** (413-684-0948). A *Massachusetts Campground Directory* to commercial campgrounds is available from the **Massachusetts Association of Campground Owners** (781-544-3475; www.campmass.com). Seasonal camping is also available at 26 wooded sites, managed by Northfield Mountain in Barton Cove in Gill (800-859-2960).

CANALS The country's first canal is said to have been built in South Hadley in 1794 (scant trace remains). The **Farmington Canal**, which ran from Northampton through Westfield and Southwick on its way to New Haven, is still visible in parts. In Holyoke power canals have become important parts of a Heritage State Park; in **Turners Falls**, near the new Great Falls Discovery Center, both power and transportation canals are still visible.

CANOEING AND KAYAKING The canoe is making a comeback, and kayaks demanding less skill are now even more popular, increasing interest in paddling Western Massachusetts ponds, lakes, and rivers. Rentals have proliferated, and we detail them in specific chapters.

CAVING Seventy solution caves or caverns are known in Massachusetts, most in the Berkshires. A few caves are found in the Connecticut River Valley. Check with the caving group Boston Grotto (www.bostongrotto.org).

CHEESE Not only is **Monterey Chèvre** (413-528-2138) delicious, but buying it at the source—Rawson Brook Farm in Monterey—also makes a great excuse to visit with the goats that contribute their milk to its cause. While you're in Monterey, also check out **Gould Farm Cheddar**, available at both its roadside store and Harvest Barn. Never mind that **Granville Cheese** is made now in upstate New York; the cheddar is aged, as it has been since 1851, in the Granville Country Store.

CHILDREN, ESPECIALLY FOR Many Western Massachusetts attractions appeal to children ages 3 to 93, but those we note under *Families, Especially for* and with the *𝒔* sign highlight things of special interest to families with young children, as well as child-friendly lodging and restaurants. Such destination attractions include **Eric Carle Museum of Picture Book Art** (www.picturebookart.org) in Amherst and **Six Flags New England** (www.sixflags.com), the region's largest theme and water park. In Old Deerfield the **Old Indian House** (www.old-deerfield.org) houses activities geared to young visitors, and Holyoke offers a fine **Children's Museum** and adjacent **merry-go-round** in the Holyoke Heritage State Park. In Springfield there's the **Forest Park Zoo** (see *Animals*); the **Quadrangle**, with its **Dr. Seuss figures** (the father of the real Dr. Seuss ran the Forest Park Zoo); and the **Science Museum** (www.springfield museums.org), with its many child-geared exhibits and dinosaurs. New since 2006 is the Amherst College Museum of Science, with its extraordinary exhibit of dinosaurs and the world's largest collection of dinosaur prints. The **Great Falls Discovery Center at the Silvio O. Conte National Fish and Wildlife Refuge**

(www.greatfallsma.org) is now open regularly in Turners Falls, showcasing the flora and fauna of the Valley. We also describe where to find real dinosaur prints in the Pioneer Valley and the "Dino Dig" that's among the many interactive exhibits at the **Berkshire Museum** (www.berkshire museum.org) in Pittsfield. The nearby **Hancock Shaker Village** (www .hancockshakervillage.org) includes a great hands-on Discovery Room—and visitors under 18 are free.

CHRISTMAS TREES The **Massachusetts Christmas Tree Association** (978-365-5818; www.christmas-trees .org), lists Christmas tree farms by county on its web site.

COVERED BRIDGES Covered bridges are found in Charlemont, Colrain, Conway, Greenfield, and Sheffield.

CRAFTS The country's largest concentration of craftspeople is reportedly in the Five-College Area and in West County. **Northampton's Main Street** showcases much of their work, as do several shops in **Shelburne Falls**. The region's outstanding crafts fairs are the **Paradise City Arts Festivals** held on the Memorial Day and Columbus Day weekends at the Three-County Fairground in Northampton. The **Deerfield Crafts Fairs** showcases traditional crafts in June and September at Memorial Hall in Old Deerfield. We list outstanding crafts galleries and studios in each chapter under *Selective Shopping*.

EVENTS This region generates several very different kinds of events.
(1) There are the seasonal happenings: sugaring sit-down breakfasts in the Upper Pioneer Valley and Berkshire

Christina Tree

Hilltowns in March, the white-water races on the Westfield in April, and crop festivals and PYO as they ripen (see *Farms, Farmer's Markets, and Farm Stands*). August is the season for small-town agricultural fairs, and September for the big ones. Then come fabulous fall foliage festivals, followed by November and early-December crafts fairs combined with holiday lighting festivals. (2) Cultural happenings staged for the general public (as opposed to the rich Five-College Area academic-year events and theater, music, and lecture offerings—which are almost all open to the public) begin in mid-June and end in August. The Tanglewood Music Festival in Lenox is the most famous of these, but there are many more, along with theater and dance, all staged primarily in south Berkshire County but also found throughout the region. (3) Town celebrations. Many of these are annual events, but some of the best are onetime celebrations. Check *Special Events* at the end of each chapter; area web sites are also rich sources of information.

FACTORY OUTLETS The **Prime Outlets** at Lee (www.primeoutlets.com)

Christina Tree

Cider Day

are an attractive grouping of five dozen fairly upscale "outlets" just off Mass Pike exit 2. Several old-fashioned outlets are found off the beaten path. In Adams, **Interior Alternative** is an outlet for Waverly fabrics and wallpaper.

FALL FOLIAGE AND FOLIAGE FESTIVALS The most colorful small-town fall festivals in the state (ranking right up there with the most colorful in all of New England) are the **Conway Festival of the Hills**, the first weekend in October, and the **Fall Foliage Festival** in Ashfield on Columbus Day weekend. **The Northern Berkshire Fall Foliage Festival** in North Adams, the first weekend in October, is a huge old event, and on Columbus Day weekend you can join residents of Adams who turn out in force to hike "their" side of the mountain.

Western Massachusetts is unquestionably as beautiful a region to explore in fall as any in New England, given its wealth of maple trees and back roads, many of them dirt. Be advised that color comes first to the higher reaches of Mount Greylock and spreads through the Berkshire Hills the first weeks of October, filling both the Berkshire and Pioneer valleys a week or two later and lingering on there through October. We decry the lodging practice of charging "foliage rates" throughout October. When it's over, it's really over.

FARMS, FARMER'S MARKETS, AND FARM STANDS "Agritourism" is big in Massachusetts. Several farms offer B&B and cottage rentals on their property. Many more farms have pick-your-own (apples, strawberries, and blueberries, for example), depending on the season; still others invite you in to see their animals, and one, Cook

Farm in Hadley, makes fabulous ice cream from the cows grazing beside its shop, Flayvors of Cook Farm. Farms in South Hadley, Hancock, and Hawley feature large collections of animals (see *Animals*).

A visit to a farm invariably gets you off the main drag and into beautiful countryside you might otherwise not find. The **Massachusetts Department of Food and Agriculture** (877-MASS-GROWN) maintains an extensive web site (www.mass.gov/agr/massgrown) detailing information about farms that allow you to pick your own vegetables and fruit. Request or download the agritourism directory of farms that welcome visitors with farm stands, PYO, B&B, or in other ways. The **Community Involved in Sustaining Agriculture** or CISA (www.buylocalfood.com) publishes an annual guide to farmers in Franklin, Hampshire, and Hampden Counties who sell directly to the public. **Berkshire Grown** (www.berkshiregrown.org) publishes an annual map/guide and performs a similar service for farmers in Berkshire County.

Look for asparagus in May in the Pioneer Valley (also known as Asparagus Valley); for strawberries throughout the area in June; for blueberries, raspberries, and sweet corn after July 4 and—through August—peaches, too. September is apple season, October is all about pumpkins, and in December it's time to cut Christmas trees. Also see *Maple Sugaring*.

FISHING Freshwater fishing options range from mountain streams in the Berkshires and Hilltowns to the wide Connecticut. For a listing of stocked fishing sites, best bets, and areas with handicapped access, call the **Massa-**

chusetts Division of Fisheries and Wildlife (800-ASK-FISH or 275-3474; www.mass.gov/dfwele. Also check *Fishing* under each of the chapters in this guide.

FISH LADDERS Northfield Mountain naturalists staff fishways at the Holyoke and Turners Falls Dams when the fish are running upstream, late May to mid-June (800-859-2960).

GOLF We have listed golf courses under *To Do* in each chapter.

GUIDANCE At the beginning of each chapter we list the regional and local sources of information for that area. The web site www.masscountryroads.com is a helpful travel resource devoted to the northern tier of Western Massachusetts towns. The Massa-

Kim Grant

chusetts Office of Travel and Tourism (MOTT; 617-973-8500 or 800-227-6277; www.mass-vacation.com) publishes the free *Massachusetts Getaway Guide*. E-mail queries to vacation @state.ma.us will be answered within 2 hours if sent weekdays between 8:45 AM and 5 PM EST.

HERITAGE STATE PARKS Conceived and executed by the state as a way of revitalizing old industrial areas, each "park" revolves around a visitor center in which multivisual exhibits dramatize what makes the community special. Though they have served as prototypes for similar parks throughout the country, the Heritage State Parks within the scope of this book have all suffered severe financial cutbacks under recent administrations. The **Holyoke** and **Western Gateway** (in North Adams) parks are, however, still operating as envisioned.

HIGHWAYS I-91 parallels the Connecticut River in its north–south passage through Western Massachusetts, and I-90—the Massachusetts Turnpike —is a quick way across the southern tier of the state (see *Massachusetts Turnpike*). Much of the area described

VISITORS CENTER

Christina Tree

in this book is, however, blessedly far from any major highway—unless you want to count Rt. 2, which is four lanes, even six lanes in places, from Boston all the way to Wendell in the Pioneer Valley. From Boston, if you are heading west to the Amherst/ Northampton area as well to most of the Berkshire Hilltowns and northern Berkshire County, Rt. 2 is actually quicker as well as more scenic and cheaper than the Mass Pike. For more on the westernmost stretch of Rt. 2, see *Mohawk Trail*.

HIKING AND WALKING The **Department of Conservation and Recreation** (DCR, formerly DEM) maintains hundreds of miles of hiking trails in the 47 state parks and forests in Western Massachusetts. The **Appalachian Trail** winds 87.7 miles through Berkshire County (see above). The **Taconic Crest Trail** offers many spectacular views along its 35-mile route, also in the Berkshires, including sections in New York and Vermont. Another dramatic, but not easy, hike follows the ridgeline of the east–west Holyoke Range (accessible from the state-run Notch Visitors Center in Granby). Elsewhere in the Five-College Area, the Amherst Conservation Department maintains some 45 miles of walking and hiking trails. Within this book several walks are suggested in each chapter (see *Hiking* and *Green Space*). The bible for hiking throughout the state is the Appalachian Mountain Club's *Massachusetts Trail Guide*.

HISTORY Within this book a fair amount of Massachusetts history is told through descriptions of many places that still commemorate or dramatize it.

The Connecticut River Valley was farmed by Native Americans for thousands of years before the first "Pioneers" arrived, but today only place-names recall their tribes: **Woronoco** (Westfield), **Agawam** (Springfield/West Springfield), **Norwottuck** (Hadley and Northampton), **Pocumtuck** (Deerfield area) and **Squakheag** (Northfield area). It's difficult to estimate how many people lived in this area before a smallpox epidemic, contracted through contact with English and Dutch traders, decimated these tribes in 1633. William Pynchon of Roxbury took advantage of this situation to establish a settlement at present-day **Springfield** in 1636, buying the land for 18 fathom of wampum, 18 coats, 18 hatchets, 18 hoes, and 18 knives. Settlers and Indians tentatively coexisted for several decades, but in 1675 the 24-year-old Wampanoag Indian chief Metacomet, better remembered as King Philip, attempted to unite all tribes east of the Hudson River to rise up against the colonists, who already outnumbered them. The uprising began in Plymouth Colony, but King Philip and more than 1,000 Wampanoags escaped to the Connecticut River Valley, killing 60 settlers at Deerfield. An obelisk in **South Deerfield** marks the site of this "Bloody Brook Massacre," and the nearby summit of **Mount Sugarloaf**, now a state reservation accessible by road and offering a spectacular view down the Valley, is still known as King Philip's Seat. Philip himself, however, barely escaped capture in a devastating ambush at **Turners Falls** (named for the English captain who directed it) and was slain soon after on the coast.

Local Indian tribes, understandably angry at being pushed off their land,

Pocumtuck Valley Memorial Association
MOCCASINS, CIRCA 1880, ON DISPLAY AT MEMORIAL HALL IN OLD DEERFIELD

began forming alliances with the French in Canada, then locked in a struggle with Britain for the control of the continent. A series of conflicts known as the French and Indian Wars (1689–1763) devastated settlements over much of Western Massachusetts despite the efforts of the citizen soldiers of the colonial militia. During one campaign the song "Yankee Doodle" was reportedly written in Charlemont by a British army doctor to poke fun at the typical unmilitary-looking militiaman, whose idea of dressing up was to "stick a feather in his cap." Ignoring the doctor's sarcasm, Americans enthusiastically adopted the song, which became one of the marching tunes of the Revolution. **Charlemont** annually commemorates its composition with a festival called **Yankee Doodle Days** in July.

The most destructive and dramatic of all the French and Indian attacks occurred at **Old Deerfield** in February 1704. A large force of French soldiers and Indian allies from several tribes swarmed over the stockade just before dawn, catching the sleeping village completely by surprise. In the ensuing battle 50 of the town's 291 inhabitants were killed and 112 were captured and carried away to Canada, while many of its houses were burned. Most of the captives were eventually ransomed and returned home, but some children, adopted by Indian or French families, remained in Canada. Serious settlement in the hills of the Connecticut River Valley commenced only after the end of the French and Indian Wars.

Deerfield was rebuilt and, although it was attacked twice more in the next 40 years, was never again captured. The stories (not just the settlers' side) of the 1704 attack are well told at **Memorial Hall Museum** and **Indian House Memorial** in Deerfield, which among other things display a door covered with gashes made by Indian tomahawks during the raid.

Native Americans in the southwestern corner of Massachusetts had been trading amicably with Dutch settlers along the Hudson for several decades before the English arrived in the 1730s. Families from the Connecticut River Valley settled **Sheffield**, and a young missionary, John Sergeant, was dispatched to **Stockbridge** from Yale College to propagate the Gospel to the Mahicans. The town's unusually wide street dates from its use as the site on which these friendly Indians built their wigwams, and Sergeant's **Mission House** survives, portraying how well a white family could survive in these backwoods in the early 18th century, but little about the Indians remains. Despite their service to Washington during the American Revolution, the Stockbridge Indians were forced west by the end of the 18th century, carrying their heavy, leatherbound Bible with them.

Berkshire residents played a significant role in the Revolution. In 1773 Sheffield townspeople gathered in the **Colonel Ashley House** to draft the

Sheffield Declaration, a petition against British tyranny, observing that "Americans are entitled to all the liberties, privileges and immunities of natural born British subjects." The following August a Berkshire Congress dedicated to taking practical action in defense of such rights met at Stockbridge, and when the British ministerial judges attempted to convene at the courthouse in Great Barrington, they found their way barred by angry locals. Tombstones of those who lost their lives in the Revolutionary War can be found throughout the area.

Boston merchants actually profited from filling war needs, but residents of rural towns in the west of the state found themselves hard hit in the years immediately following the war, especially when payment was required in hard currency, which farmers usually lacked. A farmer who could not pay was stripped of his lands and sent to prison. In 1786, at the height of this rural depression, farmers held a 3-day convention in Hatfield and decided to attack the county courthouse in Northampton. Led by Daniel Shays, a debt-ridden war hero from Pelham, they next attacked the Springfield Arsenal and failed miserably. A few little-noticed plaques tell the remaining

SUNDERLAND TOBACCO BARN

Christina Tree

story. A marker beside the **Pelham Town Hall** (just off Rt. 202, the **Daniel Shays Highway**) commemorates the spot where the rebels camped for more than two winter weeks in their stand "against unjust laws." Another monument along the **Sheffield–South Egremont Road** records the finale of the uprising: HERE 100 REBELS WERE ROUTED AFTER PLUNDERING STOCKBRIDGE AND GREAT BARRINGTON. Shays himself escaped to Vermont, and a recorded 700 families from Western Massachusetts followed him.

The first decades of the 19th century were also the era of the quintessential New England village with its steepled church and grouping of handsome houses around a common, a picture for which Greenfield architect Asher Benjamin is largely responsible. Aware of rural carpenters' need for a do-it-yourself guide, Benjamin in 1796 wrote *The Country Builder's Assistant*, then six more books that went through 44 editions and resulted in the **Greenfield Public Library**, **Memorial Hall** in Old Deerfield, and hundreds of handsome homes and churches in the area and throughout the region.

The Civil War fueled the state's industrial growth. At the **Springfield Armory National Historic Site** you learn that it also turned that city into a boomtown, the "Arsenal of the Union," which produced about half the rifled muskets used by northern troops. The story of the region's first major planned mill city built from scratch in the 1840s is told in the **Holyoke Heritage State Park**, while that of the state's last industrial-era boom city—North Adams— spawned by the 25-year construction of the then world's longest railroad

tunnel is dramatized in the **Western Gateway Heritage State Park**. Such manufacturing cities continued to prosper, thanks to immigrant labor, until the 1920s when the textile and other industries began moving out of the state. Innovative uses have been found for many old mill buildings, notably the **Massachusetts Museum of Contemporary Art** (MASS MoCA) in North Adams, which occupies most of a sprawling industrial complex originally built as a textile plant.

What's generally forgotten is the flip side to this "industrial revolution." In the agricultural era farmers rarely left their land, but city dwellers who punched clocks also took vacations. Moneyed visitors from throughout the country flocked to summer hotels; to upward of 100 summer estates such as **Naumkeag** and **Blantyre**, **Cranwell**, **Wheatleigh**, **Seven Hills**, and **Eastover** in Lenox; and to more modest country houses like the **William Cullen Bryant Homestead** in Cummington. Many blue-collar workers and their families traveled the ubiquitous trolley lines to amusement parks, all now vanished except for Riverside in Agawam (currently Six Flags New England). Less affluent folks also traveled the trolleys and rail lines to farms catering to guests throughout Western Massachusetts.

In 1910 **Jacob's Ladder**, a stretch of Rt. 20 over the hills into south Berkshire County, was constructed to accommodate autos; in 1914 the **Mohawk Trail** (Rt. 2 west over higher and more dramatic Hoosac Mountain, then down into North Adams) was created specifically as one of the country's first scenic auto touring routes. The **Hotel Northampton** opened as a "motoring destination" in

1927 featuring a mini museum village of Americana, and at the same time **Storrowton**, a larger gathering of rural historic buildings, was assembled at the **Eastern States Exposition**. In ensuing decades, as train service atrophied and car travel increased, virtually all the old summer hotels disappeared, replaced by motels.

In the last few decades of the 20th century the settlement pattern of the 19th century was actually reversed, with people moving back to the country as urban refugees found ways to support themselves in rural places. Educational centers such as Northampton and Amherst became lively destinations in their own right, creating the need for lodging in surrounding hills.

Currently many of the state's true beauty spots are far more easily accessible than they were for most of the 20th century, thanks in large part to the state's enterprising **Department of Conservation and Recreation** (www.mass.gov/dcr) and to private land preservation groups like the **Trustees of Reservations** (www .thetrustees.org), the **Massachusetts Audubon Society** (see *Birding*), and many local conservation trusts. Lodging has also once more proliferated throughout the area.

HORSEBACK RIDING Over the past decade a number of Massachusetts livery stables have closed or limited themselves to lessons and clinics. In Lenox trail rides are offered at **Undermountain Farm** (413-637-3365) and **Berkshire Horseback Adventure** (413-623-5606); in Becket at **Sunny Banks Ranch** (413-623-5606; www.sunnybanksranch.com); and in Williamstown at **DeMayo's Bonnie Lea Farm** (413-458-3149).

Trail rides are also available to guests at **High Pocket B&B** (www.high pocket.com) in Colrain.

HUNTING The source for information about licenses, rules, and wildlife management areas is the **Massachusetts Division of Fisheries and Wildlife** (617-626-1590; www.mass .gov/dfwele), 251 Causeway St., Suite 400, Boston 02114. To receive the division's newsletter *MassWildlife News* electronically, e-mail join-Mass Wildlife.news@listserve.state.ma.us.

LITERARY LANDMARKS In Amherst poet **Emily Dickinson** (1830–86) was born, lived virtually her entire life, and wrote most of her finest verse in an imposing mansion at 280 Main Street. Her second-floor bedroom has been restored to look much as it did when she was in residence. She is buried in **West Cemetery** on Triangle Street.

The **Jones Library** at 43 Amity Street has a collection of 8,000 items relating to Dickinson, including original handwritten poems. Seven panels in the research wing depict her life in Amherst. The library also has a collection devoted to poet **Robert Frost**, who lived in Amherst from 1931 to 1938 and later taught at Amherst College.

Kim Grant

Poet and editor **William Cullen Bryant** was born in Cummington in 1794. At the height of his fame, when he was editor and co-owner of the *New York Post*, he transformed the original humble family homestead off Rt. 112 into a graceful mansion, now owned by the Trustees of Reservations. Filled with memorabilia of Bryant and his era, the **Bryant Homestead** also has an expansive view of a beautiful countryside.

The Mount, novelist **Edith Wharton**'s home on Plunkett Street in Lenox, is a turn-of-the-20th-century copy of a 17th-century English mansion, but it incorporates a lot of her own ideas of gracious living (she was a wealthy New York socialite). It was here that she wrote *Ethan Frome*, which is set in the Berkshires. **Edith Wharton Restoration, Inc.**, manages the property and conducts tours.

In 1850 **Herman Melville** bought **Arrowhead**, an 18th-century Pittsfield farmhouse, where he wrote his masterpiece *Moby-Dick*. The house at 789 Holmes Road has a fine view of Mount Greylock, the mass of which may have inspired his vision of a great whale. The house is now headquarters for the Berkshire Historical Society. The **Berkshire Athenaeum** on the Pittsfield common has a Melville Room with every book he ever wrote, and most of those written about him. Artifacts displayed include the desk at which he wrote *Billy Budd*.

MAPLE SUGARING Native Americans reportedly taught this industry to early settlers in Tyringham (southern Berkshire County) in the early 18th century. Sugaring is thriving today, primarily in the Hilltowns, an area with more sugarhouses than the rest of the state put together. During sug-

aring season in March, visitors are welcome to watch producers "boil off" the sap, reducing it to the sweet liquid that is traditionally sampled on ice or snow. The *Massachusetts Maple Producers Directory*, listing dozens of sugarhouses that welcome visitors when they are boiling in March and that cater to customers year-round, is available from the **Massachusetts Maple Producers Association** (413-628-3912; www.massmaple.org), Watson–Spruce Corner Rd., Ashfield 01330.

MAPS Most of the Massachusetts this book explores has been backroaded by the limited-access highways—the Massachusetts Turnpike, Rt. 2, I-91, and I-3—and the free state road map available at this writing is of limited use. In this edition we have made a special effort to provide detailed maps to the areas that merit them, striving for accuracy both in the way back roads run and in the extensive amount of open space accessible to visitors (within each chapter, we detail it under *Green Space*). We recommend, however, that you secure copies of the 75-page DeLorme *Massachuestts Atlas and Gazeteer*, the detailed *Rubel Western Massachusetts Bicycle and Road Map* (see *Bicycling*), and the *Western Massachusetts Road Map* published by Jimapco (www.jimapco .com). Franklin County and the Hampshire Hilltowns also publish free detailed maps, available from the *Guidance* sources listed in those chapters.

MASSACHUSETTS TURNPIKE It's impossible to explore much of Massachusetts without encountering the "Mass Pike" (I-90). Completed in 1965, this superhighway cuts as straight as an arrow 135 miles across the state from Boston to the New York State line, with just 25 exits, 14 of them east of I-495. It was the first road in Massachusetts on which you could officially drive 65 miles per hour (between Auburn and Ludlow and again between Westfield and the New York line). Eleven service centers (most with fast-food restaurants) are scattered along the route, and four of these include information desks. They are located near the intersection with I-84 in Charlton (eastbound, 508-248-4581; westbound, 508-248-3853); in Lee (413-243-4929); and in Natick (508-650-3698).

MOHAWK TRAIL Traditionally this is the ancient trail blazed through the hilly northwestern corner of the state by Native Americans on their way between the Connecticut and Hudson River valleys. No one, however, pretends that it's the exact route. What's certain is the fact that on October 22, 1914, the 38-mile stretch of Rt. 2 between Greenfield and Williamstown was officially opened as New England's first "Scenic Road." At the time only a small percentage of roads in the region were paved, and this particularly hilly section was specifically designed to lure "tourists," touring in their first cars. In its namesake chapter we describe the Mohawk Trail's 1920s and 1930s viewing towers and trading posts, which are strategically spaced to permit those old autos to take on water after a steep climb. Thanks to white-water rafting and the dramatic renaissance of Shelburne Falls, visitors and residents alike are rediscovering this genuinely scenic road. The Mohawk Trail Highway has, incidentally, grown over the years and now extends a full 63 miles, beginning

in Millers Falls. Web site: www .mohawktrail.com.

MOUNTAINS Mount Greylock is the state's highest, and you can get to the top (3,491 feet) by car. You can also drive up Mount Sugarloaf, Mount Tom, and Mount Holyoke. All these offer hiking trails, as does Mount Toby.

MUSEUM VILLAGES Unlike most museum villages, both Hancock Shaker Village, a restored Shaker community in central Berkshire County, and Historic Deerfield, a street lined with more than a dozen 18th- and 19th-century homes in the Upper Pioneer Valley, are composed of buildings still in their original locations. Both therefore evoke an unusual sense of place as well as illustrating their respective stories. Both are also serious research centers. In East Springfield the much smaller Storrowton represents one of the country's earliest re-created villages; Greenfield Village, just west of Greenfield on Rt. 2, is one man's collection, housed in a building he constructed himself.

MUSIC The best known is the Tanglewood Music Festival (www.bso .org) during July and August in Lenox. Other prestigious summer series of note include the Aston Magna Festival (www.astonmagna.org) in Great Barrington, the Berkshire Choral Festival (www.choralfest.org) in Sheffield, the Sevenars concerts in South Worthington, and the Mohawk Trail Concerts (www.mohawktrail concerts.org) in Charlemont.

PETS, TRAVELING WITH The dog-paw symbol 🐾 indicates lodgings that

Hancock Shaker Village

accept pets. Most require prior notice and a reservation; many also require an additional fee.

PUBLIC RADIO Albany-based **WAMC-FM** (90.3) enjoys a wide reception throughout Western Massachusetts thanks to a transmitter atop Mount Greylock. There's also Great Barrington–based **WAMQ-FM** (105.1) and Amherst-based **WFCR-FM** (88.5).

RAIL EXCURSIONS The **Berkshire Scenic Railway** (413-637-2210; www.berkshirescenicrailroad.org) offers seasonal 20-mile round trips among Lenox, Stockbridge, and Lee. Also check out the **Chester Railroad Museum** (413-354-7778) in Chester.

ROCK CLIMBING Climbers seek out cliffs and boulders in Northfield, Ashfield, Erving, and Great Barrington. The Appalachian Mountain Club (www.amcberkshire.org) and Zoar Outdoor (www.zaroutdoor.com) lead frequent trips.

ROOM TAX In contrast with most states, which impose one state tax throughout, Massachusetts has given local communities the option of

adding an extra 4 percent—theoretically for local promotion—to the basic 5.7 percent room tax. Although resort towns tend to add the extra 4 percent, there is no hard-and-fast rule. It's worth asking. It's also worth noting that B&Bs with only two or three rooms are exempt from the room tax.

SHAKERS The Shakers are the oldest and most successful of America's many 19th-century communal religions, and interest in Shaker furniture and clothing, drawings, and entire, architecturally distinctive Shaker villages runs wide and deep. So does fascination with the people who created these "visible prayers." The Shakers once numbered 6,000 celibate brethren and sisters scattered in 20 self-contained villages from Maine to Ohio. Today only eight villages survive in good enough shape to tell their story—and the Hancock Shaker Village in Central Berkshire is one of the best.

In the 1770s Ann Lee was the leader of England's small sect of the United Society of Believers in Christ's Second Appearing, known for their expressive style of worship as "Shaking Quakers." With her husband, brother, and six followers, Mother Ann settled in Watervliet, near Albany, New York, in 1776. These were years of religious revival as well as political revolution.

Kim Grant

Zoar Outdoor

Whole communities of New Light Baptists—those in New Lebanon, New York (just over the boarder from Hancock), and Hancock—embraced Mother Ann's dictates of celibacy, shared property, pacifism, equality of the sexes, and a firm belief that life could be perfected in this world.

This last philosophy bred not only fine workmanship but also an astounding array of inventions: the flat broom, circular saw, clothespin, seed packet, and no-iron fabric, to name a few.

The Shaker Vatican, so to speak, was Mount Lebanon Shaker Village, straddling the Massachusetts–New York border just west of Hancock. Mount Lebanon elders and eldresses codified rules for all aspects of Shaker life. With 600 residents by the mid–19th century, this was the largest as well as most important Shaker community. On the Sabbath, brethren gathered to pray, sing, and dance in the theater-sized meetinghouse that had been ingeniously designed in 1824 without interior supports, and it was not unusual for more than 1,000 "World's People" (non-Shakers) to come for this "Sunday Show."

"They filed off in a double circle, one going one way, one the other— two or three abreast—laboring around this large hall with knees bent, hands

paddling like fins and voices chanting weird airs," recorded Fanny Appleton Longfellow.

Most of Mount Lebanon's surviving Shaker buildings are now part of the Darrow School, which is also the venue for summer Concerts at Tannery Pond. **Hancock Shaker Village** (www.hancockshakervillage.org), just east of New Lebanon in Hancock, is now a museum village—the area's prime showcase for all things Shaker. Another former Shaker village can be found in Tyringham, and yet another vanished community existed deep in Savoy State Forest.

SKIING, CROSS-COUNTRY Trails are noted throughout the book under *Cross-Country Skiing* and *Green Space.* The state's most dependable snow conditions are found in the Berkshire Hilltown snowbelt, which runs north–south through **Stump Sprouts** (a lodge and touring center; www.stumpsprouts.com) in East Hawley; the **Windsor Notch Reservation** (www.thetrustees.org) in Windsor; and **Canterbury Farm** (www.canterbury-farms.com) in Washington. Many state parks in Western Massachusetts offer

Hancock Shaker Village

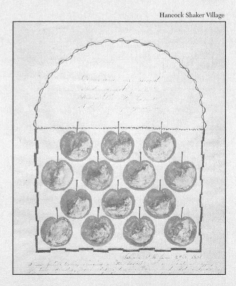

cross-country trails www.mass.gov/dcr/ recreate/skiing.htm); Northfield Mountain (800-859-2960) also offers an extensive groomed-trail system.

SKIING, DOWNHILL Within this book we have described each area. In Central and North Berkshire **Jiminy Peak** (www.jiminypeak.com) has expanded substantially in recent years; **Bousquet** (www.bousquets.com), founded in 1932, continues to offer beginner, intermediate, and night skiing. In South Berkshire, **Catamount** (www.catamountski.com) and **Butternut** (www.butternutbasin.com) both offer vertical drops of 1,000 feet and a variety of trails, while **Otis Ridge** (www.otisridge.com) is a family-geared area limiting lift tickets to 800 per day. Up in West County, **Berkshire East** (www.berkshireeast.com) bills itself as southern New England's largest ski area with 45 trails and five lifts, including a quad installed in 2004.

SNOWMOBILING The Snowmobiling Association of Massachusetts

(SAM) (413-369-8092; www.sledmass .com), P.O. Box 55, Heath 01346. SAM coordinates local clubs and offers guidance to some hundreds of miles of trails throughout the state.

SPAS Lenox is the spa capital of New England. Admittedly, there are relatively few spas in New England, and only two of the three major facilities in Lenox—**Canyon Ranch** (www .canyonranch.com) and **Cranwell** (www.cranwell.com)—are technically spas. The third, the **Kripalu Center for Yoga and Health** (www.kripalu .org), is, however, also a mainstream mecca for thousands seeking physical and mental renewal. The staff requirements at all these centers have drawn a large number of both New Age and traditional fitness practitioners to the area; several have opened small day spas catering to patrons of the many local inns, a situation worth noting, especially in winter and spring, when inn prices drop well below Tanglewood-season rates. **Mepal Manor & Spa** (www.mepalspa.com), in New

Butternut, Great Barrington

Marlborough, is the newest and smallest of the region's full-service spas. It's a gem in a beautiful setting.

STATE FORESTS AND PARKS Would you believe that Massachusetts, the sixth smallest state in the country, has the eighth largest state park system? The **Department of Conservation and Recreation** (DCR) is responsible for more than a quarter million acres of public forests and parks. It's the largest single landholder in the state. The system began in 1898 with the gift of 8,000 acres around Mount Greylock. Initially its mandate was to purchase logged-over, virtually abandoned land for $5 per acre, and during the Great Depression the Civilian Conservation Corps (CCC) greatly expanded the facilities (building roads, trails, lakes, and other recreation areas).

This book describes 47 forests and parks in their respective chapters

under *Green Space*, suggesting opportunities for hiking, camping, boating, swimming, and skiing both downhill (Butternut) and cross-country. *The Massachusetts State Parks Guide to Swimming, Camping, Hiking & Biking* is an indispensable key to this vast system, available along with the *Massachusetts Outdoor Recreation Map* (including state wildlife management areas) and the pamphlet guides *Universal Access* (detailing handicapped-accessible facilities) and *Massachusetts Historic State Parks*, from the DCR (for the Berkshires, 413-442-8928; for the Pioneer Valley, 413-545-5993; www.mass.gov/dcr).

THEATER The **Williamstown Theatre Festival** (www.wtfestival.org), late June through August, is the premier summer theater festival of the Northeast. **Shakespeare & Company** (www.shakespeare.org) in Lenox, performing May through

Kim Grant

October, is in a class of its own, and the **Berkshire Theatre Festival** (www.berkshiretheatre.org) in Stockbridge is still thriving after 75 years of summer productions. Recently moved to expanded quarters in Pittsfield, where it offers an expanded season, **Barrington Stage Company** (www.barringtonstage.org) features musicals and original productions. The **Miniature Theatre of Chester** (www.miniaturetheatre.org) offers superb small productions. **Pioneer Valley Summer Theatre** (www .summertheatre.net) at the Williston Northampton School offers performances June through mid-August in Easthampton; **New Century Theatre** (www.newcenturytheatre.org) has developed a reputation for quality performances, staged late June through mid-August on the Smith College campus in Northampton and at the **Arena Civic Theatre** in Greenfield. **City Stage** in Springfield stages professional theater September through May, as does **Shea Community Theater** in Turners Falls.

TRACKING With or without snowshoes, tracking is proving to be a new way into the woods year-round for many people. The idea is to track animals for purposes other than hunting. Naturalist **Alan Edmond** (413-624-95444) in Colrain, the local guru, offers half- and full-day tours. In the North Quabbin area check out the **Walnut Hill Tracking and Nature Center** (978-544-6083) and **David Brown's Wildlife Services** (978-249-3929). Massachusetts Audubon Sanctuaries (see *Birding*) throughout the state also now offer tracking programs.

TRUSTEES OF RESERVATIONS The nation's oldest private statewide conservation and preservation organization, the **Trustees** (413-298-3239; www.thetrustees.org), as this nonprofit is simply known, was founded in 1891 by Charles Eliot, who proposed to preserve parcels of land "which possess uncommon beauty and more than usual refreshing power . . . just as the Public Library holds books and the Art Museum pictures—for the use and enjoyment of the public." So it happens that the Trustees now own and manage hilltops, waterfalls, islands, barrier beaches, bogs, historic houses, and designed landscapes, among other things, 20 in Western Massachusetts alone. Within this book we describe properties as they appear within chapters. Note that holdings include the outstanding Guest House at Field Farm in Williamstown. Also note the beautifully maintained historic houses in Stockbridge, Ashley Falls, and Cummington.

WATERFALLS We long thought that someone should make a poster of Massachusetts waterfalls, not only because there are so many but also because most are so little known and varied. Happily, such a poster—which depicts 20 Berkshire County waterfalls in full color—is now available from **Berkshire Photos** (413-743-4326; www.berkshirephotos.com). Check out the falls in Ashfield, Becket, Blandford, Cheshire, Chesterfield, Dalton, Middlefield, Mount Washington, New Marlboro, North Adams, Sheffield, Shelburne Falls, Williamsburg, and Worthington, all of which we have visited and describe. Also check Joe Bushee's web site www .massfalls.com and his book, *Waterfalls of Massachusetts: An Explorers Guide to 55 Natural Scenic Wonders*.

WEATHER The web site www.mass countryroads.com is a good bet for 5-day weather forecasts for Western Massachusetts.

WHEELCHAIR ACCESS The wheelchair symbol ♿ indicates lodging and dining places that are handicapped-accessible. Also note the pamphlet detailing the universal-access program in state forests and parks (see above).

WHITE-WATER RAFTING Since 1989, when New England Electric began releasing water on a regular basis from its Fife Brook Dam, white-water rafting has become a well-established pastime on the Deerfield River. **Zoar Outdoor** (www.zaroutdoor.com) in Charlemont pioneered the sport in this area and offers lodging and a variety of programs. Maine-based **Crab Apple Whitewater** (www.crabapple whitewater.com) now has its own attractive base on the river down the road—stiff competition—as does

Moxie Outdoor Adventures (www.moxierafting.com), also headquartered in Maine.

WINERIES West County Winery (www.westcountycider.com) in Shelburne has been producing widely marketed and respected apple wines since 1984. **Chester Hill Winery** (413-354-2340; www.blueberrywine .com) in Chester makes three kinds of blueberry wine, as well as a white wine with grapes from New York, and welcomes visitors in its tasting room June–Dec., weekends 1–5. **Furnace Brook Winery at Hilltop Orchards** (www.hilltoporchards.com) in Richmond specializes in oak-aged cider but also offers tastings of its varietal grape and specialty wines. In New Marlborough check out **Les Trois Emme** (413-528-1015; www.lte winery.com), 8 Knight Rd., New Marlborough; it's open for tours and tasting ($5) Apr.–Dec., Thu.–Sun. noon–5. Red wines from home-grown and California grapes, also pumpkin wine.

The Berkshire Hills

BERKSHIRE COUNTY

ALONG THE MOHAWK TRAIL

THE HILLTOWNS

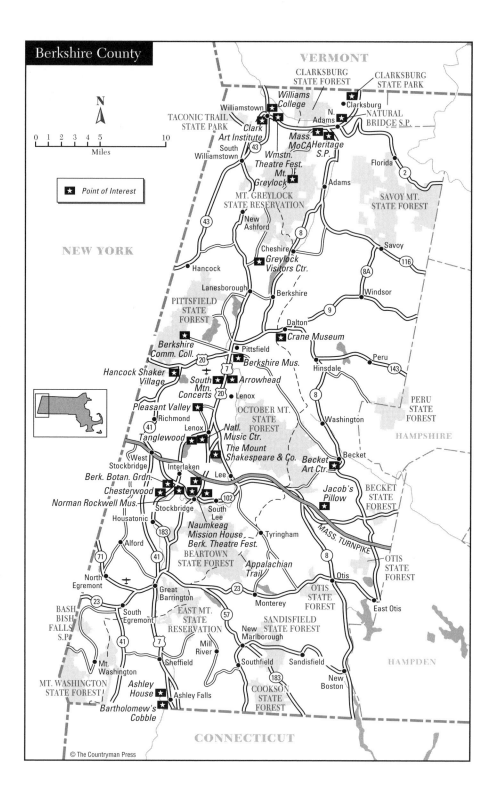

Berkshire County

BERKSHIRE COUNTY

SOUTH COUNTY
CENTRAL AND NORTH BERKSHIRE

Berkshire has the best name recognition of any Massachusetts county. Ask residents where they come from and the answer is invariably "the Berkshires," not "Massachusetts."

The Berkshires is actually a fairly recent name created to promote Berkshire County. Never mind that the Berkshire Hills themselves roll east through the Hilltowns.

This westernmost strip of Massachusetts has always been a place apart. Its first settlers were easygoing Dutchmen rather than the dour Puritans, and while parts of Berkshire County are equidistant from both Boston and New York City, visitors and ideas tend to flow from the south rather than the east.

Berkshire County is a distinctive roll of hill and valley that extends the full 56-mile length of the state. Its highest mountains, including Mount Greylock (3,491 feet) in North Berkshire and Mount Everett (2,264 feet) in South Berkshire, are actually strays from New York's Taconic Range; the county is walled from New York State on the west by the Taconics and from the rest of "the Bay State" by hills high enough for 18th-century settlers to have called them the Berkshire Barrier.

History, topography, and politics aside, what sets the Berkshires apart from anywhere else in the United States is the quantity and quality of the music, art, dance, and theater staged here during July and August. Summer festivals are scattered through a wide swath of largely forested countryside: from the Williamstown Theatre Festival in the state's northwestern corner to the Jacob's Pillow Dance Festival in South Berkshire.

GEDNEY FARM IN NEW MARLBOROUGH
Kim Grant

Writers and artists were the first Berkshire summer residents; wealthier rusticators began arriving with the trains from New York and Boston. Between 1880 and 1920 some 75 grandiose summer mansions were built around Lenox and Stockbridge. Then came the stock market crash and Depression years, but neither Boston nor New York society forgot their former summer playground. In the 1930s the Boston Symphony Orchestra selected an estate in Lenox as its summer home, and the cultural and summer social tide began to turn once more. It was interrupted, however, by World War II, and after came the years in which illustrator Norman Rockwell vividly recorded sleepy small-town America, based on what he saw within bicycling distance of his Stockbridge studio.

Unexpectedly, the Cold War boosted Berkshire County as a cultural destination. Fearing a nuclear attack on Manhattan, Singer Sewing Machine heirs Sterling and Francine Clark chose to display their legendary art collection in the ivied college town of Williamstown, building a marble museum to house it. The 1955 opening of the Clark Art Institute drew art lovers from around the world— and the steady stream continues.

Even more unexpectedly, the Vietnam War brought the Berkshires a different artistic fame. Folksinger Arlo Guthrie wrote "Alice's Restaurant," an 18-minute-long saga recounting Guthrie's arrest for illegally dumping litter and how it kept him out of the draft. The song became the antibattle cry of a generation, and the 1969 movie version brought it all visually home: the same small-town scenes and people that Norman Rockwell had depicted, and once more evoking the feel— this time a different feel—of small towns across the country.

In the 21st century Berkshire County is once more enjoying a Gilded Era, and this time it's shared by a far larger group than that of 100 years ago. Once more there's no question that Stockbridge and Lenox are not just any small towns. Visitors from everywhere rock on the porch of the Red Lion Inn (which was almost torn down to make way for a gas station at the early 1960s tourism ebb), and while the Curtis in Lenox is no longer a hotel, the town now offers dozens of princely mansions in which to sleep, and half a dozen in which you can dine at princely prices. In all, the Berkshires can now accommodate 5,000 visitors on any given night, offer them 70 cultural attractions, and feed them in 200 restaurants.

While many attractions are seasonal, few lodging places or restaurants now close for the winter. Lodging rates, on the other hand, vary wildly with the season and even with the day of the week. On weekends during "Tanglewood season" (July and August), you can pay Manhattan prices for a modest room and frequently must stay a minimum of 3 days. Weekdays, even in August, generally cost less. Rates remain high through October as foliage colors linger. Winter offers skiing at some of the country's oldest family-geared ski areas and reduced

IN SHEFFIELD

Kim Grant

prices for all those elegant rooms with fireplaces; it's also a good time to take advantage of lower rates at both the day and full-service spas that now cluster in South Berkshire.

We have divided Berkshire County in two: "South County" includes Lenox and Stockbridge as well as Great Barrington and the surrounding rural villages. The Central Berkshire communities of Pittsfield, Hancock, and Dalton we have combined with the Williamstown and North Adams in "Central and North Berkshire."

Year-round the countryside remains far more than a backdrop. Since the 1840s, both picnicking and hiking along bench-spotted paths and up gentle mountains have been considered the thing to do in summer, and now snowmobiles as well as snowshoes and cross-country skis access many trails in the county's more than 125,000 acres of public preserves.

GUIDANCE

Countywide information services
Berkshire Visitors Bureau (800-237-5747; www.berkshires.org) offers a countywide reservation service. Request *The Berkshires Official Visitors Guide*, a thick annual listing of attractions, lodgings, and dining. Lodging reservation service Mon.–Sat. 9–4: 800-237-5747, ext. 506.

Massachusetts Department of Conservation and Recreation (DCR) publishes a handy map/guide to state forests and parks and maintains the web site www.mass.gov/dcr, as well as a friendly visitor information center at 740 South St. (Rt. 7 northbound), Pittsfield (413-442-8928).

SOUTH COUNTY

The southwest corner of Massachusetts has its own distinctive beauty and pace. The Housatonic River is slower, and the roads are more heavily wooded, winding through classic old villages, by swimming holes, and past hiking paths that lead to waterfalls.

In July and August, however, this serene landscape is the backdrop for the liveliest music, theater, and dance presentations in the Northeast, arguably in the entire country. It's a phenomenon that's been more than a century in the making.

Writers Nathaniel Hawthorne, Herman Melville, and Oliver Wendell Holmes Sr. were among the first Berkshire summer residents. Their lyrical descriptions of the area's inspirational scenery helped attract wealthy rusticators, who built great summer mansions (coyly called "cottages") and terraced cornfields into formal gardens, especially in and around Lenox and Stockbridge. The stock market crash of 1929, the Depression, and the federal income tax thinned the ranks of the Berkshires' wealthy elite. The mansions remained, however, and were frequently taken over by private schools, religious orders, or cultural institutions.

In 1937 the Boston Symphony Orchestra (BSO) made Tanglewood, an estate donated by an orchestra patron, its summer home. Dancers, musicians, actors, and writers began flocking to the Lenox area, lured by the presence of the Berkshire Playhouse (now the Berkshire Theatre Festival), Jacob's Pillow Dance Festival, and the BSO—all presenting summer programs at former private estates.

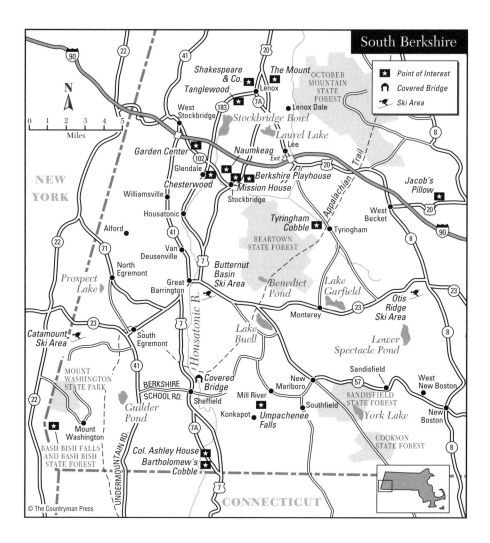

The audience for these, and the many more live performances that currently form the South Berkshire summer arts scene, is composed primarily of New Yorkers. Great Barrington is said to be equidistant from both New York and Boston—2 hours, 15 minutes (traffic permitting) from both—but New York accents predominate here. This isn't a bad thing. New Yorkers are a famously discerning audience for music, theater, and the arts and bring a discerning palate to restaurants. They not only support the arts and patronize the places to eat, to shop, and to stay but also tend to be the people operating most visitor-geared ventures.

In and around Lenox and Stockbridge, many mansions are now inns and bed & breakfasts, and three former Lenox estates are now destination resorts in their own right: Canyon Ranch is New England's premier spa, Cranwell is both a golfing resort and a spa, while Kripalu is the region's largest yoga-based retreat center. The other resort villages are South Egremont (blink and you're through), with its clutch of restaurants and antiques shops, and Sheffield, the Berkshires' oldest town and now aptly synonymous with antiques dealers.

The towns that have changed most visibly in South County in recent years are the formerly workaday Lee and Great Barrington. Paper is still made in Lee, along with lime, even a little marble; both the vintage-1855 Morgan House and 1955 Joe's Diner are still Main Street staples; and the Victorian-era buildings house a number of restaurants. Capitalizing on its status as the county's prime gateway to the Massachusetts Turnpike, a large designer outlet mall, Prime Outlets, sits on a hillside just off the Pike exit. Gracious B&Bs are scattered along the town's wooded upland roads.

Great Barrington, the largest town in south Berkshire County, has always been a place to buy a wrench, catch a bus, and see a dentist or a movie. Recently it's also become a place to shop for linen clothing and country furnishings, to purchase artist materials and vintage posters, and to choose from an ever-widening variety of menus. The tiny visitor center also houses Half Tix, selling same-day, half-price tickets for musicals and plays at the Barrington Stage Company, dance at Jacob's Pillow, and music in numerous Berkshire venues.

South from Great Barrington, the Housatonic spirals lazily through a broad valley hemmed in by rolling hills to the west and walled by the abrupt range that includes Mount Everett on the west. Sheffield's village of Ashley Falls, almost on the Connecticut line, is the site of the Colonel Ashley House in which the Sheffield Declaration, a 1773 statement of grievances against Bristish rule, was drafted. This exceptional home is owned by the Trustees of Reservations, the venerable Massachusetts organization that also maintains several of the area's outstanding historic houses and preserves.

South County harbors thousands of acres of state park and forest, acquired when land was cheap, after 75 percent of its trees were chopped down to feed either the area's lime kilns or its paper mills. In the 1890s vast estates were also acquired by private owners, and segments of these are also now preserved by the state and by the Trustees. Public lands offer camping, swimming, and fishing as well as hiking and cross-country skiing. The Appalachian Trail cuts across the Housatonic Valley, offering numerous access points, from the heights of Mount Race to Benedict Pond in Beartown State Forest.

East of the Housatonic Valley gentle hills are webbed with back roads, many still dirt, climbing through old farms and still some estates dating from land speculation before railway routes were determined. A railway never materialized, and the east–west Massachusetts Turnpike followed Rt. 20 through Becket to Lee, backroading Otis, Tyringham, and Monterey and even further backroading the 18th-century towns of Sandisfield and New Marlborough.

AREA CODE 413.

GUIDANCE **Southern Berkshire Chamber of Commerce** (413-528-1510; www.southernberkshires.com), 362 Main St., at the southern edge of Great Barrington (Rt. 23–Rt. 7), across from "Searles Castle." Open year-round, Tue.–Sun. 9:30–6. Lodging hotline: 800-269-4825.

Lenox Chamber of Commerce (413-637-3646 or 800-25-LENOX; www.lenox .org), Curtis Building, 5 Walker St., Lenox 01240-0646. Open Tue.–Sat. 10–4. A walk-in, volunteer-staffed information center providing free lodging referral, which during Tanglewood season includes many private homes, along with guidance about shopping, dining, and attractions.

Bluebird Visitor Center, Main St., Stockbridge, is open daily in summer months. The **Stockbridge Chamber of Commerce** (413-298-5200; www .stockbridgechamber.org), 6 Elm St., is good for help Mon., Wed., and Fri. Lodging hotline: 866-626-5327.

The **Lee Chamber of Commerce** (413-243-0852; www.leechamber.org), 3 Park Place, is well marked and conveniently sited just after you make the turn (northbound) onto Rt. 20 (Main St.), in a small park with plenty of adjoining parking. Open Mon.–Sat. 10–4, Sun. 1–4.

GETTING THERE *By air:* See **Albany Airport** and **Bradley International Airport** in Windsor Locks, Connecticut, under *Airports* in "What's Where."

By bus: From Boston, **Peter Pan–Trailways** (800-343-9999) serves Lee and Lenox via Springfield. From Manhattan, **Bonanza** (800-556-3815) runs up Rt. 7, stopping on the green in Sheffield, South Egremont, Great Barrington at the chamber booth, Stockbridge (Main St.), Lee at the Morgan House Inn, and Lenox (Lenox News & Variety: 413-637-2815).

By train: From New York City, **Metro-North** (212-532-4900 or 800-METRO-INFO; www.mta.info). On weekends from July through Labor Day, Friday-evening trains from Grand Central to Wassaic Station, New York, connect with buses to Great Barrington. Return service is offered Sunday afternoon. The price is surprisingly reasonable.

By car: From Boston, the obvious route is the Massachusetts Turnpike to exit 2 at Lee (2 hours on the button). For a more scenic approach take exit 6 (Rt. 291) to I-91 south to Rt. 57 west (see *Scenic Drives*).

From New York City, the obvious approach is the Major Deegan Expwy. or the Henry Hudson Pkwy. to the Saw Mill River Pkwy., then to the Taconic Pkwy.; take the South Berkshire exit, Hillsdale/Claverack, Rt. 23.

GETTING AROUND A car is the way to go, but you can hire a taxi or rent a car (check chamber listings in Lee and Great Barrington). Local rental car agencies deliver cars to the bus stops or local inns. Given the many scenic but confusing roads that web this area in particular, we recommend securing a Berkshire County map, free from the sources listed under *Guidance*.

The **Berkshire Regional Transit Authority** (413-499-2782 or 800-292-2782) links Great Barrington, Lee,

Christina Tree

Lenox, and Stockbridge with Pittsfield; hours are geared to commuters
rather than to visitors.

PARKING It's free in Lenox, Stockbridge, and Great Barrington, but
there's a 2-hour limit, strictly
enforced. In Great Barrington the big
downtown lot is at the end of Railroad St.; there's a smaller lot at the
end of Castle St.

MEDICAL EMERGENCY Dial **911**.

Christina Tree

BALDWIN HILL, SOUTH EGREMONT

✳ Towns and Villages

Egremont (population: 1,150). There is no village of Egremont; instead there's
North Egremont and South Egremont, divided by Baldwin Hill. **South Egremont** is the livelier village, one of the few in the Berkshires to retain its original,
rambling old inn. The village is also known for antiques shops. Note the fan window in the **Congregational Church** and the town hall in the southern village.
Don't miss **Baldwin Hill**, with its surviving farms and sense of serenity. **North
Egremont** offers a general store, inn, and lakeside campground.

Great Barrington (population: 7,288). The shopping hub of southern Berkshire
County, Great Barrington is known for the quality and quantity of its restaurants,
and also of its downtown shopping. Railroad Street is restaurant row; neighboring film, music, and live performance venues complement the dining and shopping. This is still a place to get your shoes or your camera fixed. There were
actually once three large and fashionable inns in town, including the Berkshire
Inn (1868–1963), which more than filled the site that's now occupied by the
Southern Berkshire Chamber of Commerce, Bill's Pharmacy, and the Days Inn.
Searles Castle, across the street, was designed by Stanford White and built of
local blue dolomite stone between 1882 and 1886 for the widow of a founder of
the Central Pacific Railroad. Main
Street's three stone churches also
evoke this opulent era.

RIVER WALK, GREAT BARRINGTON
Kim Grant

Worth noting: The ancient-looking
(and barely readable) stone marker in
front of **town hall** with the inscrip-
tion: NEAR THIS SPOT STOOD THE FIRST
COURT HOUSE OF BERKSHIRE COUNTY.
HERE AUGUST 16, 1774 OCCURRED THE
FIRST OPEN RESISTANCE TO BRITISH
RULE IN AMERICA. Worth finding:
River Walk, still evolving but offer-
ing benches and views of the
Housatonic in several segments as it

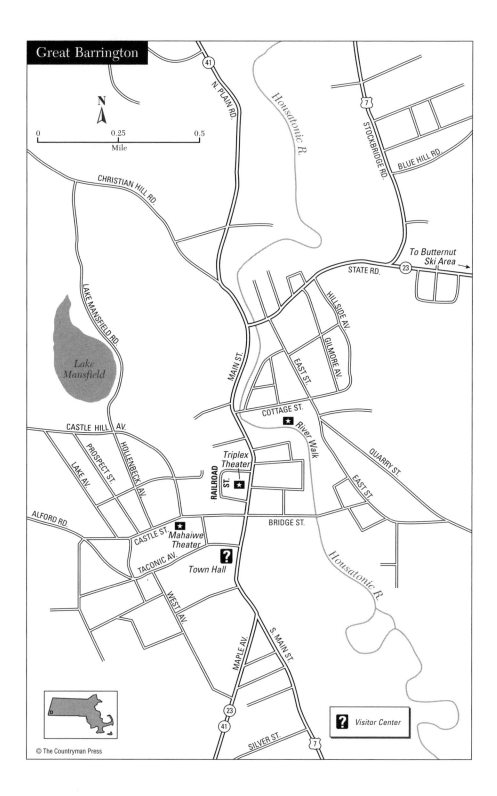

Great Barrington

N

0   0.25   0.5
Mile

© The Countryman Press

? Visitor Center

flows behind Main Street. At the entrance beside Brooks Drugs, a brief history credits William Edward Burghardt DuBois with inspiring the project, pleading with townspeople to "Rescue the Housatonic . . . restore its ancient beauty." Sociologist and civil rights activist W. E. B. DuBois (1868–1966) was born in Great Barrington by what he called this "golden river," explaining that it was "golden because of the woolen and paper waste that soiled it." The woolen and paper mills were, however, several miles upstream in **Housatonic**, a village that still has a working paper mill as well as a number of artists working in former mill buildings.

Lenox (population: c. 5,000) evolved in stages. Its 1787 status as county seat gave it graceful Federal buildings like the courthouse; the recently renovated library with its luxurious reading rooms, gallery, and outdoor reading park; the Academy; and the Church on the Hill. In the 1860s county government shifted to Pittsfield and summer visitors began buying up large holdings. By the turn of the century more than 90 elaborate summer "cottages" were scattered along every ridge in the area. Lenox's glory years as the inland Newport were brief, ended by the Great Depression and the federal income tax. The resort might have vanished entirely had it not been for the Boston Symphony Orchestra's Berkshire Music Festival. Concert halls were not yet air-conditioned, and symphony music typically ceased during summer. The orchestra selected Lenox as its summer home because Tanglewood (a forested estate named by Nathaniel Hawthorne, who wrote *Tanglewood Tales* there) was given to it by a patron.

More than 50 grand "Berkshire Cottages" still cluster in and around Lenox. The Mount, former residence of novelist Edith Wharton (whose best-known work, *Ethan Frome*, is set in the Berkshires), has been restored and is open to the public. Bellefontaine, another baronial cottage, is now a spa (Canyon Ranch), several are inns, and the site of one of the grandest—Andrew Carnegie's mansion, which unfortunately burned (though its million-dollar view remains)—is now the Kripalu Center for Yoga and Health.

Stockbridge (population: 2,300) was founded in 1734 to contain and educate the local Mahicans. Just four white families were permitted to settle, theoretically to "afford civilizing examples to the Indians." But predictably, the whites multiplied and the Native Americans dwindled. After distinguishing themselves as the only tribe to serve in the Revolution and the first to be given U.S. citizenship, the Stockbridge tribe was banished to the west, eventually to Wisconsin, where a few hundred descendants still live. Stockbridge boasts that the Laurel Hill Association was the country's first village-improvement society. Residents will tell you that the same number of notables have been summering in town for the past century; only the faces change periodically. The rambling, wooden **Red Lion Inn**, a short walk from the restored **Mission House**, forms the heart of the village. **Naumkeag**, the quintessential Gilded Age mansion, is just a short way up the hill, and the **Berkshire Theatre Festival** is on the northern fringe of town.

The village green is west of the Rt. 102–Rt. 7 junction, and many visitors miss it entirely. Here stand the imposing brick Congregational Church (1824), the pillared Old Town Hall (1839), and the Field Chime Tower, which marks the site of the original Native American mission. The Indian Burial Ground is nearby—the

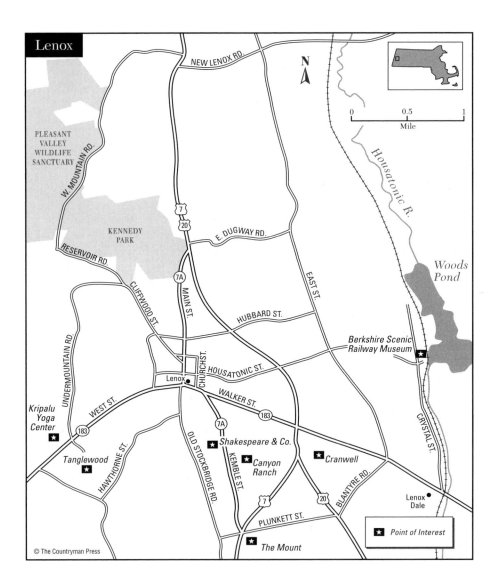

Lenox

large mound topped by a stone obelisk and overlooking the golf course. The Village Cemetery, across from the green, contains the remains of John Sergeant, Native American chief John Konkapot, 19th-century tycoons such as Joseph Choate, and town aristocrats like the Fields and Sedgwicks, the latter buried in a large circular family plot known as "the Sedgwick pie."

Monterey (population: 918). Much of this town has been absorbed into **Beartown State Forest**, and it is largely a second-home community. Lake Garfield is ringed with summer homes, and its beach is private. The **General Store** is, however, hospitable, with a deli and snacks at tables in the rear. Head north from the village center and turn onto Art School Road to find the **Bidwell House**, an exceptionally well-furnished 18th-century home with walking trails through its extensive grounds. This was once a dairy center producing more cheese than any other location in the county, and **Monterey Chèvre** from Rawson Brook Farm is still the county's best.

Mount Washington (population: 135). This town is the southwesternmost, the highest, and one of the smallest in Massachusetts. Best known as the home of **Bash Bish Falls**, the state's most photographed cascade, it is also the site of one of the highest peaks (2,600-foot Mount Everett) and the highest lake (Guilder Pond) in Massachusetts. The community is also arguably the oldest in Berkshire County (settled by the Dutch in the 1690s). The town is webbed with hiking trails—including one of the more dramatic, open ridgeline sections of the **Appalachian Trail**. Given that you can park at several trailheads that access high-elevation trails—and paths to several waterfalls (the cascades of Race Brook and Bear Rock as well as Bash Bish)—you would assume this was one of the better-known, more popular spots to hike. Not so. Mount Washington seems to be a well-kept hikers' secret. Population is less than 200 and triples in summer. The center of the village is marked by the small **Union Church** (ecumenical, open summers only) and tiny town hall. Note the old cemetery on West Street and Blueberry Hill Farm.

New Marlborough (population: 918; www.newmarlborough.org) lies within a beautiful roll of hills pocked by shallow valleys carved by the Konkapot River and its offshoots. The town is webbed with roads connecting its villages: Mill River, Southfield, Hartsville, New Marlborough Center, and Clayton. At the center stand the Old Inn on the Green and a domed white-clapboard meetinghouse, the venue for late-summer-through-fall music, films, etc., sponsored by Music and More. The town's last surviving industrial vestige is the **Buggy Whip Factory** in the village of Southfield. In operation from 1792 until 1973, it's now an antiques market housing more than 80 dealers. A small museum dramatizes the history of the village tanning industry.

Sheffield (population: 2,967). This town was the first in the Berkshires to be chartered (1733). Its wide main street (Rt. 7) is lined with stately old homes, and the town boasts the greatest number of antiques dealers of any town in the Berkshires. North of the green, the 1770s brick **Dan Raymond House**, maintained by the **Sheffield Historical Society** (413-229-2694), is open Memorial Day–Oct., Sat. 10–2, Sun. 11–3. It reflects the lifestyle of this prosperous merchant, his wife, and their nine children. It's part of a seven-building complex that includes a regional research center (Mon. and Fri. 1:30–4 and by appointment), a vintage-1820 law office, a carriage house with a tool exhibit, and an oddly shaped building once used to grow vegetables for nearby hotels, now an education center. There's also an 1830s smokehouse

COVERED BRIDGE IN SHEFFIELD

Kim Grant

Kim Grant

and the Old Stone Store housing changing exhibitions and a museum store. The 1760 **Old Parish Church** is a beauty, one of the oldest churches in Berkshire County and the site of a seasonal Friday-afternoon farmer's market (3:30–6:30) as well as of the annual 3-day **Sheffield Antiques Fair**, always the third weekend in August. Several miles south on Rt. 7 is Ashley Falls. It's well worth allotting several hours in which to tour the **Colonel Ashley House** (1735), the oldest in the Berkshires, and to walk along the glassy Housatonic in **Bartholomew's Cobble**. Note the covered bridge, built originally in 1827, just off Rt. 7 at the northern end of the village.

Tyringham (population: 375). Hemmed in on three sides by mountains, this village was the site of a major Shaker community from the 1790s until the 1870s (a group of privately owned Shaker buildings still stands on Jerusalem Road near Shaker Pond). The village then began attracting prominent summer residents, including Samuel Clemens. A number of 19th-century writers eulogized Tyringham.

Sandisfield (population: 809). With the largest area of any Berkshire County town, this was once a thriving industrial center with six taverns and churches and a population said to surpass Pittsfield's. It's difficult to believe. Land sales boomed when a railroad was proposed to run through town, but it never happened. The most visible village in Sandisfield is New Boston, at the junction of Rts. 8 and 57. The **New Boston Inn**—said to date to 1737—has a well-documented resident ghost and still offers food and lodging. Much of the town now lies within the **Sandisfield State Forest**.

✳ To See

MUSIC

Aston Magna Festival (413-528-3595 or 800-875-7156; www.astonmagna.org), Daniel Arts Center, Simon's Rock College, Great Barrington. Five Saturdays in July and Aug., three in Oct., Jan., and Mar. The country's oldest annual summer festival devoted to baroque, classical, and early romantic music, very professionally played on period instruments. Tickets $30–35.

Berkshire Choral Festival (413-229-8526; www.choralfest.org), 245 Undermountain Rd. (Rt. 41), Sheffield. Held in the concert shed of the Berkshire School, this is a summer series of concerts combining hundreds of voices with music by the Springfield Symphony. Come early for a picnic and a preconcert talk. $25 rear orchestra, $30 front orchestra, $40 box seat.

Close Encounters with Music (800-843-778; www.cewm.org) or through the Mahaiwee Box Office (413-528-0100). A respected chamber music series Sep.–Memorial Day weekend, usually at St. James Church or the Mawhaiwe in Great Barrington.

Music & More in the Meetinghouse (www.newmarlborough.org), Rt. 47, New Marlborough. An August-through-fall series of pre-dinner chamber music and other programs staged in this 300-year-old church.

THEATER Shakespeare & Company (box office, 413-637-3353; off-season, 413-637-1197; www.shakespeare.org), 70 Kemble St., Lenox. Productions late May–Oct.; tickets run $10–54, depending on seating, theater, and performance. Students, seniors, and groups get a 10 percent discount. Some free performances. In existence for more than 25 years, this exciting theater company, long based at the Edith Wharton mansion, the Mount, now has its own expansive home: a 30-acre property with two stages. The grounds are open to the public for strolling and picnicking. Although Shakespeare is the main dramatic fare, the company also does other classic plays, such as works of Chekhov, as well as plays by contemporary authors and short "salon" pieces based on stories by Edith Wharton and others. Major productions are staged at Founders Theatre, which can seat nearly 500 people. One of the company's long-term projects is a re-creation of The Rose—a three-tiered, thatch-roofed Elizabethan-era London theater. Until the money is raised to begin construction, the group makes do with "The Rose Footprint." This is a simple outdoor theater covered with a tent in midsummer (often used for productions featuring student actors) that is on the site of and has the same dimensions as the planned Elizabethan replica.

Berkshire Theatre Festival (413-298-5576; www.berkshiretheatre.org), 6 E. Main St. (Rt. 102), Stockbridge. Since 1928 the July-through-August festival has been staged in a building designed by Stanford White in 1887 as the Stockbridge Casino. The building was restored and moved to its present site in the 1920s by Mabel Choate, mistress of Naumkeag. Katharine Hepburn, Ethel Barrymore, James Cagney, and Dustin Hoffman all performed here early in their careers. The festival program is varied and usually includes one or two premieres each season. Children's theater is staged Wed.–Sat. at 11 AM at the Berkshire Museum in Pittsfield in July and the festival's 100-seat Unicorn Theatre in August.

Mahaiwe Performing Arts Center (413-644-9040; www.mahaiwe.org), 14 Castle St., Great Barrington. This ornate and intimate (700-seat) vaudeville house was built in 1905 and has been thoroughly, lovingly restored

SHAKESPEARE & CO.'S 2006 PRODUCTION OF *THE MERRY WIVES OF WINDSOR,* OFTEN CALLED SHAKESPEARE'S FUNNIEST ROMP
Kevin Sprague

TANGLEWOOD MUSIC FESTIVAL

(413-637-5165; off-season, 617-266-1492; box office, 617-266-1200 or 888-266-1200; www.bso.org), Tanglewood, entrance on West St. (Rt. 183) west of Lenox village. The Boston Symphony Orchestra's summer concert series, which opens July 4 and runs through August, has been held since the 1930s in a fan-shaped, open-sided hall understatedly referred to as "the Shed." The Koussevitzky Music Shed actually seats 5,000 people and has splendid acoustics. More than 14,000 patrons regularly converge on Tanglewood on weekends, but a concert is rarely sold out, and then it's usually for an appearance by a pop music superstar such as James Taylor. There is always room on the 500-acre grounds, though parking lots can fill up and postconcert traffic jams are legendary (which is why inns and B&Bs within walking distance of the main gate can charge premium rates). Many concertgoers actually prefer sitting on the lawn and come several hours early, dressed in high resort style (or any old way at all), bearing elaborate picnic hampers that have been known to include white linen tablecloths and candelabra. (*Note:* It does rain and bugs do bite on the lawn, so come prepared.) The lawn at Tanglewood is one of New England's great people-watching places. Many concerts are now also staged in the 1,200-seat Seiji Ozawa Hall, which also has an adjoining lawn that can accommodate several hundred.

Symphonic concerts (Fri. and Sat. evenings and Sun. afternoons) aside, the Tanglewood calendar is filled, beginning in mid-June, with chamber music and other special concerts; there's also an annual Festival of Contemporary Music and a Labor Day weekend Jazz Festival, plus almost daily concerts by young musicians of the Tanglewood Music Center (TMC) Orchestra. The Boston Pops performs each summer, and there are Friday Prelude Con-

over the past six years. It now offers a year-round schedule of film, music, dance, opera, family entertainment, and more. Check out the new marquee and the current schedule on the web site. Tip: It's pronounced *muh-HEY-we.*

Also see the **Barrington Stage Company** and **Williamstown Theatre Festival** in "Central and North Berkshire."

Jacob's Pillow Dance Festival (413-243-0745; www.jacobspillow.org), George Carter Rd., Becket (off Rt. 20, 8 miles east of Lee). America's oldest dance festival and still its most prestigious, Jacob's Pillow presents a 10-week summer program of classic and experimental dance. Located on a onetime hilltop farm, the Pillow was founded in the 1930s by the famed dancer Ted Shawn as both a school for dancers and a performance center. As well as scheduled productions, informal impromptu performances are going on all the time. Picnicking is certs and Saturday-morning open rehearsals. In 2006 round-trip bus service from Boston Symphony Hall to Tanglewood was introduced for Friday- and Saturday-night concerts. Bus tickets are $30. For information call 888-266-1200 or visit www.tanglewood.org. Prices for seats in the Shed are $18–98 depending on the place and event, while lawn seats run $8.50–20; Ozawa Hall, $31–95. Open rehearsals in the Shed are $17, and dress rehearsals in the theater are $15. TMC tickets are $8.50–36. Request a detailed schedule and order form. Children 12 and under are free on the lawn.

TANGLEWOOD MUSIC FESTIVAL

Walter Scott

allowed on the Great Lawn; the pleasant Pillow Café opens for dinner and drinks before evening performances. Tickets for performances in the Ted Shawn Theater, the first in the country built exclusively for dance, are $24–60. Inquire about performances in the Doris Duke Studio Theater, as well as children's programs and free performances.

ART MUSEUM **Norman Rockwell Museum** (413-298-4100; www.nrm.org), Rt. 183 south of its junction with Rt. 102, 3 miles west of Stockbridge. Norman Rockwell (1894–1978), America's most beloved illustrator, spent his last 50 years in Stockbridge and often used it as a backdrop and local residents as models. The museum displays some 200 of his works, including the famous World War II poster series *The Four Freedoms*, along with many original paintings done for

HOME FOR CHRISTMAS AT THE NORMAN ROCKWELL MUSEUM

covers of the *Saturday Evening Post* magazine, at the time a national institution. Even if you didn't grow up with the *Post*, Rockwell's iconic yesteryear images of small-town American life retain their charm and are a delight to look at. Also on view are powerful paintings, quite different from the folksy *Post* covers, that he did for *Collier's* magazine to illustrate articles on 1960s civil rights incidents. Although Rockwell is the focus, the museum always also has major special exhibits on other illustrators and aspects of contemporary illustration. The handsome museum building, which includes a large gift shop and a café, is on a 36-acre former estate with tranquil views from benches (and picnic facilities) overlooking the Housatonic River. Open daily 10–5 in summer; Nov.–Apr., weekdays 10–4, weekends 10–5. Rockwell's studio, located on the museum grounds, is open May–Oct. Closed Thanksgiving, Christmas, and New Year's Day. $12.50 adults, $7 students, under 18 free.

Jacob's Pillow Dance Festival

Also see the **Clark Art Institute**, **MASS MoCA**, the **Williams College Art Museum**, the **Berkshire Museum**, and **Hancock Shaker Village** in "Central and North Berkshire."

HISTORIC HOMES
Chesterwood (413-298-3579; www.chesterwood.org), Rt. 183, south of its junction with Rt. 102 in the Glendale section of Stockbridge.

Open May until mid-Oct., daily 10–5. $10 adults, $9 seniors and students, $5 ages 6–18, family rate $25. This 160-acre estate served for 33 years as the summer home of Daniel Chester French (1850–1931), whose *Minute Man* statue in Concord established his eminence as a sculptor at age 25. By 1895, when he discovered Stockbridge, he was internationally respected and able to maintain this elaborate summer home and studio, which commands, as he put it, the "best dry view" he'd ever seen. The National Trust offers guided tours of the residence, of a newly renovated barn gallery with special exhibits, and of the studio, now exhibit space for plaster casts of many of the sculptor's works, including the statue that now sits in Washington's Lincoln Memorial. Visitors are welcome to stroll the grounds, which include a wooded path—the Hemlock Glade—overlooking Monument Mountain. Frequent events are staged throughout the summer, notably an outdoor sculpture show July into October, a Summer Gala and auction in August, and a pumpkin festival in October.

Mission House (413-298-3239; www.thetrustees.org), Main St., Stockbridge. Open Memorial Day weekend–Columbus Day, daily 10–5. $6 adults, $3 ages 6–12. John Sergeant, idealistic young missionary to the Stockbridge tribe of the Mahican nation, constructed this house for his bride in 1739. He built it not on Rt. 102 where it now stands (known as the Plain at the time, this site held Native American wigwams) but up on the hill where the town's few white families lived, among them the Williamses. Sergeant's wife was Abigail Williams, a lady of pretensions, and the house is elaborate for its time and place. Salvaged and moved to this site in 1929, it's maintained by the Trustees of Reservations. An outbuilding houses an exhibit on the Stockbridge Indians. The beautiful "Colonial Revival" garden, a mix of flowers and herbs, is the work of the noted landscape architect Fletcher Steele, who also designed the famous formal gardens at Naumkeag.

Naumkeag (413-298-3239; www.thetrustees.org), Prospect Hill Rd., Stockbridge. Open daily late May–Labor Day, then weekends and holidays through Columbus Day, 10–4:15. $10 adults for house and garden, $8 for garden only; $3 ages 6–12. The Trustees of Reservations maintain this fantasy gabled and shingled 26-room "cottage." It was designed by McKim, Mead & White in 1885 for one of the leading lawyers of the day, Joseph Hodges Choate, who endeared himself to his wealthy colleagues by securing the reversal of an income tax law that Congress had passed in 1894. It's the most evocative of the region's Gilded Age mansions because it retains many of its original furnishings and because the tours are so good. The view from the terrace is one of the finest in the Berkshires. The gardens, designed by leading landscaper Fletcher Steele, are as exceptional as the house and filled with imaginative touches and surprising elements, such as the famous curving blue steps set for contrast in a grove of white birches. The gardens are also the scene of a concert series in July and August.

Frelinghuysen Morris House & Studio (413-637-0166; www.frelinghuysen .org), 92 Hawthorne St., Lenox. Open July 4 weekend through Labor Day, Thu.–Sun. 10–4; June, Sep., and Oct., Thu.–Sun. 10–4. $10 adults, $3 children. An architecturally interesting 1940s house (a starkly white Bauhaus-style building with art deco decor) on 46 acres bordering Tanglewood. The furnishings are original (cutting-edge modern for the era) and the walls hung with paintings by the owners and their contemporaries, including Picasso, Braque, Léger, and Gris.

Ventfort Hall (413-637-3206; www.gildedage.org), 104 Walker St., Lenox. Open Memorial Day through Oct., daily 10–3 (the last tour is at 2 PM). In winter admission is by appointment. An imposing Elizabethan-style mansion in the center of Lenox built in 1894 for Sarah Morgan, sister of financier J. P. Morgan, Ventfort Hall is now "the Museum of the Gilded Age." The building is used for lectures and theatrical performances and has some exhibits, but only a couple of downstairs rooms have been restored and furnished in period style. Much more needs to be done before it can fully embody the opulent era it represents. Admission with guided tour $8 adults, $4 ages 5–17.

The Bidwell House (413-528-6888; www.bidwellhousemuseum.org), Art School Rd., Monterey. Open Memorial Day through mid-Oct., Thu.–Mon. 11–4; $6 adults, $5 seniors and students, $2 under age 18. A genuine center-chimney colonial house, built circa 1750 as a parsonage by the Rev. Adonijah Bidwell, but what's special about this place is the way it's furnished. In the 1960s it was purchased by Jack Hargis and David Brush, New York interior designers who not only painstakingly restored the home but also expertly furnished it with their collections of earthenware and china,

NAUMKEAG, STOCKBRIDGE

Trustees of Reservations

THE MOUNT

(413-637-1899 or 888-637-1902;
www.edithwharton.org), 2 Plunkett
St. (junction of Rts. 7 and 7A),
Lenox. Open early May–Oct., daily
9–5; $16 adults, $8 students, free
under 12. Novelist Edith Wharton's
Georgian-style home, built in 1902,
is an English mansion designed by
Christopher Wren but incorporates
many of the ideas articulated in her
book *The Decoration of Houses*.
Wharton had a hand in designing
the formal gardens as well as the
building and also chose its furnishings. The resulting mansion is special indeed and once more looks
as it did in Wharton's day: Nearly

PORTRAIT OF EDITH WHARTON, 1902

$9 million was spent to restore the 42-room house and magnificent formal
gardens for their centennial in 2002. Also meticulously restored was Wharton's sumptuous bedroom suite—it has French marble fireplaces, oil-painted
floral wall panels, gilded mirrors, and the best views of the gardens where
she did much of her writing. In 2006 the author's original 2,700-volume library
was acquired; it's now on display as well. Included in the admission price
are 45-minute tours (given by volunteers from Edith Wharton Restoration,
Inc.) that convey a sense of her life and work.

THE MOUNT

including redware, slipware, and delft, some fine early samplers, antique quilts, pewter, domestic hand tools, and lighting devices. It's a must for anyone interested in 18th-century decorative arts. The house is set in period gardens, and footpaths lead through 196 acres of fields and woods. Inquire about lectures, workshops, and other special events.

Colonel John Ashley House (413-298-3239; www.thetrustees.org), Cooper Hill Rd. in Ashley Falls, well marked from Rt. 7, south of Sheffield Village. The grounds are open without charge daily from sunrise to sunset year-round. The house is open for guided tours Memorial Day weekend until Columbus Day, Sat.–Sun. 10–5. $5 adults, $3 ages 6–12. The oldest in Berkshire County (1735), this house was the site of the 1773 drafting of the Sheffield Declaration denouncing the British Parliament. The Ashley family had a black servant, Mum Bett, who in 1780 sued for and won her freedom on the grounds that slavery was unconstitutional in Massachusetts, the first such court case in the country. The home is beautifully paneled, restored, and furnished. Along with nearby Bartholomew's Cobble, also maintained by the Trustees of Reservations, this is one of the most interesting corners of south Berkshire County.

SCENIC DRIVES **Southwick to New Marlborough**. Take exit 6 (Rt. 291) off the Massachusetts Turnpike to I-91; continue south to Rt. 57 in Agawam. This quickly leads you to **Granville**, a classic old village with a general store that's worth a stop to pick up the Granville Cellar Cheddar that's been aged and sold on this spot since the 1850s (open most days until 6:30). It only gets prettier after that, passing though **West Granville** with its early-18th-century meetinghouse and **Tolland** with its state forest (with lakeside campsites on Otis Reservoir). Note the **New Boston Inn** that's been standing at the junction of Rts. 57 and 8 since 1737 and still boasts good food and lodging. Just over the New Marlborough line, note the turnoff for **York Lake** (swimming and fishing). Farther along in **New Marlborough**, the Old Inn on the Green, vintage 1760, also offers hospitality. From here roads radiate to most corners of South County.

Great Barrington to Lee is one of our favorite routes. Follow Rt. 23 east to Rt. 57, wandering through the historic village of New Marlborough, and turn north at the Old Inn on the Green onto the (dirt) New Marlborough–Monterey Road. It climbs up into high meadows then dips down through woods. Bear left at the fork and you soon see a sign for Rawson Brook Farm; stop to visit the goats and pick up some exceptional goat cheese. At Rt. 23 turn left into the center of Monterey and head north on the Tyringham Road (also called Main Road). A left turn will take you to the **Bidwell House**; otherwise continue into the breathtaking Tyringham Valley. Stop at **Tyringham Cobble**, parking by the cow pasture just above the village, and walk to the top of the cobble (a limestone hill); the trail also winds through forest and meadow. The road brings you into Lee, near Rt. 102 and exit 2 on the Mass Pike.

Egremont–Sheffield Road. For both history and beauty, it's difficult to beat the road from South Egremont to Sheffield. This country road runs south from the South Egremont Inn, and woods soon give way to fields with views of the hills to the west. This is the "Sheffield Plain." At the corner of Kiln Road look for the suitably ancient-looking marble monument commemorating the last battle of **Shays Rebellion** in 1787. Follow the road on down to Rt. 7 and look on your left for the **covered bridge**, originally built in 1837 and reconstructed in 1998.

✳ To Do

BICYCLING *Berkshire Bike Touring*, a version of the *Rubel Western Massachusetts Bicycle and Road Map*, is currently available from local info booths and centers. Bicycles can be rented from **Berkshire Bike & Blade** (413-528-5555), 29 State Rd. (Rt. 7), Great Barrington; or the **Arcadian Shop** (413-637-3010), 91 Pittsfield Rd., Lenox, open daily (also cross-country skis, snowshoes, backpacking equipment, and clothing).

BIRDING **Pleasant Valley Wildlife Sanctuary** (413-637-0320; www.mass audubon.org), 472 West Mountain Rd., Lenox. This Massachusetts Audubon sanctuary includes an evolving education center and year-round programs. Its 730 acres include part of Lenox Mountain, Yokum Brook, beaver ponds, a hemlock gorge, and 7 miles of trails used for cross-country skiing in winter. It harbors hooded mergansers, great blue herons, and belted kingfishers as well as beavers, snapping turtles, and many other animals. Inquire about guided canoe trips on the Housatonic, mid-May through early October.

Thousand Acre Swamp, off Norfolk Road, south of Southfield, left on Hotchkiss. A birder's delight.

BOATING The placid **Housatonic** is ideal for lazy rides down the river, especially between Great Barrington and Bartholomew's Cobble. Trips are detailed in *Discover the Berkshires of Massachusetts: AMC Guide to the Best Hiking, Biking & Paddling.*

The **Acadian Shop** (413-637-3010; www.acadian.com) in Lenox rents both kayaks and canoes. Rental kayaks, kayaking information, and tours are available at **Expeditions Outdoor Store** at Ski Butternut (413-528-2000), 380 State Rd. (Rt. 23), Great Barrington. **Berkshire Canoe Tours** (413-442-2789) also offers guided tours on the Housatonic from Decker's Landing in Lenox. More guided tours are available through **Pleasant Valley Wildlife Sanctuary** (413-637-0320; www.massaudubon .org), the **Berkshire chapter of the AMC** (www.outdoors.org), and **Berkshire South Regional Community Center** (413-528-2810; www.berkshire south.org). By far the largest lake in the area is **Otis Reservoir** in the **Tolland State Forest** (413-269-6002); rowboats can be rented at **Camp Overflow** (413-269-3036).

DOWNTOWN LEE

Christina Tree

CAMPING The obvious way to beat the high cost of lodging during the Tanglewood season is to take advantage of one of the four state park campgrounds in this area. The best bet for finding a site is in **Tolland State Forest** (93 campsites, 26 lakeside). The other options are **October Mountain State Forest** (50 sites) and **Beartown State Forest** (12 year-round sites). For reservations, phone 877-422-6762. The Department of Conservation and Recreation (DCR) maintains an excellent web site—www.mass.gov/dcr—as well as a friendly visitor information center at 740 South St. (Rt. 7 northbound), Pittsfield (413-442-8928). Each of the state forests is described in more detail under *Green Space*.

For commercial campgrounds, check out the free guides published by the **Massachusetts Association of Campground Owners** (781-544-3475; www.camp mass.com).

CAR RACING Lime Rock Park (800-722-3577; www.limerock.com), 497 Lime Rock Rd., Lakeville, CT. Open Apr.–Oct., Sat. and holidays. Known as "Road Racing Center of the East," Lime Rock hosts car shows, vintage races, and world-class sports car events. Located in a bucolic corner of northwestern Connecticut, it is the most picturesque of the major racetracks. Free parking and free on-site camping for ticket holders. Admission under age 12 is free.

FISHING Licenses for fishing are required. Log onto www.mass.gov/dfwele for a list of trout-stocked waters. South Berkshire's many trout-stocked waters include Center Pond and Yokum Pond in Becket, Prospect Lake in Egremont, Goose Pond and Laurel Lake in Lee, Benedict Pond in Monterey, Thousand Acre Swamp in New Marlborough, Benton Pond and East Otis Reservoir in Otis, and Stockbridge Bowl in Stockbridge. **The Berkshire Fishing Club** (413-243-5761; www.berkshirefishingclub.com) offers access to a private, 125-acre secluded lake stocked with largemouth bass. A "Trial Pass," including a 16-foot boat, motor, and tackle, is $250 per day. The **Berkshire National Fish Hatchery** (413-528-9761), 240 Hatchery Rd. off Rts. 57/183 in New Marlborough, raises Atlantic salmon, rainbows, and brown trout and maintains a visitor center.

FOR FAMILIES ✐ **Rainbow's End Miniature Golf** (413-528-1220), 18 holes at the **Cove Lanes**, 109 Stockbridge Rd. (Rt. 7), Great Barrington. If the kids are along, this indoor mini golf is great for evenings or rainy days.

✐ **Berkshire Theatre Festival** offers children's theater written by local children.

✐ The **Norman Rockwell Museum** is free to children under age 18.

✐ **Pleasant Valley Wildlife Sanctuary** (413-637-0320; www.massaudubon.org) in Lenox; **Berkshire Botanical Garden** (413-298-3926; www.berkshirebotanical .org) in Stockbridge; and **Bartholomew's Cobble** (413-229-8600) offer special programs for children.

✐ Both the **Stockbridge Library** (413-298-5501) and **Lenox Library** (413-637-0197) have extensive children's collections; inquire about story hours.

Also see *Farms*.

GOLF Cranwell Golf Course (413-637-1364; www.cranwell.com), Lee Rd. (Rt. 20), Lenox, is an 18-hole championship par-70 course. There's a Golf Digest School as well as a driving range, pro shop, and full-service spa. Sloane's Tavern serves lunch. Also see *Lodging*.

Egremont Country Club (413-528-4222; www.egremontcountryclub.com), Rt. 23, South Egremont. 18 scenic holes, driving range, pro shop, private lessons, moderate greens fees.

Greenock Country Club (413-243-3323), West Park St., Lee, has nine holes; moderate greens fees.

HIKING More than 100,000 acres of Berkshire County (75 percent) is wooded, and 86 miles of the **Appalachian Trail** traverse the county. The number and variety of walking and hiking trails, many dating to the 19th century, are amazing. They are described in several books, notably *Hikes & Walks in the Berkshire Hills* by Lauren R. Stevens, *A Guide to Natural Places in the Berkshire Hills* by René Laubach, and *Wildflowers of the Berkshire & Taconic Hills* by Joseph G. Strauch Jr., all published by Berkshire House, based in South Lee. The *Appalachian Mountain Club Guide to Massachusetts* is also extremely helpful, published by AMC Books. Also see the trails described in this chapter's *Green Space*.

HORSEBACK RIDING Undermountain Farm (413-637-3365; www.undermountainfarm.com), Undermountain Rd., Lenox. Year-round lessons, trail rides. $55 an hour for trail rides; no children under 12. When it comes to setting, views, and total experience, innkeepers tell us that this is by far the best local trail ride.

Berkshire Horseback Adventure (413-637-9090; www.berkshirehorseback.net), 293 Main St., Lenox. Scenic trail rides. $50 an hour, $150 half day, $250 overnight.

Sunny Banks Ranch (413-623-5606; www.sunnybanksranch.com), Rt. 8, Becket. Trail rides, lessons, shops with riding equipment and gifts. Special equestrian events on Saturday. Lessons $50 an hour, trail rides $40.

LLAMA HIKES Berkshire Mountain Llama Hikes (413-243-2224; www.hawkmeadowllamas.com), 322 Landers Rd., Lee. Guided 1- to 3-hour hikes with llamas. Rates for an hour-long hike range from a minimum of $40 for a group of up to 3 people to $70 for 10 or more. Accommodations available.

SIGN ON THE APPALACHIAN TRAIL

Kim Grant

PICNICKING **Bowker Woods**, Rt. 183 between Stockbridge and Chesterwood; drive in at the sign. There's a pine grove by a small pond, good for picnics.

Picnicking is also allowed on the grounds of **Shakespeare & Company** on Kemble Street in Lenox.

     ✿ **Berkshire Botanical Garden** (413-298-3926; www.berkshirebotanical .org), Stockbridge, junction of Rts. 102 and 183. Display gardens open 10–5 May–Sep.; gift shop through Oct. Greenhouses open year-round. The 15 acres include a pond, woodland trail, and children's garden. There are shrubs, trees, perennial borders, greenhouses, herbs, a gift shop, and periodic lectures and workshops. There are also a number of annual special events, including a plant sale in May, a flower show in August, and a harvest festival on Columbus Day weekend that is the Berkshires' oldest continuous community event. Picnickers welcome. Weddings encouraged. Admission $7 adults, $5 seniors and students. Children under 12 free.

✿ RAILWAY EXCURSION **Berkshire Scenic Railway Museum** (413-637-2210; www.berkshirescenicrailroad.org), 10 Willow Creek Rd., Lenox. On weekends and holidays from Memorial Day weekend through Oct., the museum offers two daily 90-minute excursions between Lenox and Stockbridge, as well as a 45-minute journey between Lenox and Lee. Vintage coaches and a veteran diesel locomotive are used, and a uniformed conductor narrates the scenic trip along the banks of the Housatonic River. Excursions begin from the old Lenox depot, which houses a gift shop and a museum that includes model train displays and an exhibit on the role of railroads in the Berkshires' Gilded Age boom years. $15 adults, $14 seniors, $8 children under 14 for the Stockbridge trip; $9, $8, and $5, respectively, for Lee.

SPAS AND FITNESS CENTERS The region's destination spas—Cranwell, Canyon Ranch, Kripalu, and Mepal Manor—are listed under *Lodging*. **The Berkshire South Regional Community Center** (413-528-2810; www.berkshiresouth.org) offers a pool, fitness center, and classes ($12 per day). The **Lenox Fitness Center and Spa** (413-637-9893; www.lenoxfitnesscenter.com) also offers a fitness center and daily programs plus spa treatments. Thanks to the destination spas, there are also probably more massage therapists per capita in this area than anywhere in the country. Several more day spas are around, and many inns have massage therapists on call.

SWIMMING For a fee, you can swim at **Prospect Lake Park** (413-528-4158), a private campground in North Egremont with a sandy swim beach, and at **Card Lake** in West Stockbridge. Inquire locally about swimming in the **Stockbridge Bowl** and **Laurel Lake**. Another favorite local spot is the swimming hole in the **Green River** on Rt. 23 about a mile west of Great Barrington between Rt. 71 and Alford Rd., and on Rt. 23 south of Great Barrington (look for the lineup of cars).

Under *Green Space*, check 40-acre **York Lake**, off Rt. 57 in Sandisfield State Forest; **Otis Reservoir** in Tolland State Forest; **Benedict Pond** in Beartown State Forest; and **Umpachenee Falls** in New Marlborough.

TENNIS Tennis Village School, West Stockbridge, two hard-surface courts.
Sheffield Racquet Club (413-229-7968), four clay courts, clubhouse.
Greenock Country Club (413-243-3323), Lee, two courts.

✳ Winter Sports

ALPINE SKIING 🎿 ✎ **Butternut** (413-528-2000; www.skibutternut.com), Great
Barrington; east on Rt. 23. Still owned by the same family that founded it in
1963, Butternut is known for its grooming and for the beauty of its design by
founder Channing Murdock—both on and off the slopes.

Vertical drop: 1,000 feet.
Terrain: 22 trails, 110 skiable acres; longest run: 1.5 miles.
Lifts: 3 quads, one triple, 2 double chairs, 4 surface lifts.
Snowmaking: 100 percent of area.
Programs: Children's ski and boarding programs, ski school, tubing.
Rates: Adults $49 weekends, $36 Fri., $15 Mon.–Thu. except holidays.

✎ **Catamount** (413-528-1262; snow conditions, 800-342-1840; www.catamount
ski.com), Rt. 23, South Egremont. Straddling the New York–Massachusetts line,
overlooking the rolling farm country of the Hudson Valley, Catamount has been
in business 65 years as a family area. The base lodge is pleasant.

Vertical drop: 1,000 feet.
Terrain: 32 trails including 1-mile-long (intermediate) "Sidewinder."
Lifts: Six, including a new triple chair and 3 double chairs.
Snowboarding: Megaplex with 400-foot half-pipe.
Snowmaking: 98 percent of area.
Programs: Mountain Cats for ages 4–12; also Tiny Tot lessons for ages 4–6.
Rates: Adults $48 weekends, $15 weekdays; juniors and seniors $38 weekends,
$15 weekdays; night skiing.

✎ **Otis Ridge** (413-269-4444; www.otisridge.com), Rt. 23 in Otis. A long-
established family ski area whose ski camp (ages 8–15) is the oldest in the
country and has its own dedicated tow.

Vertical drop: 400 feet.
Terrain: 11 trails.
Lifts: 1 double chair, 4 tows.
Snowmaking: 90 percent of area.
Facilities: Lodging and food at the
slope-side Grouse House (413-269-
4446).
Rates: Adults $30 weekends, $15
weekdays; $10 nights Tue.–Sun.; jun-
iors $25, $15, and $10; seniors $20,
$10, $5. Seniors 70 or older ski free.

Also see **Jiminy Peak** in "Central and
North Berkshire."

BUTTERNUT'S RAINBOW RAIL

Butternut, Great Barrington

CROSS-COUNTRY SKIING **Butternut** (413-528-2000; snow conditions, 800-438-SNOW), Great Barrington. Adjacent to the alpine area are 8 km of trails connecting with Beartown State Forest cross-country skiing.

Canterbury Farm (413-623-0100; www.canterbury-farms.com), 1986 Fred Snow Rd., Becket. Generally open Dec.–Mar., 9–5. Offers 12 miles of tracked wide trails to a lake and around a beaver pond, with an average elevation of 1,700 feet, rental equipment (including snowshoes), lessons, and a fireplaced room with drinks, hot soup, chili, snacks, or space for your own picnic.

Cranwell (413-637-1364 or 800-272-6935; www.cranwell.com), Lee Rd., Lenox, offers snowmaking along groomed golf course trails, equipment rentals, and instruction. Full-service spa.

Also see *Green Space*. Some of the best cross-country skiing is to be found in public preserves. Because of its elevation, the **Mount Washington State Forest** is a standout, as is **Bartholomew's Cobble** in Ashley Falls and **Beartown State Forest** in Monterey. **Kennedy Park** in Lenox also offers easy access to an extensive trail system; rental equipment is available next door at the Arcadian Shop.

SNOWMOBILING Several state forests and parks in this region permit snowmobiling; see *Green Space* below. For guided tours, contact Wild n'wet Sport Rentals in Lenox (413-445-5211; caseycare@peoplepc.com).

✳ Green Space

STATE PARKS AND FORESTS *Note:* The Massachusetts Department of Conservation and Recreation (DCR) publishes a handy map/guide and maintains a visitor-friendly regional office on Rt. 7 south of Pittsfield (413-442-8928; www.mass.gov/dcr).

Beartown State Forest (413-528-0904), Blue Hill Rd., Monterey; 10,555 acres. This is high tableland stretching northwest from Monterey, the upper end dropping down to the Housatonic River in South Lee. Accessible from Rt. 102 in South Lee, and in Monterey from both Blue Hill Rd. off Rt. 23 and the Tyringham Rd. In summer the big attraction is 35-acre **Benedict Pond**, an artificially formed pond good for swimming (there are sanitary but no changing facilities), picnicking, and boating (no motors). The Appalachian Trail skirts the pond, and a trail circles it. There are also a dozen campsites (open year-round; reservations are needed in summer, but Oct.–Apr. it's first come, first served) plus lean-tos along the AT. Inquire about the trail to the summit of Mount Wilcox; a 1.5-mile trail circles the pond there.

Four DCR properties cluster in the extreme southwestern corner of the state. The best known of these is at **Bash Bish Falls**, a dramatic waterfall that rushes down a 1,000-foot-deep gorge, finally plunging some 80 feet around two sides of a mammoth boulder and dropping into a perfect pool that's labeled NO SWIMMING. Needless to say this sign is frequently ignored (rangers are on duty weekends only) and, sad to say, divers occasionally die here. Don't swim, but do explore this special place. Access is via Rt. 23, Rt. 41, and Mount Washington

Rd. in South Egremont; take Mount Washington Rd. to East St., then Cross Rd. back up West St. to Falls Rd. to the parking lot. Signage here, at this writing, is dreadful. The rugged 0.25-mile trail meanders steeply down through pines to the falls. Don't lose heart at the point the blue blazes disappear (after you cross the stream); they pick up below. Locals who want to bring folding chairs and picnics usually continue down the road instead to the "lower parking lot" in New York's **Taconic State Park**. It's a longer, but level, walk in to the bottom of the falls. From this lot you can also access the steep but short trail to the upper rim of the falls—which continues (via the South Taconic Trail) to Alander Mountain in **Mount Washington State Forest** (413-528-0330), East St., Mount Washington (see directions above from South Egremont to East St.). Forest Headquarters are on East St., south of the Cross Rd. turnoff for Bash Bish Falls. Inquire about primitive, walk-in (0.5 mile) camping sites with pit toilets, springwater, and fireplaces, and about access to the Appalachian Trail. The AT is also accessible from Jug End Rd. in the **Jug End Reservation**, an extension of the Mount Everett State Reservation that's accessible both from Rt. 41 and from the Mount Washington Rd. in South Egremont. The **Mount Everett State Reservation**, accessible from East St. (north of Cross St.) in the town of Mount Washington, seems sadly neglected. At this writing the road to the top of Mount Everett, the 2,602-foot-high peak (second highest in Massachusetts) that commands an overview of Berkshire County to the north, is closed with, we are told, no plans for its reopening. Dogwood blooms in spring, mountain laurel in June and early July, and there are wild blueberries in late July and early August.

Guilder Pond, a little more than 0.5 mile up the road, is filled with pink water lilies during late July and much of August; the Appalachian Trail leads north and south of the pond along the ridgeline. Within the reservation a popular trail climbs up to the AT via **Race Brook Falls** from Rt. 41 in Sheffield. South of Mount Race, the AT skirts beautiful Plantain Pond.

October Mountain State Forest (413-243-1178), a total of 15,710 acres accessible from Rt. 20 in both Lenox and Lee. Camping (Memorial Day–Columbus Day) is the big draw here, but there are just 46 sites (flush toilets, showers, picnic tables, dumping station). **Schermerhorn Gorge** is a popular hike and has many miles of trails also used for winter skiing and snowmobiling. Much of this area was once impounded by Harry Payne

BASH BISH FALLS

Christina Tree

Whitney as a game preserve (it included buffalo, moose, and Angora goats as well as smaller animals). **Halfway Pond** is a good fishing spot.

Otis State Forest (413-269-6002), off Rt. 23 on Nash Rd. in West Otis. Boating (no motors) is permitted on **Upper Spectacle Pond**; cross-country skiing and snowmobiling on the unplowed roads, which include the original road that Henry Knox labored over with cannons in the winter of 1775–76.

Tolland State Forest (413-269-6002), off Rt. 23 in Otis, offers 92 campsites, Memorial Day–Columbus Day (most for tents; flush toilets, showers, picnic tables, fireplaces). Campsites are on a peninsula jutting out into **Otis Reservoir**. There is a picnic area with a sandy swim beach and a boat launch; also fishing and boating in the reservoir. This is a spot to hike and cross-country ski.

Sandisfield State Forest (in winter, 413-528-0904; in summer, 413-229-8212). The state forest holdings are scattered around Sandisfield; the most popular section is just over the New Marlborough line (Rt. 57) on **York Lake**, a 40-acre dammed area near the headquarters of Sandy Brook. Here you can swim, boat (no motors), and picnic (there are tables, grills, and fireplaces). The forest harbors five more lakes, all stocked with trout and accessible to nonmotorized boats. Winter trails for skiing and snowmobiling. Hunting is permitted in-season.

TRUSTEES OF RESERVATIONS Contact 413-298-3239 or www.thetrustees.org.

✧ ☀ **Bartholomew's Cobble** (413-229-8600), marked from Rt. 7A in Ashley Falls, south of Sheffield. Open year-round but closed Sun. and Mon., Dec.–Mar. The visitor center with exhibits, restrooms, and a naturalist on duty is open 9–4:30. Admission for non-Trustees-members is $4 per adult, $1 per child. This 329-acre tract takes its name from the high limestone knolls or cobbles of marble and quartzite that border the glass-smooth Housatonic River. We recommend the pine-carpeted Ledges Trail, a (theoretically) 45-minute loop with many seductive side trails down to the river or up into the rocky heights. The Cobble is noted for the diversity of its fern species and woodland wildflowers, at their best in April and May. A booklet guide is available from the naturalist. Leashed dogs welcome. Inquire about special kayaking and nature programs. Note that the Colonel Ashley House (see *Historic Homes*) is just up the road.

Monument Mountain on Rt. 7 north of Great Barrington. This peak is one of the most distinctive in the state: a long ridge of pinkish quartzite, scarcely 15 feet wide in some places, 1,700 feet high. The climb is lovely any day, whether by the Hickey or the Monument Trail. The hillside is covered with red pine and, in June, with flowering mountain laurel. A Bryant poem tells of a Native American maiden, disappointed in love, who hurled herself from Squaw Peak. Nathaniel Hawthorne, Herman Melville, and O. W. Holmes all picnicked here in 1850.

Tyringham Cobble, 0.5 mile from Tyringham Center on Jerusalem Rd. Open daily, year-round. The Appalachian Trail crosses a portion of this 206-acre property: steep upland pasture and woodland, including a part of Hop Brook, with views of the valley and village below.

Ashintully Gardens, Tyringham. Sodem Rd., marked from the Main Rd. between Tyringham Center and Monterey. Open mid-June to mid-Sep., Wed.

and Sat. 1–5. Free to individual visitors; group tours by appointment. These elaborate gardens are sited on a 120-acre property below the ruins of the "Marble Palace," a pillared white mansion completed in 1912 as the centerpiece of 1,000-acre Ashintully Estate. This design of the garden is described as "episodic"—an artistic creation incorporating paths, fountains, bridges, stairs, gates, and lawns.

McLennan Reservation, Fenn Rd., off Main Rd. south of Tyringham Center. Open daily, year-round. This 491-acre property adjoins Ashintully Gardens (see above) and was once part of the same 1,000-acre estate. Round Mountain and Long Mountain are the backdrop for paths through the woods, along brooks, and by a beaver pond.

Questing, New Marlborough. Open daily, year-round. From New Marlborough Center, take New Marlborough Hill Rd. for 0.6 mile. A 2-mile loop trail threads hardwood forest, upland field, pockets of wetlands, and the Leffigwell settlement where the first non–Native American children were born in Berkshire County. The farmhouse remains private.

OTHER **Kennedy Park** in Lenox on Rt. 7. The grounds of the former Aspinwall Hotel offer trails for hiking, biking, and cross-country skiing.

Bowker Woods, Rt. 183 between Stockbridge and Chesterwood; drive in at the sign. There's a pine grove by a small pond, good for picnics.

Laurel Hill, Stockbridge. A path leads from the elementary school on Main Street to a stone seat designed by Daniel Chester French. Marked trails continue across the Housatonic to Ice Glen (a ravine) and to Laura's Tower (a steel tower); another trail leads along the crest of the spur of Beartown Mountain.

⚘ **Berkshire Botanical Garden** (413-298-3926; www.berkshirebotanical.org), Stockbridge, junction of Rts. 102 and 183. Gardens and gift shop open

MONUMENT MOUNTAIN

May–Oct., 10–5. Greenhouses open year-round. The 15 acres include a pond, woodland trail, and children's garden. There are shrubs, trees, perennial borders, greenhouses, herbs, and periodic lectures and workshops. Picnickers welcome. Admission charged mid-May to mid-October.

WATERFALLS Bash Bish Falls. The area's most famous and dramatic waterfall—a 60-foot cascade plunging through a sheer gorge (see also *State Parks and Forests*).

Race Brook Falls in Sheffield: a series of five cascades and a picnic area. From the turnout on Rt. 41 north of the Stagecoach Inn, follow red blazes for 1.5 miles.

Becket Falls, 0.2 mile up Brooker Hill from the Becket Arts Center (Rt. 8 and Pittsfield Rd.); there is a shallow turnout in which to park. It's a steep scramble down to view the 25-foot-high cascade.

Umpachenee Falls. At the New Marlborough Church in the village center, turn south; follow signs to Mill River. Just before the metal bridge there is a dirt road forking right; from here follow signs. While this is the least dramatic falls, it's the best swimming hole.

Campbell Falls State Park, accessible from Rt. 57 in New Marlborough, then a forest road to this site. The Whiting River pours over a split ledge and cascades 80 feet down a precipitous declivity. There are picnic tables, toilets, and foot trails.

Sages Ravine. A strikingly cut chasm with a series of falls, best accessed from Salisbury Road in Mount Washington and from Rt. 41 between Sheffield and Salisbury, CT.

✳ Lodging

Note: Tax varies from town to town, so inquire when making a reservation. Most places also have a 2- or 3-day requirement for weekends July through October, and many inns offer midweek discounts, even in July and August. B&Bs with fewer than four rooms are not required to charge tax. Check with local chambers of commerce for seasonal B&Bs and apartments.

RESORTS

All resorts are in Lenox 01240
&. **Blantyre** (413-637-3556; www .blantyre.com), Blantyre Rd. Built in 1902 to replicate an ancestral home in Scotland, this magnificent, Tudor-style mansion—open year-round—was lovingly restored to its original glory in 1980 by Jack and Jane Fitzpatrick, owners of the Red Lion Inn in Stockbridge. There is a baronial entry hall and a truly graceful music room with crystal chandeliers, sofas covered in petit point, a piano, and a harp. Guests enjoy their meals in the paneled dining room, around the long formal table, or in the adjoining, smaller, octagonal room. (See *Dining Out*.) The 25 guest rooms are impeccably furnished with antiques, and most have a fireplace. There are 117 well-kept acres with four tennis courts, a swimming pool (with Jacuzzi hot tub and sauna), a spa, and compe-

tition croquet courts. Including continental breakfast, rates begin at $550 for a room and run to $1,600 per night for the two-bedroom Ice House Cottage.

✒ **Cranwell Resort, Spa & Golf Club** (413-637-1364 or 800-272-6935; www.cranwell.com), Lee Rd. (Rt. 20). A 380-acre resort with 107 units—rooms, suites and town houses—scattered in five varied buildings. An imposing, Tudor-style 1890s summer mansion is the centerpiece, and both its common and guest rooms are large and luxurious, furnished with period antiques. Less formal options in other buildings include family-friendly suites with large bedrooms, a living room with a sleeper sofa, and a galley kitchen. Buildings reflect the property's varied history, including its use for much of the 20th century as a famous Jesuit prep school. There are three restaurants, a lounge, meeting rooms, four claylike Har-Tru tennis courts, heated indoor and outdoor pools, and cross-country skiing in winter.

The big attractions, however, are the 18-hole, PGA championship golf course and a luxurious spa complex, built at a cost of $9 million and one of the largest resort spas in the Northeast. The spa offers some 50 different treatments and has a 60-foot-long indoor heated pool along with a fitness room, sauna, whirlpool, juice bar, fireplace lounges, and café. Glass-enclosed heated passageways connect it with several resort buildings so that guests in about half the rooms can access the spa without going outdoors —a welcome convenience in winter. Room rates are $275–575 a night in high season, $175–475 low season. Rates include full use of the spa,

exclusive of spa and fitness services. The resort offers a number of packages, including golf and spa. Weddings and meetings are a specialty; before booking you might want to ask what else is booked for your stay.

Wheatleigh (413-637-0610; www.wheatleigh.com), Hawthorne Rd. This yellow-brick palazzo was built in 1893 and set in 22 acres that now include a heated outdoor swimming pool and a tennis court. Tanglewood is around the corner. There are 19 large and elegantly decorated rooms, all with private bath, about half with fireplace. The restaurant is expensive (see *Dining Out*) and award winning. Rates are $575–1,800, without breakfast.

✒ 🐾 ♿ **Seven Hills Inn** (413-637-0060 or 800-869-6518; www.sevenhills.com), 40 Plunkett St. Open year-round. This 1911 Tudor Revival mansion with its wonderfully ornate carved woodwork is set in 27 terraced and landscaped acres, next door to Edith Wharton's former home, the Mount. The manor itself has 15 various-sized bedrooms, some with working fireplace and jet tub. A restored carriage house has six suites, all with fireplace,

THE POOL AT CRANWELL RESORT
Cranwell Resort, Spa & Golf Club

jet tub, and kitchenette; 37 more rooms (motel-style doubles) are in the adjoining Terrace building (several are handicapped-accessible). Room 1 in the manor is a corner room with leaded-glass windows and sleigh bed, where we would read in front of the fireplace in the Victorian love seat, and Room 4 is a pleasant suite with sitting room and a sofa bed for children. Facilities include a landscaped pool and tennis courts; a path leads down to Laurel Lake. Pets and children are welcome. Rates with breakfast (continental only off-season) are $95–340 in the manor house and carriage house, $85–240 in the annex. Ask about MAP rates and packages.

✍ **Eastover** (413-637-0625 or 800-822-2386; www.eastover.com), 430 East St. This 1,000-acre hilltop estate has been offering "old-fashioned fun" since 1947. There are 165 rooms, some in a turn-of-the-20th-century gilded "cottage," most in motel-style annexes. Facilities include a small ski slope with a chairlift, an ice rink, a driving range, a toboggan slide (the longest in New England), tennis courts, horseback riding and hayrides, archery, basketball, indoor and outdoor pools, sauna, and exercise room, and a crenellated castle with swings for the kids. Other amenities include a huge dance hall, a Civil War museum, and a herd of buffalo! Weeks and weekends are tightly scheduled, with some programs geared exclusively to singles, others to families, still others to couples. Liquor is not served, but guests may bring their own. Weekend nightly rates for couples are $250 for a room, $384 for a suite, with a minimum 2-night stay. Included are all meals and almost all activities except horseback riding, massage, and cross-

country ski and trail bike rentals. Special single, family, and children's rates.

SPAS AND A YOGA CENTER Lenox is the spa center of the Northeast and said to have one masseuse for every 60 residents. Augmenting the residential centers described below are several day spas, a resource for all visitors, especially in the off-season when inn prices are so reasonable. Nowhere else in New England is it so possible to combine the comforts of an inn or B&B with so many services that improve the health of both body and spirit.

Canyon Ranch in the Berkshires (413-637-4100 or 800-326-7080; www.canyonranch.com), Bellefontaine, 165 Kemble St., Lenox 01240. Sister to the famous spa in Arizona, this spectacularly deluxe, 150-acre fitness resort is blessed with a superb setting. The focal point is a grand 1890s manor house that is a replica of the Petit Trianon of Louis XVI. Guests sleep in the adjoining 120-room inn, a clapboard building in traditional New England style. Just about every health and fitness program imaginable is offered, and instruction and equipment are state of the art. The setting is luxurious, but the emphasis on wellness is serious. The staff-to-guest ratio is about three to one. Meals are dietary but also gourmet and delicious. Guests (who have included many celebrities) almost invariably depart glowing and enthusiastic. Three-night packages run $2,470–4,740 in high season, $1,740–4,090 off-season. Packages include meals and a wide variety of spa and sports services. Inquire about special deals such as discounts for returning guests who bring a first-timer friend or relative with them, and off-season 1-day "Spa Renewal" programs.

⚘ Kripalu Center for Yoga and Health (800-741-7353; www.kripalu .org), Rt. 183, Lenox 01240. This yoga-based holistic health center offers a structured daily regimen and a variety of weekend, weeklong, and longer programs. A mecca for spiritual and physical renewal, nonprofit Kripalu is housed in a former Jesuit seminary (once the estate of steel magnate Andrew Carnegie) on 150 acres overlooking Stockbridge Bowl and just a stone's throw from Tanglewood. Founded as a guru-centered yoga ashram (*kripalu* means "compassion" in Sanskrit), it is now staffed primarily by paid professionals, and the atmosphere is more relaxed and mainstream New Age than formerly. The country's largest holistic health center, Kripalu accommodates more than 400 guests and has a national reputation for training instructors in its own style of yoga. It also attracts nationally known lecturers and teachers. Facilities include whirlpools, saunas, hiking and cross-country trails, a beach, boats, and tennis; also a children's program during summer months.

A variety of variously priced programs are offered, which include healthy meals, workshops, yoga classes, and use of all facilities. The cost of a 2-night "personal retreat," a popular introduction to Kripalu, ranges from $244 for dormitory accommodations weekdays off-season to $700 in a single room with private bath on weekends. A 3-day "Yoga Immersion" package including clinics on meditation and holistic healing as well as yoga classes, is $693 in peak season. Kripalu also has a day-guest program priced at $50, which includes lunch,

Kripalu Center for Yoga and Health

YOGA ON THE LAWN AT KRIPALU

all retreat and renewal activities, and use of facilities.

Cranwell Resort, Spa & Golf Club (see *Resorts*) has an elaborate spa facility that boasts a 60-foot-long heated indoor pool and offers some 50 different spa treatments. Both day and overnight spa packages are available.

⊙ **Mepal Manor & Spa** (413-229-8236; www.mepalspa.com), 100 Stone Manor Dr., New Marlborough 01230. The latest and most ambitious undertaking by Brad Wagstaff and Leslie Miller, who also restored New Marlborough's Old Inn on the Green and transformed Gedney Farm into a fantasy wedding venue, this vintage-1906 stone mansion was a boy's prep school when the couple bought it. In just a few years it's been lavishly reborn, the former gym transformed into an elegant and imaginative spa. The setting for the inn is key. The manor sits high above sweeping lawns with a view of hills rolling away south into Connecticut. Paths through meadows lead to a beaver pond and on into the neighboring nature preserve.

There are just 12 guest rooms (private bath), some in the round towers and some with wood-burning hearth and arches, all with many small-paned windows. Even the smallest have been individually, richly, and comfortably decorated using William Morris wallpapers, rich colors and fabrics. Common space includes several smaller rooms as well as the formal parlor and a breakfast room. All rooms may be reserved on weekends for weddings, but just as frequently they aren't, and spa packages are the specialty. A number of rooms have twin beds, the better for two women to share. The spa includes a salon and outdoor whirlpool and offers a variety of massages, a full menu of spa treatments, and a schedule of yoga and Pilates classes. There is also a complement of fitness machines and a gym. $225–395 includes breakfast; less midweek and off-season.

MEPAL MANOR & SPA

Christina Tree

INNS

In Stockbridge

♂ ☀ ₺ **The Red Lion Inn** (413-298-5545; www.redlioninn.com), Main St., Stockbridge 01250. Probably the most famous inn in Massachusetts, the Red Lion is a rambling white-clapboard beauty built in 1897. Staying here is like stepping into a Norman Rockwell painting. Even the cheapest, shared-bath rooms are furnished with real and reproduction antiques and bright prints of Rockwell's *Saturday Evening Post* covers, and there are some splendid rooms. In summer the inn's long porch, festooned with flowers and lined with rockers, is the town's true center. This is also true of the lobby hearth in winter. There is a large, formal dining room, an inviting tavern, nightly entertainment in the Lion's Den (never a cover charge), and, in summer, a popular garden café (see *Where to Eat* for all). In all there are 108 guest rooms (90 with private bath, two handicapped-accessible) in the main inn and six annexes, one of them the old Stockbridge firehouse that Rockwell painted. From $89 for a shared-bathroom with breakfast on a weekday off-season. Rooms in the inn with private bath are $190–235 in-season (June 30–Oct. 22); two-room suites with connecting bath are $285–375, and rooms in the annexes are $190–445 (cheaper midweek than weekends). Children are free, but there's a charge per cot. Well-behaved pets are welcome but cost another $40. Inquire about **Meadowlark at Chesterwood**, a studio hideaway built by sculptor Daniel Chester French in 1905, off across the road and down a wooded road from the present public part of his estate. The living and dining area features a big skylight and a view of Monument Mountain from its deck, and the cottage includes two bedrooms, a bath, and small kitchen. It's a graceful and comfortable as well as a historic space.

∞ **Williamsville Inn** (413-274-6118; www.williamsvilleinn.com), Rt. 41, West Stockbridge 01266. Kandy and Erhard Wendt have renovated this old (1797) inn, among other improvements adding a new kitchen wing to house their culinary school. The dining room, open to the public for dinner (see *Dining Out*), is a showcase for gourmet cuisine. There are nine rooms in the main house, four in the restored 18th-century barn, and two cottages, all with private bath. The 10-acre grounds include flower and herb gardens, a tennis court, swimming pool, and seasonal sculpture garden. $165–260 includes a full breakfast and afternoon tea.

In Lenox 01240

& **Village Inn** (413-637-0020 or 800-253-0917; www.villageinn-lenox.com), 16 Church St. Dating to 1771 and the oldest house in Lenox, this is an authentic old New England inn but after many enlargements and renovations has all the modern conveniences. All of the 32 rooms have private bath (some with Jacuzzi tub) and are comfortably furnished with antiques or reproductions, period prints, and country quilts. Many rooms have four-poster canopy beds, and some also have a working fireplace. The restaurant, Rumplestiltzkin's (see *Dining Out*), is open for breakfast and dinner but not lunch. The tavern, Rumpy's, is a popular hangout. $189–284 in high season and $114–189 off-season, with breakfast (continental only, weekdays in winter and spring).

⌀ **Apple Tree Inn** (413-637-1477; www.appletree-inn.com), 10 Richmond Mountain Rd. This century-old house sits high on a hill overlooking the waters of the Stockbridge Bowl, near the main entrance to Tanglewood. The main house offers 12 rooms and two suites, four with a working fireplace. The 21 rooms in the modern lodge are motel-style but pleasant and handy to the pool, which has the best view from any pool around. Landscaping includes a wide variety of roses that bloom from spring into fall, as well as apple trees. Well-behaved children are welcome. $200–400 in the main house in high season, $100–235 in low; in the guest house, $180–200 high season, $50–70 low.

Gateways Inn (413-637-2532 or 888-492-9466; www.gateways.inn.com), 51 Walker St. Built by Harley Procter of Procter & Gamble in 1912, the inn has been said to resemble a cake of Ivory soap, but it is more elegant than that, with black shutters and central skylit mahogany staircase designed by the firm of McKim, Mead & White. Owners Fabrizio and Rosemary

THE PORCH AT THE RED LION INN

Kim Grant

Chiariello have made many improvements and are welcoming hosts. The 12 guest rooms all have a private bath, telephone, television, and individually controlled central air-conditioning. Three, the only ones where children are accepted, are on the first floor, along with a restaurant, terrace café, and popular bar (see *Dining Out*). Second-floor rooms include a suite with two fireplaces that was Arthur Fiedler's favorite place to stay when he conducted at Tanglewood; another room has a fireplace and wonderful Eastlake furnishings; and a third, named for Romeo and Juliet, features a king-sized sleigh bed under a small skylight. High-season rates are $110–325, low-season $60–200, with full breakfast.

In New Marlborough
The Old Inn on the Green (413-229-7924; www.oldinn.com), Star Rt. 70, New Marlborough 01230. This is a classic, double-porched 1760 stagecoach inn at the center of a gem of a small village. Restored by previous owners, it's now received a new lease on life from Peter Platt and Meredith Kennard. Platt was executive chef for a dozen years at Wheatleigh in Lenox and the atmospheric old tavern rooms are reputedly the setting for some of the best food to be had in the state (see *Dining Out*). The 11 guest rooms are divided between the inn with its appropriate antiques (all private bath) and neighboring Thayer House, a 19th-century home with six elegant rooms and more privacy. Room rates are $225–365 in summer, fall, and holiday weekends but drop to $99 per person midweek, dinner included, even in slightly slower but lovely periods like mid-September.

 Gedney Farm (413-229-3131 or 800-286-3139; www.gedneyfarm .com), Rt. 57, New Marlborough 01230. In the 1970s Bradford Wagstaff and Leslie Miller (now husband and wife) restored the Old Inn (see above), then moved on to transform the nearby Norman-style barn at Gedney Farm into 16 fantasy guest rooms (our favorite is Room 138) and suites, many with a fireplace and tiled whirlpool. The neighboring barn is a reception and banquet center and both the farm and barn are booked most weekends for weddings. Midweek, however, this remains a great getaway spot. Dinner (except Tue.) is next door at the Old Inn on the Green. $240–350 includes a continental breakfast; frequently cheaper midweek.

Also see **Mepal Manor & Spa** under *Spas*.

 The Egremont Inn (413-528-2111; www.egremontinn.com), Old Sheffield Rd., Box 418, South Egremont 01258. This four-story, double-porched landmark is in the middle of a classic crossroads village. The structure dates, in part, to 1780, but in the late 19th century it expanded into a rambling country inn with wide and welcoming porches. Visitors enter a spacious reception area with an 18th-century fireplace; there are two more comfortable sitting rooms, each with a fireplace, stocked with books and board games. Innkeepers Steven and Karen Waller have totally renovated the inn, furnishing the 20 second- and third-floor guest rooms with real and reproduction antiques, private bath (some Jacuzzi, some traditional clawfooter), and phone as well as new mattresses, most queen sized, and varied furnishings. Three rooms are family-geared suites. There's a tavern with its own menu as well as a delightfully old-fashioned dining room that features both a good reputation and jazz on Thu. and Sat. year-round (see *Dining Out*). Amenities include a pool and two tennis courts. Catamount ski area is just down the road. $100–250, more during foliage; weekend MAP packages available in July, August. Three-night minimum required on summer weekends. Add 10 percent tax and service.

🍴 🐾 **New Boston Inn** (413-258-4477; www.newbostoninn.com), junction of Rts. 8 and 57, Sandisfield 01255. This authentic 1737 inn is sited at the junction of two country roads. It's pleasant and informal. Present innkeeper Barbara Colorio is a chef, so tables fill more of the common space than in the past (see *Eating Out*). The seven upstairs guest rooms have wide floorboards, private bath, and furnishings a bit funky but comfortable. The former second-floor ballroom with its matching fireplaces (one is now gas) at either end of the room was set up for a banquet when we stopped by but still contained a corner with armchairs. The resident ghost—a 19th-century bride shot at the top of the stairs by her thwarted lover—is sighted regularly, usually around 3:30 AM. $149 double, $128 off-season. $35 per extra person; $35 per pet.

BED & BREAKFASTS

In Great Barrington
❀ **Windflower** (413-528-2720 or 800-992-1993; www.windflowerinn.com), 684 South Egremont Rd. (Rt. 23), Great Barrington 01230. We keep returning to this gracious, turn-of-the-20th-century country mansion set in expansive grounds. The common rooms are just the right combination of elegance and comfort. All 13 guest rooms have private bath and queen-sized bed (most are canopy or four-poster), and five have a working fireplace. Check out the deep claw-footed tub in Room 5 and the vintage, many-needled shower in Room 7— which is actually our favorite with its window seat, fireplace, and maple cottage furniture. Our second favorite is ground-floor Room 12 with its huge stone fireplace and easy access to the big screened porch and its wicker furniture. Several of the rooms have both queen and twin beds. But what really makes this place is the welcoming family that runs it: veteran innkeeper and sensational chef Claudia Liebert with her green-thumbed and handy husband, John Ryan. Whether you are traveling solo, as a family, or as a couple looking for a romantic getaway, this is one place that works for all—plus tunes you in to local dining and happenings. The grounds include a landscaped pool; golf and tennis are across the road at the Egremont Country Club. $110–265 in-season, from $100 off-season, with a full country breakfast—

THE OLD INN ON THE GREEN

Christina Tree

maybe cottage cheese pancakes with yellow raspberries from the garden—and afternoon tea featuring home-made cookies. The charge for an extra person in the room is $25, less for infants. Checks or AmEx please.

Dragonsfield B&B (413-644-9338; www.dragonsfield.com), 365 State Rd. (Rt. 23), Great Barrington 01230. Sited on a rise almost directly across from the entrance to Ski Butternut, this 1980s house offers four spanking clean, sunny, elegantly comfortable rooms (AC/TV/VCR, private bath) and great views of the ski hill across the way. Weather permitting, a full breakfast is served on the terrace overlooking the back lawn and woods; otherwise it's in the cheerful dining room. There's a fireplace in the living room and a three-room suite that sleeps up to four people. $87–207.

𝄢 ☂ **Turning Point Inn** (413-528-4777; www.turningpointinn.com), corner of Rt. 23 and Lake Buel Rd., RD 2, Box 140, Great Barrington 01230. Open year-round. Built as the Pixley Tavern in 1800, this striking brick inn, 3 miles west of downtown Great Barrington, has been nicely renovated, with six guest rooms (four with private

Christina Tree

bath) in the main house and a cottage that sleeps five. The wide-plank floors survive, and owners Rachel, Dennis, and Teva O'Rourke have enhanced the simple lines of the old inn with country charm, Shaker-plain but elegant furniture and quilts, and great colors (each room is different). While there's a pleasant sitting room, it's the old tavern room with its fireplace and long dining table that is the center of the house—appropriately, since the innkeepers are accomplished chefs who put their all into breakfast and are happy to rent and cook for the entire house. They also offer Saturday-night dinner by arrangement and cater. Pets are accepted in the neighboring two-story, two-bedroom cottage with its full kitchen, living room with cable TV, and heated sunporch. Children over age 3 are also accepted in the inn. Lake Buel is just down the road, and Butternut Basin ski area is a few minutes' drive. $120–170 per room May–Oct.; inquire about the cottage.

𝄢 ♿ **Wainwright Inn** (413-528-2062; www.wainwrightinn.com), 518 S. Main St. (Rt. 7 south of town), Great Barrington 01230. Said to date to 1766, this large, Victorian-looking house was expanded to its present shape by Franklin Pope, an electrical genius recognized for a number of inventions (a couple in partnership with Thomas Edison) who died while tinkering with a transformer in his basement here. A place to stay for many decades, it's been thoroughly renovated and brightened by present innkeeper Marja Tepper. There's an attractive living room with an upright piano and fireplace, and a crisp, sunny breakfast room. The nine guest rooms vary from fireplaced to family geared, so we suggest asking for details when booking. You might want one in the quieter, rear wing of the building. $135–299 in-season, from $100 off-season, includes a three-course breakfast.

☙ Christine's Bed & Breakfast (413-274-6149 or 800-536-1186; www .christinesinn.com), Rt. 41, Housatonic 01236. Christine and Steve Kelsey are Berkshire natives who know their way around. The house, which dates in part to the 18th century, is surrounded by gardens and farmland, off by itself but technically in Housatonic, the mill village within the town of Great Barrington. The four guest rooms are each very private and have TV, phone, and air-conditioning. Common space includes a large sitting room and screened porch, with a special area reserved for tea. Christine is well-known locally for her baking skills and serves high tea by reservation. Children over 11 only please. $187–217, less off-season.

♫ ♿ Acorn's Hope (413-528-2573; www.theacornshope.com), 85 Alford Rd., Great Barrington 01230. This expanded 1930s shingle Cape sits surrounded by large oak trees, across from the Simon's Rock campus. There are expansive lawns and a rear guest room with private entrance that is good for families. Another attractive ground-level room with private entrance is handicapped-accessible. The remaining two upstairs rooms are also inviting, all with private bath and AC. Both the living and dining room have working fireplaces. A full breakfast is served. A resident grey parrot contributes to conversation. $105–185.

In Lee
Historic Merrell Tavern Inn (413-243-1794 or 800-243-1794; www

.merrell-inn.com), 1565 Pleasant St. (Rt. 102), South Lee 01260. This is a standout: a double-porched inn built in 1794 with a third-floor ballroom added in 1837, the first place in Berkshire County to be placed on the National Register of Historic Places. A stagecoach stop for much of the 19th century, it stood vacant for 75 years before previous owners painstakingly restored and furnished it appropriately. Present owners George and Joanne Crockett appreciate what they have and maintain the place lovingly. All guest rooms have private bath and have been carefully decorated with an eye to comfort as well as style. All have TV. The Riverview Suite in a separate wing at the back has a king-sized bed, a wood-burning fireplace, and a private balcony overlooking the grounds and the Housatonic River. Real wood fires glow in the old keeping room where guests breakfast (choosing from a full menu), and in the taproom with its original birdcage bar in the corner, now a cozy sitting room. Grounds slope gently in back to a gazebo beside the Housatonic. $109–155 in

THE HISTORIC MERRELL TAVERN INN

Christina Tree

high season ($195 for the suite), $90–155 off-season with full breakfast. $25 per extra guest.

Applegate Bed and Breakfast (413-243-4451 or 800-691-9012; www .applegateinn.com), 279 W. Park St., Lee 01238. This place is a winner: a 1920s mansion with a pillared portico that's spacious and comfortable. Gloria and Len Friedman, longtime Staten Island residents, bring people skills acquired in their previous careers to innkeeping. The living room is huge, bright, and comfortably furnished, with built-in bookcases and window seats, a fireplace, and space for reading or playing backgammon. Welcoming touches include flowers and chocolates in the rooms. The five rooms in the main house vary in size from huge (Room 1, with its king-sized four-poster, fireplace, and steam shower with two showerheads) to snug but cozy. There are also three suites in the house. Two more suites, along with a two-bedroom "cottage" apartment, are in the adjacent carriage house, all with patio and whirlpool tub. Amenities include a pool, a guest fridge, borrowable bicycles, and plenty of lawn. $155–360 in-season, from $120 off-season. Inquire about winter and spring packages.

Federal House Inn (800-243-1824; www.federalhouseinn.com), 1560 Main St. (Rt. 102), South Lee 01260. This is a graceful Federal-era house, built of mellow brick with white columns in 1824. The guest rooms—two downstairs and six upstairs—all have private bath, WiFi, TV, and AC; three have a gas fireplace, and most have a four-poster bed. Guests have the use of a downstairs parlor. Owners Barbara and Philip Broyles and Megan O'Connor offer a warm welcome to guests. A full breakfast is served, always with a hot entrée. $190–250 high season, $105–180 off-season.

Devonfield (413-243-3298 or 800-664-0880; www.devonfield.com), 85 Stockbridge Rd., Lee 01238. A mansion set in a 29-acre estate, with an 18th-century core and turn-of-the-20th-century lines (it was landscaped and modernized by George Westinghouse Jr.). Rooms and suites are all furnished in antiques and have a private bath; several have a working fireplace and Jacuzzi, and a one-bedroom cottage by the large outdoor pool has kitchen facilities and a fireplace in the living room. There is a tennis court, and rates include full breakfast. Children over 10 welcome. Rooms are $190–320 during Tanglewood season; $175–275 Memorial Day through mid-November; otherwise $140–250. The cottage is $250–350.

🦌 ✐ 🐾 **The Inn at Laurel Lake** (413-243-9749; www.laurellakeinn .com), Rt. 20 west, Lee 01238. This inn has served Berkshire travelers since 1900. One of its nicest features is the small private beach just 150 feet downhill from the house. Tom Fusco bought the inn in 1996 and has improved and brightened it considerably. Of the 19 rooms and suites, 17 have a private bath. Facilities include a music room with over 1,000 classical recordings, tennis court and sauna, picnic tables on a bluff overlooking the lake, and a paddleboat and canoe. A well-behaved dog can be accommodated in the room with a separate entrance. The Cork 'n Hearth restaurant (see *Dining Out*) is next door. Supervised children are welcome. Rates include continental breakfast. Picnics and dinner can be ordered.

$95–195 in-season, $95–205 in foliage season, otherwise $50–125.

&. **Chambery Inn** (413-243-2221 or 800-537-4321; www.berkshireinns .com), 199 Main St., Lee 01238. This unlikely lodging place, a parochial school built in 1885, was rescued from the wrecker's ball and moved to its present site by Joe Toole (whose grandfather was in the first class to attend the school). As you might suspect, the rooms are huge, with 13-foot-high tin ceilings, 8-foot-tall windows—and blackboards (chalk is supplied). Separate stairs are marked for girls and boys, but guests don't get their knuckles rapped with a ruler if they take the wrong one. A continental breakfast is delivered to your room. $85–289, depending on the season and day.

In Lenox 01240
Stonover Farm (413-637-9100; www.stonoverfarm.com), 169 Undermountain Rd. Stonover Farm is a luxurious gem of a place with a setting to match: a quiet woods- and meadow-lined rural road just 0.6 mile from the entrance to Tanglewood. After spending more than 20 years in Los Angeles (where he was a successful rock record producer), Tom and Suky Werman moved to the Berkshires for a complete change of scene and lifestyle. They bought what had been the farmhouse of a former grand estate, a stone-and-shingle building built in the 1890s, and spent a year restoring and remodeling the house and its outbuildings. They also cleared and landscaped the 8-acre grounds, which include a spring-fed duck pond. The result is an elegant small B&B that has lots of character and tasteful touches and all the high-tech comforts. Walls are decorated with

original paintings and prints—there is also an art gallery on the grounds—and guests have the use of a library, a greenhouse solarium, and a computer with high-speed Internet access. Units are air-conditioned and have cable TV and phones with voice mail. There are three large suites in the main house. The adjacent Rock Cottage has a large, sunny living room (one wall is lined with windows), a kitchen, a master bedroom, and a smaller twin-bedded room in a turret, accessed by circular staircase, that makes an ideal children's room. The new School House suite adjacent to the pond is a renovated 1850s schoolhouse with heated floors for winter use, gas fireplace, and a luxurious bathroom that includes a Jacuzzi for two. The rate for house suites is $275–375; Rock Cottage $385–515; and the School House $375–485. There is a 3-night minimum over weekends at peak times, a 2-night weekend minimum the rest of the year. Rates include afternoon wine and cheese and a full, cooked-to-order breakfast.

The Summer White House (413-637-4489 or 800-832-9401; www .thesummerwhitehouse.com), 17 Main St. Originally called "The Lanai" (Hawaiian for "veranda") because of its many inviting porches, this is an authentic Berkshire cottage built in 1885 for a wealthy New Yorker. President Chester K. Arthur is supposed to have stayed here when the Curtis Inn was full, hence the name. The decor is distinctly—almost overwhelmingly—Gilded Age, with lots of period furniture, paintings, and antiques. There are two guest parlors and a formal dining room where a full breakfast is served. The seven large bedrooms, all air-conditioned and with private bath, are named for the wives of U.S. presidents, including Eleanor Roosevelt and Abigail Adams. $195–225 high season, $160 off-season.

✂ ☀ ♿ **Rookwood** (413-637-9750 or 800-223-9750; www.rookwoodinn .com), 11 Old Stockbridge Rd. A turreted, 20-room Victorian inn within walking distance of Tanglewood. All rooms have a private bath, some have a small private balcony, and 12 have a fireplace. We liked Victorian Dream on the second floor with its fainting couch, fireplace, and bath with both claw-footed tub and extra-large shower, but our favorite was Revels Retreat, a third-floor room with queen bed, gas fireplace, and an octagonal space with daybed four steps up in a turret with oval windows and incredible views. Suites have phone and TV. Well-behaved, supervised children are welcome, and two first-floor rooms are handicapped-accessible. Dogs are allowed in two ground-floor suites. A three-room suite is available for rentals of a week or more. Rates, which include afternoon refreshments as well as a full, "heart-healthy" breakfast, are $160–400 in summer, $110–300 the rest of the year, except holidays.

♿ **Hampton Terrace** (413-637-1773 or 800-203-0656; www.hampton terrace.com), 91 Walker St. Stan and Susan Rosen have completely renovated this handsome white frame turn-of-the-20th-century house, filling it with antiques, many family heirlooms. A 1929 Steinway grand piano graces the living room, for instance, and a hand-painted cabinet holds the family doll collection. The 14 rooms all have a private bath. Some units have whirlpool tub; every room has

TV, VCR, and CD player. WiFi access is free. Guests can relax in the parlor of the main house; there is a separate lounge area in the carriage house. Breakfast is served in the dining room and sunporch of the house. $175–325 high season, $160–225 the rest of the year.

The Cornell Inn (413-637-0562 or 800-677-0562; www.cornellinn.com), 203 Main St. This inn on the edge of the village has 28 rooms in three very different structures: a Gilded Age mansion built in 1888; the adjacent MacDonald House, dating to 1777; and a restored former carriage house. Most rooms have fireplace; all have a private bath and some, a Jacuzzi tub. The decor in the mansion is Victorian, but the decorative theme is Colonial in MacDonald House and "country primitive" in the carriage house. Amenities include a pub-style guest lounge with access to a deck looking out on the Japanese rock garden. $150–300 in high season, $80–200 low, with full breakfast.

Garden Gables (413-637-0193 or 888-243-0193; www.lenoxinn.com), 135 Main St. (Rt. 7). This triple-gabled, white-clapboard house dating in part to 1780, is set well back from the road but within walking distance of the village shops and restaurants. New owner John Vittori has made a number of improvements and plans more. Nice touches include fresh flowers in rooms and afternoon sherry in the parlor. The 18 rooms are bright and comfortable, all with private bath, telephone (with answering machine), and air-conditioning, several with whirlpool, many with fireplace or private porch. Our favorites are in the back of the main house, but four suites in the orchard cottages have cathedral ceilings and sitting areas. The ample grounds convey a sense of being out in the country, and the outdoor, guests-only pool is one of the biggest in Berkshire County. Breakfast, at a common table in the gracious dining room or at individual tables out on the porch, includes fresh fruit, yogurt, and cheeses as well as a hot dish. $160–450 in-season, $125–425 off-season.

& **Birchwood Inn** (413-637-2600 or 800-524-1646; www.birchwoodinn .com), 7 Hubbard St. Ellen Gutman Chenaux has brought out the best of this grand old house (the oldest in Lenox), which dates in part to 1767. There are nine rooms in the main house, all with private bath and telephone, and two in the carriage house. The library parlor—the real thing with four walls lined with books, many recent purchases of Ellen's—is a gracious, welcoming room with window seats, a fireplace, and tea and a plate of brownies in the afternoon for guests. The front porch, with its homey wicker furniture, is a popular gathering place in summer. Kennedy Park (good for walking and cross-country skiing) is across the street. All rooms are nicely furnished, some with canopy bed; six have a fireplace. Rates are $180–295, including a full breakfast (fondue Florentine is a particular specialty) prepared by a trained chef.

Brook Farm Inn (413-637-3013; www.brookfarm.com), 15 Hawthorne St. A handsome yellow Victorian house on a quiet byway south of the village, Brook Farm has been tastefully furnished to fit its period (1889) by owners Phil and Linda Halpern. There are 15 guest rooms, all with private bath, six with a fireplace. The carriage house annex has two rooms and

a suite, all with whirlpool tub. Breakfast, featuring homemade baked goods, is buffet-style in the elegant green dining room overlooking the garden, and afternoon tea is served. There is a heated outdoor pool, a comfortable lounging parlor with fireplace, and a large library of poetry books and tapes. Linda, a storyteller, sometimes entertains at teatime. $150–395 in-season, $120–300 the rest of the year.

& **Harrison House** (413-637-1746; www.harrison-house.com), 174 Main St. This handsome old house on the northern fringe of Lenox village, across from Kennedy Park, is named for innkeeper Andrew Fishbein's late beloved dog, whose portrait is on the distinctive inn sign. The six guest rooms are nicely decorated with an eclectic mix of art and antiques. All are air-conditioned and have private bath, cable TV, and fireplace. A suite offers a canopy bed, sitting room, and splendid Victorian bathroom. A first-floor room with fine views is also fully handicapped-accessible. A wraparound porch and a combination sitting/breakfast room look out on the garden. $210–340 high season, $110–240 off-season, with a full breakfast buffet.

& **The Kemble Inn** (413-637-4113 or 800-353-4113; www.kembleinn .com), 2 Kemble St. This Georgian Revival mansion was built in 1881 by U.S. secretary of state Frederick Freylinghuysen and is named for tart-tongued actress Fanny Kemble, a frequent Lenox visitor in the 19th century. New owner Bosa Kosovic has renovated and redecorated from top to bottom using period colors—and the inn has never looked better. The 14 guest rooms, named for writers with local connections such as Edith Wharton, all have private bath, telephone, and air-conditioning, and some have marble fireplace and Jacuzzi. Children over 12 are welcome. A continental breakfast is served in a grand dining room whose picture window offers a superb view of the Berkshires. $195–395 in high season, $155–280 the rest of the year.

Whistler's Inn (413-637-0975; www.whistlersinnlenox.com), 5 Greenwood St. (corner of Rt. 7A). A mostly Tudor-style mansion with large common rooms including a ballroom, library, music room, and baronial dining room. The decor is high Victorian. It's across from the Church on the Hill and an easy walk from both village shops and Kennedy Park. The grounds include 7 acres of garden and woodland. The 14 guest rooms all have private bath. In the carriage house, a very large room on the second floor has wide pine floors, two sitting areas, a TV, a small refrigerator, and lots of light, as well as African artifacts, and books; the rustic suite on the first floor has a woodstove, a sitting/sleeping/TV room, and a private deck. Continental breakfast is served. The library is well stocked, the walls hung with interesting art, and the atmosphere distinctly cultural. It's also rumored to have a ghost, like so many of the English country houses it emulates. $110–275 in summer and fall, $90–225 off-season.

Cliffwood Inn (413-637-3330 or 800-789-3331; www.cliffwood.com), 25 Cliffwood St. On a quiet street just a block off Main, Cliffwood is the home of Joy and Scottie Farrelly—who speak four languages—and a Yorkshire terrier named Charlie. Built in 1888–89 as the summer home of a

former American diplomat, the inn is airy and elegant with seven guest rooms, six with a working fireplace. You might ask for the third-floor room with skylight and a king-sized bed from which you can enjoy the fireplace just inside the bathroom, with its oak floor and Oriental rug. Only coffee is served in the morning, but there are several good breakfast places nearby. Children from 11 years are welcome, but credit cards are not. $159–273 in-season, $114–173 the rest of the year.

♣ ❦ **Walker House** (413-637-1271 or 800-235-3098; www.walkerhouse.com), 64 Walker St. This expanded Federal-era (1804) house in the heart of town is decorated with interesting art, has a lot of common space, and features amenities such as a large library of videos and DVDs guests can watch on a 12-foot-high screen. Peggy and Richard Houdek have been innkeepers for more than 25 years, and Walker House has a somewhat cluttered, lived-in feeling—there are five cats in residence, among other things—more like that of a private home than most Lenox B&Bs. A long flower-garnished and wicker-furnished veranda overlooks the expansive back garden. Five of the eight guest rooms, each named for a composer, have a fireplace, and all have charm. A continental breakfast with fruit, served at the dining room table, and afternoon tea are included in the rates: $90–220 June–Oct., $90–160 the rest of the year.

In Sheffield 01257

Broken Hill Manor (877-535-6159; www.brokenhillmanor.com), 771 West Rd. Many try but few are equal to the challenge of converting ponderous Edwardian mansions to truly inviting places to stay. Mike Farmer and Gaetan Lachance, however, have both the savvy and the furniture it takes. The colors and many details are authentically Edwardian, and while the furniture is comfortable, much of it is exotic, appropriate to the pervading sound and theme of opera music. The eight guest rooms are each named for an opera's heroine. Tosca, as you might suspect, is the most elegant, featuring an Egyptian brass canopy bed, but our favorite is Violetta with its golden walls and coverlet and slightly less ornate (also Egyptian) bed. We could spend hours in the Great Room with its mix of comfortable and exotic furnishings (most rugs are also Egyptian) around the stone hearth. The dining room is formal, but there are also tables on the back terrace, beyond the totally revamped kitchen, surrounded by landscaped gardens. The house was built in 1900 and was previously home to the two writers of the radio soap opera *Young Doctor Malone*. Farmer and Lachance spent 4 years rewiring, plumbing (they installed five bathrooms), and landscaping. The 12 hilltop acres are just minutes from either Rt. 7 or Rt. 23 but seem totally removed. $150–200 includes a full breakfast.

🐾 ✿ ❀ **Staveleigh House** (413-229-2129 or 800-980-2129; www.staveleigh .com), 59 Main St. (Rt. 7). Ali Winston offers exceptional hospitality at this gracious B&B, a vintage-1817 parsonage just off the Sheffield village green. She has a sure touch with colors, and the seven guest rooms (five with private bath) are furnished with a mix of well-chosen antiques and an eye to comfort. Our favorite is one of the two ground-floor side rooms with private entrances (the other is

reserved for guests with pets), but there isn't a room in the house we wouldn't love staying in. There's a hearth in the parlor and a breakfast room filled with flowers and sunlight. We dropped by at teatime and the aroma of fresh-baked chocolate chip cookies was heady. Ali is an enthusiastic cook whose breakfasts are special, perhaps a home-grown melon and light little pancakes drizzled with baked apples, served with locally raised and cured bacon. $125–165 May–Oct.; $85–135 off-season. Add $25 for a pet.

The B&B at Howden Farm (413-229-8481; www.howdenfarm.com), 303 Ronnapo Rd. When we first met artist Bruce Howden, he was operating the (then) only bed & breakfast in Burlington, Vermont. He has since inherited the family homestead, a Victorianized Greek Revival farmhouse and a 250-acre pumpkin farm, famous for having developed its own varieties and for its pick-your-own policy. It's all beautifully sited in Ashley Falls near Bartholomew's Cobble and the Colonel Ashley House. Guests can launch a canoe on the river and hike in the fields and woods. There are four rooms, two with private bath, two sharing. All are nicely furnished, but the beauty is Room 104, which offers a sitting room with bow windows overlooking fields. $99–149 includes a very full breakfast, perhaps featuring eggs from resident chickens.

∞ ✿ ❀ **Race Brook Lodge** (413-229-2916; www.rblodge.com), 864 S. Undermountain Rd. (Rt. 41). Architect David Rothstein has transformed a 1790s barn into one of Berkshire County's more distinctive places to stay. "This is a chintz-free zone," Rothstein quips about the lack of antiques and frills in his 32 guest rooms (14 in the barn, many with private entry; 6 in the brick Federal-era Coach House; and the rest divided among cottages). The open beams and angles of the rustic old barn remain, but walls are white and stenciled; rooms are furnished with Native American rugs and quilts or spreads. As you would expect in a barn, the common room is large and multi-leveled, with some good artwork; a wine bar is in one corner. The lodge caters to hikers and walkers (as individuals and couples as well as groups), encouraging guests to climb the Race Brook Trail, which measures 1.5 miles in distance and rises almost 2,000 feet in elevation—past a series of five cascades—to Mount Race. There's a landscaped pool and a Meeting Barn (also used for wedding receptions). Innkeeper Allegra Scott Graham offers an abundant continental breakfast with one hot special. Children are welcome, as are well-behaved dogs (in certain rooms). Dinner is served in the Stagecoach Tavern (see *Dining Out*). $115–245 in high season; $95–198 in summer, slightly less in winter.

❦ Birch Hill Bed & Breakfast
(413-229-2143; www.birchhillbb.com), 254 S. Undermountain Rd. (Rt. 41). Formerly Ivanhoe House, this gracious old country house is now owned by Wendy and Michael Advocate and is a real find for hikers or cross-country skiers and their dogs (subject to strict rules). Nearby hiking trails lead up to the five cascades along the Race Brook Trail, on up to a spectacular stretch of the Appalachian Trail across Mount Race; in winter you can poke around the inn's own 25 acres on skis. Guests are welcome to play games or

the piano, watch TV, or dip into the library of the paneled Chestnut Room. The seven centrally air-conditioned rooms are nicely furnished, and all have private bath. There is also a pool, and guests enjoy access to a small lake across the road. Children over 9 years only please. Memorial Day through Labor Day and October, from $130 weekdays to $215 on the weekends.

1802 House (413-229-2612; www .berkshire1802.com), P.O. Box 395, 48 S. Main St. This much-expanded early-19th-century house rambles back from Rt. 7 in the village of Sheffield. Nancy Hunter-Young and Rick Kowarek offer a choice of seven rooms with queen or double bed, five with private bath (two small rooms share). There's a screened porch and nicely landscaped gardens in the rear. The full breakfast may include ice cream with your French toast. $110–165 single or double May 15–Nov. 1, $100–145 off-season, $25 extra for a third person in a room.

In Stockbridge
The Taggart House (413-298-4303; www.taggarthouse.com), 18 Main St., Stockbridge 01262. "For a big house, it's warm and there's plenty of light," remarks August Murko, who since acquiring this grand village manor has installed a new heating system, a new roof, and storm windows, redone chimneys, and generally injected it with informality and comfort. The rambling mid-19th-century "cottage" has some grand common rooms. The four upstairs guest rooms are lush, with decor to match their names: the French, Russian, Willow Bough (with William Morris paper and matching curtains and linens), and Clara Bow Rooms. Guest amenities include deep

soaking tubs, a butler's pantry stocked with complimentary beverages, and a small beach as well as both canoes and kayaks on the Housatonic River, which winds along below the grounds. Breakfast is served in the formal dining room. $250–350 in-season, $175–250 Nov.–May.

&. **The Inn at Stockbridge** (413-298-3337; www.stockbridgeinn.com), Rt. 7, Box 2033, Stockbridge 01262. This white-pillared mansion was built in 1906 and set on 12 acres with ample woods and meadow. Alice and Len Schiller preside over afternoon wine and cheese, served by the hearth in the pleasant living room. Common space also includes a library and a more private computer/writing room; there's WiFi throughout. The wicker-and flower-filled back porch overlooks a garden and pool. Full breakfast is served by candlelight at the formal dining room table. In addition to the guest rooms in the main house—each different, most with king bed, and all with private bath—there are eight large, luxurious rooms in two new annexes, the "Cottage House" beside the pool and the "Barn Suites" set farther back amid greenery. These all are themed and fitted with gas fireplaces; six have baths featuring deep, two-person whirlpool tubs. All rooms have air-conditioning and telephone. There's also a well-equipped fitness center and a massage room. $170–360 in-season, $140–260 off-season.

Conroy's Bed & Breakfast (413-298-5188 or 888-298-4990; www .conroysinn.com), Rt. 7, P.O. Box 191, Stockbridge 01262. Set up and off Rt. 7 in 3 acres of lawn and woods, this 1830 brick farmhouse has a homey feel. There is a bright dining room and a small sitting area; the eight rooms—five in the main house (two with private bath) and three (all with private bathroom) in the old post-and-beam barn—are all country comfortable. Two of the barn rooms have decks, and the third offers a patio. The real treasure here, however, is the seasonal apartment in the barn with a deck, a sleeping loft, and a great downstairs space with fully equipped kitchen, great for families (four people). Amenities include a pool in landscaped grounds that include the foundations of the former dairy barn. $135–180 for rooms in summer, $325 for the apartment; in winter rooms from $85, apartment $225. Breakfast is served in the dining room.

Blue Willow (413-298-3018; www .bluewillowbb.com), 2 Lincoln Lane, P.O. Box 843, Stockbridge 01261. Open May–Oct. Lila and Joseph Ruggio have created a gem of a place to stay. Within walking distance of the village, the 19th-century house is on a quiet street in the shade of a shagbark hickory tree, with a back lawn that slopes to the Housatonic River. The three guest rooms, all with TV, AC,

THE INN AT STOCKBRIDGE

and private bath, are comfortably, tastefully decorated. The standout is the Blue Room with its cannonball queen bed and gas fireplace. A full candlelit breakfast is served on blue willowware. $110–185. Inquire about the cottage room.

The Stockbridge Country Inn (413-298-4015; www.stockbridge countryinn.com), Rt. 183, Box 525, Stockbridge 01262. Handy to Chesterwood and the Norman Rockwell Museum in the Glendale section of Stockbridge, this 1856 farmhouse offers an unusual amount of common space, including an elegant living room with fireplace, a less formal sitting room, and a sunporch overlooking the garden. The seven guest rooms all have private bath and are tastefully furnished with four-poster queen-sized bed, antiques, Laura Ashley fabrics and prints, bright chintzes, and hooked rugs. The walls are hung with original Audubon prints—which are for sale, as is much of the furniture, because innkeepers Diane and Vernon Reuss are antiques dealers. There is a large, heated outdoor pool. The full breakfast is cooked to order and in summer served on a screened porch looking out on the garden. $160–399 in summer and fall, less off-season.

Elsewhere

The Inn at Freeman Elms Farm (413-229-3700; www.vgernet.net/ freeman), 566 Mill River, Great Barrington Rd., New Marlborough 01230. This is a find: a handsome farmhouse still in the same family that's owned it for nine generations. Obviously it was built very grandly in 1797. Later additions are limited to a spacious, screened front porch, furnished with plenty of rocking chairs, and a rear ell

with a classic Mission-style dining room. The six guest rooms (private baths) are furnished in family antiques and quilts, the kind most innkeepers covet. We especially like the "cottage" room with its mint-condition Cottage furniture. Breakfast is full, and the property totals 600 acres with fields, woods, gardens, orchard, and cattle. Children must be 12 or older. $135–210 includes breakfast.

🦢 ♿ **The Silo B&B** (413-528-5195), 6 Boice Rd., P.O. Box 5444, North Egremont 01252. What a great spot! This is an artfully designed home attached to an authentic silo, atop a knoll and surrounded by fields. The airy living room maximizes the view, beyond flowers and ever-popular bird feeders. Two guest rooms share an upstairs sitting area, and a third is on the ground floor. $115 midweek, $125 weekends year-round, includes a full breakfast either in the breakfast room or on the screened porch. While there's an away-from-it-all feeling, the Silo is within walking distance of the North Egremont general store and of Elm Court Inn (see *Dining Out*). It's also handy to wading in the Green River and to swimming in Prospect Lake. No credit cards.

The Inn at Sweet Water Farm (413-528-2882; www.innsweetwater .com), P.O. Box 196, 1 Prospect Rd. and Rt. 71, North Egremont 01252. This early-19th-century building—the former North Egremont Grange—is sited at a country crossroads, part of a cluster that also includes the village general store/post office and the Elm Court Inn (see *Dining Out*). Innkeeper Lynda Fisher is an artist and cook, offering guests the wherewithal to sketch or paint and a choice of elaborate breakfasts. We like the open-timbered living room with its bright walls and hearth and the guest rooms we saw. *Sweet water* refers to the taste of the inn's own water, served fresh to guests each day in delectable blue bottles. At this writing the inn has been opened so recently that we're unsure how it will shake out. Breakfast, for instance, is currently an additional charge. Inquire about dinner by reservation. Rooms are $145–165.

Linden-Valley (518-325-7100), P.O. Box 157, Hillsdale, NY 12529. Sited on the New York–Massachusetts border at Catamount ski area, but really in a landscaped world of its own. Linda Breen has created an exceptional hideaway: seven large, nicely designed and decorated rooms, the upper units with cathedral ceilings and those on the garden level with small terraces. Each has a TV, coffeemaker, and wet bar with icemaker. A full breakfast is served in the dining room, an inviting space with a fireplace, or, weather permitting, on the garden terrace. The magnificently landscaped grounds include a spring-fed pond with a sandy beach, a swimming pool, and two tennis courts. The previous owner of the nearby Swiss Hutte (see *Dining Out*), Linda is Bavarian, clearly a scrupulous housekeeper and an enthusiastic cook. $145–155 midweek, $165–175 on weekends, includes a full breakfast.

✍ **Cobble View Bed and Breakfast** (413-243-2463 or 800-467-4136; www.cobbleviewbandb.com), 123 Main Rd., Tyringham 01264. Located across the road from Tyringham Cobble (hence the name), this handsome early-19th-century house is just 4 miles from the Mass Pike exit but has a way-off-the-beaten-path feel. Life-

long Berkshire residents Lynn Bertelli and Alan Wilcox offer four large guest rooms with air-conditioning and private bath, also a studio with its own kitchen and a separate entrance, good for families. A large loft in the barn can accommodate four people. Decor throughout is a pleasantly appropriate mix of antiques and reproductions. Guests have the use of two downstairs parlors and the grounds, which include flower gardens and a croquet course. Rooms are $95–180, studio $130–220, loft $225–285. The enhanced continental breakfast is served by candlelight.

Hallig Hilltop House (413-644-0076; www.hallighilltophouse.com), 68 West St., Mount Washington 01258. In the very southwestern corner of Massachusetts, this is about as away-from-it-all as you can get. The turn-of-the-20th-century Dutch Colonial–style house is surrounded by thousands of acres in the Mount Washington State Forest, handy only to some of the region's best hiking trails and to Bash Bish Falls. Oskar Hallig is a chef and happy to prepare lunch and dinner, as well as picnic versions of both—which is a good thing, because once you get here you won't want to leave, and you certainly won't want to have to find the place again after dark (it's 12 miles to South Egremont). There are three guest rooms, all with private bath; other amenities include a stone fireplace in the living room, a porch lined with rockers, a swimming pool, and a wood-burning cedar sauna. In winter there can be good cross-country skiing—you're at 1,300 feet, and there are plenty of trails through the woods. $125–250 per room includes a full breakfast; $15 for a picnic lunch; $40 for a five-course dinner. Inquire about renting the whole house.

Lakeside Terrace (413-528-3371; off-season, 631-242-5547; www.lake sideterracebb.com), 24 Lakeside Terrace, P.O. Box 33, Monterey 01245. Open July 4 weekend through Labor Day weekend. This is a 150-year-old summer house on Lake Garfield with rockers on the screened porch and a fireplace in the living room, set in 9 acres. It's been in Merry Oislander's family since 1962 and catered to paying guests long before that but was a closely guarded secret. "Now most of the guests who came every year are gone, and we need to let people know we're here," Merry says about why this hidden gem has finally surfaced. There are six bedrooms, all with private bath (the two smallest rooms share or are rented together). $125–145 per room includes breakfast, served on the porch when possible, otherwise in the dining room. There's a swim dock with a rowboat, and guests are welcome to bring kayaks. Children only over age 5 please.

✳ Where to Eat

DINING OUT

In Great Barrington

Castle Street Café (413-528-5244; www.castlestreetcafe.com), 10 Castle St. Open for dinner except Tue. Reservations advised. Next door to the Mahaiwe Performing Arts Center, Michael Ballon's casually elegant restaurant was the first high-end place to dine in Great Barrington, and it remains one of the best. Linen-draped tables and changing art set the tone for a frequently changing menu that features local farm products. Entrée choices ($21–28), served with

green salad, might include sautéed breast of duck with braised apples, pears, cranberries, and black currant sauce, or sea scallops in lemongrass broth with crisp vegetables; pasta, burgers, and a vegetarian plate are also available. Live music in the **Celestial Bar** (no cover charge).

&. **Pearl's** (413-528-7767; www.pearls restaurant.com), 47 Railroad St. Open for dinner and Sunday brunch. Reservations advised. A former auto parts store at the head of Railroad Street has been transformed into one of the most sophisticated restaurants around. Dark and richly paneled, it evokes the dining room on a vintage ocean liner. The original emphasis was on steaks but the menu is large and varied, ranging from pan-seared venison with sweet potato fritters, oven-roasted Vidalia onions, and pecan glaze, to vegetarian ravioli (entrées $18–27). The bar is separate and features comfortable seating facing the plate-glass window overlooking the length of Railroad Street. Come evening, these are the most coveted seats in town. The bar menu might include chili, clams casino, and fried calamari.

&. **Bizen** (413-528-4343), 17 Railroad St. Open for lunch and dinner daily. Michael Marcus opened this restaurant and sushi bar in 1997 to serve the food for which his pottery is intended. Marcus studied the distinctive pottery of Bizen in Japan for four years and has been creating it since 1982 in his Joyous Spring Pottery in Monterey. The restaurant has expanded several times and now includes a sake bar and an area of traditional tatami rooms specializing in "Kaiseki" cuisine with a prix fixe menu. The main menu features three dozen varieties of sushi, sashimi, and maki, all made from the freshest fish, seafood, and organic vegetables. Dinner entrées ($8.95–18.95) include seafood, chicken, vegetables, tempura, and noodles.

Helsinki Tea Room (413-528-3394), 284 Main St. Open daily for lunch, dinner, and Sunday brunch. There's also a separate bar and nightclub, a venue for live entertainment. *Colorful* is an understatement for the decor of this café that has, unfortunately, diluted its original Scandinavian and Russian menu with quasi-Thai and southern items. Happily, the "mad Russian" (crisp potato latkes headed with gravlax, sour cream, and caviar, served with berry compote, $20) survives, but we were disappointed in the "Finnish meatballs"($18), and the wine list was overpriced. The lunch menu now includes "quesadilla of the day" and falafel as well as a Helsinki salad.

Verdura Cucina Rustica (413-528-8969), 44 Railroad St. Open for dinner. Reservations advised. Chef William Webber is an advocate of "slow food" and of local ingredients. The former store is richly colored and inviting. The menu is theoretically northern Italian but varied. The "primi" course might include handmade tagliatelle with foraged mushroom, asparagus, and truffle essence ($14); "secondi" might be house gnocchi with spring vegetables, arugula pesto, and lemon, or wood-roasted quail with spaghetti squash and balsamic sage brown butter. Entrées $23–31. This menu is also available in neighboring **Dué Enoteca**, open to the street in summer and open until 1 AM, serving "dué" (Mediterannean-style tapas) and panini. Italian wines are the house specialty in both places.

Union Bar and Grill (413-528-6228), 293 Main St. Open for dinner except Tue.; also for Saturday lunch and Sunday brunch. Exposed pipes, stainless steel, and bleached tabletops with lime-green trim give this new storefront a loft-in-SoHo feel, but the ambience is relaxed and family-friendly, and the menu nouvelle country. Now owned by a Manhattan restaurateur, this remains a reliably good bet among the area's high-end dining choices. The Caesar salad is excellent. Dining entrées might include pan-seared tuna with basmati rice, bok choy, and spicy soy wasabi sauce, or steak *au poivre* with sun-dried mashed potatoes, braised greens, and cognac Dijon shallot au jus. Entrées range from $12 for a grilled portobello sandwich to $34 for grilled sirloin.

✂ ♿ **Aegean Breeze** (413-528-4001; www.aegean-breeze.com), 327 Stockbridge Rd. (Rt. 7). Reservations advised. Open 11–10 daily. The winning combination here is a light, bright, and airy decor and good service plus unusual Greek appetizers and a wide variety of pastas and of very fresh fish entrées. You might begin

A VIEW OF RAILROAD STREET FROM PEARL'S IN GREAT BARRINGTON

Christina Tree

with *prasopita* (baked stuffed filo with fresh leeks, feta cheese, dill, and scallions), and dine on the Aegean Breeze Platter (baked Chilean sea bass with Vidalia onions, tomato, feta, and fresh herbs, served in a clay pot). Children's menu. Dinner entrées $15.95–35.

Shiro (413-528-1898), 105 Stockbridge Rd. (at the junction of Rts. 23 and 7). Closed Tue. This is a local favorite, a Japanese restaurant with two hibachi tables (reserve if you want one) and an attention to presentation. Over 20 varieties of sushi are featured, along with hibachi-grilled steak and seafood, tempura dishes, and noodle dishes. Full bar. Most dinner entrées are around $20.

In Lee

Chez Nous (413-243-6397; www .cheznousbistro.com), 150 Main St. Open for dinner daily in summer, fewer days off-season; closed in March. French chef Franck Tessier and pastry chef Rachel Portnoy have created one of the hottest dining venues around. You may have to reserve a night or two in advance. The setting: three romantically lit dining rooms in a rambling village house. The à la carte menu usually includes frog legs with garlic-herb butter, and escargots roasted on a skewer and served with garlic-herb butter and locally grown mushrooms. Main courses ($17.95–28.95) might include pan-fried crabcakes with sage-cranberry mayonnaise and a ragout of green French vegetables, or various cuts of certified Black Angus beef. This is not a place to pass up dessert—perhaps a dark chocolate hazelnut crunch torte or maple crème brûlée. The wine list is extensive and moderately priced.

✍ **Cork 'n Hearth** (413-243-0535; www.corknhearth.com), Rt. 20. Open for dinner except Mon.; call ahead in the off-season. Dine overlooking Laurel Lake if you can get a table near the large glass windows in the Lake Room; there's also a stone fireplace in the barnboard-sided Brass Room, hung with brass antiques. Chef-owner Chris Ryan offers a varied à la carte menu. Try the pan-roasted seafood medley with ginger teriyaki sauce, the veal Oscar, or the boneless roast prime rib. Children's menu. Entrées are $17.50–24.

Sullivan Station (413-243-2082), 189 Railroad St. Open for lunch and dinner. Housed in the old Lee railroad depot (still a stop on the Lenox-based Berkshire Scenic Railway), this has been a local institution for more than 25 years. It features stick-to-the-ribs fare such as prime rib, baked stuffed shrimp, and grilled pork chops with applesauce. Dinner entrées (from 4:30) $15.95–21.95. Burgers and sandwiches are also available at dinner.

In Lenox

Church Street Café (413-637-2745; www.churchstreetcafe.biz), 45 Church St. Open daily for lunch and dinner May–Feb. Billing itself "An American Bistro," this lively, popular restaurant has an eclectic and always interesting menu. There is a pleasant dining patio and several connecting dining rooms, the walls of which are hung with paintings by local artists. Lunch on pulled-pork BBQ or Mediterranean salad, dine on Maine crabcakes or pan-roasted Moroccan spiced free-range chicken with couscous. Dinner entrées $19.50–32.50.

Bistro Zinc (413-637-8800), 56 Church St. Open daily for lunch and dinner except Tue. Very popular, with a contemporary decor and cuisine but a cozy bistro atmosphere. Dine on grilled lamb loin or Maine lobster with vegetable spaetzle. Entrées $24–35. The bar is known for its martinis and other cocktails and serves 14 different wines by the glass. Usually crowded and lively in the evening, it's separate from the main dining room but very visible—an impressive array of bottles behind the bar is dramatically illuminated—through a floor-to-ceiling glass wall.

Café Lucia (413-637-2460), 80 Church St. Open for dinner Tue.–Sat. A remodeled art gallery is the setting for appreciating fine regional Italian dishes such as *osso buco con risotto* or boneless breast of duck with soft polenta, brandied pear sauce, and sautéed greens. The Caesar salad is rich and garlicky. Try the tiramisu for dessert. Good wine list. Deservedly popular, and reservations are recommended. Entrées $24–39.

Spigalina (413-637-4455; www.spigalina.com), 80 Main St. Open for dinner daily in-season, closed Tue. and Wed. off-season. A very popular presentation of the flavors and colors of the Mediterranean. Besides the main restaurant—several connecting rooms—there is also a dining porch that looks out on Main Street. Dinner entrées ($18–29) could be vegetarian risotto, homemade tagliatelle, veal scaloppine, or spaghetti with clams.

Village Inn (413-637-0020; www.villageinn-lenox.com), 16 Church St. The restaurant, Rumplestiltzkin's, is open to the public for dinner year-round and lunch in summer and fall. Entrées ($17.95–27.95) include dishes such as Shaker-style cranberry pot roast and pistachio-encrusted rack of lamb. **Rumpy's**, the basement tavern, serves pub food and has entertainment on weekends.

Gateways Inn (413-637-2532), 751 Walker St. Open daily for dinner, plus lunch and brunch on weekends (except Tue. in winter). The warm colors and crisp settings of the formal dining room are the appropriate setting for excellent meals that might begin with pan-seared Hudson Valley foie gras, then move on to roast Maine lobster with Chardonnay sauce, or New Zealand baby lamb chops with heirloom tomatoes. Entrées $24–32. In summer light fare is served in **LaTerraza**, the terrace café. The bar adjacent to the dining room stocks 200 different kinds of malt whiskey.

Blantyre (413-637-3556; www.blantyre.com), 16 Blantyre Rd. Blantyre is a baronial mansion that epitomizes the Berkshires' Gilded Age glory. Dining in its grand restaurant is a memorable and rather formal experience. (Men are required to wear jackets and ties.) The cuisine is French, of course, prepared with care and served with flair. The wine list is vast and varied. The prix fixe three-course menu is $85 per person, the four-course menu $100, the five-course menu $115–170 with wine tasting. A 20 percent gratuity is added. Dinner is by reservation only. The restaurant is closed to the public on Mon. In July and Aug. lunch is also served, on the terrace overlooking the splendid formal garden. A three-course prix fixe menu is $42.

Wheatleigh (413-637-0610; www.wheatleigh.com), W. Hawthorne Rd. Open for lunch and dinner; check off-season. By reservation only. The formal dining room in this Florentine palazzo, within walking distance of Tanglewood, features a contemporary American interpretation of classic dishes such as olive oil poached king salmon or heirloom Challans duck, served with blood orange, cipollini onion, and dandelion. The three-course prix fixe dinner menu is $85, and the four-course one $115, not including a 20 percent service charge. The wine list is long and includes some superb vintages.

Cranwell (413-637-1364; www .cranwell.com), Rt. 20. Breakfast, lunch, and dinner. "Wyndhurst," the main dining room of the baronial manor (Wyndhurst was its original name), is grandly appointed and its cuisine appropriately first rate. Menu choices include the likes of sake-marinated breast of chicken, and grilled gremolata-painted salmon. Entrées $27.75–33. **Sloane's Tavern**, a seasonal English-style pub, is on the golf course; the **Music Room** offers live entertainment on weekends as well as a grill menu at lunch in winter. The spa also has a café serving light fare.

Prime Italian Steakhouse & Bar (413-637-2998; www.primelenox .com), 15 Franklin St. Still in the same family, this is the successor to Antonio's, an unpretentious Italian restaurant that had a strong local following. Proprietor Jerry Gallo, who started working in the restaurant when he was 8 years old, has given the old place a sleek contemporary decor with black tile, red leather, polished wood, glass-enclosed booths, and colorful artwork. Unchanged, however, are the shingled exterior and outdoor patio. The emphasis is obviously on beef—the signature steak is the 40-oz. Bone-in Cowboy, a rib-eye French cut that serves two—but traditional Italian dishes such as eggplant parmigiano and shrimp scampi are also on the menu. The wine list

includes more than 1,000 vintages. Most entrées are $17–39; the Bone-in-Cowboy is $62.

Fin Sushi & Sake Bar (413-637-9171) 27 Housatonic St. Open daily 5:30–9:45 PM. Varied as its restaurant scene has been, for a long time Lenox lacked a good sushi bar. That void has been more than filled by Fin Sushi & Sake, which has a genuine Japanese menu that includes tuna, salmon, and yellowtail sushi and sashimi along with items such as squid salad, barbecued eel, sea urchin roe, and miso soup. The decor is uncluttered but pleasant in the Japanese style. Beer and wine as well as sake are served. Entrées $17–21; sushi, $5–9; sashimi, $8–14.

Firefly (413-637-2700; www.firefly lenox.com), 71 Church St. Open daily for dinner in summer; closed Tue. and Wed. off-season. Live music Thu. nights. This cheery, popular place has an uncluttered contemporary decor and an eclectic "world fusion" menu. Summer diners have the option of eating inside or outside on the porch. Tapas are served in the popular but often noisy bar, which also mixes high-octane drinks such as Tequila Cosmopolitans and Prickly Pear Margaritas, starting at 3 PM on Sat. and Sun. Entrées $12–27.

Lenox 218 (413-637-4218; www .lenox218.com), 218 Main St. (Rt. 7A). Open daily for lunch and dinner. The contemporary art deco decor is warm and welcoming, as is the wood-burning fireplace in the lounge. The specialty is northern Italian cuisine, represented by dishes such as chicken cacciatore served on polenta, and angelhair pomodoro with meatballs, but New York sirloin, rainbow trout fillet, and a hamburger smothered with caramelized onions are also on the menu. Dinner entrées $14–28.

Trattoria il Vesuvio (413-637-4904; www.trattoria-vesuvio.com), 242 Pittsfield Rd. (Rts. 7/20). Though the exterior has little character (the building is a remodeled barn), this pleasant restaurant, owned and run by the Arace family, has a devoted following. The bread and pasta are homemade, and the menu features authentic Italian specialties such as roast breast of veal stuffed with prosciutto and spinach, or penne tossed in a sauce of tomato, basil, garlic, red peppers, and olive oil. Entrées $14–32.

In Stockbridge

The Red Lion Inn (413-298-5545; www.redlioninn.com), 30 Main St. Breakfast, lunch, and dinner served daily. Reservations recommended. The formal and fabulous old main dining room bans blue jeans and shorts for dinner. You might lunch on salmon cakes or a grilled chicken salad, and dine on vanilla-cured pork loin or lemon-thyme roasted pheasant breast. For dessert we recommend the Red Lion Indian pudding. The wine list is extensive. Dinner entrées $23–30. Also see Widow Bingham's Tavern under *Eating Out*.

Rouge Restaurant and Bistro (413-232-4111), 3 Center St., West Stockbridge. Open for dinner only Wed.–Sun. 5–10. Up a side street in a small wooden building on the banks of the Williams River, Rouge draws diners by the droves with its Americanized international cuisine and elegantly casual atmosphere. Chef de cuisine William Merelle's moderately priced but imaginative menu includes dishes such as persillage of frog legs, pan-sautéed with sauce à la Rouge and polenta; and seared tuna encrusted

with peppercorns and ginger with ratatouille. Tasting menus are available. The cozy bar serves memorable martinis, among other drinks, as well as tapas, a "croque madame," and mini burgers. Entrées $21–24.

Once Upon a Table (413-298-3870), 36 Main St. Tucked away in the Mews, around the corner from the Red Lion Inn, this popular place is open for lunch and dinner daily in July and August, variable days at other times. The menu changes with the seasons. Dinner entrées $19–24.

Williamsville Inn (413-274-6118; www.williamsvilleinn.com), Rt. 41, West Stockbridge. Dinner by reservation Thu.–Sun. Kandy and Erhard Wendt (he is a certified master chef and culinary instructor) also offer cooking classes. While the à la carte menu includes a choice of dishes, the specialties are German—perhaps Rhenish beef sauerbraten with raisin sauce, red cabbage, and potato dumplings. Desserts inlude Bavarian-style warm apple strudel. Appetizers $7–18, entrées $20–32.

Trúc Orient Express (413-232-4204), 3 Harris St., West Stockbridge. In summer open daily for lunch (11–3) and dinner (5–9). Off-season open for dinner only, every day except Tue. Nguyen and Drai Duong still offer the personalized service they have been known for since opening this Vietnamese restaurant in 1979. On a recent visit we arrived a few minutes before our friends and soon became absorbed in the coffee table books about Vietnam piled beside comfortable seating. The large dining room is pleasant, decorated with woven straw, Vietnamese art, and white tablecloths. Dishes can be as spicy as you specify. Specialties include Trúc's special triangular shrimp rolls (with crab, pork, and vegetables surrounding a large shrimp, wrapped in crisp, golden rice paper) and many vegetarian selections. Our hot-and-sour soup was outstanding. We also recommend the Banh Xeo ("happy pancake"), a crispy rice flour crêpe stuffed with shrimp, pork, mushroom, onions, and bean sprouts. Dinner entrées range from $11.95 for Trúc's special fried rice (combined with peas, carrots, onions, shrimp, pork, chicken, and sausage) to $22.75 for "Bo Luc Lac" ("shaking beef"). Another specialty is lemongrass duck: crispy boneless duck topped with chopped lemongrass and chili sauce and served with fine rice noodles ($25). A gift shop selling Vietnamese crafts is attached to the restaurant.

Oeno (413-232-7277), 1 Harris St., West Stockbridge. Open for dinner except Wed. This is a new effort for La Bruschetta, a restaurant-turned-gourmet-takeout that's now serving meals again: osso buco Milanese with saffron risotto, crispy rotisserie free-range duckling with fennel and garlic, and much more. Entrées $19–24. Well-chosen wines remain a part of the draw.

In Egremont

The Old Mill (413-528-1421), Rt. 23, South Egremont. Dining nightly; closed Mon. off-season. First come, first served. Chef-owner Terry Moore has been creating some of the most reliably superb fare in the county since 1978. The vintage-1797 gristmill by Hubbard Brook makes a rustic but elegant setting for a meal that might begin with steamed mussels in Cinzano with garlic, herbs, and scallions. Entrées ($17–30) might include grilled organic Scottish salmon with wild rice risotto cake, roasted local mushrooms, and grilled asparagus. Other choices: lasagna with eggplant, grilled onions, ricotta, and mozzarella; and grilled Angus New York steak with foie gras butter and truffle oil fries. The cozy tavern area has its own reasonably priced menu. Special care is taken to make single diners feel at ease in either venue.

Elm Court Inn (413-528-0325), Rt. 71, North Egremont. Dinner Wed.–Sun. (reserve). The large, low-ceilinged dining room of this 1790 inn is filled with white-clothed tables. Chef-owner Urs Bieri serves mouth-watering blackened fish of the day on a bed of arugula salad with mango salsa; he also earns high praise for his classic German-Swiss dishes like Wiener schnitzel and veal à la Suisse, both with roesti potatos. The menu changes daily. There is an extensive wine list. Entrées $18–31.

John Andrews (413-528-3469; www .jarestaurant.com), Rt. 23, South Egremont near the New York line. Open for dinner nightly; closed Wed. in winter. We love the warm, earth-toned walls and soft lighting, not to mention the menu that includes so many of our favorite foods: starters like lobster ravioli with lemon, pine nuts, and fried parsley ($10), followed by sautéed duck breast, crisp duck confit, mashed potatoes, braised greens, and balsamic maple syrup ($24). Pastas such as fettuccine with mushrooms, parsley, and pine nuts begin at $17, and other entrées are $22–30. Leave room for dessert.

The Egremont Inn (413-528-2111; www.egremontinnrestaurant.com), 10 Old Sheffield Rd., South Egremont. Open for dinner Wed.–Sun. Local residents vouch for the excellence of the food served in this classic old hotel dining room. You might begin with a slightly spicy tomato bisque ($7.50), then dine on crispy ribs served with greens. Entrées $19–25. Live jazz Thu. and Sat. year-round. You can also order a burger, and the tavern has its own menu ($10–20). The wine list is outstanding.

Swiss Hutte Inn & Restaurant (413-528-6200), Rt. 23 at Catamount ski area in South Egremont. Open in the winter and summer seasons for lunch on weekends and dinner Wed.–Sun. We should explain that "at Catamount" simply means within the grounds, which are delightfully green and landscaped in summer. The present chef-owner is Swiss, and choices include Wiener schnitzel and "bundnerteller"—but it's a varied menu. Entrées may range from seafood curry to herb-crusted rack of lamb with a red wine glaze. The ambience is polished wood and linen. There's also an outdoor patio, weather permitting. Dinner entrées $23–29.

Elsewhere
The Old Inn on the Green and Gedney Farm (413-229-7924; www .oldinn.com), Rt. 57, village green, New Marlborough. Open for dinner except Tue. Also closed Mon., Nov.–June. Reservations advisable. This is a beautifully restored 18th-century inn set in the middle of a gem of a village. The four small, candlelit (the only other light is from the hearth) dining rooms are furnished with worn Windsor chairs and mahogany tavern tables. In July and August there's additional seating on a tented terrace. Chef-owner Peter Platt, former executive chef at Wheatleigh, gets some of the best reviews of any restaurateur in New

England. He offers a $68 prix fixe menu (there are three choices per course) on Saturday. On other nights it's an à la carte menu (entrées $22–35) that changes frequently and features locally grown produce. A recent spring menu included Taft Farms asparagus with morels and truffle vinaigrette, followed by a memorable seared pepper-crusted yellowfin tuna Niçoise with a tapenade beurre blanc. The wine list is outstanding. Wish we had room for the chilled rhubarb soup. A $70 tasting menu is also available, and a $30 prix fixe is offered Wed.–Thu., along with a reasonably priced MAP package.

Stagecoach Tavern (413-229-8585; www.stagecoachtavern.net), 845 S. Undermountain Rd. (Rt. 41), Sheffield. Open for dinner Thu.–Sat. This handsome brick Federal-style house became a tavern in 1829 and has been many things since—but never anything better than its current look and use. Now owned by neighboring Race Brook Lodge, the timbered, candlelit tavern is both informal and romantic, the setting for dining on a menu that ranges from cheeseburgers (100 percent grass fed) to pan-seared wild salmon with herb salsa and grilled hanger steak. Chef Sarah Dibben describes it as comfort food prepared with the finest local ingredients. Entrées $10–23.

EATING OUT

In Great Barrington
20 Railroad Street (413-528-9345), 20 Railroad St. Open daily for lunch and dinner, also for Sunday brunch. Railroad Street was still dingy in 1977 when this friendly pub opened. Since then the side street has filled with boutiques and restaurants, but this

one still stands out. The menu is huge, ranging through soups, chilis, nachos, salads, pocket sandwiches, burgers, and Reubens, and featuring daily specials like chicken Marbella. The ornate, 28-foot-long bar was moved from the Commodore Hotel in Manhattan to Great Barrington in 1919 and served as the centerpiece of a speakeasy until 1933—when it became one of the first legal bars in town.

✧ **Martin's** (413-528-5455), 49 Railroad St. Open daily 6–3 for breakfast and lunch. Breakfast is an all-day affair, the omelets are a feast, and the burgers are outstanding, too. Beer and herbal teas are served, and crayons are at every table; inspired customers of all ages can design their own place mats. Martin Lewis worked in several of New York's most famous restaurants, but his wife is from Sandisfield and 15 years ago he opened this spotless, family-run diner-with-a-difference, good for a veggie sandwich or Berkshire Breeze (avocado, cucumber, tomato, sprouts, and Swiss or cheddar on farmer's bread) as well as a BLT or burger.

DOWNTOWN GREAT BARRINGTON

Kim Grant

✧ **Baba Louie's Sourdough Pizza Restaurant** (413-528-8100), 286 Main St. Open Tue.–Sun. for lunch and dinner. Unusual wood-fired pizzas ("Pizza Festival" is topped with broccoli rabe, fresh tomatoes, roasted peppers, yellow squash, zucchini, mozzarella, and oregano) are the specialty, but there are also a surprising variety of salads and a hearty antipasto.

✧ **Siam Square** (413-644-9119), 290 Main St. Lunch and dinner. This is a deep, deep storefront with a pleasant decor. In addition to a choice of reasonably priced and quickly prepared curry and noodle dishes, you'll find an intriguing array of house specialties and Thai hot-and-sour salads. Try the Chicken Volcano: marinated Cornish hen with herbs, spices, and a sweet hot chili sauce. Wine and beer is served.

Barrington Brewery & Restaurant (413-528-8282), 420 Stockbridge Rd. (Rt. 7) in Jennifer House Commons. Open for lunch and dinner. Both the brew and the food are good, and the scruffy barn atmosphere works. "Barn Brewed" is the original microbrew here; there are usually half a dozen on tap. The menu includes a plowman's lunch and hearty classics like shepherd's pie.

✧ **Four Brothers** (413-528-9684), Rt. 7. This restaurant is part of an upstate New York chain, but it doesn't seem that way. The decor is classic Greek, complete with plants and fake grape arbor. Generally regarded as having the best pizzas, Greek salads, and lasagna around; there's also fried fish and eggplant casserole. Dinners range from a small pizza to honey-dipped fried chicken.

✧ **The Great Barrington Bagel Company** (413-528-9055), 777 S.

Main St. (Rt. 7 south), across from Guido's Market. Open 7–4 daily; Fri.–Sat. until 5. Our New York friends tell us these are the best you can get north of Manhattan. We counted 19 varieties, from sesame to jalapeño to chocolate chip. This is a small, attractive deli with daily-made soups, eight kinds of smoked fish, and more than a dozen spreads, good to eat in or take out. Breakfasts served until 11 AM.

East Mountain Café at the Berkshire Co-op Market (413-528-9697; www.berkshirecoop.org), 42 Bridge St. Open Mon.–Sat. 8–8, Sun. 10–6. The parking is easy, the food is good, and so, amazingly, is the view. For visitors this is also a place to pick up a range of local produce and products.

♪ **Route 7 Grill** (413-528-3235; www.route7grill.com), 999 S. Main St. (Rt. 7) near the Sheffield line. Open daily for dinner and takeout. We want this family-owned grill to succeed, but at this writing it's new and not quite right. Decor is attractive but a little formal and pricey for barbecue, which is what this place is all about. There's a full bar.

The East (413-528-8850), 305 Stockbridge Rd. (Rt. 7). Open daily for lunch and dinner. The menu includes sushi and sashimi; the specialties are Chinese, fresh and flavorful vegetarian and seafood dishes.

In Lee

♪ **Salmon Run Fish House** (413-243-3900), 78 Main St. The decor is minimal but the price is right and the seafood menu, extensive. We enjoyed the fish-and-chips, but the specialty really is salmon, and it's served 10 different ways. There's also a choice of chicken and steak and a good kids' menu.

Joe's Diner (413-243-9756), 63 Center St., South Lee. Open Mon.–Sat. 5:30–9, Sun. 7–2. The scene of a famous Norman Rockwell *Saturday Evening Post* cover (the one where a burly but kindly state trooper counsels a runaway small boy sitting at the counter), this is still a local hangout. So choose from a counter stool or a booth and watch the town saunter in and out. The food is good, and when particular specials are on the menu, such as corned beef or slow-roasted prime rib, there can be a line waiting to get in.

Pho Sai Gon (413-243-6288), 5 Railroad St. This new Vietnamese restaurant is sparking clean, cheerful, and so good that we wish we lived within take-out range. We feasted on a lunch special ($7.95) of pan-fried salmon with black bean sauce that was exquisite, the salmon marinated in chunks and delicately spiced. A cup of piping hot jasmine tea arrived in a very large, bright cup. The extensive menu features a number of noodle soups and noodle stir-fries as well as seafood, meat, and vegetarian dishes. Another diner raved about the crispy spring rolls, each served in a wrapping of lettuce.

Cakewalk Bakery and Café (413-243-2806; www.cakewalkbakery.com), 56 Main St. Open daily except Tue., 7–5. The cakes—mocha cream, carrot, lemon raspberry, and many more—are the thing here, but so are breakfast scones, muffins, croissants, and bread on which you can get a sandwich. Everything is made from scratch.

Paradise of India Restaurant (413-243-0500), 5 Railroad St. Just off the main drag, a pleasant place for curries and tandoori dishes—and a real bargain at lunch and dinner, too. BYOB.

Morgan House Inn (413-243-0181; www.morganhouseinn.com), 33 Main St. The center of town since stagecoach days, this place is a sure bet for either lunch or dinner. It has been lucky over the years, regularly acquiring energetic owners who pour their all into the place. Both the tavern and more formal dining room are wood paneled, welcoming, and deservedly popular. Dine on blackened Atlantic salmon garnished with sun-dried tomato pesto or pan-seared pork paillards topped with caramelized apple brandy sauce. Open daily. Entrées $12.95–16.95.

In Lenox

✦ **Napa** (413-637-3204), 34 Church St. Open daily for lunch and dinner. This popular casual restaurant has an open kitchen off the main dining area and a dining porch that's a great place to watch the scene on Lenox's restaurant row. The bar serves Mexican beers. An eclectic "California cuisine" menu includes burritos and quesadillas but also ahi tuna with Asian vegetables along with potato-and-cheese pierogi and Chilean sea bass. Dinner entrées $15–28.

Dish Café Bistro (413-637-1800), 37 Church St. Open 11–3 daily for lunch and 5:30–9 for dinner. Dish's modest boast is that it serves "uncomplicated food that tastes good." This includes soups, salads, and sandwiches as well as menu items such as pecan-encrusted rainbow trout and roast baby rack of lamb. Entrées $18–26.

The Olde Heritage Tavern (413-637-0884) 12 Housatonic St. Open for lunch and dinner. A no-nonsense pub housed in an 1881 building. There are tables out front in summer, while the dining room and bar areas are cozy and unpretentious. The burgers are

the best we found in Lenox; wraps, steak, and fish-and-chips are reputed to be very good, too. Dinner entrées $9.99–14.99.

Dakota Steak House (413-499-7900; www.dakotarestaurant.com), 1035 South St. (Rt. 20), Pittsfield. Open daily 4–10 for dinner, Sunday brunch 10–2. Although the Dakota is in Pittsfield, it's just over the line from Lenox, which provides most of its customers. A big, cheery place, it specializes in beef and seafood and does both well, often together. Signature dishes include Crabby Filet (a petite filet mignon topped with sweet blue crabmeat), teriyaki sirloin, steak kebab (chunks of sirloin skewered with bell peppers, mushrooms, and tomatoes, then grilled), shrimp scampi, and Steak & Cake (grilled sirloin with a Maryland-style crabcake). Entrées $17.99–26.99.

In Stockbridge

Widow Bingham's Tavern at the Red Lion Inn (413-298-5545), Main St. Open for all three meals. More casual and intimate than the formal dining room and good for lighter fare. The Red Lion burgers are legendary, and dinner stews are a good bet. You might also want to try the "plowman's plate" of local Camembert, dried sausage, and Berkshire Mountain bread. In summer the garden itself is a pleasant café. The **Lion's Den**, opening at 4 on weekdays and noon on weekends, features live entertainment, no cover, and reasonable prices.

Elm Street Market (413-298-3634), 4 Elm St. A good little grocery store with hand-cut meats and a deli menu with a choice of sandwiches, a few tables. When Stockbridge is flooded by a bus group, this is a find.

Also see **Once Upon a Table** under *Dining Out.*

In Sheffield

✍ **Limey's** (413-229-9000), 650 N. Main (Rt. 7). Open Mon.–Sat. 4:30–9, Sun. noon–9. A great roadhouse/family restaurant with deep booths and an English accent. Specialties include bangers and mash, shepherd's pie, and steak-and-kidney pie as well as standout burgers.

Elsewhere

Mom's Restaurant (413-528-2414), Rt. 23, South Egremont. A great little way stop that's open for breakfast, lunch, and dinner, with a shady deck in back overlooking a stream. A good choice of burgers, sandwiches, soups, and salads for lunch. For dinner, 4–10, the chef and menu change entirely, to Italian classics like pasta, pizza, and veal scampi. Beer and wine are served.

New Boston Inn (413-258-4477; www.newbostoninn.com), junction of Rts. 8 and 57, New Boston. Open Thu.–Sun. for lunch and dinner. This genuine 18th-century inn was beautifully restored not long ago, and the present owner, Barbara Colorio, is a former corporate chef. Now not only the old taproom but also three large, light-filled rooms are filled with tables. You can opt to dine in the pub on Philly cheese steak or meat loaf, or in the formal dining rooms with a full menu ranging from BBQ ribs to surf and turf. Most dinner entrées remain priced under $20 and include pot roast, fried oysters, pan-seared trout, and chicken Florentine as well as pasta dishes served with homemade garlic bread. We lunched on a delicious minestrone soup and half sandwich of Italian cold cuts on a flaky roll.

Roadside Store and Café at Gould Farm (413-728-2633), Rt. 23, Monterey. Open daily in summer months for breakfast and lunch, 7–2. There are six tables plus counter seating; on weekends the line is frequently out the door because everything is so good. Specialties include pancakes (both the mix and syrup are made here) and Gould Farm's own cheddar cheese and homemade breads.

✍ **Jack's Grill & Restaurant** (413-274-1000; www.jacksgrill.com), Main St., Housatonic. Open for dinner except Mon. Owned by the Fitzpatricks of Red Lion Inn fame, this is a former company store for workers at the textile mills in this classic mill village. It's decorated with nostalgia items like tube radios and a model railroad. The menu is self-consciously small town with chicken potpie and pot roast sandwich, "mac & cheese" and lumpy applesauce, even "mom's meatloaf dinner" and spaghetti with meatballs and sausages "like at home—except we do the dishes." Frankly, it all seems a bit much, including the prices ($5 for fries?).

The Village Oven (413-232-7269), 30 Main St., West Stockbridge. Open for lunch and dinner but closing some days off-season. This is a cheery, attractive eatery, specializing in pizza, also serving panini, burgers, and salads.

The Southfield Store Café (413-229-5050), Southfield Village. Open (except Tue.) for all three meals, plus Sunday brunch. Follow signs from Rt. 27 in New Marlborough for the Buggy Whip Antiques Market, a popular destination and excuse to drive back roads into this beautiful corner of the county. This is the former village store, pleasant inside with tables in front and an ambitious menu, daily specials.

✳ Entertainment

MUSIC Guthrie Center (413-528-1955; www.guthriecenter.org), 4 Van Deusenville Rd., Great Barrington. This is the actual church immortalized as "Alice's Restaurant," and it now belongs to folksinger and writer Arlo Guthrie, who periodically performs here himself as well as staging other well-known and not-so-well-known performers.

Club Helsinki (413-528-3394), 284 Main St., Great Barrington. South Berkshire's leading venue for live music, from reggae to folksingers to jazz, it gets the best, periodically staging big names at the Mahaiwe Performing Arts Center. The club itself is dark, narrow, and funky with a great bar and a bar menu from the same kitchen as the adjoining café (see *Dining Out*).

Celestial Bar at the Castle Street Café (413-528-5244; www.castle streetcafe.com), 10 Castle St. Live music nightly (except Tue.): piano, guitar, jazz groups. Check to see who's on. No cover. An attractive bar with its own menu. Also see *Dining Out*.

Egremont Inn (413-528-2111), 10 Old Sheffield Rd. Live jazz Thu. and Sat. year-round. Also see *Dining Out*.

Dream Away Lodge (413-623-8725), 1342 County Rd., Becket. Open Wed.–Sun. (for brunch) from Mother's Day to Halloween, weekends only from New Year's to Valentine's Day. An old roadhouse that once had a funky reputation, Dream Away has in recent years (under the ownership of Daniel Osman) become a very hip music and dining venue with a diverse and devoted clientele. The decor is eclectic, as is the music and also the cuisine, which Osman—a former Shakespeare & Company of Lenox actor—describes as "a daily happening." Name performers are booked on weekends, but the very popular Wednesday "open acoustic" night in the intimate music room attracts area musicians who can include, among others, local boy Arlo Guthrie. Reservations are encouraged and often essential. Credit cards not accepted.

FILM Triplex Theater (413-528-8886; www.thetriplex.com), 70 Railroad St., Great Barrington. First-run and some art films, surround sound.

✳ Selective Shopping

ANTIQUES SHOPS South Berkshire County is one of the antiques centers of New England. Visit www.berkshire antiquesandart.com. A pamphlet listing Berkshire County antiques dealers is available from antiques stores and from the sources listed under *Guidance*. **Sheffield** alone has more than a dozen dealers and is home to **Bradford Galleries** (413-229-6667; www .bradfordauctions.com), with monthly auctions of quality furniture and accessories and special rare-book and ephemera auctions five times a year.

The Buggy Whip Antiques Market (413-229-3576; www.buggywhip antiques.com), Rt. 272, Southfield. Open May–Dec., daily 10–5; Jan.–Apr., closed Tue. and Wed. This long, vast, picturesque wooden tannery, said to date to 1792—it remained an ongoing business, producing the leather for buggy whips and other products, until 1973—now houses more than 70 antiques dealers, resulting in genuine variety. Currently the "market" is divided, with one multigroup dealership downstairs and another, featuring

French Canadian antiques and reproductions, up. Even if you aren't looking for anything in particular, this is a
great place to browse and an excuse to
drive down some beautiful back roads.
Displays now include a museum corner, with exhibits and video depicting
the history of the factory. The Southfield Country Store (see *Eating Out*)
is across the road.

Jenifer House Commons, Rt. 7, a
small shopping complex housed in old
New England buildings north of
downtown Great Barrington, is the
site of 100-dealer **Coffman's
Antiques Market** (www.coffmans
antiques.com).

ART AND ARTISANS

In Lenox

DeVries Fine Art Gallery (413-637-
3462; www.andrewdevries.com), 62
Church St. This gallery mainly displays sculptures, reliefs, sketches,
watercolors, and pastels by Andrew
DeVries. However, other well-known
artists are also on view. This is a visitor-
friendly gallery where touching the
sculptures is actually encouraged.
Open Sat.–Sun. noon–4 in spring;
daily in high season, and by appointment the rest of the year.

Ferrin Gallery (413-637-4414; www
.ferringallery.com), 69 Church St.
Displays contemporary ceramic art,
painting, photography, and sculpture.
Frequent changing exhibitions. Open
11–5 daily in July and Aug.,
Thu.–Sun. the rest of the year.

Weaver's Fancy (413-637-2013) 65
Church St. Specializes in handcrafted
clothing and accessories by leading
fabric artists, including owner
Katharine Pincus. Open year-round,
always on weekends, but check for
weekday hours off-season.

In Great Barrington

Great Barrington Pottery (413-
274-6259: www.greatbarrington
pottery.com), Rt. 41, Housatonic. The
handsome, nicely glazed pieces are
fired in a Japanese wood-burning kiln.
Visitors are invited to view demonstrations of *ikebana* or the tea cere-
mony between 1 and 4 in the
Kyoto-style teahouse.

October Mountain Stained Glass
(413-528-6681), 343 Main St., Great
Barrington. Closed Mon. A variety of
quality stained glass: lamp shades,
bottles, jewelry, custom work.

Mill River Studio (413-528-9433),
8 Railroad St., Great Barrington.
This long-established gallery specializes in fabulous vintage posters and
other "vintage art" as well as archival
framing.

S.K.H. Gallery (413-528-3300), 46
Castle St. Housed in the old Great
Barrington train station, this is a
showcase primarily for fabrics by
internationally known weaver Sam
Kasten, as well as other weavers and
artisans. At this writing it's open during the Saturday-morning farmer's
market that takes place in front of the
station.

AT THE BUGGY WHIP ANTIQUES MARKET
Christina Tree

In West Stockbridge

Hotchkiss Mobiles Gallery (413-232-0200; www.artmobiles.com), 8 Center St. Joel Hotchkiss likes to watch jaws drop as unsuspecting tourists step into his gallery and register the dozens of moving sculptures suspended from the ceiling and gloriously colored artifacts spaced through the rooms, beyond which stretches a vast studio. Hotchkiss makes more mobiles than anyone in the country, supplying museum shops with a variety of models (from $55 to $2,000). He also creates original mobiles on commission. A stunning array of glass and glass-beaded jewelry selected by Sandra Hotchkiss is also sold.

Tokonoma Gallery (413-232-8505), 5 Central St. Generally open in summer, less so off-season. Formerly in Housatonic, Robin Schmitt's gallery exhibits contemporary fine arts and crafts including jewelry, glass- and ironwork, and hand-painted fabrics.

Clay Forms Studio (413-232-4339; call ahead for hours), the source of Leslie Klein's ceramic visions, is on Austerlitz Rd., about a 10-minute drive from the village on winding roads lined with farms and fields.

Hoffman Pottery (413-232-4646; www.ehoffmanpottery.com), south of the village at 103 Rt. 41, is a must-stop. Open daily during summer, weekends during the school year. Elaine Hoffman's brightly colored house/studio/shop stands in a flower garden peppered with pottery masks, representing the good spirits guarding the house. Check her web site for a sense of the variety of patterns and colors in which she has created plates and mugs, bowls, vases, and other functional pottery over the years.

Elsewhere

Holsten Galleries (413-208-3044; www.holstengalleries.com), 3 Elm St., Stockbridge. Open daily, year-round. Established in 1978, this was one of the first art glass galleries in the country. Well worth finding (it's hidden behind a bank), this is a showcase for some of the finest contemporary glass sculpture around.

Joyous Spring Pottery (413-528-4115), Art School Rd., Monterey. Open daily 10–5 in summer; otherwise call ahead. Striking unglazed vases and other decorative pieces, fired once a year day and night for 12 days, an ancient Japanese technique called *yakishime*. At the same time, visit the neighboring Bidwell House.

Sheffield Pottery (413-229-7700; www.shefield-pottery.com), Rt. 7, Sheffield, north of the village. This

AT THE HOTCHKISS MOBILES GALLERY

Christina Tree

family-owned business began in 1946 by supplying Sheffield clay to make "redware" pottery and now imports clays from across the country, blending them for use by potters throughout the East. The showroom displays and sells work by a wide range of the craftspeople it supplies.

The Loring Gallery (413-229-0110; www.loringgallery.com), Rt. 7, Sheffield. May–Oct., 11–5 except Tue. Changing shows featuring the gallery's stable of established artists.

BOOKSTORES The Bookstore (413-637-3390), 9 Housatonic St., Lenox. An inviting independent bookshop of the kind that's getting harder to find with a large, well-chosen, and varied selection of new and used books. Regional interest and authors with local connections are featured, but there's something for just about every kind of reader.

The Bookloft (413-528-1521), Barrington Plaza, Rt. 7, Great Barrington. A large, long-established, attractive independent bookstore with a knowledgeable staff.

Stockbridge Booksellers (413-298-3329; www.stockbridgebooksellers .com), 10 Elm St., Stockbridge. Open daily except Wed. An inviting, independently owned bookstore stocking new and used books; inquire about frequent author events.

ANTIQUARIAN BOOKS Farshaw's Fine Old Books (413-528-1890), 43 Main St., South Egremont. Long a fixture on Railroad Street in Great Barrington, this remains an inviting shop in its new location, still specializing in the rare and unusual. Michael and Helen Selzer founded www .bibliofind.com, the Internet's largest

Christina Tree

AT HOFFMAN POTTERY

marketplace for old and used books, when they sold out a few years back. Call before coming.

North Star Rare Books (413-644-9595), 684 S. Main St. (Rt. 7), Great Barrington, specializing in 18th-through 20th-century historical and literary manuscripts and rare volumes. Sited unexpectedly in a mini shopping mall, Randy Weinstein's shop seems as much gallery as bookshop, a serene space displaying valuable vintage manuscripts and illustrations, all said to come from local collections.

Yellow House Books (413-528-8227), 252 Main St., Great Barrington. Open Mon.–Sat. 10:30–5:30, Sun. noon–5. Bonnie and Bob Benson's store fills several rooms in a house. They specialize in rare books, photographs, children's illustrated books, and folklore and encourage browsing. We always come away with something we never meant to buy but are grateful we did.

Berkshire Book Company (413-229-0122), 510 S. Main St. (Rt. 7), Sheffield. A broad range of titles but emphasizing children's books, cookbooks, first editions, history, and military.

SPECIAL SHOPS Country Curtains (413-298-5565; www.countrycurtains .com) at the Red Lion Inn, Stockbridge (see *Lodging*). A phenomenon rather than just a store, nationally known through its catalog, Country Curtains is a source of a wide variety of matching curtains, bedding, and pillows, beautifully displayed in the rear of the inn. Open daily.

Charles H. Baldwin & Sons (413-232-7785; www.baldwinextracts.com), 1 Center St., West Stockbridge. This aromatic emporium has been in the same family since 1888 and on the same spot since 1912, making and selling its own "table syrup" (a blend of maple and cane sugar syrup), pure vanilla extract, and other cooking extracts and flavorings. The shop is chock-full of gifts and souvenirs, but most customers are looking for extracts, particularly the hard-to-find pure vanilla. Check out the family's fabulous hardware store across the street.

Kenver, Ltd. (413-538-2330), Rt. 23, South Egremont. Housed in an 18th-century tavern, a long-established source of skiwear.

Guido's Fresh Marketplace (413-528-9255), 760 S. Main St. (Rt. 7), Great Barrington. The standout place to shop for a full line of vegetables, health food, and deli items as well as seafood and meat; great baked goods, too.

The Snap Shop (413-528-4725), 14 Railroad St. Open Tue.–Fri. 9–5:30, Sat. 8:30–4. Steve Carlotta and his nephew Tony Carlotto have been running this friendly camera shop since 1972. We tried to buy an expensive new card for our digital camera and instead were given a lesson in how to work with what we had.

Byzantium (413-528-9496), 32 Railroad St., Great Barrington. Our favorite for women's clothing and accessories.

Gatsby's (413-528-9455), 25 Railroad St. The neon HOTPOINT sign suggests that this was recently an appliance store, but this emporium, selling everything from bras to lawn chairs, has been here since the 1970s. It's still fun to browse, though prices have risen steeply in recent years.

Old Country Store (413-637-9702), 67 Church St., Lenox. Open daily May–Dec. An eclectic emporium that seems to stock a little bit of everything, from toys, books, cards, and T-shirts (some with mildly naughty messages) to interesting souvenirs and handicrafts.

OUTLET MALLS Prime Outlets at Lee (413-243-8186 or 800-866-5900; www.primeoutlets.com) at Mass Pike exit 2 in Lee. A nicely grouped array of more than five dozen outlets offering upscale and everyday wares, from Liz Claiborne and Polo Ralph Lauren to Reebok and OshKosh B'Gosh. There is a central food court and plenty of parking. In summer a shuttle bus runs to and from downtown Lee.

✳ Farms

Note: **Berkshire Grown** (www .berkshiregrown.org) is the community group promoting locally grown food, flowers, and plants. Their web site lists farmer's markets for each town.

In Great Barrington

Farmer's market, at the old train station, corner of Castle St. and Taconic Ave. (behind town hall). Early May–Oct., Sat. 9–1. Organic vegetables, fruit, dairy products, prepared foods, special events.

Windy Hill Farm (413-298-3217), 686 Stockbridge Rd. (Rt. 7), Great Barrington. Open Apr.–Christmas, daily 9–5. Pick-your-own apples (more than 25 varieties), pies, and fresh-pressed cider in fall, extensive container-grown nursery stock, and hardy perennials; staff are very knowledgeable.

Taft Farms (413-528-1515 or 800-528-1015; www.taftfarms.com), corner of Division St. and Rt. 183. Over 400 produce items, baked goods, and free-range chickens. Call to find out what's in-season in the way of PYO fruits and vegetables.

In Monterey

Gould Farm's Harvest Barn (413-644-9718; www.gouldfarm.org), marked from Rt. 23. Memorial Day to late Oct., weekdays 9–4. Produce, maple syrup, Monterey Mint Tea (made from organically grown apple mint leaf, dried and packaged in tea bags) herbs, salsa and sauces, and an artisan cheddar cheese that's a big draw.

Lowland Farm (413-528-0728), 128 New Marlborough Rd. Open year-round daily with mulch hay, maple syrup, PYO raspberries in-season.

✿ **Rawson Brook Farm** (413-528-2138), off New Marlborough Rd., 2 miles from Rt. 23 in Monterey. Getting there is half the fun, since the back roads to the farm are beautiful. Wayne Dunlop and Susan Sellew have chosen to supply local restaurants and customers rather than go big time—an option that is very real given the quality of their **Monterey Chèvre** goat cheese, The cheese is available in various sizes from the fridge at the dairy at prices well below what you pay in local stores. Children will love seeing the baby goats, but adult supervision is a must.

In Sheffield

Howden Farm (413-229-8481; www.howdenfarm.com), 303 Rannopo Rd. From Rt. 7 in Ashley Falls, follow signs for Bartholomew's Cobble and the Ashley House. Rannopo Rd. runs north between these two sites. Also off Rt. 7A south of Sheffield. Home of the Howden Pumpkins, two varieties developed by John A. Howden. Family run since 1937; PYO pumpkins on weekends and holidays starting in late September. PYO blueberries and raspberries in July and August. Good for sweet corn and eggs, too. Also see *Lodging*.

Equinox Farm (413-229-2266), 489 Bow Wow Rd. Open daylight hours, Memorial Day–Labor Day. From Rt. 7 south, turn right onto Cook Rd., then right onto Bow Wow. A variety of greens, mesclun, salad greens, herbs, heirloom tomatoes.

Moon in the Pond Organic Farm (413-229-3092), 819 Barnum St. A wide variety of organic meats, eggs, greens, and herbs.

Elsewhere

Les Trois Emme Winery & Vineyard (413-528-1015; www.ltewinery.com), 8 Knight Rd., New Marlborough. Open for tours and tastings ($5) Apr.–Dec., Thu.–Sun. 1–5. The newest Berkshire winery, producing red wines and a blush from their own California grapes, also a pumpkin wine.

Blueberry Hill Farm (413-528-1479; www.austinfarm.com), Mount Washington Rd., Mount Washington. If you don't happen to have your own blueberry patch, this is the next best thing: pick-your-own wild blueberries (late July through frost, 9–5 except Wed.) in one of the Berkshires' most beautiful settings.

High Lawn Farm (413-243-0672), 535 Summer St., Lee, is a source of the creamiest milk around. Visitors are welcome.

✻ Special Events

March: **Southern Berkshire Chamber of Commerce Winterfest Auction** (www.southernberkshires.com).

May: **Chesterwood Antique Auto Show**, Stockbridge. **Memorial Day Parade**, Great Barrington.

July: **Fireworks** and Independence Day music at Tanglewood. **Butternut**

Crafts Fair (413-499-0856).

August: **Berkshire Crafts Fair**, at the high school, Great Barrington. **Annual Antiques Show** at Berkshire Botanical Garden (*midmonth*).

Late September: The **Tub Parade** in Lenox is a re-creation of the Gilded Age end-of-summer procession in which carriages and carts were decked with flowers.

October: **Housatonic Heritage Walks** (www.heritagehikes.org) features guided walks in and around town (*Columbus Day weekend*). **Berkshire Botanical Garden Harvest Festival**, Stockbridge (*Columbus Day weekend*). **Halloween Walk through Ice Glen** is a Stockbridge tradition, usually followed by a bonfire. **Spirits of Sheffield Rise Again** is a dramatized tour of the town's 14 cemeteries on Halloween weekend.

December: **Stockbridge Main Street at Christmas** is decorated to re-create the way it looked in Norman Rockwell's famous painting (*first weekend*). **Naumkeag** is also decorated for Christmas. **Lenox Holly Fair**.

CENTRAL AND NORTH BERKSHIRE

North Berkshire is a ruggedly beautiful landscape of steep-sided, wooded valleys cut by the rushing Hoosic River, divided and dominated by Mount Greylock. In 1800 Timothy Dwight, president of Yale University, described the view from Greylock's 3,491-foot summit as "immense and of amazing grandeur." Dwight's widely read guidebook may have inspired many subsequent visitors, including Nathaniel Hawthorne, who compared the "high mountain swells" of the Taconics on the west to "immense, subsiding waves," and Henry David Thoreau, who bushwhacked up and spent the night on top, waking to "an ocean of mist . . . and undulating country of clouds." The view from the summit extends 70 to 100 miles on a clear day.

Mount Greylock isn't an isolated peak but part of a range that includes three of the highest mountains in Massachusetts, rising from the countryside on four sides. It's said that Herman Melville, gazing at Mount Greylock from his home in Pittsfield, was inspired to write about a whale.

The entire mountain is webbed with hiking trails, and the new Ashuwillticook Rail Trail runs south along Cheshire Reservoir (from which the Hoosic River flows north). The range divides the north–south flow of traffic in this region the way a big boulder divides the flow of a narrow stream. Rt. 7, running from Williamstown down to Pittsfield on the western side of the range, is the main road, while Rt. 8, from North Adams south through Adams and Cheshire, is the road less taken. Below Cheshire and Lanesborough the landscape opens expansively into a broad valley with Pittsfield at its center. The two branches of the Housatonic River and all roads meet in Pittsfield,

Williamstown is the area's "village beautiful," home to prestigious Williams College and to the Sterling and Francine Clark Art Institute, internationally known for its collection of paintings by French impressionists and 19th-century American masters. The Williams College Museum of Art also displays several icons of American art, and in summer the Williamstown Theater Festival— staged in a stunning, recently expanded theater—draws theater buffs from throughout the Northeast.

For decades this cultured northwestern corner of the state has been perceived as isolated—but that's changing. MASS MoCA (the Massachusetts Museum of Contemporary Art), one of the world's largest contemporary art and performance centers, is now housed in former mill buildings in neighboring North Adams and has sparked a genuine renaissance in that proudly gritty little city, which now also offers upscale dining and lodging.

Williamstown and North Adams *are* a couple dozen of miles north of Lenox. Recently, however, the distance seems less because Pittsfield, the original heart and hub of Berkshire County, is once more emerging as a destination in its own right. Barrington Stage Company has moved here from South County, restoring a 1912 music hall as their main stage. The Colonial Theatre, the city's elaborately decorated vintage-1903 vaudeville house, has also been meticulously restored and offers a lively performance schedule. The neighboring Berkshire Museum continues to draw families from surrounding regions. Long-empty storefronts along North Street are filling fast with restaurants, cafés, and new shops while upper floors are hatching condos and studios.

Hancock Shaker Village, 5 miles west of Pittsfield, represents the largest collection of Shaker artifacts on any original Shaker site and evokes a sense of the rare and beautiful places (not just things) that Shakers created.

AREA CODE 413.

GUIDANCE Discover the Berkshires Visitor Center (413-743-4500 or 866-444-1815; www.berkshires.org), Berkshire Visitors Bureau, 3 Hoosac St., Adams. Open daily; hours vary seasonally. Lodging reservation service Mon.–Sat. 9–4: 800-237-5747, ext. 506.

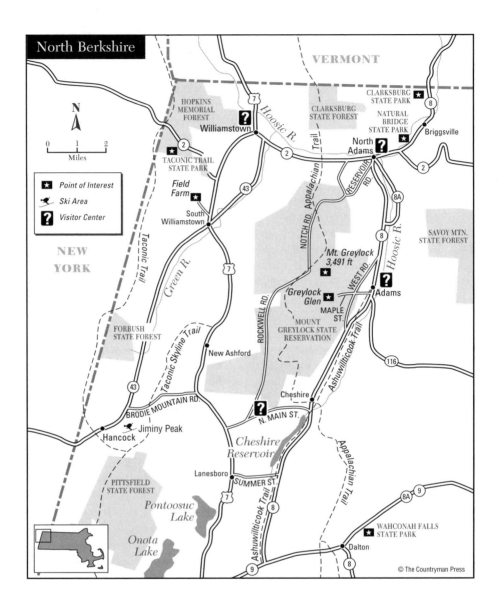

Pittsfield Visitors Center (413-443-9186, ext. 323 or 324), 111 South St. in the Colonial Theatre Annex. Open Mon.–Sat. 9–5, Sun. 10–5. Closed Sun. off-season. Also see www.pittsfield.com and www.berkshireeagle.com.

North Adams. Phone inquiries: **Mayor's Office of Tourism** (413-664-6180; tourist@bcn.net). Walk-in information: **Western Gateway Heritage State Park** (413-663-6312), marked and accessible from State St. (Rt. 8 south). Open year-round, daily 10–5. A seasonal information booth at **Windsor Mill** is on your right as you enter the city on Rt. 2 (Union St.) from the east.

Williamstown Chamber of Commerce (413-458-9077 or 800-214-3799; www .williamstownchamber.com) maintains a well-stocked, unstaffed information booth with restrooms at 100 Spring St., across from the village parking lot, and another at the junction of Rts. 2 and 7.

GETTING THERE *Note:* An **Intermodal Transportation Center** (413-499-2782 or 800-292-2782), corner of Columbus Ave. and North St. in downtown Pittsfield, serves local and long-distance buses as well as Amtrak under one roof.

By bus: From New York City, **Bonanza** (800-751-8800) serves Williamstown via Pittsfield (413-442-4451); **Peter Pan/Trailways** (800-343-9999; www.peterpan bus.com) serves Pittsfield via Lenox, Lee, and Springfield. *From Albany,* Bonanza and **Greyhound** both offer service to Pittsfield. *From Boston,* Peter Pan/Trailways serves Pittsfield.

By train: **Amtrak** (800-USA-RAIL) stops at convenient times in Pittsfield en route from Boston to Chicago.

By car: From Boston, Rt. 2 (see "Along the Mohawk Trail") is a half-hour shorter and far more scenic way to north Berkshire County than the Mass Pike.

GETTING AROUND Williamstown, North Adams, Adams, Cheshire, and Lanesborough are all served by buses of **BRTA**, the **Berkshire Regional Transit Authority** (413-499-2782 or 800-292-BRTA).

PITTSFIELD MURAL

Christina Tree

MEDICAL EMERGENCY 911 reaches police, fire departments, and ambulances throughout this area.

Berkshire Medical Center (413-447-2834), 725 North St., Pittsfield.

North Adams Regional Hospital (413-664-5256), Hospital Ave.

✳ To See

TOWNS AND CITIES Pittsfield (population: 45,793). "Pittsfield was, and will be, the downtown of the Berkshires" maintains the city's mayor, James M. Ruberto, explaining that while the old downtown was about retail, what's evolving is a mix of restaurants and shops, with offices, lodging, and creative enterprises on upper floors and side streets. It's happening thanks in good part to a 2005 zoning change creating a downtown arts district that encompasses the city's commercial core.

Until recently Pittsfield was a company town that had lost its company. In the 1950s some 15,000 General Electric employees worked in Pittsfield; today it's one-tenth that number. There is, however, a silver lining to GE's legacy of toxic waste and deflated property values: a $250 million settlement that includes $1 million a year for 10 years. A healthy percentage of this discretionary fund is seeding cultural projects—such as the splendid **Colonial Theatre**, closed since 1949, beautifully restored and reopened in 2006.

The **Barrington Stage Company** has also taken advantage of the city's financial incentives, moving up from South County, restoring another major theater and mounting smaller productions in other venues around this town that is now studded with public art. Around Park Square and along North Street long-vacant storefronts are filling with cafés, restaurants, and galleries beside long-established utilitarian stores.

This isn't the first time Pittsfield has reinvented itself. First settled in 1752, the town grew in the late 18th century around the common that still survives as Park Square, a centerpiece from which radiate streets aptly named North, South, East, and West. It was in Park Square that in 1807 Elkanah Watson introduced the first merino sheep to New England, inaugurating an era in which this particular breed transformed the region's landscape from woods to open pasture, dotted with mills to process their wool. Watson founded the Berkshire Agricultural Society and in 1811 held one of the country's first agricultural fairs on the square.

In the second half of the 19th century the arrival of the railroad changed Pittsfield from agricultural center to industrial metropolis, transporting its burgeoning products, principally textiles and paper, and bringing visitors to stay in its hotels and build summer homes. This boom was also fueled by

ART IN DOWNTOWN PITTSFIELD

Christina Tree

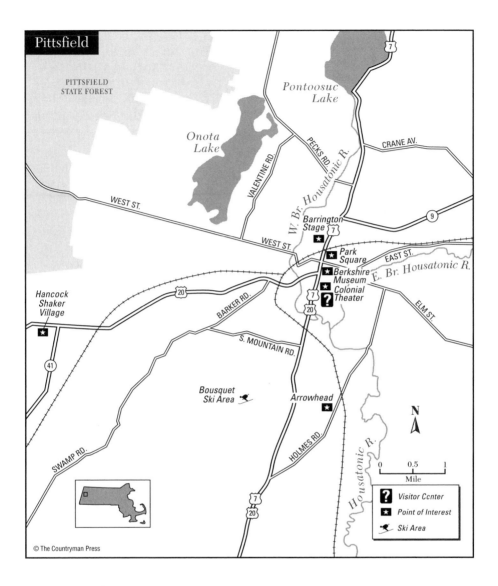

local inventors like William Stanley, who developed the electric transformer and employed 5,000 people before General Electric bought him out in 1903. For a sense of the city's Gilded Era, walk up quiet, gracious Wendell Avenue (visitors are welcome in the Women's Club of Pittsfield at No. 42) and around the common, noting the Victorian Gothic Athenaeum (now the registry of deeds), the courthouse built of Sheffield marble, and St. Stephen's Church with its stained-glass windows by Louis Comfort Tiffany. Most of these buildings date to 1870–1903, years during which the population grew from 11,000 to 40,000.

Pittsfield remains headquarters for GE's Plastics Division, which has, in turn, spawned a number of local plastics companies. It's also recently become corporate headquarters for several other companies of various sizes, and the feel is that of a small city rather than a tourist destination. Still, it's far more visitor-friendly than it was just a few years ago. Note the new **Pittsfield Visitor Center** (with parking) on South St. (Rt. 7) town. It's in the Colonial Theatre Annex, steps from the **Berkshire Museum** with its fine art and family-friendly exhibits. Given its central location, within easy striking distance of all the county's art, theater, and music, this is also becoming recognized (as it was a century ago) as a good place to stay.

Williamstown (population: c. 8,400). From its earliest years Williamstown has been an orderly, elegantly planned, and education-minded community. It was founded in 1753 as West Hoosac, and at their first meeting the seven original proprietors passed what would now be called zoning laws. Meadows and uplands were divided, and settlers were required to clear a minimum of 5 acres of land and build a house at least 15 by 18 feet—a substantial dwelling by frontier standards. An exact replica of one of these "regulation" houses, built as a town bicentennial project using mid-18th-century tools and methods, stands in **Field Park**, a remnant of the original town green. Two years after the settlement was founded, Colonel Ephraim Williams Jr.—who had commanded the local fort and first surveyed the area—wrote a will endowing "a free school forever," provided that the township fell within Massachusetts (New York claimed it) and was renamed Williamstown. Shortly after making his will, Williams was killed in upstate New York fighting the French, but the conditions of his will weren't met for many years.

Because the border between Massachusetts and New York was long disputed, the school, now **Williams College**, couldn't be founded until 1791. It quickly became central to town life, however. In 1815, when finances were shaky and the trustees considered moving the school to a less isolated location, local people pledged enough money to keep it in town. **Williams College** (413-597-3131; www.williams.edu) presently enrolls some 2,000 students, almost equally divided between men and women and drawn from throughout the United States and more than 40 countries. Tours of the 450-acre campus are available at the admissions office (next to the Adams Memorial Theater). Few other colleges are as entwined with their communities. Be sure to pick up the *Guide to the Campus*, with a map that covers half of town. Buildings of interest to the general public (in addition to the art museum) include **Chapin Library** (413-597-2462) of rare books in Stetson Hall, which sits behind Thompson Memorial Chapel, across Main Street from the Museum of Art. It's worth visiting to see the college's priceless collection of documents from the American Revolution. Original copies of the Declaration of Independence, the Articles of Confederation, two

WILLIAMSTOWN'S CLARK ART INSTITUTE OFFERS ENGAGING ACTIVITIES FOR ALL AGES.

Sterling and Francine Clark Art Institute, Williamstown, MA

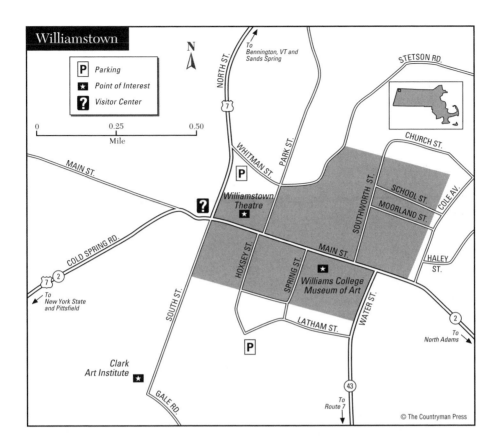

early versions of the Bill of Rights, and a draft of the Constitution are exhibited. Closed Sat.–Sun. **Hopkins Observatory** (413-597-2188), dedicated in 1838, is one of the first observatories in the country. Free shows are offered here in the Milham Planetarium most Fridays; since space is limited, make reservations.

The town has been a tourist destination since the mid–19th century. As early as the 1830s, local mineral springs began attracting visitors, and by the Civil War, Williamstown was an established resort with some large hotels and palatial summer homes. The old resort hotels are long gone, but there are many appealing places to stay. Bucolic South Williamstown still has a number of gentlemen's farms, some quite grand. **Sterling and Francine Clark Art Institute** alone is worth a trip to Williamstown, and its world-class collection is complemented by that of the first-rate **Williams College Museum of Art**.

The **Williamstown Theatre Festival** is one of the best of its kind in the country. Also check out the **Williamstown House of Local History** in the Elizabeth S. Botsford Memorial Library (413-458-2160), 1095 Main St. (open Mon.–Fri. 10–noon and 1–3, or by appointment: nancywb947@aol.com). Built in 1815 as a residence for the college treasurer, this homey library building retains many original features, including a curved staircase and graceful fireplace mantels. The

House of Local History wing contains an extensive and eclectic collection that includes spinning wheels, Civil War uniforms, old ice skates, photos, and much more.

All in all, Williamstown, a jewel of a village set within a circle of mountains, deserves more than a quick stop.

North Adams (population: 15,038). Few communities in Massachusetts have had a more dramatic death and rebirth than its smallest city. A 1939 guide, *The Berkshire Hills* (American Guide Series), described a Main Street lined with "mid-Victorian blocks, small drygoods stores, taverns, colorful fruit stands and markets, and ten-cent stores." "There is a constant hum of noise and a confusion of tongues: French-Canadian, Italian, nasal Yankee. . . . North Adams is nervous with the energy of twentieth century America."

The energy that powered North Adams—the railway, the vast Arnold and Windsor Print Works and other textile mills, along with other small manufacturing— all ebbed away. Arnold Print Works was supplanted by Sprague Electric Company, which flourished during World War II and came to dominate the economy, producing circuitry that, among other things, was used to detonate atomic bombs and later helped launch systems for Gemini and moon missions. Sprague finally closed completely in 1985, but it had atrophied long before and the downtown had already been decimated by "urban renewal." One entire side of Main Street was razed. At the time—and for a decade thereafter—the idea that a contemporary art museum could revive this city full of vacant mills and sagging mill housing seemed scarcely believable.

Luckily both MASS MoCA director Joseph Thompson and North Adams mayor John Barrett III believed in it deeply enough to hang on through thick and thin. Aside from the museum itself, the former Sprague complex now houses a growing number of enterprises, and several more former mill buildings downtown now house artists' studios. Facades along Main and Eagle streets have been restored and half a dozen quality restaurants have opened along with specialty shops, complementing long-established eateries, bakeries, and stores. Much of the old railyard is now the **Western Gateway Heritage State Park**, with sophisticated displays dramatizing construction of the Hoosac Tunnel—the phenomenon that created this brick city in the first place. Because the Hoosac Range, just east of North Adams, is so steep, early locomotives were unable to climb it, which meant a railroad couldn't run directly westward from Boston. Massachusetts's industries were handicapped, and Boston's future as a major port was in doubt until 1875, when—after 25 years of nonstop work, at a cost of nearly 200 lives—a 4.75-mile-long railroad tunnel was finally blasted through the Hoosac Range.

Beyond the narrow downtown, North Adams's streets climb steeply up the hills. At the foot of Main Street, turn at the Blackinton Mansion (now the public library) onto Church Street, lined with turn-of-the-20th-century mansions. Follow it up by the Massachusetts College of Liberal Arts and turn onto Kemp Avenue to find **Windsor Lake**.

Adams (population: 9,213). In McKinley Square at the center of Adams stands a bronze statue of President William McKinley, arms outstretched pleadingly as they were when he asked Congress to pass a tariff protecting American textile manufacturers from foreign competition. The protective tariff was responsible for Adams's period of greatest prosperity and directly benefited a local industrialist and longtime friend of McKinley, William Plunkett, owner of the Berkshire Cotton Manufacturing Company. A grateful and grieving Plunkett erected the statue after McKinley's assassination in 1901.

Adams was founded by Quakers, and their 1782 meetinghouse still stands on Friend Street. The town's most famous daughter is Susan B. Anthony (1820–1906), the daughter of Quakers who became a leading suffragist, instrumental in passing legislation that gave married women legal right over their children, property, and wages. A plaque at the southern end of Main Street commemorates her as the only woman to have ever graced the face of an American (silver) dollar.

Approaching Adams from the north on Rt. 8, you pass an unsightly operation mining calcium carbonate from Mount Greylock—but persevere. At the McKinley statue turn onto Hoosac Street to find the town's prime outlet and the **Discover the Berkshires Visitor Center**. Or head up Maple Street through orchards to **Greylock Glen** with its trails and views. Bicyclists note the new **Ashuwillticook Rail Trail** running south through Cheshire.

MUSEUMS ❧ **Berkshire Museum** (413-443-7171; www.berkshire museum.org), 39 S. Main St. (Rt. 7, just south of Park Square), Pittsfield. Open Mon.–Sat. 10–5, Sun. noon–5; $8 adults, $6.50 seniors and students, $5 ages 3–18. An example of what a regional museum should be. Founded in 1903 by Dalton philanthropist Zenas Crane, its no less than eight galleries display both permanent and changing exhibits. Check the web site for current special exhibits, as these are invariably elaborate.

There are frequent films, performances, lectures, and concerts in the **Little Cinema**, a 300-seat theater. The permanent collection includes American and European paintings, 15th- to 18th-century European works, and contemporary art, along with ancient artifacts that include a 2,000-year-old mummy. There are also interactive exhibits based on toys by Alexander Calder, and children love the "Dino Dig" in the Gallery of Dinosaurs; the natural history collection of shells, gemstones, and fossils; and the aquarium featuring fish from throughout the world, as well as reptiles, spiders, local animals, and birds. Note the annual Festival of Trees in Nov.–Dec.

❧ **Western Gateway Heritage State Park** (413-663-6312), Furnace St., North Adams. Open year-round, daily 10–5. Housed in a former railroad freight shed, its sophisticated

OUTSIDE THE BERKSHIRE MUSEUM

Christina Tree

& **Sterling and Francine Clark Art Institute** (413-458-2303; www.clark art.edu), 225 South St., Williamstown. Open daily July–Labor Day 10–5; otherwise closed Mon. Free Nov.–May and $12.50 per adult June–Oct.; also free under age 18 and students with ID. Inquire about the combination ticket with MASS MoCA. The increase in price in recent years reflects the quality of special exhibits. The permanent collection rivals those of many city museums. There are medieval works like a 15th-century panel painting by Piero della Francesca and works by such masters as Fragonard, Turner, and Goya. The museum is best known for its French impressionist paintings (Monet, Degas, Pissarro, and more than 30 Renoirs) and for its American period pieces by Winslow Homer, John Singer Sargent, and Frederic

LITTLE DANCER OF FOURTEEN YEARS BY EDGAR DEGAS (MODELED 1880–81; CAST 1919–21)

WEST POINT, PROUT'S NECK, BY WINSLOW HOMER (1900)

MORNING IN THE CITY BY EDWARD HOPPER (1944)

Remington. R. S. Clark (1877–1956), grandson to a founding partner in the Singer Sewing Machine Company, settled in Paris and began collecting art in 1912. When he met Francine (1876–1960), she was an actress with the Comedie Française. The couple collected avidly for their own pleasure but considered donating everything to the Metropolitan Museum of Art before determining in 1950 to build a museum to house it in this serene, safe town, far from the threat of nuclear war then felt in New York City. The white-marble building at the center of the present museum was opened in 1955. It has since been substantially expanded, and another major expansion by the Japanese architect Tadao Ando is planned. The Clark Art Institute is set in 140 acres of lawns, meadows, and walking trails, spotted with picnic tables and benches. Inquire about concerts and other special programs, including a series of films and lectures.

♿ **Williams College Museum of Art** (413-597-2429; www.wcma.org), Rt. 2. Open Tue.–Sat. 10–5, Sun. 1–5. Free. This is one of the finest college art museums in the country, too often overlooked by visitors. It's easily accessible from Spring Street (Williamstown's shopping drag) as well as from Main Street (Rt. 2). The striking building combines a vintage-1846, two-story octagon with a major three-story addition designed by Charles Moore, filled with unconventional spaces. The museum has an outstanding permanent collection of American 19th- and 20th-century works by Eakins, Hassam, Feininger,

Kim Grant

MASSACHUSETTS MUSEUM OF CONTEMPORARY ART (MASS MOCA)

Rivers, and Hopper, and represents the world's largest collection of works by Charles and Maurice Prendergast. Exhibits change frequently.

✦ ♿ **Massachusetts Museum of Contemporary Art (MASS MoCA**; 413-662-2111; www.massmoca.org), 87 Marshall St., North Adams. Open daily 11–5, closed Tue. except in July and Aug., when it's open every day 10–6. $12 per adult, $5 ages 6–16, $9 students. Inquire about Kidspace, an interactive area with special exhibits for kids, open daily in summer months noon–4 and weekends off-season (but call to check). Also inquire about the seasonal combination ticket with the Clark Art Institute. Check the schedule of upcoming programs, which might include weekend films, Saturday-night Dance Parties, and varied special exhibits and events. *MASS MoCA* stands for "Massachusetts Museum of Contemporary Art." So what's it like? It's fun. Exhibits change so constantly that it's pointless to describe what we last saw here, but one thing we notice consistently is that as we wander from gallery to gallery, our perceptions alter. In contrast with a traditional museum in which you focus on one painting or sculpture after another, here the size of the viewing space itself changes constantly: One moment you are in a small blackened room mesmerized by a computer-composed choreography, and the next you are faced with a gallery as big as a football field, its walls stamped and streamed with myriad shapes and colors. Finally stepping outside, you may see actors filming while in another millyard workers may be installing a stage for the night's performance. The mill's old bell tower tolls the quarter hour in muted tones (the volume of this "sound art" varies with the intensity of the sun), while in front of it upside-down trees, presented by the Clark Art Institute as a welcoming present, appear to thrive. If conventional museums are boxes, MASS MoCA is more of an open platform. The lines between the exterior and interior of the building, between art and urban reality, blur. The 15 galleries fill 4 large buildings in this 25-building complex connected by the courtyards, viaducts, and elevated walkways that evolved to house Arnold Print Works (1860–1942), one of the world's leading textile producers. Sprague Electric Company occupied the complex from 1942 to 1985, at its height employing 4,137 workers. In 1986, when Williams College Museum of Art director Thomas Krens was searching for a space to display large modern art pieces, North Adams

mayor John Barrett III showed him the vacant Sprague mill buildings. (Krens went on to direct the Solomon R. Guggenheim Museum, which is devoted primarily to modern art.) The ups and downs of the project, shepherded by MASS MoCA's present director Joseph Thompson over the next dozen years, easily fill a book. **Lickety Split**, the museum's café, is open for breakfast (you can come in before the museum opens) and lunch as well as during after arts events; **Café Latino** (see *Dining Out*) is next door. Inquire about guided tours and audio guides. Local historian Paul W. Marino (413-663-3809; historyman@fiam.net) offers free, seasonal tours of downtown.

UPSIDE-DOWN TREES AT MASSMOCA

Christina Tree

displays tells the epic story of the construction of the 4.75-mile-long Hoosac Tunnel, one of 19th-century America's greatest engineering feats. The tunnel took 25 years to build, from 1850 to 1875, claimed nearly 200 lives, pioneered use of the explosive nitroglycerine, and cost $20 million—a vast sum for the time. An audiovisual presentation takes visitors back in time with the sounds of dripping water, pickaxes striking stone, nitroglycerine explosions, and a political debate about the merits of the massive project. Displays also depict other aspects of North Adams's history and include a miniature railroad with a precise diorama of the city in its heyday. There are changing arts and crafts exhibits, too. Other buildings in the "Park" contain the Freight Yard Pub, shops, and the volunteer-operated **North Adams Museum of History and Science** (413-664-4700). Open Apr.–Dec., Thu.–Sat. 10–4, Sun. 1–4; off-season, Sat. 10–4, Sun. 1–4. Free. This fascinating museum fills three floors of a former coal storage shed with exhibits on North Adams history and industry. Hands-on history and science discovery rooms are geared to children, and working model trains will delight rail buffs. Donations requested.

Crane Museum of Papermaking (413-684-6481; www.crane.com), off E. Housatonic St. (Rts. 8/90), 30 South St., Dalton. Open early June to mid-Oct., weekdays 1–5. Free and worth a stop. Housed in the rag room of the **Old Stone Mill** (1844) in a garden by the Housatonic, the displays and a video tell the story of papermaking from rags and include a fascinating variety of paper money. Crane Paper is the sole supplier of "money paper" to the U.S. Mint; the company has been in the family for five generations.

THEATER AND MUSIC Williamstown Theatre Festival (413-597-3400; www.wtfestival.org), Williamstown. Since 1955 this festival has offered some of the best theater in the Northeast, staging some 200 performances of classic and new plays from the last week of June through August. In 2002 the WTF was the country's first summer theater to receive a Tony Award for sustained excellence. In 2005 it acquired a sleek, glittering new Main Stage when Williams College opened the '62 Center for Theatre and Dance. Full-scale productions aside, you'll also find Downstage performances, late-night musical cabarets, staged readings, and Free Theatre.

WESTERN GATEWAY HERITAGE STATE PARK
© DCR/John Crispin

Barrington Stage Company (413-236-8888; www.barringtonstageco.org), 30 Union St., Pittsfield. MainStage tickets $15–52; senior and student discounts; children free. Artistic director Julianne Boyd has orchestrated a number of major musical hits, most notably *The 25th Annual Putnam County Spelling Bee*, which went on from Berkshire County to Broadway where, as we go to press, it is still playing to packed houses. In 2006

Boyd moved the company from Sheffield to Pittsfield, restoring a 500-seat vaudeville theater as its main stage and extending the season. In addition to MainStage productions, BSC mounts two Stage II productions, a Youth Theatre production, and a New Works Festival of staged readings.

Colonial Theatre (413-997-4444; www.thecolonialtheatre.org), 111 South St., Pittsfield. Built in 1903, the playhouse in its heyday hosted a dazzling array of performers, from the Barrymores and Sarah Bernhardt to Will Rogers. Eventually refitted for movies, it closed in 1949 and for half a century was preserved as a warehouse by the Miller family, who sold art and paint supplies from a storefront they added on. In 1998 Hillary Clinton declared the Colonial "a national treasure," which triggered initial efforts to reclaim the theater's glory. It was finally and completely restored in 2006, opening with a performance of *Rent*. At this writing performances include children's productions, jazz (T. S. Monk), Arlo Guthrie, *The Nutcracker* by the Albany Berkshire Ballet, and the Irish Rovers.

Williams College

THE NEW '62 CENTER FOR THEATRE AND DANCE AT WILLIAMS COLLEGE

Berkshire Opera Company (413-442-9955; www.berkshireopera.org) 297 North Street, Pittsfield. Venues for productions include the Mahaiwe Performing Arts Center in Great Barrington, the Koussevitzky Arts Center at Berkshire Community College in Pittsfield, Chapin Hall at Williams College in Williamstown, and Lee High School in Lee.

Albany Berkshire Ballet (413-445-5382; www.berkshireballet.org), 51 North St., Pittsfield. Performances of classic and contemporary ballet are staged periodically year-round at a variety of venues, reviewed respectfully in New York and Boston.

South Mountain Concerts (413-442-2106; www.southmountainconcerts.com), Rts. 7/20, 2 miles south of downtown Pittsfield. A series of five Sunday-afternoon concerts September to early October, featuring internationally known chamber ensembles, performed in an acoustically fine, vintage-1918 music hall seating 440. Top performers and serious patrons characterize the series.

SANDY DUNCAN IN THE BARRINGTON STAGE COMPANY'S 2006 PRODUCTION OF *MAME*

Kevin Sprague

Christina Tree

HANCOCK SHAKER VILLAGE

✎ **Hancock Shaker Village** (413-443-0188; www.hancockshakervillage.org), 5 miles west of Pittsfield on Rt. 20, at its junction with Rt. 41; use the Mass Pike West Stockbridge exit (take Rt. 41 north to Rt. 20 west). Open daily, year-round. Winter hours are 10–4 until Memorial Day weekend, then 9:30–5 through Oct. 15. Closed Thanksgiving, Christmas, and New Year's Day. Admission: $15 adults in summer, $12.50 late October until the Friday before Memorial Day weekend when village is fully staffed and there is a program of demonstrations and activities. Free year-round for children 12 and under; $4 ages 13–17. Inquire about frequent special events. Oct. 16–Dec. 31, guided tours of the Brick Dwelling and Round Stone Barn are offered. Call ahead to check times.

Founded in 1783, this "City of Peace" was the third of what would eventually number 19 Shaker communities stretching from Maine to Kentucky (see *Shakers* in "What's Where"). In the mid-19th century it numbered some 250 brethren divided among six "families," farming 3,000 acres. It survived until 1959.

In 1961 the village's buildings were about to be sold to a neighboring racetrack when a group of Pittsfield residents rallied and bought the entire community—including 1,000 acres—from its last Shaker sisters. Since then it has evolved into a 20-building museum housing the largest collection of Shaker artifacts on any original Shaker site. The buildings have been restored, including the much-copied and -photographed round stone barn, and the five-story Brick Dwelling House, built in 1830 to house 100 Shaker brethren and sisters.

CLOAKROOM IN THE 1830 BRICK DWELLING

A scattering of tidy buildings surrounded by its own orchards and meadows, the village looks like some primitive painter's vision of the heavenly kingdom. The guides, craftsmen, and furnishings all tell about the dancing monks and nuns who turned farming, craftsmanship, and invention into visible prayers. Note the frequent special events staged throughout the year. During fall and on holiday weekends Shaker dinners are served in the brick building (call for reservations). The visitor center includes a Center for Shaker Studies and a gallery displaying the village's spirit drawing collection as well as an orientation theater, a changing exhibit gallery, and a gift shop selling yarn, herbs, and baked goods made on the premises. It also includes a café with a children's menu. Families should take care not to miss the hands-on Discovery Room in the 1910 barn: Visitors can weave and spin, try on Shaker-style clothes, milk MaryJane (a life-sized replica cow), sample 19th-century toys and games, and check out the beehive and newly hatched chickens. Inquire about the **Shaker Trail** leading to the adjacent **Pittsfield State Forest**, traveling past the sites of old Shaker dwellings and religious ceremonies. During summer months inquire about the day's schedule of thematic tours and crafts demonstrations.

OVAL-BOX-MAKING DEMONSTRATION

Massachusetts Museum of Contemporary Art (MASS MoCA; 413-662-2111; www.massmoca.org), 87 Marshall St., North Adams. See *Museums*. MASS MoCA sponsors a year-round series of live concerts and other performances.

Main Street Stage (413-663-3240; www.mainstreetstage.com), 57 Main St., North Adams. Year-round performances are given in a storefront theater.

Tannery Pond Concerts (880-820-1696; www.tannerypondconcerts.org), New Lebanon, NY 12125. The setting for these six outdoor chamber music concerts, staged on selective Saturday evenings late May through mid-October, is beautiful: the pond on the grounds of the former Mount Lebanon Shaker Village, now the Darrow School, a coed boarding school with a campus that occupies and sensitively enhances the former Shaker Village, just over the New York line from Hancock and off Rt. 20.

SCENIC DRIVES Mohawk Trail. Even if you don't drive to the northern Berkshires via Rt. 2, better known as the Mohawk Trail, be sure to drive from North Adams up along Rt. 2 to the Western Summit and park at the Wigwam Gift Shop to take in "the three-state view" before plunging back down the well-named Hairpin Turn as it zigs and zags its way into North Adams.

Williamstown to Pittsfield. Along Rt. 7 south through South Williamstown, the views are of high meadows and mountains. Turn at the Five Corners Store onto Rt. 43 and follow it through the steep, mostly wooded Jericho Valley to the village of Hancock; continue on into New York State and turn south onto Rt. 22. At the high school in New Lebanon make a sharp left east onto Rt. 20 and continue over Lebanon Mountain. Stop by **Hancock Shaker Village**, then continue east to Pittsfield.

Greylock Glen, Adams. Rt. 8 is the main north–south drag through Adams, but find your way up to parallel West Rd. and then Gould Rd. This quiet old road climbs up and up to the glorious high meadow that's been the object of a series of development schemes, including a ski area, a gambling casino, then a high-altitude cross-country resort. At present, however, Gould Road ends at the Gould farmhouse, and while the area is webbed with hiking and biking trails, few are marked. A Department of Conservation and Recreation (DCR) pavilion by a small pond (good for a dip) is the site of periodic educational programs. It's a magical spot.

✳ To Do

BIKING Ashuwillticook Rail Trail (www.berkshirebikepath.org) is an 11-mile bike path with the first 5 miles, from Berkshire Mall Road in Lanesborough to Cheshire, now paved. The remaining 6 miles exist as a path, and plans call for paving it. The currently completed portion is unusually scenic, paralleling Rt. 8 but also following the shores of Berkshire Pond and Cheshire Reservoir for several miles. It replaces tracks first laid in 1845 and used until 1990.

Rental bikes are available at **Berkshire Outfitters** (413-743-5900; www .berkshireoutfitters.com) on Rt. 8 south of Adams.

The Mountain Goat (413-458-8445; www.themountaingoat.com), 130 Water St. in Williamstown, is an excellent source of biking information in the

Herman Melville (1819–91) spent 13 of his happiest, most productive years at Arrowhead, a farm on the southern edge of Pittsfield that's now headquarters for the Berkshire County Historical Society. Forced to work after his father's bankruptcy and death, Melville held a number of jobs, joined the merchant marines, and—at age 22—set sail on the whaler *Acushnet.* He jumped ship in the Marquesas Islands and spent time in Hawaii before returning to Boston, where he wrote *Typee,* followed by several more South Seas–based novels. Established as a writer, he married and in 1850 brought his wife, Lizzie, and baby son Malcolm to spend the summer at his uncle's fine house (now the Pittsfield Country Club) on Rt. 7.

It was on a famous rainy picnic atop Monument Mountain that he met Nathaniel Hawthorne (then living at Tanglewood in Lenox). The two young writers bonded instantly, and Melville was influenced by Hawthorne to become a year-round Berkshire resident. He bought a farm just up the road from his uncle, one commanding the same splendid view of Mount Greylock—which is said to have inspired his grandly conceived story of the great white whale and the mad sea captain. Melville penned *Moby-Dick* in a study overlooking the mountain. In all he wrote four novels, a collection of short stories, and 10 magazine pieces as well as beginning a book of poetry in this wonderfully rambling 18th-century house with its central hearth (described in the short story "I and My Chimney"). Unlike his far more famous neighbor, Oliver Wendell Holmes, Melville seems to have kept somewhat aloof, preferring to farm and write rather than to party.

Arrowhead, which is furnished with many original pieces, evokes Melville the author and father—who had difficulty supporting his wife and four children despite his prodigious literary output. Melville eventually sold the farm to his brother and moved to New York, where he worked in the Customs House for more than 20 years, earning $4 per hour and finding time to write only poetry and, eventually, *Billy Budd,* published in 1924, 33 years after his death.

AN 1861 PHOTO PORTRAIT OF HERMAN MELVILLE

Rodney Dewey, courtesy of Berkshire Athenaeum

Arrowhead (413-442-1793; www.mobydick.org), 780 Holmes Rd. (off Rts. 7/20), Pittsfield, is open daily Memorial Day–Columbus Day, tours on the hour 11–3; otherwise by appointment. $12 adults, $5 students, $3 children. The 44-acre grounds include a walking trail. Inquire about special exhibits.

Note: Melville buffs should also find the **Herman Melville Memorial Room** in the **Berkshire Athenaeum** (413-499-9480, ext. 204), Pittsfield's public library at 1 Wendell Ave. on Park Square. It contains every book about, as well as by, the author and such artifacts as the desk on which he wrote *Billy Budd.* **Canoe Meadows**, the former property of Oliver Wendell Homes (see *Birding*), is just up Holmes Road.

Williamstown area. Recommended: Rt. 43 along the Green River. **Plaines Bike & Ski** (413-499-0294; www.plaines.com), 55 W. Housatonic St. (Rt. 20) in Pittsfield, rents bikes.

Jiminy Peak (413-738-5500; www.jiminypeak.com) rents mountain bikes in summer, along with use of lifts and 14 trails, some singletrack and some downhill cruises. Helmets are required. An all-day trail and lift access pass is $24 (bikes and helmets not included).

Berkshire Cycling Association (www.berkshirecycling.org), based in Pittsfield, schedules frequent rides.

Rubel Western Massachusetts Bicycle and Road Map (Rubel Bike Maps) is highly recommended for its in-depth coverage of the area. At this writing an excellent, free *Berkshire Bike Touring* map/guide, based on Rubel, is available from the regional information sources listed under *Guidance*.

BIRDING **Canoe Meadows Wildlife Sanctuary**, Holmes Rd. off Rt. 7, south of Pittsfield. This 290-acre Massachusetts Audubon sanctuary offers a mix of wetlands and croplands with 5 miles of trails. A great place to jog. No restrooms.

Dorothy Frances Rice Wildlife Refuge in Peru, on South Rd. off Rt. 143 from the town center. Three hundred acres, walking trails, and self-guiding trails owned by the New England Forestry Foundation.

CAMPING

State Forests and Parks
The Massachusetts Department of Conservation and Recreation (DCR) publishes a handy map/guide and maintains a visitor-friendly regional office on Rt. 7 south of Pittsfield (413-442-8928; www.mass.gov/dcr). For reservations, phone 877-422-6762. Campsites are sited in **Clarksburg State Park** (50 campsites near Mauserts Pond; flush toilets and showers but no hookups), in the **Mount Greylock State Reservation** (34 wooded campsites, five group campsites, five backpacker shelters; no flush toilets, showers, or hookups), and in **Pittsfield State Forest** (13 rustic campsites on Berry Pond at the top of Berry Mountain, 18 at the Parker Brook campground at the mountain's base; flush and nonflush toilets, no showers or hookups). See *Green Space* for details about these preserves; also see **Savoy Mountain State Forest** in "Along the Mohawk Trail."

Historic Valley Park Campground at Windsor Lake in North Adams (413-662-3198), 10 Main St., North Adams, open May 15–Oct. 15, a city-

THE ASHUWILLTICOOK RAIL TRAIL
A. Blake Gardner/Berkshire Visitors Bureau

operated facility on a quiet lake, minutes from downtown North Adams and Rt. 2, offers 100 campsites ranging from water and electric hookup sites to "wilderness," tent-only sites; some wilderness (walk-in) tent sites and some lakeside. Even in August there are usually vacancies midweek. No motorcycles permitted.

For other private campgrounds, contact the **Massachusetts Association of Campground Owners** (781-544-3475; www.campmass.com).

CANOEING AND KAYAKING The **Hoosic River** flows north from Cheshire Lake, offering some good kayaking and canoeing along the way. Check in with **Berkshire Outfitters** (413-743-5900; www.berkshireoutfitters.com), Rt. 8 south of Adams, for canoe and kayak rentals as well as sales and guidance (closed Mon.).

Canoes and boats can also be rented at **Windsor Lake** (413-662-3198) in North Adams.

Cheshire Reservoir (also known as Hoosac Lake) on Rt. 8 in Cheshire offers a good launch area, as does **Richmond Pond**, Swamp Rd., Richmond. **Berry Pond** in **Pittsfield State Forest** (see *Green Space*), one of the highest ponds in the state, is also accessible for kayaks and canoes.

Berkshire Rowing and Sculling Association (413-496-7769; www.berkshire sculling.com), Pittsfield. Lew Cuyler rents and offers instruction in an unusually lightweight and stable scull for use on Onota Lake.

On **Pontoosuc Lake**, Rt. 7 in Pittsfield, **Wild'N'West Snow & Water** (413-445-5211) offers a variety of boat rentals. On neighboring **Onota Lake**, **Onota Boat Livery** (413-442-1724) rents motor- and pontoon boats as well as sailboats, kayaks, and canoes.

FISHING Licenses for fishing (currently $11.50 ages 15–17, otherwise $12.50 for a resident and $23.50 for a nonresident for 3 days) are required for everyone age 15 or over. They are available at local sporting stores and by contacting the Division of Fisheries and Wildlife (413-447-9789), 400 Hubbard Ave., Pittsfield. Log onto www.mass.gov/dfwele or www.masswildlife.org. The **Green River** is a famous trout stream. Anglers should also check out **Cheshire Reservoir** in Cheshire, **Mauserts Pond** in Clarksburg, **Windsor Lake** in North Adams (where you can rent a boat), **Onota** and **Pontoosuc lakes** in Pittsfield, and **Richmond Pond** in Richmond. **Points North Outfitters** (413-743-4030), 111 Forest Park, Adams, sells fly-fishing gear, runs fly-fishing schools, and offers guided trips on the Deerfield River. Also see **Savoy Mountain State Forest** in "Along the Mohawk Trail"; it's accessible from Rt. 2 just east of North Adams.

FOR FAMILIES ✍ **Jiminy Peak Mountain Adventure Park** (413-738-5500; www.jiminypeak.com), Corey Rd. (between Rts. 7 and 43), Hancock. Open daily Memorial Day–Labor Day, 11 AM–9 PM; weekends in May and Sep., 11–6. Eleven attractions including the Mountain Coaster—the only one in the Northeast—which provides a thrilling ride through the woods down several thousand feet of twisting track; an Alpine Slide; the Giant Swing; and a rock climbing wall.

Kim Grant

PONTOOSUC LAKE IN PITTSFIELD OFFERS
EXCELLENT BOATING AND FISHING.

🚣 **Play Bousquet** (413-442-8316; www.bousquets.com), Dan Fox Dr., Pittsfield. Open Memorial Day–Columbus Day. This small ski area is a summer family fun park with water-slides and activity pool, a miniature golf and a driving range, a go-cart track, a climbing wall, and chairlift rides.

🚣 **Family Fun Center** (413-499-0051), 10 Williamstown Rd. (Rt. 7), Lanesborough. Go-carts, bumper boats, miniature batting cages, and a snack bar.

🚣 **Buster's Entertainment Center** (413-499-7500; www.bustersforfun .com), 457 Dalton Ave., Pittsfield. More than 100 games for kids of all ages.

Also see *Museums*, *Farms*, and *Special Events*.

GOLF **Bas-Ridge Golf Course** (413-655-2605), 151 Plunkett Ave. (off Rt. 8), Hinsdale. 18 holes, challenging but user-friendly.

North Adams Country Club (413-663-7887), River Rd., Clarksburg. Nine holes.

Pontoosuc Lake Country Club (413-445-4217), Kirkwood Dr., Pittsfield. 18 holes, reasonable rates, snacks, beverages.

Skyline Country Club (413-445-5584), Rt. 7, Lanesborough. 18 holes. Dining area with pub menu.

Taconic Golf Club (413-458-3997), Meachem St., Williamstown. Open daily mid-Apr. to mid-Nov. but only Tue.–Fri. to the public.

Waubeeka Springs Golf Links (413-458-8355), Rt. 7, South Williamstown. Open daily Apr. to mid-Nov.

Wahconah Country Club (413-684-1333), Orchard Rd. in Dalton. 18 holes, after 2 PM on weekends.

HIKING AND WALKING **Mount Greylock**. The 60 miles of trails in the Mount Greylock Reservation include more than 11 miles of the Appalachian Trail. The (literally) top hike in North Berkshire is from the summit of Mount Greylock (currently closed to motor traffic; see *Green Space*), which has been newly land-scaped with trailheads clearly marked and quotes from literary and historic fig-ures who walked this way inscribed on "interpretive stones" scattered along the trails. Wear sensible shoes and clothing and enjoy the views. *Note:* Food and lodging are *not* available during current road contruction.

Hopkins Memorial Forest (413-597-2346), Northwest Hill Rd., Williamstown, is a 2,050-acre preserve owned by Williams College with a network of hiking (and, in winter, cross-country skiing) and nature trails. The **Hopkins Farm Museum** and a botanical garden are also here.

Field Farm (413-458-3135; www.thetrustees.org), Sloan Rd., South Williamstown. Foot trails (more than 3 miles) wander through meadows, crop-land, marsh, and forest with spectacular views of Mount Greylock to the east. Waterfowl frequent the pond, and the lime-rich soil nurtures an abundance of wildflowers. There are two buildings on the property, an outstanding 1950s home (see the Guest House at Field Farm in *Lodging*) and "The Folly," a small house designed by noted architect Ulrich Franzen and open to the public by appointment. From the intersection of Rts. 43 and 7, take Rt. 43 west and then make an immediate right onto Sloan Rd.; the reservation is 1 mile down the road. This is also a favorite local cross-country skiing venue.

Sheep Hill (413-458-2492; www.wrlf.org), 671 Cold Spring Rd., Williamstown. This 50-acre spread of woods and meadows offers trails, access to more trails, and the Mary and Craig Lewis Center for Nature (open Mon.–Fri. 9–5)—a farmhouse by Josiah's Pond that's home to the Williamstown Rural Lands Foundation and offers educational nature programs for all ages.

Taconic Crest Trail. The 35-mile ridgeline trail along the western rim of Berkshire County is accessible from Hopkins Memorial Forest, from Field Farm, and several other trailheads in North Berkshire, but it should not be attempted without a trail map. Serious hikers should pick up a copy of the *North Berkshire Outdoor Guide* published by the Williams Outing Club and available at The Mountain Goat (see *Bicycling*). *Nature Walks in the Berkshire Hills* by Charles W. G. Smith (AMC) and *Hikes & Walks in the Berkshire Hills* by Lauren Stevens (Berkshire House) are both very useful.

Also see *Green Space*

HORSEBACK RIDING DeMayo's

Bonnie Lea Farm (413-458-3149), Rt. 7, Williamstown. Guided cross-country trail rides for riders over 13 and by appointment only. **Berkshire Equestrian Center** (413-698-3200), 802 State Rd. 9 (Rt. 41), Richmond. Lessons for all level riders, in the ring and on the trail.

TRAILS IN THE MOUNT GREYLOCK RESERVATION

Kim Grant

SWIMMING ♂ **Sands Spring Pool and Spa** (413-458-5202), Sands Spring Rd. (off Rt. 7, north of Williamstown; turn at the Cozy Corner Motel and Restaurant). Open May–Sep., 11–7. This attractive 50-by-75-foot pool is fed year-round by mineral springs that were well-known to the Native Americans for centuries. It's surrounded by lawn on which patrons spread their towels; there are picnic tables and some lawn sports. Billed as the oldest spa in the United States, it was formally established in 1813 and in 1842 became the centerpiece for a resort hotel. The century-old pavilion survives and includes a snack bar, changing rooms, and whirlpool. The pool is sparkling clean, 74 degrees, and genuinely exhilarating. There's a separate wading pool for preswimmers, and a sauna. Inquire about fitness classes and swim lessons.

Windsor Lake (413-662-3198), off Kemp Ave., North Adams. This pleasant city-run beach is set in a 180-acre preserve and seems miles from the mills that are just blocks away. There's a pavilion, lifeguards, and, just off the lake, 100 campsites (see *Camping*). Nonresidents pay a nominal fee per car.

Margaret Lindley Park (Rts. 2 and 7), Williamstown, is a well-kept town pool with changing rooms and picnic tables; daily charge for nonresidents. Open summer and school vacation, daily 11–7.

See also **Clarksburg State Park** and **Pittsfield State Forest** under *Green Space*, and **North Pond** in **Savoy Mountain State Forest** under "Along the Mohawk Trail."

TENNIS There is a free town court off Main St., across from the **Maple Terrace Motel**, Williamstown. **Williams College** (413-597-3131) maintains 12 clay and 12 hard-topped tennis courts (fee and reservations). **Berkshire West Athletic Club** (413-499-4600), Dan Fox Dr., Pittsfield, has four outdoor and five indoor courts. **Ponterril/YMCA** (413-499-0687), Rt. 7, Pontoosuc Lake, Pittsfield, offers six clay courts; fee for nonmembers.

✳ Winter Sports

CROSS-COUNTRY SKIING Rentals are available in Williamstown at the **Mountain Goat** (413-458-8445) and **Goff's Sports** (413-458-3605). Cross-country skiers are welcome on the **Taconic Golf Course**, and on the **Stone Hill** trails. Also see *Green Space*.

A GREAT SPOT FOR PICNICKING ON MOUNT GREYLOCK

Christina Tree

DOWNHILL SKIING ♂ **Jiminy Peak** (413-738-5500 or 888-4-JIMINY; www.jiminypeak.com), Corey Rd., Hancock, open mid-Nov. to mid-Apr. Set high in the Jericho Valley, a narrow corridor that runs east–west between Rts. 43 and 7. Jiminy Peak is a self-contained four-season resort— the largest ski and snowboarding resort in southern New England—

with rental two- to four-bedroom condos. You'll also find a 105-suite inn (see *Lodging*); **John Harvard's Restaurant and Brewery**; and **Hendricks Lodge** on the summit.

Vertical drop: 1,150 feet.

Terrain: 44 slopes and trails.

Lifts: 1 six-passenger, 2 quads, 3 triples, 1 double chair, 1 Magic Carpet lift.

Snowmaking: 95 percent of area.

Facilities: The Children's Center accommodates up to 350 SKIwee and Explorer program participants with their own rental shop and cafeteria; it also offers a playroom for children not skiing.

Rates: $57 adults, $51 teens, $41 seniors on weekends; $50, $40 during the week; less for 4 hours and younger kids. Lodging-skiing packages.

✍ **Bousquet** (413-442-8316; www.bousquets.com), Pittsfield. Marked from Rts. 7/20 south of town. The Berkshires' oldest ski area, founded in 1932, and the one that pioneered both the ski train and night skiing. Noted for friendly slopes ideal for beginning and intermediate skiers. Open daily in winter for skiing, snowboarding, and tubing, also nightly except Sunday for skiing and boarding. Inquire about condo lodging on the adjacent property.

Vertical drop: 750 feet.

Terrain: 21 trails.

Lifts: 3 double chairs, 2 surface lifts.

Rates: $32 weekends and holidays; Mon.–Thu. $15; night $20 skiing.

SNOW TUBING Snowy Owl (413-443-4752; www.jiminypeak.com) 36 Williamstown Rd. (Rt. 7), New Ashford. Just a few minutes' drive from Jiminy Peak, the snow-tubing resort occupies the former Brodie Mountain ski area site. For $15, anyone 3 or older can tube on the slope for 90 minutes. The number of tubers at any given time is limited; reserving time slots is recommended.

Also see **Bousquet**.

SNOWMOBILING Snowmobiling is permitted in many local state parks. Check with the Pittsfield office of the DCR (see below). Guided snowmobile tours are offered by Wild'N'Wet Snow & Water, Inc. (413-445-5211; caseycare@peoplepc.com).

✳ Green Space

STATE PARKS AND FORESTS *Note:* The Massachusetts Department of Conservation and Recreation (DCR) publishes a handy map/guide and

SANDS SPRING POOL AND SPA IN WILLIAMSTOWN

Christina Tree

maintains a visitor-friendly regional office on Rt. 7 south of Pittsfield (413-442-8928; www.mass.gov/dcr).

☞ **Natural Bridge State Park** (413-663-6392), Rt. 8, North Adams. Open Memorial Day–Columbus Day. $2 parking fee. The centerpiece of this 47-acre park is an unusual natural formation, a white-marble bridge spanning a steep gorge that's attracted tourists since the 1830s, when Nathaniel Hawthorne compared the stream churning through its depths to "a heart that has been rent asunder by a torrent." A series of dramatic (but child-safe) paths and stairways offer views of the waterfall and stone formations. There are picnic tables, nature trails, and a visitor center with restrooms; in summer a park interpreter is on hand to explain the geological forces that created the bridge. It's also a popular local fishing spot.

Clarksburg State Park and **Clarksburg State Forest** (413-664-8345), 1199 Middle Rd., Clarksburg. Off Rt. 8 north from Rt. 2. Together the park and forest cover 3,250 wooded acres that are particularly beautiful in foliage season. The park's **Mauserts Pond** has a day-use area with swimming, picnic facilities, and a pavilion. There is a scenic nature trail around the pond and 50 campsites nearby (nominal fee). (In "Along the Mohawk Trail," also see **Savoy Mountain State Forest**, with its beautiful **Tannery Falls**, swimming in North Pond, and camping at South Pond, all not far from Adams.)

♿ **Pittsfield State Forest** (413-442-8992) totals 9,695 acres. From the corner of Rts. 20 and 7 in Pittsfield, drive west on West St., north on Churchill St., and west on Cascade to the entrance. A 5-mile circular paved road follows Lulu Brook to high, scenic **Berry Pond**, good for boating (no motors); swimming, however, is in smaller **Lulu Pond**. A pavilion that can be rented by groups in summer serves as a warming hut in winter. **Tranquillity Trail**, a paved, 0.75-mile loop through spruce woods, has been designed for wheelchair access. There are taped descriptions of flora and fauna. In June the forest harbors 40 acres of azaleas. **Balance Rock**—a 165-ton boulder poised on another rock—is accessible via Balance Rock Road from Rt. 7 in Lanesborough.

Wahconah Falls State Park (413-442-8992), off Rt. 9 in Dalton, 3 miles east of the town center. A 2-minute walk brings you from the parking area down to picnic tables, scattered among the smooth rocks above the falls; swimming is permitted in the small pool at their base.

The Cascades, a waterfall formed by Notch Brook as it tumbles into a pool

NATURAL BRIDGE STATE PARK
Christina Tree

below, is a popular 1-hour hike from Rt. 2: Park on Marion Ave. and pick up the path at the end of the street. Cross the footbridge and follow the trail.

Peru State Forest (413-442-8992), off Rt. 143 in Peru; south on Curtin Rd., 1 mile from Peru Center. Garnet Hill (2,178 feet) yields a good view of the surrounding country, and there is fishing in **Garnet Lake**.

PICNICKING **Stone Hill**. A 55-acre town park, accessible from Stone Hill Rd. off South St., Williamstown, offers wooded trails and a stone seat with a view.

✷ Lodging

INNS

In Williamstown 01267

✎ ♿ **The Williams Inn** (413-458-9371 or 800-828-0133; www.williamsinn.com), Main St. (junction of Rts. 2 and 7). Carl and Marilyn Faulkner are thoroughly capable innkeepers, and their 125-room hostelry serves as the heart of town. At first glance you might wonder how such a prominent site—across from the green, at the junction of Rts. 2 and 7—came to be filled by a boxy motor lodge. In fact, a white-pillared mansion built with the Procter & Gamble fortune stood here and served for decades as a fraternity house until one bitter-cold night in 1979 when it burned to the ground. Its picture hangs in the lobby, a spacious, comfortable space with the feel of a country campus hotel. Rooms are comfortable, motel-style, crisply, attractively furnished in reproduction antiques, with full bath, TV, phone, computer hookup, and air-conditioning; the 24 "premier rooms" in the new wing are better than comfortable. Request a corner room. Amenities include an indoor swimming pool, sauna, and hot tub. The dining room is open for breakfast, lunch, and dinner, and lighter fare is served in the tavern lounge, known for its burgers. This is, incidentally, the ideal place to stay without a car—it's a short walk from the museums and steps from the Adams Memorial Theater (venue for the Williamstown Theatre Festival), and its outer lobby (open 24 hours) doubles as the Bonanza bus stop. Rooms are $170–300 per couple. No charge for children 14 and under in the same room.

♿ **The Orchards** (413-458-9611; www.orchardshotel.com), 222 Adams Rd. (off Rt. 2). Walled away from a commercial strip on the eastern edge of town, the Orchards faces inward, on a flowery, inner courtyard with a patio dining by a reflecting pool. The feel is of a small, elegant country hotel, and tea is served in a spacious sitting room fitted with Oriental rugs, crystal chandeliers, and antiques. The tone is formal. There are 45 rooms and two suites, each different, many with fireplace and window seat, all furnished with English antiques, goosefeather and down pillows. Amenities include a fridge, full bath, and separate dressing area. The restaurant is highly rated (see *Dining Out*). One complaint: Staff are drawn from foreign countries and are understandably unaware of the locale. Amenities include a pool and an exercise center with a sauna. $205–350 Memorial Day weekend to early Nov.; less off-season.

Mount Greylock State Reservation

Until spring 2009 the 3,491-foot-high summit is open only to hikers. The two roads to the summit are closed due to construction, but you can still drive the 1.8 miles from Rt. 7 in Lanesborough (north of Pittsfield) to the **Mount Greylock Visitor Center** (413-499-4262; open year-round, daily 9–4, later in summer). Snowmobiling, snowshoeing, and cross-country skiing are permitted.

In 1898, 400 acres on Mount Greylock was the first property acquired by the state's forest and park department. The reservation now comprises more than 12,500 acres with 70 miles of trails. The summit is landscaped and capped

Berkshire Visitors Bureau

THE SUMMIT VETERANS MEMORIAL TOWER ATOP MOUNT GREYLOCK

with the state's **Veterans War Memorial Tower**. On a clear day five states are visible. The Appalachian Trail crosses the summit, and several other trails beckon. The Thunderbolt Ski Shelter was built in the 1930s at the top of a ski trail by the Civilian Conservation Corps (CCC), which also built the handsome, fieldstone Bascom Lodge—unfortunately closed until the road reopens in 2009.

Note the "interpretive stones" scattered along trails near the summit

BED & BREAKFASTS

In Pittsfield 01201

♿ **Thaddeus Clapp House** (413-499-6840 or 888-499-6840; www.clapphouse.com), 74 Wendell Ave. Just a block off South St. (Rt. 7) and a leafy stroll from Park Square, this 1871 mansion evokes a sense of what Pittsfield once was and promises again to be. Innkeeper Beck Smith is herself at the heart of the city's current renaissance and enjoys plugging guests into the best of all the city has

to offer. A dilapidated apartment house when Smith began renovations in 2001, this is now an elegant B&B with eight suites. Each has a fireplace, cable TV, fridge, AC, and dataport; all are spacious and airy, furnished in handsome antiques. Several have a whirlpool bath as well as shower. Woodwork is extraordinary throughout, set off by Oriental rugs. An enthusiastic historian, Smith likes to tell guests about Thaddeus Clapp, the president of the Pontoosuc Woolen Mill but with a passion for acting.

recalling the experiences here of notables who have come this way in the past. Our favorite remains the description by Henry David Thoreau, who spent a July night up here in 1844 when only a "rude observatory," built by Williams College students, stood on the top. In *A Week on the Concord and Merrimack Rivers*, Thoreau describes the way he built a fire and "encased" himself in boards to keep warm. At dawn he found himself above the clouds, which he described as "floating on this fragment of the wreck of the world, on my carved plank, in a cloud land." Imagine the novelty of sitting above the clouds before the era of airplane windows.

MOUNT GREYLOCK IN WINTER

Kim Grant

These spacious public rooms were designed as venues for musical performances, poetry, and theatrical readings as well as elaborate dinner parties (inquire about occasional theatrical presentations in the parlor). In warm weather the wicker-filled front porch is a favored gathering spot. Breakfast and tea are served in the dining room. $125–250 includes a full breakfast.

✈ **White Horse Inn** (413-442-2512 or 877-442-2512; www.whitehorsebb .com), 378 South St. (Rt. 7). Two gen-

erations of Pittsfield's McGovern family have worked together to totally renovate this handsome century-old home, adding a spacious deck and landscaping the ample back garden. Host Gary McGovern, former assistant manager at a San Francisco hotel, puts his all into breakfast, which is served on the deck or in a sunny breakfast room, heated by a wood-pellet-fed stove. A similar stove also glows in the comfortable, uncluttered living room. The eight guest rooms (one on the ground floor) all have the same unfussy feel. The emphasis is on comforts such as a good mattress (from full to king), new (private) bathroom, and small TV in each room. $120–195 in high season, $85–100 in low.

In Williamstown 01267
Williamstown Bed and Breakfast (413-458-9202; www.williamstown bandb.com), 30 Cold Spring Rd. Since 1989 Lucinda Edmonds and Kim Rozell have been welcoming guests to this spacious 1880s house nicely but unfussily furnished in period style. It's steps from Field Park (the town green) and within walking distance of downtown restaurants and shops. There's a sitting room opening onto the oak-furnished dining room, the setting for a full breakfast that always includes a hot entrée and home-baked breads. Guests tend to talk to one another over breakfast or while relaxing on the porch or lawn. The four good-sized guest rooms, each with private bath, are furnished with a mix of well-chosen antiques and a sure eye to comfort. We especially like the upstairs front room with its small-patterned paper, marble-topped dresser, and coral couch set in a window bay. Children over 12 please. $135–150 double, less off-season.

Steep Acres Farm (413-458-3774; jmgangemi@adelphia.net), 520 White Oaks Rd. High on a hill with splendid views and bird life, this handsome, spacious, vintage-1900 home, set in 50 acres, has been home to Mary and Marvin Gangemi since 1978, one that they have shared with guests since 1983. Special features include the ample sunporch filled with white wicker and flowers, from which you can watch birds feeding just outside, and the 2-acre pond down in back,

good for swimming, fishing, and boating. Over the years the Gangemis have obviously merged smaller rooms into flowing downstairs spaces. Our favorite guest room, upstairs in back, features an Eastlake bed handed down through the family. There are four rooms all told, three baths. $70–160 includes a full breakfast and taxes. **The Birches** (413-458-8134), a new home built along traditional lines by Mary and Marvin's son Daniel, is just downhill and also part of the property. It offers three more rooms, including one with a king-sized bed, fireplace, and whirlpool. $100–175 includes a full breakfast and afternoon refreshments.

Upland Meadow House (413-458-3990), 1249 Northwest Hill Rd. This contemporary house is set in 160 acres, high on a hill adjacent to Hopkins Forest but less than 3 miles from the middle of town. It's very much Pan Whitman's home, but the two rooms (sharing one bath) are private, with their own sitting room and a splendid view east to the Green Mountains. It's a great spot for birders, cross-country skiers, and hikers as well as anyone who savors mountain meadows and views. Pan is, incidentally, known for her blueberry and raspberry jams. $100 includes breakfast served, when possible, on the big deck. Two-night minimum only on major weekends.

Le Jardin Restaurant & Inn (413-458-8032; www.lejardininn.com), 777 Cold Spring Rd. (Rts. 2/7). Always best known for its dining room (see *Dining Out*), this is now less of an inn, more of a restaurant than in years past. Still, the six recently renovated upstairs rooms are faultlessly comfortable, four with working fireplace and one with a small deck, all with bath, TV with DVD/VHS player, small fridge, and wireless Internet. The suite has a sitting room with a pullout sofa and a Jacuzzi. $125–225 in-season; from $85 Dec.–Apr.

The House on Main Street (413-458-3031; www.houseonmainstreet .com), 1120 Main St. This lovely, centuries-old house has been taking in "guests" since the 1930s. Thoroughly remodeled and modernized by the Riley family, it now offers six large, sunny, and cheerfully decorated guest rooms, three with private bath and the others sharing a bath and a half. A full breakfast is served in the country-style kitchen. Guests have the use of a parlor and a large screened porch. $95–140 includes a full breakfast.

In North Adams 01247
Also see the Porches Inn sidebar.

Blackinton Manor (413-663-5795; www.blackinton-manor.com), 1391 Massachusetts Ave. Obviously a mill owner spared no expense in building himself this exquisite Italianate mansion in 1832 in the middle of the small, leafy mill village that bears his name. It was restored as a B&B under previous owners, but Laura and Paul Micionus have substantially raised the comfort level. Common space includes elegant living/dining rooms with floor-to-ceiling windows and a grand piano. The grounds include an inviting pool. There are two ground-floor guest rooms and three more up the graceful staircase; all have private bath and one (the Parlor), a Jacuzzi. From $120 weekdays off-season for the Blue Room to $190 on a summer weekend for the Parlor. Rates include a full breakfast.

Jae's Inn (413-664-0100; www.jaes inn.com), 1111 S. State St. At the end of a long driveway south of town, off Rt. 8, this old inn (formerly Two Sisters) has been thoroughly revamped. Jae Chung grew up in North Adams and owns several Boston restaurants. His attractive, informal restaurant here (see *Dining Out*) is also justly popular. The 12 rooms are nicely furnished and air-conditioned, with gas fireplace, Jacuzzi, and TV with DVD. Facilities include a tennis court, heated swimming pool, basketball court, and spa. $95–150 includes continental breakfast. The attached spa offers a full menu of body treatments: massage, manicure, etc.

HISTORIC WILLIAMSTOWN B&BS
Riverbend Farm (413-458-3121), 643 Simonds Rd. (Rt. 7), Williamstown 01267. Open late Apr.–Oct. Many B&Bs try to cultivate a colonial ambience, but Riverbend Farm doesn't have to try: It's an authentic 1770 former tavern listed on the National Register of Historic Places. The present parlor is the original tavern taproom in which the Battle of Bennington was planned. Owners David and Judy Loomis have lovingly restored the place, uncovering and preserving the wood paneling, wide floorboards, and massive central chimney serving five working fireplaces. Whenever it's cool enough, a fire glows afternoons and evenings in the parlor and is lit in the old "keeping room" or kitchen in time for breakfast. The two common rooms are as comfortable as they are historic, and there is a fridge for guest use. Each of the four guest rooms (one downstairs and three up) reflects careful, scholarly restoration: Period lighting fixtures, latch doors, and

RIVERBEND FARM

Christina Tree

exposed original wallpaper lend authenticity. One of the two shared baths has a claw-footed tub; the other, downstairs, has a slate-lined shower and shelves filled with antique glass bottles, pottery, and jugs. A substantial continental breakfast featuring homemade breads and granola is served in front of the hearth. This is a great place to rent as a whole for reunions. $120 per room, $20 for a third person in a room; $600 for the entire house.

The Guest House at Field Farm (413-458-3135; www.guesthouseat fieldfarm.org), 554 Sloan Rd. (off Rt. 43, near the intersection with Rt. 7), Williamstown 01267. Owned and maintained by the Trustees of Reservations. In 316 upland acres, with a spectacular view of Mount Greylock, Lawrence Bloedel had a house built in 1948 by Edward Goodell that represents, both inside and out, the best of 1950s design. He filled it with furniture to match and with a priceless collection of modern art. Many of the artists were, however, little known at the time they were patronized by Bloedel, a 1923 graduate of Williams College and heir to a fortune earned in the Pacific Northwest and Canada.

Bloedel himself designed and made furniture, some of which survives in the house. He died in 1976; on the death of his wife, Eleanor, the most valuable paintings found their way into museums. Most went to the Whitney in Manhattan, but one of the most moving—*Morning in the City* by Edward Hopper—usually hangs in the Williams College Museum of Art. The property was donated to the Trustees, but without funds to maintain the house. Initially the idea was to tear it down, but preservationists David and Judy Loomis, who had meticulously restored Williamstown's 18th-century tavern as a bed & breakfast, suggested that they might do the same with this exceptional home. Luckily they prevailed, serving as its initial hosts.

Guests will appreciate the enormity of the loss this house would have been. Field Farm's meadows and woods are beautiful, webbed with 4 miles of trails, good for cross-country skiing as well as walking (see *Green Space*), but to stay in this house is a gift. We sat mesmerized at the dining room table, facing the picture window through which clouds quickly shaped and reshaped above Mount Greylock, drifting toward us above the pond and

THE GUEST HOUSE AT FIELD FARM

Trustees of Reservations

landscaped lawns below the house. Beside the living room picture window, which commands the same view, there's a telescope and Eames chair. The room is sparely, comfortably furnished with cleanly lined, bright, and comfortable pieces, some sculpture and paintings. The simple hearth here, as in other rooms, features unusual hand-painted tiles. The cork floors are warmed by copper pipes, corners are rounded, and lighting is recessed. In all there are five guest rooms, and at this writing all except the ground-floor room (a former study, with its own balcony) retain their original furnishings. The large master bedroom with its balcony and glass-faced hearth is the indisputable gem. $150–250 includes a full breakfast and use of the guest pantry to store a picnic and drinks. While weekends are booked far in advance, midweek nights are frequently wide open.

Elsewehere

⊗ ❦ **The Inn at Richmond** (413-698-2566 or 888-968-4748; www.inn atrichmond.com), 802 State Rd. 9 (Rt. 41), Richmond 01254. Handy to Hancock Shaker Village, an attractive inn with three comfortable, elegant guest rooms, three suites, and three cottages on this gentleman's horse farm. Formerly separate from the farm, it's now under the same ownership; guests can take lesssons and ride (see Berkshire Equestrian Center under *Horseback Riding*). All rooms have air-conditioning and phone as well as private bath and queen- or king-sized bed. And there's WiFi throughout the inn. Landscaped grounds include perennial gardens and woodland trails; inside there's an attractive parlor and library. Cottages have fully equipped kitchens, and some suites and cottages have fireplaces and whirlpools. High-season rates are $180–240 for rooms, $190–350 for suites; cottages are $250–380 per night; weekly rates available. All rates except weekly cottage rentals include a full breakfast.

Harbour House Inn (413-743-8959; www.harbourhouseinn.com), 725 N. State Rd. (Rt. 8), Cheshire 01225. Eva and Sam Amuso are warm and welcoming hosts at this mansion-sized country house in the shadow of Mount Greylock. As a stop on the Albany–Springfield stage, it first welcomed guests in 1793, but it was substantially expanded in the 1880s as the manor of a 500-acre gentleman's farm. The name *harbour* refers to safety— this was a known stop for fleeing slaves on the Underground Railroad. With its immense, long sitting room and six guest rooms, it works well as a B&B. The master suite with its fireplace, many windows, and paneling (it was the former library) is beloved by brides, and there is a two-room suite with fireplace and balcony on the third floor. We thoroughly enjoyed a night in Country Sunshine, a comfortable room cleverly decorated in lemon yellow and Wedgwood blue. A full breakfast is served at the long dining room table. The Ashuwillticook Rail Trail, just down the road, runs along Cheshire Reservoir, and the main access road up Mount Greylock and hiking trails in Greylock Glen are both handy. Come to think of it, while it's quite far from anywhere else to stay, Harbour House is handy (because of the way the roads run) to most of Berkshire County and to much of the Hampshire Hilltown area as well. $110–250 in summer and fall; less offseason.

The Porches Inn (413-664-0400; www.porches.com), 231 River St., North Adams 01247. These six wooden row houses, each containing four apartments, were built facing the vast brick Arnold Print Works around 1900. With slate roofs, some shingle detailing under their sharply peaked gables, and distinctive, continuous porches, they were a cut above the city's typical, no-frills workers' housing. The mill across the river (then Sprague Electric) closed in 1985, and the by-then dilapidated row houses continued to deteriorate. Luckily, however, they remained clearly visible from a major gallery in the mill, which reopened in 1999 as MASS MoCA (see *Museums*). Thanks to foresight and funding ($6 million) by Williams College graduate Jack Wadsworth and Berkshire hotelier Nancy Fitzpatrick, the wooden row houses were thoroughly but sensitively renovated to form one of New England's most unusual lodging places. Each building is now painted a different, tasteful color (red, yellow, sage, gray, and blue); together they house 52 guest rooms, including 25 suites.

In contrast with the other Fitzpatrick family properties (the Red Lion Inn in Stockbridge and Blantyre Castle in Lenox), the decor is a combination of sleek contemporary and 1950s funky. Specially designed steel cupboards hiding TVs, DVD players, and mini bars resemble mill lockers; windows are bare except for natural linen ingeniously hung. In the luxurious bathrooms large mirrors, set into the original, battered window frames, hang above marble sinks. Furnishings are simple and comfortable, hung with paint-by-the-number oils, and bedside tables are topped with 1950s futuristic lamps. Top-floor rooms as well as suites feature skylights; suites have a Jacuzzi tub and separate living room; two-bedroom suites feature two baths with

MOTOR INNS AND MOTELS Crowne Plaza Hotel (413-499-2000 or 800-2-CROWNE), Berkshire Common at West St., Pittsfield 01201. This is the Berkshires' only high-rise and very much a part of the county seat. There are 179 rooms, an attractive indoor pool, and **Dewey's Restaurant**. Rooms: $120–289 in summer and fall, off-season $99–149.

🐾 ✈ **North Adams Holiday Inn** (413-663-6500 or 800-HOLIDAY; www.holidayinnberkshires.com), 40 Main St., North Adams 01247. This seven-floor, 87-room hotel, the only place to stay during North Adams's darkest era, has risen to the city's change in status. It's been thoroughly, tastefully renovated. On a downtown site that has been occupied by a hotel since the city's inception, it continues to serve as the heart of town. Rooms vary in configuration, with king beds or two queens. Steeples (see *Eating Out*) serves three meals a day, and there's an indoor pool, sauna, game room, and weight room in the basement. No minimum 2-day stay on

Jacuzzis as well as bedrooms, connected by a spiral staircase, plus a sitting room.

Halls throughout the inn are hung with vintage souvenir plates and memorabilia from the Mohawk Trail. Guests check in at a central reception desk in a row house that also offers two comfortable sitting rooms, one with a fireplace stocked with local reading material, and a large, sunny breakfast room. There's a sauna in the small 1850s River Street house out back, beside the landscaped lap pool that's usable year-round. River Street itself has not been rehabbed, but it's a short, safe walk to downtown restaurants, shorter still to MASS MoCA with its many evening performances.

THE PORCHES INN, NORTH ADAMS

Nicholas Whitman

Frankly, however, enthusiastic as we are about MASS MoCA, we wearied of looking at its vast brick presence and will request a room with a view of the green hill right behind the inn on our next visit. From $170 for an off-season room to $445 for a two-bedroom suite in high season.

weekends except during college graduations. $89–150. Some smokers' rooms.

The 1896 House Inn & Country Motels (413-458-1896 or 888-999-1896; www.1896house.com), Rt. 7, Williamstown 01267. Brookside Motel, the neighboring red barn that housed a restaurant for many decades but has been expanded to include luxury suites, and the Pondside Motel across Rt. 2 are now all under the same ownership. The six "Barnside" suites are elaborately decorated, each evoking a different era or theme. All have a sitting area, gas fireplace, spacious bath with dual whirlpool tubs, TV, DVD/CD player, dataport, and more. They are, however, all rather dark, with windows only at the entrance ($219–289 in-season; off-season from $179). Rooms in the neighboring Brookside Motel are crisp and cheerful. Across the road, Pondside units have been decorated to look more like B&B than motel rooms; the Sweetheart Room has a canopy bed and whirlpool, and a three-room suite has a full kitchen and whirlpool bath ($64–169 for motel rooms; $189–219 for the suite).

✒ ☂ **Jericho Valley Inn** (413-458-9511 or 800-537-4246), 2541 Hancock Rd., Williamstown 01267. This family-owned and -geared motel is 5 miles south of Williamstown on Rt. 43, minutes from skiing at Jiminy Peak. There's a fireplace in the breakfast room off the reception area. The 24 units range from one to three bedrooms, some with efficiencies. There are also several cottages with full kitchens and fireplaces. $68–138 for rooms, $198–288 for suites. Inquire about cottages.

♨ ✒ **Northside Motel** (413-458-8107; www.northsidemotel.com), 45 North St. (Rt. 7), Williamstown 01267. On a prime location in the heart of Williamstown, the motel offers 30 clean units with individually controlled heat and air-conditioning, direct-dial phone, and cable TV; there's a swimming pool. Rooms from $90, including a continental breakfast, served in the original house. Less off-season. No pets, but children under 10 are free; cribs and cots available.

Other Lodging

✒ **The Country Inn at Jiminy Peak** (413-738-5500; outside Massachusetts, 800-882-8859; www.jiminypeak.com), Jiminy Peak, Corey Rd., Hancock 01237. At the base of the ski mountain, this facility offers one-bedroom efficiency suites, also a restaurant and lounge, an outdoor pool, indoor and outdoor whirlpools, and exercise and game room. Each suite has a master bedroom with a king-sized bed, a living room with a queen-sized sleep sofa, two cable TVs, a bath, a powder room, and a fully equipped kitchen. Two- and three-bedroom condominiums are also available. Units are nicely laid out and furnished. $159–229; larger units run $229–599. Rates are based on double occupancy. Children 13 and younger stay free. See *Skiing*, *Biking*, and *For Families*.

✳ Where to Eat

DINING OUT

In Williamstown

Mezze Bistro & Bar (413-458-0123; www.mezzeinc.com), 16 Water St. Open for dinner nightly, until 9 weekdays, 10 on weekends. Reserve. Nancy Thomas's popular bistro has a seasonal deck overlooking the Green River, and the decor is sophisticated and appealing. It's been awhile now since Mezze burned down, reopened a few doors up, and once more established itself as the town's most popular dining venue. Staff are adept at getting patrons out before the curtain rises, but if you aren't seeing the night's play you might want to book *at*, not before, 8 PM. Chef James Tracey draws as heavily as possible on local produce. You might begin with red, golden, and candy-striped beets with goat cheese and tarragon ($9), then dine on pepper-crusted duck legs with mustard greens and figs. Entrées $22–29. "Casual Fare," available in both the bar and main dining room, is $13–16. There's also a wide choice of wine by the glass as well as the bottle, plus delectable desserts.

♨ ✒ **Hobson's Choice** (413-458-9101), 159 Water St. Open 5–9:30 for dinner. A friendly, unpretentious roadhouse-style restaurant with old-fashioned wooden booths. The ground floor of an 1830s house is the setting for the most popular, moderately priced place to dine in town. Recently expanded, it's now easier to get into than in years past and just as good. The menu is vast, ranging from vegetarian pasta to prime rib, with plenty of seafood and chicken options. All dinners include the big salad bar as well as starch and vegetable. Beers and specialty drinks. Entrées are $14–24.

Yasmin's Restaurant at The Orchards (413-458-9611), 222 Adams Rd. (Rt. 2). Open for lunch and dinner, Sunday brunch. An elegant formal dining room serving basically Continental cuisine. Tables are set with Irish linen and decorated with fresh flowers; there is also patio dining in the garden, weather permitting. The menu changes frequently but might include quails stuffed with sweet potatoes and cashews on mango-chili chutney, or mustard-crusted rack of lamb. Dinner entrées $19–31.

Le Jardin (413-458-8032), 777 Cold Spring Rd. (Rt. 2 west of the village). We're delighted to see Chef Walter Hayn still in charge of this long-famous kitchen that's recently seen a renovated building and an infusion of capital from Jae Chung (of Jae's Inn fame) and other investors. The menu includes tournedos of beef Bordelaise and sole meunière, but there's also plenty of pasta. Lunch options include blackened tuna salad and a BLT (for $8.95). Dinner entrées $15.95–21.95. The wine list—which includes French champagnes—ranges widely, including choices by the glass.

The Williams Inn (413-458-9371), Main St. The formal inn dining room remains a favorite with many. It's a traditional American menu with such entrées as roast pork tenderloin Shaker-style ($17.25), New England scrod baked with tomatoes and smoth-ered leeks topped with choron sauce ($17.50), and roast rack of lamb ($24.95). Sunday brunch is a buffet and huge.

In North Adams
🦐 **Jae's Inn** (413-664-0100), 1111 South St. (Rt. 8 south). Open for lunch Mon.–Sat. and for dinner nightly. Jae Chung is a North Adams native who established a reputation as a restaurateur in Boston. His brightly, sleekly decorated, popular restaurant features broadly Oriental dishes, spicy Korean beef stew, pad Thai, noodle dishes, and tempura as well as a wide choice of sushi. Entrées $8.95–25.

Gramercy Bistro (413-663-5300), 24 Marshall St. Open Mon.–Thu. 5–9, until 10 Fri.–Sun. Closed Tue. Sandy Smith's storefront restaurant sits invitingly across from MASS MoCA. It's been recently expanded to fill a second storefront featuring a creative American menu with local ingredients. A recent menu offered eight entrée choices, from smoked mozzarella ravioli with red pepper, spinach, and grilled eggplant ($18) to a seafood paella ($23). Good bread and herb olive oil, and nice atmosphere.

🍴 ♿ **Café Latino** (413-662-2004), 1111 MASS MoCA Way. Open for dinner Tue.–Sat. 5–9; for lunch daily 11:30–3. Dinner reservations recommended. In the museum courtyard but a separate entity, this zany bistro is under the same ownership as popular Mezze in Williamstown. Lunch on crispy calamari or a quesadilla with roasted tomatoes, yellow chiles, and goat cheese. A similar menu is available at dinner, featuring family-style meals like slow-roasted Peruvian-style chicken ($26) and grilled guava skirt steak ($30), serving two to four people.

Gideon's Fine Dining (413-664-9449; www.gideonsrestaurant.com), 34 Holden St. Open for dinner Tue.–Sat. Plenty of atmosphere and a large à la carte menu. Appetizers range from BBQ duck spring rolls to eggplant cannelloni. Entrées ($10.95–27.95) include gnocchi Alfredo with chicken and spinach, grilled vegetable strudel, rib-eye steak, and herb-encrusted rack of lamb. Also see Gideon's Luncheon and Nightery under *Eating Out*.

Milan 55 Restaurant (413-664-9955), 55 Main St. Open for dinner except Sun. and Mon. This is an à la carte northern Italian menu with antipasto and a choice of "insalata," many pastas, and some veal and steak dishes. Entrées $17–26.

In Pittsfield

☞ **Spice** (413-443-1234; www.spice-restaurant.com), 297 North St. Reserve. Open Mon.–Sat., later in the lounge. In 2006 Spice became the first upscale restaurant on North Street, the city's main drag. According to owner Joyce Bernstein, it all began because she offered a free space to Starbucks in her building—and they turned her down. So she decided to open her version, but "went crazy." The 135-seat restaurant is hung with striking paintings by local artists, and tables are dressed in linen. Chef Douglas Luf, formerly of the Red Lion Inn, offers "familiar food with a twist." The dozen or so entrées ($16–29) might include a tomato-saffron fish stew with chorizo and spring vegetables, and a maple-glazed duck breast with caramelized fennel and confit hash. A lighter menu is served in the lounge, which features an extensive list of wines by the glass; the children's menu is $5. Initially there were complaints of inept service, but we assume all will be smooth by the time you read this.

Trattoria Rustica (413-499-1192), 26 McKay St. Open for dinner daily except Tue. Reservations suggested. Davide Manzo hails from Pompeii and is a purist when it comes to things Italian (even the floor tiles); likewise, the authenticity of everything, bread included, emerging from his brick oven. The menu might include just half a dozen choices of antipasti, pasta, and "secondi." You might begin with Caprese (homemade mozzarella, fresh basil, tomato, and olive oil), then dine on homemade ricotta-stuffed ravioli in tomato basil sauce, or oven-roasted veal loin chop. Entrées range from $12 (for penne in tomato sauce) to $28 (for oven-roasted rack of lamb). Nightly specials frequently include exotica such as buffalo steak or wild boar.

Sabor Bar & Grill (413-445-5465; www.saborbarandgrill.com), 17 Wendell Ave. Extension. Open for dinner except Mon. Chef-owner Paul Saldana, a veteran of top Berkshire restaurants, has opened his own place, featuring his native Ecuadorian

GRAMERCY BISTRO

Kim Grant

fare. Judging from the Pernil—a traditional dish of roast pork served with cheese potato cake, fava beans, and encebollado—this is a winner. Our choices included BBQ ribs with mango radish salsa, a classic paella, and several fish dishes. Entrées $13.50–25. Inquire about club nights, featuring Latin music ($5 cover).

Brix Wine Bar (413-236-9463; www .brixwinebar.com), 40 West St. Open nightly from 5 PM. As authentic as a French wine bar can be in the Berkshires: The zinc bar was hand carved in Paris by one of the last craftsmen to produce them, and red as well as white wines are kept at their proper temperatures in a "cave" behind the bar. Some 40 wines are offered by the glass; each bottle is air-sealed after opening to prevent degeneration. Some 200 labels are available. Needless to say, no one is rushed here, and friends meet for "wine flights" (samplings of four wines), hors d'oeuvres, "les sandwiches," and light entrées such as tuna Niçoise or shredded duck with white bean salad over field greens ($9–12).

Kim's Dragon Restaurant (413-442-5594), 1231 West Housatonic St. Open daily 4–10; closed Mon. in winter. A great spot! The ingredients are fresh and local, and the flavors are distinct. You might begin with Saigon noodle soup or a bowl of lemongrass soup, then dine on scrod crisped with fresh tomatoes, onions, and nuoc mam on a crêpe filled with seasonal vegetables, or on shrimp sautéed with curry, onions, noodles, coconut milk, and peanuts. Beer and wine are served.

Mazzeo's (413-448-2095), 7 Winter St. Open for dinner Wed.–Sun. Reservations suggested. A local favorite, secreted just off the main

Christina Tree

SPICE, A PITTSFIELD RESTAURANT

drag. To find it, turn off East Street at Wendy's. An old-fashioned Italian restaurant with many antipasti and house specialties that include eggplant Parmesan and vegetable lasagna. Entrées $13.95–21.95.

Elizabeth's Café Pizzeria (413-448-8244), 1264 East St. (across from the GE plant). Open Wed.–Sun. for dinner. Expanded from its original modest beginnings, still an interesting eatery. Soups are great; real Italian polenta is a specialty. There are marvelous salads.

Dakota Steak House (413-499-7900), Rt. 7, Lenox–Pittsfield line. Open for dinner daily and Sunday brunch. There is a fieldstone fireplace in the dining room, which is supposed to resemble an Adirondack lodge. Specialties include seafood, hand-cut steaks, and mesquite-grilled fish, along with some heart-healthy choices. Dinner entrées range from $10.95 for ground sirloin to 20.95 for prime rib.

Elsewhere

Mill and the Floss (413-458-9123), Rt. 7, New Ashford. Dinner nightly except Mon. A long-established favorite among Berkshire regulars, this 18th-century farmhouse with an open kitchen specializes in French country cuisine. Entrées might include crabcakes in Dijon sauce, tournedos béarnaise, and rack of lamb; $23–28.

EATING OUT

In Pittsfield

Pittsfield Brew Works (413-442-3506), 34 Depot St. Open 11 AM–midnight except Mon. The yeasty aroma from the brewing vats hits you as you open the door into this large and appealing pub, which offers a vast, varied, and reasonably priced menu as well as 10 of its own constantly changing brews.

The Lantern (413-448-2171), 455 North St. Open for all three meals except Sunday. A landmark local eatery, great hot corned beef and New York pastrami sandwiches, soups, and salads.

On a Roll Café (413-236-5671), 75 North St. Open weekdays 7–3. Hidden away in the middle of the "Central Block" (a shortcut from the parking garage to North Street), this is a cheery space with a great choice of salads, quesadillas, and individual pizzas as well as a frittata of the day.

Hot Dog Ranch (413-499-0055), 20 Linden St., Pittsfield. Open from 11 for lunch and dinner daily, serving until 11 PM Sat. and Sun. A must for hot dog connoisseurs. These are baby hot dogs, served in the flakiest of buns, slathered with onions, mustard, and the mystery sauce that has made this a local favorite for generations. We lunched on two hot dogs and a Coke for a grand total of $3.

Brazillian Restaurant and Pub (413-236-9100), McKay Street. Open for lunch 11–3, dinner 5–10. What's available here varies with the day and is all presented cafeteria-style so that you can select what you like the looks of. The selection might include chicken with rice, beans and bacon, cabbage, yucca, sausage, and such.

Café Reva (413-442-6161), 238 Tyler St. Open Wed.–Mon. 6–2. Chef-owner Aura Whitman established her reputation at Seven Hills in Lenox but decided to call her own hours when she became a mother. The cheerful storefront eatery is frequently packed but worth a try. Breakfast all day on a "frittata of the moment" or a huge choice of omelets, pancakes, and waffles.

Bellissimo Dolce (413-443-1792), 444 North St. Open daily 6–6 weekdays, from 7 Sat. and 11 on Sun. Open later on summer weekends. "I grew up here through the boom years and then the depressed years and I'm watching the city come alive again," says Beverly Dubiski, co-owner of this popular café where everyone gathers. The atmosphere is genuine European-style with plenty of baked goods—including cannolis, sfogliatelle, and biscotti—as well as (seasonal) salads and "mouth-watering brown bag lunches to go"—or stay.

House of India (413-443-3262), 261 North St. Open daily for lunch and buffet, and for dinner. This is a local favorite with a great selection of lamb and vegetarian dishes, kebabs, and Indian breads. Lunch specials are $6.95 and the lunch buffet, $8.55.

Court Square (413-442-9896), 95 East St., Pittsfield. Open daily for breakfast, lunch, and Sunday brunch. Full breakfast menu and many salads and sandwiches; also known for pies.

Patrick's Pub (413-499-1994), 26 Bank Row. Open for lunch and dinner; closed Sun. Dark, pubby atmosphere. Sandwiches and wraps at lunch, reasonably priced staples such as baked stuffed sole and honey-Dijon chicken at dinner.

The Highland (413-442-2457), 100 Fenn St. An oasis for the frugal diner since 1936. Open for lunch and dinner; closed Mon. Reasonably priced road food, fully licensed. No credit cards, no reservations, no pretensions.

In Williamstown
See **Hobson's Choice** under *Dining Out*. It's the best dinner value.

Papa Charlie's Deli and Sandwich Shop (413-458-5969), 28 Spring St. Open from breakfast through dinner. Overstuffed sandwiches and bagels, many named for actors at the Williamstown Theatre Festival and other notables, are what this place is about, and in off-hours it's a great place to play student, even if you aren't one, sipping slowly and reading a book in a deep wooden booth. The overflow basement area is less inviting.

Helen's Place (413-458-1360), 60 Spring St. Open Tue.–Fri. 11–6:30, Sat. 11–4; open summer Sun. 11–4 but otherwise closed Sun. and Mon. A spacious, friendly haven specializing in Boar's Head deli sandwiches, a variety of salads, and a vegetable and juice bar.

Sushi Thai Garden (413-458-0004), 27 Spring St. Open for lunch and dinner daily. An attractive atmosphere and reasonably priced, fresh, and tasty food are an irresistible combination. The menu features both Thai and Japanese dishes. Dine on tamarind tofu or duck, steamed ginger salmon, or a variety of sushi and sashimi.

☙ **Chef's Hat** (413-458-5120), 905 Simonds Rd. (Rt. 7, north of town). Open for breakfast from 6:30 (7 on Sun.) and lunch until 3; closed Mon. The Pudvar family will tell you that if you know where to look, the original diner car is still here, but they have expanded, adding knotty pine and booths. Locals crowd in on weekends to breakfast on hash and eggs (steak and eggs is also on the menu) and a wide choice of omelets and pancakes, diner classics like a hot turkey sandwich, and liver and onions; also salads, stir-fries, and a surprising variety of fish and seafood. The children's menu features a foot-long hot dog with fries.

Cozy Corner Restaurant (413-458-3854), 850 Simonds Rd. (Rt. 7). Breakfast, lunch, and dinner daily. An unpretentious roadhouse with low prices and a loyal following. Fish-and-chips and pizza; also Greek specialties

BEVERLY DUBISKI, CO-OWNER OF PITTS-FIELD'S POPULAR BELLISSIMO DOLCE

Christina Tree

including a great eggplant. A selection of beers. Our Mediterranean-style cod was delicious.

Tavern Menu at the Williams Inn (413-458-9371), 1090 Main St. Served 11:30 AM–10 PM, Sun. until 9:30. The large tavern area is known for its "Berkshire burger"; also good for tavern stew, the plowman's plate, and soups and sandwiches.

✒ **Michael's Restaurant** (413-458-2114), 460 Main St. (Rt. 2). Open Tue.–Sun. for dinner from 4. Charles (the original Papa Charlie) opened this place as an A&W root beer stand more than 40 years ago. Now his children, Cindy and Michael, continue to run the area's favorite Greek restaurant. Friendly atmosphere, booths, good beers on tap, and all the classics: spanakopita, salads, seafood with kalamata olives and garlic, terrific soups. Honestly, however, we were disappointed in the eggplant.

Spice Root (413-458-5200), 23 Spring St. Open daily for lunch and dinner. Lunch on mulligatawny soup and honey sesame nan or poori. You'll also find plenty of lamb and vegetarian dishes, a $6.95 buffet lunch, and dinner-to-go for the same price.

Purple Pub (413-458-3306), Bank St. (just off Spring St.). Open for lunch and dinner, until 1 AM weekends. This hospitable little place really feels like a pub. You'll get good sandwiches and burgers, daily specials, and fast and friendly service. There is a small outdoor dining area.

✒ **Misty Moonlight Diner** (413-458-3305), 408 Main St. (Rt. 2). A family restaurant with a contrived but pleasant 1950s atmosphere with a jukebox. Open 7 AM–10 PM, and serves breakfast all day as well as a large choice of burgers, sandwiches, vegetarian dishes, BBQ ribs and chicken, pastas, and fried seafood, also daily specials. Fancy rum as well as nonalcoholic smoothies and margaritas are also house specialties, and there's a choice of beer on tap.

Lickety Split (413-458-1818), 69 Spring St. This lunch place offers good soups, sandwiches, and salads.

Tunnel City Cafe (413-458-5010), 100 Spring St. Open 6:30 AM–6 PM. With coffees, teas, light snacks, and WiFi, this big, pleasant café at the far end of Spring St. is understandably a big student hangout.

Chopsticks (413-458-5750), 412 Main St. (Rt. 2). Open daily for lunch and dinner. An established and popular restaurant with a large menu featuring Japanese, Chinese, and Korean dishes. The lounge specializes in "exotic tropical drinks" and also carries imported Chinese beers. Lunch specials are $5.35.

Water Street Grill (413-458-2175), 123 Water St. Open for lunch and dinner. A more formal Grill and an informal Tavern. There's a weekday lunch buffet in the Grill as well as sandwiches, salads, and burgers. Dine on grilled chicken, or have a grilled eggplant dinner in the Tavern. We had a bad experience, however, on our last visit and found that no one we mentioned it to was surprised. Hopefully this old standby will rebound.

Also see **The Store at Five Corners** under *Selective Shopping*.

In North Adams

✒ **Boston Sea Foods** (413-663-8740), 100 American Legion Dr. Open for lunch and dinner except Mon. Just off Main St., this is a classic family-style seafood restaurant, which doesn't mean you can't get a burger, Reuben, or chicken teriyaki. Specialties include baked salmon with lobster stuffing and a seafood casserole, Same menu all day. Beers on tap and full liquor.

Gideon's Luncheon and Nightery (413-664-0404), 23 Eagle St. Lunch and dinner Tue.–Sat. The former storefront is deep, dimly lit, and attractive, with a long bar and comfortable seating. The all-day menu includes a wide choice of panini, sandwiches, and light entrées such as white lasagna and chicken fra diavolo. The same menu works upstairs, a venue for live entertainment.

Freight Yard Pub (413-663-6547), Western Gateway Heritage State Park. Open 1:30–11. An informal place, this pub has something of a sports-bar atmosphere. Burgers, ribs, seafood, and Italian dishes are always on the menu. Locally made kielbasa is a specialty, and there is an outdoor dining patio.

✐ **Jack's Hot Dogs** (413-664-9006), 12 Eagle St. (off Main St.). Lunch, dinner, and noshing in between. A local institution that's been in the same family for more than seven decades. If you like hot dogs with all the trimmings (including sauerkraut), Jack's is the place.

✐ **Steeples** (413-664-6581), 40 Main St. (the Holiday Inn). Open for all three meals. A big, cheerful dining room with terrace tables in summer, checked tablecloths, friendly waitstaff. The menu is family geared and priced, from tenderloin tips to baked stuffed shrimp. All entrées include pasta fasoli, house salad, vegetable, and starch.

✐ **Isabella's** (413-662-2239), 896 State Rd. (Rt. 2 next to Stop & Shop). Open for dinner except Sunday. A cheerful atmosphere with dining on the outdoor deck, weather permitting.

Brewhaha (413-664-2020), 20 Marshall St., North Adams. Daily except Wed., 7–5. An attractive café across from MASS MoCA. Breakfast all day with espresso and teas.

Hickory Bill's Barbeque (413-663-6665), 20 Holden St. Open 11:30 AM–8 PM. This is a tiny place with a big take-out following but also room to sit down and tackle BBQ kielbasa as well as spare- and baby back ribs and sweet potato pie.

Elsewhere

✐ **Miss Adams Diner** (413-743-5303), 53 Park St. (Rt. 8), Adams. Open weekdays 10–10, Fri. 10–2 AM, Sat. 8 AM–2 AM, Sun. 8–2:30 PM. After a stint as a Jack's Hot Dogs spin-off, this landmark has been recently expanded and restored. The 1940s classic (Worcester lunch car No. 821) is now owned by Jae Chung but with a traditional diner menu, homemade shepherd's pie, blue plate specials.

✳ **Entertainment**

Also see *The Arts*.

Williamstown Community Theatre and the college's **Williams Theater** perform during winter months.

Sterling and Francine Clark Art Institute presents a variety of films, lectures, and plays throughout the year.

Little Cinema (413-443-7171), 39 South St., Pittsfield. This 300-seat theater in the Berkshire Museum features art and classic films.

Images Cinema (413-458-5612), 40 Spring St., Williamstown. A classic college-town movie house showing foreign films and interesting domestic ones.

✳ Selective Shopping

ANTIQUES SHOPS The Library Antiques (413-458-3436 or 800-294-4798), 70 Spring St., Williamstown. Open daily. An ever-expanding series of spaces filled with fine antiques of all sorts, as well as many unusual gifts. Browsers welcome.

Saddleback Antiques Center (413-458-5852), 1395 Cold Spring Rd. (Rt. 7), Williamstown. Closed Wed. in winter. A dealers' group shop in an old schoolhouse. All manner of antiques, including furniture, pottery, and posters.

Collector's Warehouse (413-458-9686), 105 North St. (Rt. 7), Williamstown. Open Wed.–Fri. 10–3, Sat. 10–5. Miscellaneous antiques and collectibles, including glassware, jewelry, frames, dolls, linen, and furniture.

BOOKSTORES Papyri Books (413-662-2099; www.papyribooks.com), 49 Main St., North Adams. Lois and Michael Daunis now maintain this oasis for book lovers: mostly used books but some new titles with inviting seating and a full schedule of readings, signings, and music. There's also art on the first Friday of every month, and open mike on the second Saturday. Check out literary events sponsored by neighboring Inkberry (www.inkberry.org).

Water Street Books (413-458-8071), 26 Water St., Williamstown. The town's independent, full-service bookstore.

Barnes & Noble (413-496-9051), Berkshire Crossing Mall, Rt. 9, Pittsfield. A superstore and a Starbucks.

GALLERIES

In North Adams

Kolok Gallery (413-664-7381; www.kolokgallery.com), 121 Union St. (Rt. 2), Suite 1E. Open Thu.–Sun. afternoons. This classy new contemporary gallery in the Windsor Mill mounts changing exhibitions of contemporary work.

MCLA's Gallery 51 (413-662-5362), 51 Main St., North Adams. Open daily in summer, Wed.–Sun. off-season. Shows change monthly, featuring works by faculty and students at the Massachsuetts College of Liberal Arts, also locally based artists.

Eclipse Mill (413-664-9101; www.eclipsemill.com), 234 Union St. (Rt. 2). This new complex of artist lofts and galleries holds gallery hours on weekends, noon–5.

Contemporary Artists Center (413-663-9550 or 413-663-9555; www.thecac.org), Historic Beaver Mill, 189 Beaver St. A nonprofit studio and workshop facility. On the way to the Natural Bridge. Call for hours for this and the adjacent **Dark Ride Project**,

PAPYRI BOOKS IN NORTH ADAMS

Kim Grant

a 10-minute ride on the "sensory integrator" during which hooded passengers view abstract imagery. Eric Rudd is the creator of this and of **A Chapel for Humanity**, an installation of 150 life-sized figures and more than 50 ceiling panels in a former 1890s church at 82 Summer St.

In Pittsfield

Lichenstein Center for the Arts (413-499-9348), 28 Renne Ave., Pittsfield. Open Mon.–Fri. 11–5, Sat. from noon. Just behind the vest-pocket park on Main St., a handsome gallery hosting exhibitions by nationally known professionals; also the setting for performances and concerts.

Berkshire Fine Handcrafts (413-441-6926), 431 North St. This large new gallery features a surprising variety of items, most of them locally crafted. Well worth a stop.

Gallery Boreas (917-743-6548; www.galleryboreas.com), 439 North St. Open Thu. 3–7, Fri. 1–5. The newest, edgiest gallery in town, so fresh from Brooklyn it doesn't have a Berkshire phone.

In Williamstown

The Harrison Gallery (413-458-1700; www.theharrisongallery.com), 39 Spring St. Changing exhibits of work by a stable of established artists.

Plum Gallery (413-458-3389; www.plumgallery.com), 112 Water St. Changing exhibits of contemporary art and ceramics.

SPECIAL STORES

In Williamstown

Where'd You Get That? (413-458-2206), 100 Spring St., Williamstown. Open daily. Ken and Michele Gietz are enthusiastic purveyors of some

wild toys geared to children of all ages: strategy games, gizmos, gadgets.

The Mountain Goat (413-458-8445), 130 Water St. The founding store in what's become an upcountry chain specializing in outdoor clothing, equipment, and bicycles (rentals, too); also local books and plenty of advice about where to do whatever you do outdoors. Inquire about special events including rock climbing and mountain bike camp.

The Store at Five Corners (413-458-3176 or 800-261-4245), in South Williamstown at the junction of Rts. 7 and 43. This hip general store has a good deli (and café tables); specializes in gifts, gift baskets, and specialty foods.

In Pittsfield

Jim's House of Shoes (413-442-0781), 235–239 North St., Pittsfield. This family-owned and -geared shoe store is a real find, especially for people with hard-to-fit feet. Stock ranges from children through oldsters with a large bargain section in the middle of the store. We had searched through the Boston area for shoes we found here at a prices we couldn't believe.

USBluesware (413-442-5533; http://usbluesware.com), 141 North St., Pittsfield. Open Mon.–Fri. 9–4. Essentially a warehouse stocked with "new," preowned designer clothing—Chanel, Christian Dior, Prada, Versace, and the like—most of it sold online throughout the world but also off the rack here. Both quality and prices are outstanding.

Wild Sage (413-447-7000), 333 North St., Pittsfield. This eclectic combination of reasonably priced "antiques," used books (7,500 titles), and original art (in a room titled "Le Petit Musee") is a good rainy-day stop.

Elsewhere
Galabriel's (413-664-0026), 105 Main St., North Adams. Closed Mon. Comfortable, wearable, reasonably priced women's clothing, mostly natural fibers; also beaded and sterling-silver jewelry.

The Interior Alternative (413-743-1986), 5 Hoosac St., Adams. A genuine factory outlet with a wide selection of Waverly fabrics, also some wallpaper, bedding, Oriental and area rugs.

✳ Farms and Flowers

In Cheshire
& **Lightwing Farms** (413-743-4425), Rt. 8, site of Saturday farmer's market, 10–4. Also open July–early Oct. for vegetables, flowers, and honey. No pesticides or herbicides.

✺ **Whitney's Farm Stand** (413-442-4749), Rt. 8, 2.5 miles north of Berkshire Mall. Open Easter to Christmas,

USBLUESWARE IS A POPULAR NEW DESTINATION CLOTHING STORE IN PITTSFIELD.
Christina Tree

home-grown fruits and vegetables including melons, sweet corn, and apples; also bedding plants, perennials, a deli, a bakery, a dairy bar, and a petting zoo. PYO blueberries and pumpkins in-season.

In Hancock
✺ **Ioka Valley Farm** (413-738-5915; www.taconic.net/IokaValleyFarm), 3475 Rt. 43, near Jiminy Peak. Call ahead for seasonal hours. Uncle Don's Barnyard and seasonal events, especially at Halloween with a corn maze outside and a very dark hay bale maze inside the barn. Major fun. Also seasonal maple syrup and a pancake café. PYO strawberries mid-June through mid-July, pumpkins in fall, cider and apples, farm-theme playground, picnic area.

In Lanesborough
Lakeview Orchard (413-448-6009; www.lakevieworchard.com), 34 Old Cheshire Rd. Open early July–Thanksgiving. From Rt. 8, take Old State Rd. to Summer St. to Old Cheshire Rd.; from Rt. 7, take Summer St. to Old Cheshire. Sixteen varieties of apples, sweet cherries, peaches, plums, blueberries, shallots, onions, homemade doughnuts, pies and turnovers, jams, apple butter, sweet cider pressed in-season. A beautiful location.

Mountain View Farm (413-445-7642), Old Cheshire Rd. (see directions above). Open mid-June through Oct. Sweet corn, PYO tomatoes and strawberries in-season. Another beautiful location.

In Williamstown
✺ **Green River Produce** (413-458-2470), on Rt. 43 at its junction with Rt. 7. PYO strawberries, blueberries, tomatoes, and peppers. Full green-

house and nursery. Corn, summer squash, tomatoes, winter squash, Indian corn, pumpkins, and cider press in-season. Petting farm and hayrides.

In Richmond
Bartlett's Orchard (413-698-2559; www.bartlettsorchard.com), 575 Swamp Rd. Four miles south on Barker Rd. from Rt. 20. Open year-round, daily, 8–5:30. Generations of Bartletts have grown, sold, and shipped apples from these 52 hillside acres. There are 18 varieties of apples plus a full bakery (try the cider doughnuts) and specialty foods; also milk, bread, ice cream, and more.

Furnace Brook Winery at Hilltop Orchards (413-698-3262; www.hill toporchards.com), 508 Canaan Rd. off Rt. 41 (look for sign). Open Fri.–Sun. 9–5. Wine tasting. Varietal grape and specialty wines and Johnny Mash Hard Cider. PYO apples, pears, plums in summer and fall, picnics encouraged, special events. Also apple brandy, preserves, vegetables in-season, sweet corn, eggs, and dairy products. Johnny Mash (www.johnny mash.com) is oak-aged hard cider.

✳ Special Events
February: **Winter Weekend at Hancock Shaker Village** (www.hancock shakervillage.org) offers hands-on ice harvesting and special activities for children.

April: **Williamstown Jazz Festival** (www.williamstownjazz.com) features world-class performers, college jazz bands, jazz dance, lectures, and more.

🐑 *April–mid-June:* **New Life on the Farm**. A barn is filled with baby sheep, hatching chicks, kids, piglets, and other new livestock with mothers.

Exhibition organized by New England Heritage Breeds Conservancy.

May: **Memorial Day Parade** in North Adams.

June–December: **First Friday Art Walks** (413-664-6180) with music and food, late-night shopping.

Late June: **North Berkshire Food Festival** (413-664-6180), North Adams. **Sheep Shearing Weekend** at Hancock Shaker Village illustrates the entire sheep-to-shawl process with hand spinning, shearing, weaving and dyeing, sheep show, ice cream socials.

July 4: Pittsfield boasts one of the biggest **Fourth of July parades** in the country, nationally televised.

Mid-July: **Eagle Street Beach Wednesday** (413-664-6180), North Adams. The length of Eagle Street is turned into a beach, sand from curb to curb. Sand sculpting competition.

July–August: **Concerts** Tuesday evenings at the Clark Art Institute in Williamstown; every Wednesday at 7 in North Adams by Windsor Lake (rain date the following Sunday); and Thursday at 7 at the Western Gateway Heritage State Park.

Late July–early August: **Susan B. Anthony Days** commemorate the suffragette, who was born in Adams. Main Street is closed off and filled with booths, games, and food stalls.

August: **Adams Agricultural Fair. Hancock Shaker Village Antiques Show**, with a major array of Shaker, American, and European antiques displayed in the Round Stone Barn (*mid- to late month*). **Berkshire Children's Circus** (413-499-4660), Patterson Field House, Berkshire Community College, North Adams. A one-ring circus culminates the summer camp's skill building: tumbling, cycling, juggling, trapeze skills, etc., by performers ages 8–15 (*late month*).

Late September: **Country Fair and Crafts Festival at Hancock Shaker Village**, featuring New England Heritage Breeds Conservancy Exhibition of Heritage Livestock, crafts, lawn games, daily parade of animals.

October: **Northern Berkshire Fall Foliage Festival** in North Adams includes races, games, suppers, and sales and culminates with a big parade that traditionally coincides with peak foliage colors (*first weekend*). **Mount Greylock Ramble** is a traditional mass climb of "their" mountain by Adams residents (*Columbus Day weekend*). **Williamstown Film Festival** (www.williamstownfilmfest.com) honors major figures in American cinema (*mid- to late month*).

First weekend in December: **Christmas at Hancock Shaker Village** boasts free afternoon oxen- and horse-drawn wagon and sleigh rides, demonstrations, and make-your-own toys.

ALONG THE MOHAWK TRAIL

Beyond North Adams the Berkshire Hills rise steeply on the east, traversed by one of the country's first roads designed specifically for auto touring.

The Mohawk Trail, as this stretch of Rt. 2 is known, loosely (very loosely) shadows an ancient Indian trail that ran from the Hoosac Valley up over the Hoosac Range and along a wooded ridge, then dropped down into the wide Deerfield River Valley and followed the Deerfield to the Connecticut River Valley. In the late 18th century both a toll road and a "shunpike" traversed this high country, an era evoked by the fine old houses along the Deerfield in Charlemont and by the Charlemont Inn, built in 1787 to accommodate stagecoach traffic.

"Peaks of one or two thousand feet rush up either bank of the river in ranges, thrusting out their shoulders side by side . . . I have never driven through such romantic scenery, where there was such a variety and boldness of mountain shapes as this," Nathaniel Hawthorne wrote in 1850.

For all practical purposes, however, north Berkshire County continued to be isolated from eastern Massachusetts until the opening of the 4.75-mile-long Hoosac Tunnel in 1875. In the first decades of the 20th century the speediest, safest way from Boston to North Adams was still by train through the Hoosac Tunnel. By then, however, rail travel was old hat.

Everyone wanted to escape the narrow dictates of the rails and to get off on their own four wheels. Cars could drive from Greenfield to Charlemont and then along the Deerfield River, but there they met the same mountain that had stumped railroad builders for so long. Already motor traffic (almost all recreational at the time) was flowing along "Jacob's Ladder" (present Rt. 20) and into South Berkshire instead. The city fathers of North Adams rose to the challenge and on October 22, 1914,

THIS POSTCARD DEPICTS A VERMONT FAMILY ENJOYING A PICNIC ON WHITCOMB SUMMIT SOON AFTER THE 1914 OPENING OF THE MOHAWK TRAIL.

Muddy River Press

LIFE'S A PICNIC ON THE MOHAWK TRAIL

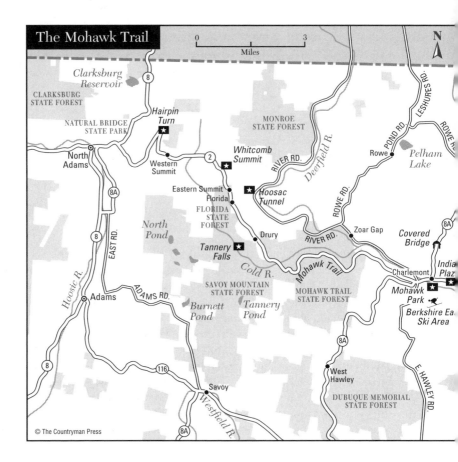

The Mohawk Trail

15 miles of carefully graded (no more than 7 percent), unpaved, but well-oiled road over Hoosac Mountain was formally dedicated and hailed by the *North Adams Transcript* as a "symphony of sylvan delight." In 1921 the eastern end of this "Mohawk Trail" was rerouted from less dramatic Shelburne Road to climb over a high shoulder of Greenfield Mountain. Given the absence of official route numbers (the U.S. Highway System was adopted in 1926), white-and-red-striped markings for the Mohawk Trail extended east much of the way to Boston. The present Mohawk Trail officially extends from Williamstown to Millers Falls.

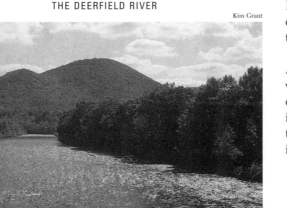

THE DEERFIELD RIVER

Kim Grant

It's the 38 miles between North Adams and Greenfield, however, that we focus on here. This was the stretch of the trail recognized as a destination in its own right from the 1920s through 1950s, a period during which it sprouted tea shops and gift shops,

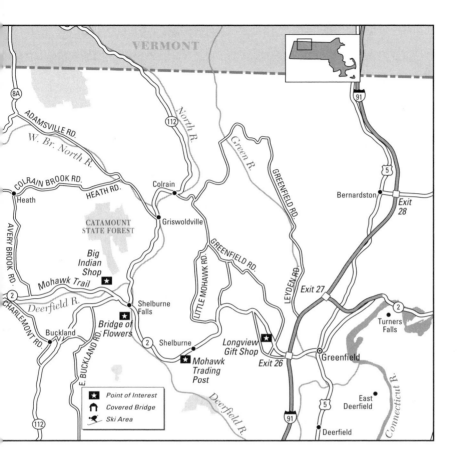

motor courts, motels, and campgrounds (both private and state), and seasonally accommodated more than 1,000 tourists.

Take its very name and theme. Ignoring the century in which this route evolved as an 18th- and 19th-century way west, *Mohawk Trail* conjures up the narrow path blazed by Indians, not even local Indians (the Mahicans on the western side and Pocumtucks on the eastern side of the Hoosac Range) but the more famous marauders from (present) upstate New York who used it as a warpath.

In 1914 America's first affordable cars were just beginning to transform the way ordinary folks vacationed (between 1908 and 1927, 15 million Model T's were produced). In the 1920s motor touring along the Mohawk Trail increased dramatically, and many of the surviving trading posts were built. "Tourists" drove their first cars over the trail and returned year after year.

Over the years the road broadened and was further rerouted, and cars picked up speed. Always to some degree a day trip, the Mohawk Trail gradually lost its status as a destination, and today it's promoted primarily as a foliage route. Several of the old motor courts were replaced by motels but most simply disappeared, along with vintage restaurants and tearooms. Attractions along the Trail are small, family-owned businesses, and in many cases they have just been hanging on.

The tourist tide is once more turning. White-water rafting on the Deerfield River now fills motels and cabins as well as a number of B&Bs and the 18th-century Charlemont Inn. The village of Shelburne Falls, known since the 1920s for its "Bridge of Flowers," is now the major dining and shopping center for the Trail, which went straight through the middle of the village until the 1950s. With its long-overdue recognition as a scenic corridor has come funding for making the Trail more visitor-friendly, but at this writing there are no signs suggesting where to turn off for the best views or how to find natural attractions such as Tannery Falls.

Like the Mohawk Trail itself, this chapter links Berkshire and Franklin Counties, describing what's to be found on and just off the Trail. Our description runs from west to east, but only because that's the way the book goes. Either way, it remains one of the most scenic drives in New England.

GUIDANCE Mohawk Trail Association (413-743-8127; www.mohawktrail.com), P.O. Box 1044, North Adams 01247, publishes a free brochure to the attractions along its length.

Also see **Shelburne Falls Village Information Center** and **Franklin Country Chamber of Commerce** in "West County." And check out www.mass countryroads.com and www.shelburnefalls.com.

Note: The Mohawk Trail Historic Auto Trail Guide by Clint Richmond (Muddy River Press, Brookline, $9; inquiries@muddyriverpress.com) is illustrated with many vintage postcards and photos of the Trail.

❋ To See and Do

ALONG THE MOHAWK TRAIL (ROUTE 2) WEST TO EAST In 1914 the Mohawk Trail officially began in **North Adams** at the intersection (now marked by Dunkin' Donuts and McDonald's) of Union and Eagle Streets.

✎ **Natural Bridge State Park** (www.mass.gov/dcr) is the first sight to see, marked from Rt. 2 westbound. Certainly worth the short detour, this is a series of waterfalls, chutes, and pools in an abandoned marble quarry, viewed from a series of bridges and stairways. There's also a visitor center (restrooms). See *Green Space* in the previous chapter for details.

"FAMOUS HAIRPIN TURN" POSTCARD
Muddy River Press

The **Hairpin Turn**, the most dramatic reverse curve in all New England, zigs and zags its way up to the **Western Summit** (2,020 feet), where there are turnouts at the **Golden Eagle Restaurant** and the **Wigwam & Western Summit Gift Shop & Cot-**

tages (413-663-3205), 2350 Mohawk Trail. The shop and cottages with a "three-state view" date to 1914, when a tearoom and a (long-gone) observation tower opened. The shop, under new ownership, is open spring–Dec.; it stocks a variety of collectibles, souvenirs, and gifts. Five cottages (most with double bed) are open May–Oct. ($70; $80 in Oct.).

In **Florida**, one of the coldest towns in the state (it was named in 1805 just as the United States was purchasing Florida from Spain), the road levels out.

Savoy Mountain State Forest (413-663-8469; www.mass.gov/dcr) is accessed by Central Shaft Road (it angles off to the right). The forest's 11,118 acres harbor some fascinating history and evocative places. A Shaker colony was among the early-19th-century settlements for which now only cellar holes exist. The most developed corner, around North and South ponds, was later the Haskins Club, a private resort. You can swim and fish for trout in North Pond, which offers changing rooms and restrooms. There's also a boat ramp, and there are 45 campsites (open Memorial Day–Columbus Day) in a former apple orchard along with four log cabins (open year-round) by South Pond. The forest offers 24 miles of hiking trails, two ski touring loops, and a "crooked forest" of deformed trees. The waters are stocked with fish.

Whitcomb Summit, Florida, is the highest point on the trail (2,173 feet). The spectacular "100 mile view" is west over wave upon wave of hills and mountains; a steel (and lower) version of the vintage-1915 tower survives. The bronze elk, placed here by the Massachusetts Elks in 1923, is magnificent. At its dedication, speakers included Boston's Mayor Curley.

✍ ☃ **Whitcomb Summit Motel, Cabins, and Cafe** (413-662-2625 or 800-547-0944; www.whitcombsummit.com), 229 Mohawk Trail, Florida. Open mid-May to mid-Nov. Ed and Carol Drummond have given this historic property a fresh lease on life. They have salvaged eight of the cabins (which once probably numbered three times as many) and are in the process of refurbishing the 18 units in the two-story motel, room by room ($55–110 in summer, depending on the room, which includes a suite; $45–65 in cabins, more in foliage season; children 12 and under are free; extra charge for pets, which are allowed only in the cabins). The cabins are rustic, accommodating from three to six people, each with a heater and shower. One began life as "the Hairpin turn tourist shop" and was hauled the 5 miles uphill one winter in the 1920s. The grounds include a pool, but the big attraction here is the view. The café is open (same season as the motel) for breakfast and lunch. This once housed the "largest souvenir and gift shop in America," and a small shop is planned, along with a tower (much reduced in height), from which you look back down the narrow Deerfield

THE TOWER ON WHITCOMB SUMMIT WHERE YOU CAN SEE THE "100 MILE VIEW"

Kim Grant

Valley. A path leads off to **Moore's Summit** (2,250 feet), the highest point on the Mohawk Trail.

Scenic detour: **Whitcomb Hill Road/the Eastern Portal and River Road**. East of the elk statue, Whitcomb Hill Road plunges off to the north, corkscrewing downhill at a grade that vintage-1912 cars simply could not handle. This is the old road up (and down) Hoosac Mountain, the one the Mohawk Trail was designed to replace. At the bottom of the hill turn left and drive a mile or so to the railroad tracks. Park just beyond them to see the "Eastern Portal" of the Hoosac Tunnel.

If you continue on this road a little more than 3 miles, passing a series of fishing and boating access points, until you reach the Fife Brook Dam, in another mile you will see the **Bear Swamp Visitor Center** (closed at this writing; for information, call 413-424-7219). The **Dunbar Picnic Area** with restrooms and swings is another mile up the road, across from the trailheads for hiking in the **Monroe State Forest** (413-339-5504; www.mass.gov/dcr). You can loop back on Monroe Hill Road past the decommissioned Yankee Rowe Nuclear Power Plant, into the village of **Rowe**, and on back down the Zoar Road to Rt. 2.

If you return to the bottom of Whitcomb Hill, you can follow the Deerfield River east (chances are you will see trout fishers) to the lovely, pine-shaded, riverside **Zoar Picnic Area** and on through mountain-walled **Zoar Gap** to Charlemont. This makes a nice loop from the east if you only want to drive as far west as Whitcomb Summit.

The **Eastern Summit Gift Shop** (413-663-6996), 367 Mohawk Trail, is the next Mohawk Trail landmark (westbound lane, but worth the crossover). The view, north and west over tier on tier of mountains, is similar to that from Whitcomb Summit. The shop has been owned by the Devanney family for more than 30 years, and the complex, which began with a shop and now defunct cabins across the road, dates back at least another 40.

Dead Man's Curve is just beyond Brown's Garage ("no gas") in the village of Drury. The overhead warning sign with its flashing lights suggests many fatal accidents over the years. It marks the beginning of the descent down the "Eastern Slope" of the Hoosac Range, following the Cold River.

AT THE EASTERN SUMMIT

Christina Tree

Detour: **Tannery Falls**. It's more difficult to catch the turnoff traveling eastbound than it is west, but just east of the bridge that marks the Florida–Savoy line, make a right turn onto Black Brook Road and drive for about 10 minutes; take a left onto unpaved Tannery Road, which, after another 10 minutes or so, brings you to the parking area for Tannery Falls (the sign may be down—it's a local collectors' item—but the path from one end of the parking area is well marked). Just be sure not to go alone (it's steep), and don't try to climb the falls itself. It looks so tempting that people try, and several have died in the process.

The trail follows a narrow stream that rushes steeply downward beneath fir and spruce trees to a lookout at the top of the falls, fenced with wire cable. What you see below is a glorious cascade, swirling through variously shaped rock pools, a pattern repeated again and again. In spring or after a big rain this series of cascades is replaced by a thunderous, continuous rush of water. The path continues steeply downward, but instead of shadowing the cascade it now follows another stream that suddenly appears, plunging down through a rocky gorge. New, broad steps, fashioned from rail ties, ease the descent, and more massive old granite steps lead to an islandlike promontory at the confluence of the two brooks, the floor of the hollow and end of the trail. A circle of stone seats suggest a picnic spot fashioned by and for druids, and the

Kim Grant

THE VIEW FROM THE EASTERN SUMMIT GIFT SHOP'S PORCH

view back up the waterfall is spellbinding.

🥾 ♿ **Mohawk Trail State Forest** (413-339-5504; www.mass.gov/dcr), Rt. 2, Charlemont, covers 6,457 acres and offers 56 campsites and seven log cabins (one wheelchair-accessible). There's swimming in a human-made pool in the Cold River, complete with bathhouse, scattered picnic tables, and many miles of hiking trails, including a portion of the original Indian path. Camping here is permitted year-round; in winter there are snowshoeing and cross-county ski trails. The remnants of the original Mohawk Trail can be seen as a hiking trail with a series of switchbacks ascending Lookout Mountain from the west end of the camping area. *Note:* There's a $5 parking fee May to mid-Oct.

Mohawk Park in West Charlemont is the official centerpiece of the trail. A bronze statue with its arms raised, the unofficial symbol of the trail, was placed here in 1932 by the Improved

TANNERY FALLS IN SAVOY MOUNTAIN STATE FOREST

© Kindra Clineff/DCR

Order of Red Men. The arrowhead-shaped tablet at the base of the statue reads: HAIL TO THE SUNRISE—IN MEMORY OF THE MOHAWK INDIAN. There is a wishing pool with 100 inscribed stones from the various tribes and councils from throughout the country. Note the Mohawk Park Cabins across the way, a vestige of what once was.

Note: The **Rowe Road** is a left off Rt. 2 here, and the next left puts you on River Road leading back along the Deerfield River to **Zoar Gap**. We have described it coming from the other direction from Whitcomb Summit. If you continue north (instead of turning left), you come to **Rowe** (see "West County").

The Shunpike Marker by the river is dedicated to THE THRIFTY TRAVELERS OF THE MOHAWK TRAIL WHO IN 1797 HERE FORDED THE DEERFIELD RIVER RATHER THAN PAY THE TOLL AT THE TURNPIKE BRIDGE AND WHO IN 1810 WON THE BATTLE FOR FREE TRAVEL ON ALL MASSACHUSETTS ROADS. It's worth noting that the marker was placed here in 1957 as

HAIL TO THE SUNRISE IN MOHAWK PARK
Shelburne Falls Area Business Association

construction of the Massachusetts Turnpike was getting under way. The Mass Pike has substantially reduced traffic on Rt. 2.

☙ **Zoar Outdoor** (www.zaroutdoor.com). This is home base for the area's oldest, most diversified white-water sports company. See *White-Water Rafting* in "West County." The outfitter also offers campsites, platform tents, and inn rooms.

Moxie Outdoor Adventures (www.moxierafting.com), based at the Berkshire East ski area, also offers rafting and funyak rentals.

☙ ❦ **Charlemont Inn** (413-339-5796), Main St., Charlemont. This is the landmark inn along the Mohawk Trail and continues to offer three daily meals as well as spirits and lodging. See *Lodging* in "West County."

The **Federated Church** in Charlemont has excellent acoustics and for almost 35 years has been the venue for the **Mohawk Trail Concerts** (413-625-9511 or 800-MTC-MUSE; www.mohawktrailconcerts.org).

☙ **Indian Plaza Gift Shop & Pow Wow Grounds** (413-339-4096), 1475 Mohawk Trail. Dating from 1933 and site of the tragic death of the owner's wife during the Hurricane of 1938, which flooded the Deerfield River. It has been in Harold Roberts's family for 40 years, best known as the site of periodic powwows from early May through the Columbus Day weekend. This is also the site of the **Catamount Farmer's Market**, Fri. 1–6 and Sat. 9–2.

☙ The **East Charlemont Picnic Area** (eastbound) along the Deerfield River is a charmed spot with tables and a view of fields across the river

Christina Tree

INDIAN PLAZA GIFT SHOP & POW WOW
GROUNDS

and the venerable Hall Tavern Farm
down the road. (The original Hall
Tavern now serves as the reception
center for Historic Deerfield.)

Several motels—the **Red Rose** (formerly cabins), the **Olde Willow
Motel and Restaurant**, **The Oxbow**
resort motel (see *Lodging* in "West
County"), and the **Hilltop Motel**
(formerly Rio Vista)—are holdovers
from the Trail's glory days. For more
about Stillwaters Restaurant, see *Dining Out* in "West County."

Crab Apple Whitewater (www
.crabapplewhitewater.com) has renovated and expanded what's left of a
vintage cabin complex. Inquire about
funyaks. See *White-Water Rafting* in
"West County."

☙ **Tubing** (floating downriver in rubber tire tubes) is a popular summer
pastime on this stretch. Look for seasonal signs for TUBES.

☙ **Big Indian Shop** (413-625-6817),
2217 Mohawk Trail. Open year-round
daily, 9–5 May–Dec., shorter hours
off-season. Named for the 28-foot-tall
Indian that guards its door, this is an
old-fashioned souvenir shop and
proud to be one. It's been in Joan
Estes's family for more than 70 years,
and Kim Estes is usually behind the
counter to sell you a rubber drum or
tomahawk, a cowboy hat, maple prod-

ucts, or moccasins. A must-stop for
kids.

Shelburne Falls (www.shelburne
falls.com). The Trail no longer passes
through the middle of town as it once
did, but this unusual village is now
the hub, offering the only visitor center (with restrooms) along the Trail
and most of its places to eat. Eastbound you turn onto State Street and
follow it to the **Bridge of Flowers**.
Park and walk. Note the **Sweetheart
Restaurant** on Rt. 2A just off Rt. 2.
Its name recalls the heart-shaped
maple sugar candies Alice Brown
began selling from her home here in
1915. The spot went on to become
The Sweet Heart Tea Room, eventually a full-service restaurant, and
served as a driving destination for
generations of families.

Gould's Sugar House (413-625-
6170), Rt. 2, Shelburne. Open in sugaring season (Mar.–Apr.) and during
foliage (Sep.–Oct.), daily 8:30–2. A
great roadside stop that's been in the
family for generations; specialties

KIM ESTES AT THE BIG INDIAN SHOP WITH
ITS 28-FOOT-TALL WOODEN INDIAN

Christina Tree

include pancakes, waffles, and fritters laced with the family's maple syrup and fabulous pickles. We also recommend the BLT.

The Mahican-Mohawk Trail runs for 7.5 miles between Shelburne Falls and Deerfield. Several years ago the Berkshire writer and naturalist Lauren Stevens initiated a study that revealed not only the location of the old riverside path but also the fact that it was still roughly maintained by the New England Power Company to access a series of hydroelectric dams. Thanks to the concerted efforts of local environmental groups, this trail is now accessible to sturdily shod hikers. The entire hike takes at least 4 hours, but the most impressive and rugged few miles are at the Shelburne Falls end. Details are in the "West County" chapter; see *Green Space*.

The **Mohawk Trading Post** (413-625-2412; www.mohawk-trading -post.com), 874 Mohawk Trail, Shelburne. Open Memorial Day through foliage season 10–5; closed Tue.; off-season open Thu.–Mon. The easternmost Indian-themed shop on the Trail, this is less dramatic on the exterior than others (the fiberglass buffalo is smallish but big enough for a small boy to sit on), though inside there's plenty to please: a wide selection of books about Native Americans and quality soapstone carvings and pottery, sterling Indian jewelry and moccasins. Laurie York is the current owner, and it's been in her family since 1985. The stuffed bear by the entrance, she explains, evokes the memory of the live bears for which the trading post was long known, and the genuine fossil by the counter was "liberated" from the Connecticut River by the son of the previous owners.

Goodnow's Chip'n'Putt (413-625-6107), 1211 Mohawk Trail, Shelburne. Open seasonally, 9–dusk. Fun for beginners and advanced players.

The Outpost (413-625-6806 or 800-541-5086), 1385 Mohawk Trail, Shelburne. Open year-round, daily 10–5. Looks can be deceptive. This shop (eastbound) looks both smallish and new. It was originally "Indian Park" but is now substantially expanded and specializes totally in sheepskin products (car seats, slippers, mittens, and more); also fine leather products. Beware. We left with a pair of gloves.

Longview Tower Specialty Shops, 497 Mohawk Trail. Opened in 1923 as the "Long Vue" by the same Misses Mansfield who also owned the Western Summit observation and gift shop. It's on the westbound side and frequently difficult to stop either way— but worth the effort. Locals bring their picnics up (there are benches). Currently a crafts shop is here, too, but what it's still about is the "three-state view" (New Hampshire, Vermont, and Massachusetts). Rebuilt in steel in 1952, this five-story observation tower is the only one left along the Trail that's still its original height.

Old Greenfield Village (413-774-7138), 368 Mohawk Trail. Open mid-May to mid-Oct., Sat. and holidays 10–4, Sun. noon–4; weekdays by appointment. $5 adult, $4 seniors, $3 ages 6–16; free under age 6. This is a genuine, Yankee kind of phenomenon, a collection of thousands of artifacts formerly found in stores, in dental offices, churches, barbershops, and tool shops around the turn of the 20th century, all collected over 30 years by retired schoolteacher Waine Morse.

THE HILLTOWNS

WEST COUNTY
HAMPSHIRE HILLTOWNS

The rolling farm and forest between the Connecticut River Valley and Berkshire County is known, among other things, as the Hilltowns. These glacially rounded hills and river-sculpted valleys are, in topographic fact, as much a part of the Berkshire Hills as Berkshire County to the west.

Early settlers dubbed it the "Berkshire Barrier," but Native Americans knew how to traverse the region. They followed its two major rivers—the Deerfield and the Westfield—which have cut three parallel east–west valleys, now obvious traffic conduits. Rt. 2 (the "Mohawk Trail"), the northernmost east–west high road (*highway* would be an overstatement) shadows the ancient Mohawk Trail along the Deerfield River. Rt. 9 (the "Berkshire Trail") follows the main stem of the Westfield River across the middle of the state, while Rt. 20 ("Jacob's Ladder"), now shadowed by I-90 (the Mass Pike), hugs the west branch of the Westfield. This high ground is also the watershed between the two major north–south valleys in the Northeast. It's said that raindrops falling on the western slant of the Congregational church roof in hilltop Peru ultimately flow into the Hudson, while those on the eastern slant fall into the Connecticut.

Few regions this beautiful and accessible are this unspoiled.

Much of this area looks the way Vermont did a couple of decades ago: Valleys are steep, alternately wooded and patched with open fields. In winter cross-country skiers, snowshoers, and snowmobilers drive from Boston and Hartford to take advantage of the highest, most dependably snow-covered trails south of Vermont. Early spring brings sit-down breakfasts in sugarhouses and tours of the sugarbush (there are more maple producers here than in all the rest of the

A SCENIC VIEW OF ASHFIELD

Kim Grant

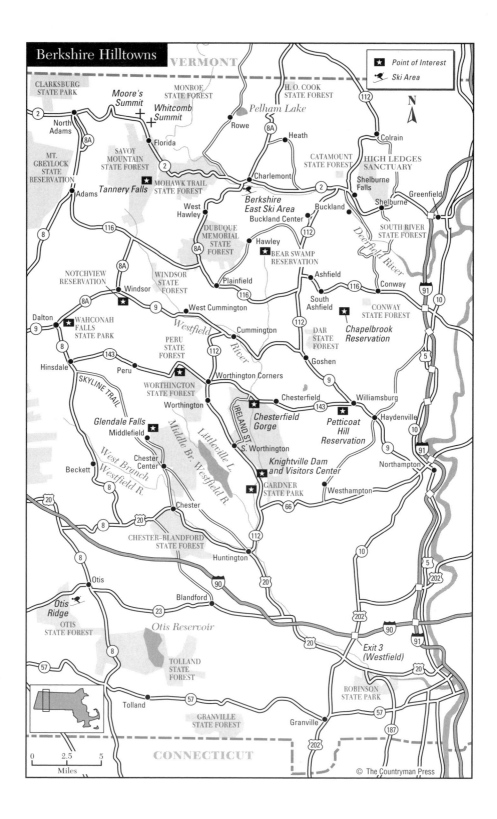

Berkshire Hilltowns

state put together). In late spring white-water rafters begin converging on the Deerfield River, and nationally ranked white-water canoeists compete on the Westfield. Anglers find trout in both rivers. In summer back roads beckon bicyclists, while hikers follow trails to hilltop lookouts and deep-in-the-woods waterfalls. In fall the Mohawk Trail is thronged with leaf-peepers, but back roads receive surprisingly little use.

Despite the fertile bottomland along the Deerfield and Westfield Rivers, this area was very sparsely settled until the end of the French and Indian Wars in 1756. Most towns were incorporated shortly before the Revolution, and many hill farms were deserted as early as the 1820s, when the Erie Canal opened the way to greener, less rocky western pastures. The stone walls pioneers built now lie deep in the area's many state parks and forests. Currently the Hilltowns are home to one of the state's largest concentrations of artists, craftspeople, and musicians.

Hilltown residents cherish the elusive, firefly-like quality of the area's attractions, a quality that, admittedly, can be frustrating to casual visitors who may not be in the right place at the right time on the right day. With a little planning, however, you can hear famed musicians perform in an old church in Charlemont and a former academy in South Worthington, world-class actors perform in the town hall in Chester, and legendery performers such as Odetta hold forth at Memorial Hall in Shelburne Falls. Throughout summer and fall hand-drawn signs steer visitors to farms offering pick-your-own berries; in August country fairs feature horse pulls, oxen draws, and local produce. In October, Conway and Ashfield hold two of the most colorful foliage festivals in New England, while November brings Cider Day and open studio tours in Colrain. All these cultural and community happenings are, moreover, held primarily for local residents rather than for New Yorkers or Bostonians.

Though the Hilltowns may all look much the same to visitors, locals will tell you that the region is clearly divided along county lines. Ashfield, Buckland, Charlemont, Hawley, and the towns to the north all fall into "West (Franklin) County," whereas Plainfield, Cummington, Worthington, and towns to the south consider themselves the "Hampshire Hills," or "Hidden Hills," both names coined by the area's bed & breakfast association. Conway seems to fall in between.

Present lodging options in the Hilltowns include roughly three dozen widely scattered B&Bs, including several farms. At present the region's only staffed information center is in Shelburne Falls, a lively dining and crafts town that's the hub of West County and the obvious way stop on the Mohawk Trail.

WEST COUNTY

West Franklin County, better known as "West County," has been attracting artists, craftspeople, and musicians for many decades and now also harbors a fair share of contemplative communities. Locals speak of a special energy emanating from this particular roll of hill and valley. One thing's certain: Wherever creative and questing spirits gather, you are sure to find exceptional peace and beauty.

"Everything that I do and make is interconnected, influenced by this view," internationally respected glass artist Josh Simpson once told us, spreading his arms to the hills that circle his studio. Simpson's deeply colored "planets" and other art pieces are featured in the Salmon Falls Artisans Showroom, a former granary in Shelburne Falls, a village formed by the centers of two towns, linked by two bridges.

Nothing in Shelburne Falls works quite the way it does in other places. Its old trolley bridge is now a walkway awash with more than 500 species of colorful flowers, and its vintage-1913 iron bridge, the main thoroughfare, is the venue of an annual community banquet. An old trolley has been rehabbed and again rumbles back and forth up at the old depot, restored by volunteers.

Always a modest shopping and dining hub for the surrounding hilltowns, Shelburne Falls is evolving as a restaurant and gallery town, but with a difference. The several "upscale" restaurants are heavy on greens and grains rather than your wallet, and galleries are artist and artisan owned. Shelburne Falls is also still a mill village with a cutlery factory (sadly up for sale at this writing) dating back to 1837, an independently owned pharmacy with a soda fountain, and an old-fashioned news store.

Just north of Shelburne Falls, hills hump abruptly and roads climb steeply through Heath and Colrain and on to Vermont. West of the village the Mohawk Trail follows a stunning stretch of the Deerfield River to Charlemont; to the south Rt. 112 leads south through Buckland's magnificent farmland to Ashfield. Back roads wind up into hills to classic clapboard villages, 50-mile views, and unexpected finds: here a farm with yaks and camels, there a woodworker's or weaver's studio, a winery or waterfall, and always a river or brook. Hiking trails abound and lodging places, while frequently hard to find, are equally hard to leave.

"It's what you don't see here that's striking," an Ashfield resident observes. Over the past 20 years the Ashfield-based Franklin Land Trust alone has preserved some many thousands of acres, just one sign of the ways local residents, few of them wealthy, feel about the look of this land.

AREA CODE 413.

A COLRAIN SIGN

William A. Davis

GUIDANCE Shelburne Falls Village Information Center (413-625-2544; www.shelburnefalls.com), 75 Bridge St., P.O. Box 42, Shelburne Falls 01370. The visitor center is open May–Oct., daily 10–4, Sun. noon–4; catch as can the rest of the year. A friendly, well-stocked information source (with restrooms), for the surrounding area as well as the village, is in a former fire station at the center of town.

Franklin County Chamber of Commerce (413-773-5463, daily;

www.franklincc.org) operates the Upper Pioneer Valley Visitor Information Center just off I-91 (exit 26) at the Rt. 2 rotary behind Applebee's on Rt. 2A east, open daily 9–5 (until 8 on Fri.), with restrooms and local products as well as information. You can also request a helpful map/guide from the chamber at P.O. Box 898, 395 Main St., Greenfield 01302.

Kim Grant

AN ARTIST PAINTS A VIEW OF THE SHELBURNE FALLS' BRIDGE OF FLOWERS.

GETTING THERE *From Boston:* There is no bus or train service. The obvious way by car is Rt. 2, which technically becomes the Mohawk Trail in Orange but really begins looking like a tourist route west of Greenfield. From points north and south, take exit 26 off I-91 at Greenfield. From Amherst, take Rt. 116 north; from Northampton, Rt. 9 north to Rt. 112.

GETTING AROUND A good map is a necessity because the state map and larger New England maps will leave you assuming that many of the most beautiful roads in this region don't exist. Franklin County publishes an excellent free, detailed map, and the *Rubel Western Massachusetts Bicycle and Road Map* covers the territory well.

MEDICAL EMERGENCY Dial 911.

✳ Villages

Ashfield. This unusually spirited town of some 1,900 people publishes its own newspaper. A large, former summer hotel still stands in the middle of the village, but most traffic now stops at Ashfield Hardware and Countrypie Pizza. The pride of Ashfield remains the Wren-style steeple on its town hall (built as a church in 1814) and its unusual number of both maple producers and craftspeople, most of whom exhibit at the annual fall festival on Columbus Day weekend. Ashfield is the birthplace of movie director Cecil B. DeMille (his parents happened to be staying at the hotel) and has been home for a number of artists and writers, making for an unusually interesting **Ashfield Historical Society** (413-628-4541; www.ashfieldmuseum.org; open by appointment). Ten rooms of exhibits include the glass-plate photos of New England towns and working people taken by the two Howes brothers of Ashfield around the turn of the 20th century. In summer there is swimming at the small town beach (transients discouraged), right in the village on Ashfield Lake, and there are two outstanding Trustees of Reservations properties (see *Green Space*). The Ashfield Fall Foliage Festival, always held Columbus Day weekend, is one of the most colorful in New England.

Buckland (population: c. 2,000). Buckland's town hall stands just across the Bridge of Flowers in the heart of Shelburne Falls (the town's northern boundary is the Deerfield River). The village center of Buckland—a gathering of a classic little church, a historical society, a small brick library, and aristocratic, 18th-century homes (one of them now a bed & breakfast), all set high on a hill—is less than 3 miles south of Rt. 2, off Rt. 112. The **Buckland Historical Society Museum** (413-625-9763; open on the second and fourth Sundays in July and August, 2–4, as well as for special programs) is housed in a historic building near the Mary Lyon Church in Buckland Center. Inquire about special events at its **Wilder Homestead** on Rt. 112, a 1775 saltbox with five working fireplaces and a barn filled with equipment, weaving looms, and a shoemaker's shop. The society's collection features exhibits about Mary Lyon, the Buckland woman who pioneered education for women in the early 19th century and is remembered as the founder of both Mount Holyoke College in South Hadley and Wheaton College in Norton. It was in the ballroom of the four-square, four-chimneyed **Major Joseph Griswold House** on Upper Street that Mary Lyon opened her first academy in 1823, teaching the family and neighborhood children (open by appointment through the Mary Lyon Foundation: 413-625-2555). The way to the site of Mary Lyon's birthplace is marked from Rt. 112 (E. Buckland St.).

Charlemont (population: 1,358). The Deerfield River rushes down from Vermont, then slows, widens, and turns east in Charlemont, creating fertile floodplains that clearly have been farmed since the mid-18th century, judging from the age of several proud farmhouses.

THE BRICK MEETINGHOUSE IN COLRAIN ON NOVEMBER'S CIDER DAY

Christina Tree

The 18th-century **Charlemont Inn**'s tavern and restaurant mark the heart of town, along with **A. L. Avery & Son General Merchandise**, still stocking everything from cheese to hardware, boots to beef. This town is the only one in New England known for both alpine skiing (**Berkshire East**) and white-water rafting, introduced by **Zoar Outdoor**. Rafting has, in turn, introduced many visitors to the high backcountry north of Rt. 2. **Bissell Covered Bridge** spans Mill Brook just off Rt. 2 on Rt. 8A (currently just pedestrian traffic). The **Charlemont Historical Society Museum** fills a theater-sized room in the town hall. It's open Tue. 5:30–7:30 and through the neighboring **Tyler Memorial Library**, itself worth a stop. In July and August the **Mohawk Trail Concerts** in the Federated Church draw a sophisticated audience from throughout the Northeast.

Charlemont **Yankee Doodle Days** in July commemorate the fact—perhaps apocryphal—that it was at a local muster here in the 1750s that America's first famous song was written, by a British doctor who was part of a British regiment to poke fun at the local militia. Local historians tells us there is no basis for this story.

Colrain (population: 1,813). This hilly town boomed with sheep raising, cotton mills, and an iron foundry in the mid-19th century, all linked to the train at Shelburne Falls by trolley. The old foundry is still in Foundry Hollow, and by the time this book appears, its rebuilt covered bridge should be back in place, spanning the North River. Catamount Hill is said to be the site of the first schoolhouse to fly the American flag, so it's appropriate that the town now harbors *Glowing Glory* (www.glowingglory.com), the country's largest neon American flag, designed by local neon artist Pacifico Palumbo and set on a hilltop across from Pine Hill Orchards on the Greenfield Road soon after 9/11 to honor U.S. veterans. The **Colrain Historical Society** (413-624-8818) is housed in the **G. William Pitt House** on Main Street. The village center with its three churches and common is at the junction of four scenic routes, including Rt. 112 north to Vermont. Colrain lists a a number of sugarhouses, and **Pine Hill Orchards** showcases apple wines from **West County Winery**. There are an exceptional number of craftsmen scattered through this sleepy town, and most hold open studio on a weekend in November (www.craftsofcolrain.com); many of these also exhibit at the annual village fair, third Saturday in September.

Conway. Turn off Rt. 116 and stop long enough at the triangular green to admire the domed **Marshall Field Memorial Library** (413-369-4646), gift of the native son who founded a Chicago department store. There's a marble rotunda and elaborate detailing within; the historical collection is open selected days. The heart of town is easy to miss: **Baker's Country Store** serves lunch, great pie, and all the local news you need. Note the covered bridge across the South River off Rt. 116. A Main Street (Rt. 116) storefront now houses the **Conway Historical Society**, open July–Labor Day, Sun. 1–4.

Heath (population: 805). Heath is worth finding, just for the fun of it: a classic hilltown with a common surrounded by the usual white-clapboard buildings. What's amazing (going and coming) are the long views. Heath is known for its wild blueberries, and the **Heath Fair**, held two weekends before Labor Day, features horse pulling, ox draws, music, food, and an old-time square dance in the dirt-floor cattle barn.

Shelburne Falls. Usually rivers divide towns, but in this case the Deerfield has united the 19th-century dining and shopping areas of two

HELEN BAKER SERVES LUNCH, GREAT PIES, AND ALL THE LOCAL NEWS IN BAKER'S COUNTRY STORE, CONWAY VILLAGE.

Christina Tree

Shelburne Falls Area Business Association

THE ANNUAL BRIDGE DINNER ON THE
IRON BRIDGE IN SHELBURNE FALLS

towns (Buckland and Shelburne) to form Shelburne Falls, one of the most unusual and lively villages in New England. Instead of a common, there's the Bridge of Flowers (see *To See*). An iron bridge, which the community has restored rather than replacing the way most communities do (claiming that they will be rarer than covered bridges in a couple of decades), also links the main streets on both sides of the river. An aberration from its rural setting, this totally Victorian shopping center has become a showcase for art and crafts work produced in the surrounding hills. The **Glacial Potholes** at the foot of Salmon Falls (Deerfield Ave., off Bridge St.) are a many-colored and unusually shaped phenomenon, worth a look. The **Shelburne Historical Society** (413-625-6150), in the Arms Academy Building (corner of Maple and Church Sts.), is open July–Oct., Wed. 10–4 and Sun. 2–5. The second-floor Opera House in vintage-1897 **Memorial Hall** has been restored and once more serves as the town's movie house (Pothole Pictures) as well as the stage for live entertainment and the Hilltown Folk music series, featuring remarkably well-known groups (Odetta is one of the performers at this writing). A **Riverwalk** runs along the Buckland side of the river. Also see the **Mahican-Mohawk Trail** along the Deerfield under *Green Space*.

Rowe (population: 381). The **Rowe Historical Society Museum** (open July through the third weekend of Oct., Sun. 2–5, otherwise by appointment; 413-339-4238) showcases the town's unusual history given its position high on a ridgeline dividing Vermont and Massachusetts (elevation ranges from 1,350 to 2,140 feet). It includes construction of the Hoosac Tunnel (the Eastern Portal); of power dams, beginning in 1911; and of New England's first atomic energy plant (1961–92) as well as the Bear Swamp Pumped Generation Station, completed in 1974. The town's population topped 800 in the 19th century; at various times there were sulfur and talc mines, several mills, a satinet factory, and some 3,000 sheep. With the arrival of train service came summer boarders. Today this is a hauntingly beautiful area with many wildflowers, including 21 species of orchids. Pick up a copy of *Wildflowers of Rowe* by Susan Alix Williams at the historical society. The **Rowe Conference Center**, originally a Unitarian Church summer camp, features workshops led by authorities on a broad spectrum of subjects. There are picnic tables in **Pelham Lake Park**.

✳ To See

The Bridge of Flowers. The Shelburne Falls Area Women's Club began plant-
ing this last remaining five-arch concrete trolley bridge in 1929 when the trolley
line was abandoned. Still meticulously tended by the club and reserved for foot
traffic, it may well be the world's floweriest bridge, abloom from April through
October with 500 varieties of flowering plants including a number of trees. This
all began with a local desire to do something about an eyesore in the middle of
the village. It's especially beautiful at dusk with the reflections in the quiet river
on its western side.

Shelburne Falls Trolley Museum (413-625-9443; www.sftm.org), 14 Depot
St., Buckland (in the railyard). Open weekends May–Oct., also Mon., July–Oct.
1–5. There is memorabilia in the visitor center, with model trains for "young
folks" to operate. The big attraction here is a vintage-1896 trolley, which for 20
years carried passengers and freight the 7 uphill miles to Colrain and back down.
It's up and running at the depot, having been restored by volunteers—after serving as Marshall Johnson's chicken coop for 70 years, which everyone agrees
saved it, both because it was up off the ground and because the chicken manure
kept the wood lubricated. The present ride may be short, but it's enlivened by
conductor Sam Bartlett's narration. Passengers learn that they are en route to
visit relatives in Colrain, having come in on the B&M (freight trains still use the
adjacent tracks). They hear about passing factories, picking up schoolkids and
shoppers on the way to "Colrain City" and its four-story (long since vanished)
inn. There is also an old railroad handcar that vigorous visitors can help pump up
and down the trolley tracks.

Glacial Potholes in Shelburne Falls. Over 50 glacial potholes—one of the
largest known concentrations of these natural sculptures, scoured into the meta-
morphic rock layers—are clustered at the bottom of the hydro dam, best viewed
from the end of Deerfield Avenue. They range in size from 6 inches to 35 feet
across.

🖋 Also see **Tregellys Fiber Farm**
under *Farms*. The farm features a
menagerie of some 200 animals,
including two-humped camels, llamas,
yaks, and rare and heritage breeds of
many other animals.

SCENIC DRIVES **Along the Mohawk
Trail**. See the previous chapter.

River Road to Whitcomb Summit
is a worthwhile deviation from the
Mohawk Trail. Take the road marked
ROWE just west of the village of
Charlemont, but bear left almost
immediately at the fork (marked by a
dead tree with numerous signs tacked
to it) along **River Road**. Follow it

THE POTHOLES IN SHELBURNE FALLS

Christina Tree

along the river, by the **Zoar Picnic Area** in a pine grove. Continue along the river as the valley walls steepen, past Whitcomb Summit Road, over the railroad tracks. Look here for the Eastern Portal of the Hoosac Tunnel, opened in the 1870s by blasting through granite.

Shelburne to Conway. There are two scenic ways from Shelburne to Conway, both good bicycle routes. The first is simply to take the Conway Road south along the river from the Buckland side; the second is to go south from Rt. 2 at the sign for Shelburne Center, where you pick up Bardwell's Ferry Road, one of the prettiest roads we know anywhere. At one high point you can see Mount Tom in Holyoke off across hills before it dips across the railroad tracks and crosses the Bardwell Ferry Bridge. Wiry and graceful, it's one of the most unusual little bridges in Massachusetts and a popular fishing spot. The Conway stretch of the road is also beautiful and joins the Shelburne Falls Road not far north of Conway Village.

Peckville Road from Rt. 2 up to the Apex Orchards offers a spectacular view of the hills.

Other suggested routes

Circle through Colrain village. Take Greenfield Road to Colrain Center, then head back down to Rt. 2 on the Shelburne Falls Road, or vice versa.

Route 112 between Buckland and Ashfield threads a beautiful valley.

Get lost. There are so many beautiful roads in this area that you really can't lose—and the best way to explore them is to get lost. Again we recommend the *Rubel Western Massachusetts Bicycle and Road Map*, as well as the free map published by Franklin County.

✳ To Do

BICYCLING Zoar Outdoor (see below) in Charlemont rents mountain bikes, suggesting routes and mapping self-guiding tours. Also see **Stump Sprouts** under *Lodging* and *Cross-Country Skiing*. Trails are open to mountain bikers. Owner Lloyd Crawford is an avid bicyclist who advises on road routes and trails in local state forests. All the *Scenic Drives* described above are good for bicycling, and many more are scenic, curving, and little trafficked.

CANOEING AND KAYAKING Zoar Outdoor (800-532-7483; www.zoaroutdoor.com), Rt. 2 in Charlemont, rents canoes and kayaks for use on several stretches of the Deerfield. Shuttle service, canoeing and white-

ZOAR OUTDOOR OFFERS FREQUENT WHITE-WATER RAFTING ON THE DEEERFIELD RIVER.

Zoar Outdoor

water clinics, and sit-on-top kayaks for the calmer reaches of the river are also offered. Inquire about "family trips." This is also a destination store for white-water kayakers.

Crab Apple (800-553-7238; www.crabpplewhitewater.com/deerfield) offers inflatable kayak ("funyak") rentals with a shuttle to the put-in point.

Moxie Outdoor Adventures (www.moxierafting.com), based at Berkshire East ski area, also offers rafting and funyak rentals.

FISHING The 12-mile stretch of the Deerfield River in Charlemont lures anglers from across the Northeast. There is a catch-and-release section in the village of Hoosac Tunnel. Beware the changing depth of the water throughout this area due to releases from the dam. The **Catamount State Forest** (413-339-5504) harbors a 27-acre trout-stocked lake. **Davenport's Mobil** (413-625-9544), Rt. 2 in Shelburne Falls, and **Avery's General Store** (413-339-4915), 127 Main St., Charlemont, stock fishing supplies.

GOLF Edge Hill Golf Course (413-628-6018), Barnes Rd. in Ashfield. This former dairy farm is now a nine-hole course with the golf shop, snack bar, and lounge in the former barn overlooking a pond. It will have 18 holes by this book's next edition.

Goodnow's Chip'n'Putt (413-625-6107), 1211 Mohawk Trail (Rt. 2), Shelburne. Open seasonally, 7:30–dusk. Fun for beginners and advanced players.

HORSEBACK RIDING See **High Pocket B&B** under *Lodging*. **Flames Stables** (802-464-8329), Rt. 100 south, Wilmington, VT. Western saddle trail rides, pony rides for young children (just over the border from Rowe).

ROCK CLIMBING ✐ **Zoar Outdoor** (www.zoaroutdoor.com), Rt. 2, Charlemont, runs a rock climbing school that emphasizes toprope climbing with the rope anchored by an instructor; there is a low student:instructor ratio. One- and 2-day novice and intermediate clinics are offered, including special parent–child clinics and climbs geared to ages 10–15.

SWIMMING See "Along the Mohawk Trail" for the **Mohawk Trail** and **Savoy Mountain State Forests**; ask locally about swimming holes in the Deerfield River.

TRACKING Alan Edmond (413-624-5115; alanedmond@mtdata.net), 12 Wildon Hill Rd., Colrain. A local tracker who is a naturalist, farmer, and writer, Alan offers half- and full-day guided tracking and mentoring.

TUBING Bring your own, or pick up an inner tube at **Davenport's Mobil** (413-625-9544) on Rt. 2 in Shelburne Falls, and coast down the Deerfield River (Charlemont is the local hub for tubing).

WHITE-WATER RAFTING "When I first approached New England Electric they said 'No. You can't raft the river,'" Bruce Lessels recalls, adding that over the next few years, the power company became increasingly cooperative. In 1989 the company began releasing water from Fife Brook Dam with a regularity that makes rafting possible on most days April through October on a 10-mile stretch of Class II and III whitewater—from Florida, through steep, green-walled, boulder-strewn Zoar Gap, and on down to Charlemont. Admittedly not as visually and viscerally exciting as parts of Maine's Kennebec or Penobscot Rivers, it offers a great introduction to rafting. The day we ran it, a third of our group was under age 16 (minimum weight: 50 pounds). The Upper Deerfield Dryway, a stretch of Class IV whitewater above the Fife Brook Dam, is also now rafted on specific days (adding up to more than 30 each season). The lower river is great for family float trips, canoeing, and recreational kayaking and tubing.

♂ **Zoar Outdoor** (800-532-7483; www.zoaroutdoor.com), based in a 1750s house with 80 acres on Rt. 2 in Charlemont, is headed by Bruce Lessels, a former member of the U.S. Olympic white-water team. The complex presently includes a bathhouse with changing rooms and hot showers, an orientation pavilion, cabin tents, primitive tent sites, and Hawk Mountain Lodge (see *Lodging*), an attractive B&B. Trips range from challenging rides down the dryway and clinics for expert white-water kayakers to family float trips. Rates vary with the day, trip, and age of the person involved. Also see *Caneoing and Kayaking*, *Bicycling*, *Rock Climbing*, and *Lodging*.

Crab Apple Whitewater (413-625-2288 or 800-553-7238; www.crabapple whitewater.com), Rt. 2, Charlemont. A well-established family-owned outfitter with a home base on Maine's Kennebec River, Crab Apple has been offering raft trips on the Deerfield since 1989. It features the full range of rafting trips and rents "funyaks" (inflatable kayaks). Its base is a former Mohawk Trail restaurant. Inquire about 2-day packages.

Moxie Outdoor Adventures (800-866-6943; www.moxierafting.com), with its home base on Maine's Kennebec, is based here at Berkshire East ski area in Charlemont. It offers both dryway (Class IV whitewater, minimum age 14) and Zoar Gap ($70 weekdays, $85 weekends) runs.

✳ Winter Sports

CROSS-COUNTRY SKIING AND SHOWSHOEING Stump Sprouts (413-339-4265; www.stumpsprouts.com), West Hill Rd., West Hawley. High on the side of a mountain, this 450-acre tract offers some memorable cross-country skiing on wooded trails at 1,500- to 2,000-foot elevations. Snacks and rentals are available in the warming hut, which is part of Lloyd and Suzanne Crawford's home (see *Lodging*). There are 25 km of trails, lessons, and guided tours.

Also see *Green Space* for trails in **Kenneth Dubuque Memorial State Forest**, and "Along the Mohawk Trail" for those in the **Savoy Mountain State Forest**.

DOWNHILL SKIING Berkshire East (413-339-6617; www.berkshireeast.com), South River Rd., Charlemont. Known affectionately as "Berkshire beast," this is an unusually challenging mountain for its size. *Vertical drop:* 1,180 feet. *Terrain:* 45 trails, 40 percent expert, 40 percent intermediate. *Lifts:* Five lifts, including a quad installed for the 2003–04 season. *Snowmaking:* 100 percent of terrain. *Facilities:* Nursery, 2 base lodges, ski school, shop; open daily; night skiing Wed.–Sat.; snowboarding.

SNOWMOBILING **The Snowmobiling Association of Massachusetts** (413-369-8092; www.sledmass.com) happens to be headquarted in Conway, but the web site offers guidance to some 500 miles of trail throughout the state, a little more than half on private and the remainder on state land. There are no rentals in the Hilltowns, but there's no doubt that this area offers some of the best sledding in the state. Snowmobilers are advised to check the web site and contact local clubs.

✳ Green Space

STATE FORESTS *Note:* See www.mass.gov/dcr for details about all of the following:

Monroe State Forest (413-339-5504) covers 4,000 acres in the towns of Florida and Monroe. Access is on Monroe Road off Rt. 2 (just east of Whitcomb Summit; see River Road under *Scenic Drives*). Nine miles of hiking trails and several "pack-in" campsites are on the **Dunbar Brook Trail**; about 2 miles is in one of the last stands of old-growth forest, with a beautiful stand of red spruce and a 300-year-old hemlock. The Roycroft Lookout takes in a panorama of the Deerfield River Valley. Watch out for the many moose droppings.

Mohawk Trail State Forest (413-339-5504), Rt. 2, Charlemont. See "Along the Mohawk Trail" for details.

Catamount State Forest (413-339-5504), Rt. 112, Colrain. Fishing is the big attraction in this 1,125-acre forest in southwestern Colrain and eastern Charlemont. Streams and a 27-acre lake are stocked. There are also hiking and riding trails.

H. O. Cook State Forest (413-258-4774), Rt. 8A, Heath. The lure here is fishing for trout in more than 5 miles of streams. There are also hiking and riding trails. Access is off Rt. 8A on State Farm Rd. in northeastern Heath, 1 mile south of the Vermont line.

Kenneth Dubuque Memorial State Forest, also known as **Hawley State Forest** (413-339-5504), northwest of Plainfield on Rt. 8A, offers a fine loop hike starting at Moody Spring, a genuine mineral spring with a metal pipe spouting water. A sign proclaims: THIS WATER HAS PROVEN HELPFUL IN CASES OF SORE THROAT, STOMACHACHE, INTESTINAL DISORDERS, RHEUMATISM AND ALL SCROFULA DISEASES. Not far from the spring, just off East Hawley Rd., stands a well-preserved charcoal kiln. The forest's many miles of dirt roads make for fine winter ski touring and summer dirt biking.

HIKING AND WALKING **Bear Swamp Reservation**, maintained by the Trustees of Reservations (www.thetrustees.org), is in Ashfield on Hawley Road (less than 2 miles west of the junction of Rts. 116 and 112). It has 171 acres with roads and trails and is known for wildflowers: lady's slipper, painted trillium, cowslip, marsh marigold, blue gentian, wild azalea, and flowering dogwood.

High Ledges, Shelburne. A 300-acre preserve with superb views of the surrounding countryside. From Rt. 2 in Shelburne, turn onto Little Mohawk Rd., then follow Audubon Society signs.

The Mahican-Mohawk Trail. Based on a study and volunteer labor, a stretch of the ancient Indian path between Shelburne Falls and Deerfield is accessible to sturdily shod hikers. The entire hike takes at least 4 hours and entails wading the river, but the most rugged and impressive few miles are at the Shelburne Falls end—and just 1 mile can feel like a satisfying outing. The trailhead is marked on Rt. 2 at the pullout just east of the police station. Visitors are advised to ask directions and pick up a trail map at the Shelburne Falls Village Information Center (see *Guidance*). Another segment of this trail can be hiked in the **Mohawk State Forest** in Charlemont.

The stone tower on Massamett Mountain was built by the town of Shelburne. You can climb the stairs inside to some wonderful views through big open windows. The view encompasses Mount Greylock on the west, Mount Snow and Stratton Mountain in Vermont, Mount Monadnock in New Hampshire, and the Holyoke Range to the southwest. The easiest way to get there from Rt. 2 is up Cooper Lane behind Gould's Sugar House, through Gould Farm to Davenport Maple Farm at the end. Be warned that although this looks like a one-way road, it definitely is not. You can park at Davenport Maple Farm and walk the fire road the mile to the tower.

Riverwalk, Shelburne Falls. This pleasant walkway begins on the Buckland side of the Deerfield River opposite McCusker's Market at the end of the Bridge of Flowers and offers a view of the Salmon Falls and Potholes.

Also see **Dunbar Brook Trail**, described under **Monroe State Forest**, above.

PICNICKING **Gardner Falls, Shelburne Falls Recreation Area**. Follow North Street along the river until you see the sign. The old power canal here is a great fishing spot, and it's also a fine place for a picnic (go past the picnic tables, down by the river).

South River State Forest (413-268-7098 or 413-339-5504; www.mass.gov/dcr), north from Conway village on the Shelburne Falls and Bardwell's Ferry roads (see *Scenic Drives*), **South River Station** offers picnic tables and grills scattered along the gorge of the South River to its confluence with the Deerfield. Near the parking area, notice the South River Dam, once used to power the trolley line.

Malley Park on the Buckland side of the Deerfield River (near the Lamson & Goodnow factory) offers a good view of the Potholes.

Also see **High Ledges**, above.

WATERFALLS **Chapelbrook Reservation** (www.thetrustees.org), maintained by the Trustees, is in South Ashfield. (Where Rt. 116 doglegs east, continue south on the Williamsburg Road for 2.25 miles.) Turn left to find the series of shallow falls that spill into a deep pool, perfect for sliding down. Across the road, the Chapelbrook Ledges offer long views.

Tannery Falls. Take Black Brook Road off Rt. 2 just east of the bridge that marks the Florida–Savoy line. One of the most spectatular waterfalls in the state. For directions and description, see "Along the Mohawk Trail."

✳ Lodging

INNS AND BED & BREAKFASTS

In Ashfield 01330

✐ **Bull Frog Bed & Breakfast** (413-628-4493), Rt. 116. Open year-round. Lucille Thibault's 200-year-old Cape sits back from Rt. 116 with a lovely back garden, a frog pond, and five kinds of berry bushes. The organically grown blueberries, strawberries, blackberries, several kinds of raspberries, gooseberries, and currants are the ingredients for the homemade jams that are part of a full country breakfast so special, we had to take a picture of it on our last visit. Maple syrup is also a family product. The big country kitchen with its antique, wood-fired Glenwood stove (in constant use) is the gathering place for the house; there's also an upstairs TV room. There are four guest rooms and two baths, but the baths are only rented for the use of one room, unless it's family or friends who share. One former parlor now features a round, king-sized bed and fireplace. Lucille irons the sheets. $115 double, $75 single year-round.

In Buckland

Johnson Homestead Bed & Breakfast (413-625-6603; thejohnsonhomestead@msn.com), 79 East Buckland Rd., Shelburne Falls 01370. Susan Grader's grandparents took in boarders for a full 40 years in this gracious 1890s farmhouse; now Susan and her husband, David, have revived the tradition. Sited on a quiet road, this is a gracious, pleasant place with a big inviting country kitchen and two more comfortable common rooms. The three attractive guest rooms (we like the one with the 1805 maple bed and hand-loomed coverlet) have private bath. Breakfast is an event, seated with a clear view of the garden bird feeders —and the hummingbirds, goldfinches, and woodpeckers. You may feast on a mushroom and basil omelet in puff pastry, fresh fruit cup including home-grown peaches, and walnut-pumpkin muffins with homemade jam. Susan is an exceptionally hospitable host, also a writer with a flair for rhyme. $75–110 double, $20 per extra person; children 12 and over welcome. The house features an unusual outdoor fireplace and flower gardens and is set in 80 acres with a brook. A ways off Rt. 112, it's on the way to nowhere except Mary Lyon's birthplace.

Bird's Nest Bed & Breakfast (413-625-9523), 2 Charlemont Rd., Buckland 01338. This hospitable house was

BREAKFAST AT THE BULL FROG B&B IN ASHFIELD

Christina Tree

built in 1797 at the head of Buckland Center's handsome street, across the road from the striking, white Mary Lyon Church, known for its carillon. Mary Lyon, who founded Mount Holyoke and Wheaton Colleges, taught a Winter School for Young Ladies here 1830–32. Guests enter the house through a comfortable brick-floored room, and common space includes the original keeping room and a big, sunny dining room. Cindy Weeks is a sculptor and painter who gives workshops, Edith Dolby is a weaver, and three generations of this family are represented in the furniture, rugs, paintings, pottery, and other decorations in the house. There are three upstairs guest rooms, each with private bath. Rooms vary in size and ambience but all are pleasant. $95–125 includes a full breakfast. Well-behaved children over 10 are welcome.

In Charlemont 01339
🐾 ☀ **Charlemont Inn** (413-339-5796; www.charlemontinn.com), Rt. 2 (Mohawk Trail). Hospitality here dates back to a decade or so before 1787, the year Ephraim Brown formally declared his house an inn. Charlotte Dewey and Linda Shimandle continue preserving (as their brochure proclaims) "a place with character." There's a kayak above the porch and a suit of armor in the back dining room; the Full Moon Tavern offers local brews and a pool table. The inn serves all three meals every day of the year (see *Eating Out*). A dozen or so clean, antiques-furnished upstairs guest rooms (some permit smoking) flank a narrow hall; eight rooms share semiprivate baths, and five others share two hall baths. Past guests have included Benedict

Arnold, General John Burgoyne, Mark Twain, and President Calvin Coolidge. Present guests tend to be fishermen, white-water rafters, history buffs, snowmobilers, and skiers as opposed to the Jacuzzi-and-gas-fireplace crowd. From $45 single, $75–100 double.

⊗ **The Warfield House Inn at Valley View Farm** (888-339-8439; www.warfieldhouseinn.com), 200 Warfield House Rd. The two guest facilities here are a white-clapboard country house with green awnings and a smaller country cottage. Together they offer nine rooms and a suite. Both buildings have living rooms and views of Berkshire East across a steep valley. The 530-acre hillside spread set high above Rt. 2 includes a barnyard with llamas, emus, goats, and chickens, but the centerpiece of the property is a restaurant and pub (see *Dining Out*), and the complex lends itself to reunions and weddings. $99–150 for a suite, includes a full breakfast.

In Colrain 01340
🌸 **Penfrydd Farm B&B** (413-624-5516; www.penfrydd.com), 105 Hillman Rd. Thom Griffin, an opera singer and farmer, is your host at this 160-acre hilltop farm, ringed by more hills. Resident animals include llamas and horses; guests are invited to hike along paths through woods and meadows. There are four guest rooms, three sharing a bath ($75 per couple); one, far larger and more attractive than the others, has a whirlpool tub ($90). Plans call for reducing the number of bedrooms and increasing the number of baths. Common space is informal and attractive. There's a baby grand piano, a Franklin fireplace, many plants and books; rates include breakfast.

✐ ☀ **High Pocket B&B** (413-624-8988; www.highpocket.com), 38 Adams Place Rd. Sarah and Mark McKusick live down the road from this 160-year-old clapboard house with three guest rooms (all with private bath), a game room in the barn, and a hot tub on the porch with a 50-mile view. On the day we visited, dozens of goats were lazing in a neighboring field, but the specialty of this house is horseback riding. The McKusicks have more than a dozen steeds and offer trail rides, but only to their guests. Beginners are welcome, as are more accomplished riders, and guests are invited to bring their own mounts. The adjoining properties add up to 650 acres; singletrack trails traverse surrounding fields and woods as well. This is a full house with a living room (with TV and woodstove), laundry room, and full kitchen, but breakfast is included in $100 per room; horses are boarded for $25 per night; there's a $10 fee for pets.

✐ ☀ **Olde Cary House** (413-624-0062; www.oldecaryhouse.com), 7 York Rd., P.O. Box 313. Built in 1846 as a 22-room double house on 12 acres, up a rural road. Anneliese Zinn and her family live in the other part of the house, leaving not only the four guest rooms (two with king-sized bed) and two shared baths to guests but also their own dining and common room with a piano and TV, and the kitchen to which they have access. It's here that Anneliese prepares a full breakfast, perhaps stuffed French toast. There's an inviting porch and yard, set in 12 acres. $65–85 double (from $60 single). No credit cards. Children and pets are accepted by special arrangement.

In Conway 01341

✐ ☀ **House in Pumpkin Hollow** (413-369-6007), 173 Whately Rd. Just a mile or so off Rt. 116 stands the town's original church and a cluster of 19th-century homes around its original, now serene green. Diane Poland, former owner of the Restful Crow in Ashfield, devoted 9 months to restoring this 1860s house, filling it with antiques that she has spent a lifetime acquiring. A fire glows in the wood-pellet stove in the parlor, the kind of place you want to linger and pick up a book you otherwise would never read. There are two guest rooms, the larger furnished with early Empire antiques including a cannonball bed; a smaller back room has a spool bed. $110–150 includes a full breakfast, perhaps a frittata with goat cheese or peach cobbler.

In Heath 01346

Alice's Place (413-337-6671), 207 Colrain Stage Rd. This distinctive 1850s brick house with its Gothic entry has been in Rollo Kinsman's family for generations; his mother took in summer boarders. Parts of the house date to the 1790s. The whole is suffused with light, furnished with antiques, taste, and an eye to comfort, set high in 125 acres of rolling field and forest with cross-country ski trails and a spring-fed book for wading and fishing. Rollo Kinsman left home to pursue a career as a concert singer but was drafted, spending the next 35 years in the army's entertainment and recreation divisions, living in many places around the world. He and his wife, Alice, returned to this old homestead and opened it as a B&B—but Alice has since passed on, hence the name. Two guest rooms are on the ground floor. $85–135 per night includes a full breakfast.

In Rowe 01367

❧ **Maple House Bed and Breakfast** (413-339-0107; www.maple housebb.com), 51 Middletown Hill Rd. A 200-year-old farmhouse that took in summer boarders a century ago, Maple House sits high on a hill surrounded by fields. Becky and Michael Bradley welcome families. Common rooms are comfortable any time of year, and the sunroom has a brick oven fireplace. The four guest rooms feature pine floors, exposed posts and beams, and bright quilts; they range from a king with private bath to a two-room family suite. Full breakfasts feature homemade syrups (blueberry and raspberry as well as maple) and locally grown produce. Guests can swim in Pelham Lake, fish or raft, canoe or kayak on the Deerfield River, and ski downhill at nearby Berkshire East or cross-country out the back door, around the lake, and into Rowe Forest. There's also year-round trail riding 4 miles up the road in Vermont—sleigh rides, too. $60–80 single, $80–100 double; dinner is available for groups of eight or more. Inquire about special packages.

In Shelburne 01370

Kenburn Orchards B&B (413-625-6116 or 877-KENBURN; www .kenburnorchards.com), 1394 Mohawk Trail. Susan Flaccus's father and grandfather planted the apple trees in the 40-acre orchard on this 160-acre farm. Susan and her husband, Larry, have planted many more fruit trees as well as Christmas trees and have transformed the old homestead into a delightful B&B. The three guest rooms (with private bath), the dining room, and the sitting room are all sparely, nicely furnished. Nothing froufrou but everything in keeping with the character of the house: a pencil-post canopy bed in the Isadore Pratt Room upstairs and a cherry king-sized bed in the downstairs bedroom, quilts and Oriental carpets, wood and gas Vermont Castings stoves (air-conditioning in summer), lovely new baths, plenty of light, and exceptional views. All rooms have AC, CD clock radios, robes, and ironing boards as well as teakettles. There are rockers on the porch; a gazebo lets you enjoy dusk without the bugs it brings. $125–155 per couple includes a full, candlelit breakfast served at the formal dining room table. For slightly more, the Isadore Pratt Room can be rented as a suite with a sleep sofa in an adjoining room.

Six Maple Street (413-625-6807), 6 Maple St. Open weekends May to Nov. Judy Hoyt grew up in this 18th-century house, the oldest standing home in the village of Shelburne Falls. It's been in her family since the late 19th century, and the two upstairs guest rooms (sharing one and a half baths) are furnished in family antiques. The larger one retains a marble sink. There's a gracious living room with a fireplace and a big kitchen and yard. Given the superb restaurants in Shelburne Falls, it's nice to stay somewhere you can walk home to. $90–100 includes a continental breakfast.

❧ **Dancing Bear B&B** (413-623-9281), 22 Mechanic St. Remodeled by new owners Phil Bragdon (former manager of New Hampshire Public Radio) and his wife, Edith Bingham. The couple have lived many places and speak several languages. There were three rooms when we stopped by but four were promised. This is a village house, nothing fancy but pleasant. Shared or private baths; continental breakfast with fresh fruit and espresso if so desired. Children are welcome. $89–99 per couple.

Shelburne House Bed & Breakfast (413-625-9955; www.shelburne house.com), 66 Colrain Rd. Just a minute off Rt. 2 but with a view of orchards and a beaver pond. The three second-floor guest rooms (private baths) are uncluttered. We spent a restful night in the Baldwin Room (each room is named for an apple). Elaine Hinz is a thoughtful host, serving a full breakfast. The paneled parlor is unusually large, a venue for workshops and gatherings, some small weddings. $90–125.

Inn the Village (413-625-2324), 17 High St. Marybeth Koreman offers two guest rooms with private baths, radiant heat floors, and TV, a parlor with gas fireplace, a game room, and front porch with rockers. A full breakfast served in the dining room or on the deck. $130 per room.

OTHER LODGING ⚭ 🐾 ✍ **Stump Sprouts Guest Lodge** (413-339-4265; www.stumpsprouts.com), West Hill Rd., Hawley 01339. In 1977 Lloyd Crawford built a contemporary, hilltop lodge almost entirely with his own hands, from timbers he found standing on this 450-acre spread. He also built the bunks and much of the furniture inside. There are 10 rooms, sleeping from two to five, and the common spaces are on many levels (there are lofts and corners to sit in with skylights and stained glass). Windows maximize the view of tier upon tier of wooded hills. The former barn is a great rec room with table tennis, pool, and a piano; the ceiling drops down for warmth in winter and can

be raised to allow even more space (the old silo is a great aerie) in summer. There's a wonderful view from the sauna, too. Vegetable gardens supply the table, which Suzanne Crawford sets family-style, or you can cook for yourself. It's possible to come singly or in couples, but it's most fun to come as a group. The repeat rate is 90 percent. In winter there are the 25 km of cross-country ski trails (also used for snowshoeing) for which this place is well-known, and in summer the trails are still there to walk or bike. In winter $149 per person per weekend includes six meals; from $224 on 3-day holiday weekends includes six meals. Spring through fall a 2-night weekend with three meals is $129, and if you cook and clean for yourself rates begin at $34 midweek, $69 on weekends.

✍ **Rowe Camp & Conference Center** (413-339-4954; www.rowe center.org), Kings Highway Rd., Box 273, Rowe 01367. The Unitarian-Universalist center consists of a farmhouse and assorted camp buildings on a quiet back road. There are 18 private and semiprivate rooms with a total of 125 beds, mostly dorm-style. On most weekends throughout the year there are speakers (many of them well-known) on topics ranging from "Writing from the Heart," to "Herbs, Holiness, and Menopause," to "Gardening: Making and Keeping a Private Eden." Seven summer weeks are also reserved for school-age, adult, and family camps. There are two costs for each conference: The first is housing, which includes six meals and ranges from $90 for 2 nights' camping to $250 for single occupancy in a private room; the second is the program cost, which is based on family income and runs $175–275. Bill fondly remembers his wake-up call here: "'Tis a gift to be simple" played at his door on a recorder.

Hawk Mountain Lodge (800-532-7483; www.hawkmountainlodge.com), P.O. Box 245, Charlemont 01339. This 19th-century farmhouse offers a pleasant alternative to the camping and cabin tent options at Zoar Outdoor. There are four rooms and a full-room suite, some shared and some private baths, all comfortably furnished and sharing a living room with WiFi. Bicycle and kayak rentals as well as white-water lessons, rafting, and rock climbing are all offered here (see *To Do*). Off-season a series of tracking and historical workshop weekends are offered; this also makes a good base for skiing at Berkshire East. Breakfast is only included in workshop weekend packages; otherwise there's the Coffee Bean (open from 6 AM), with a full breakfast menu, just down the road. May–Oct. $85–155 per room, otherwise $65–125.

✦ ♿ **Blue Heron Farm** (413-339-4045; www.blueheronfarm.com), Warner Hill Rd., Charlemont 01339. Bill and Norma Coli offer a choice of lodging options on their 140-acre organic farm with a pond and walking/ski trails. Five rentals: a self-contained cottage (two bedrooms, two baths, fireplace, sleeps up to eight), a log cabin (sleeps up to four, one bedroom), an attractive apartment attached to the sugarhouse (sleeps up to three), a bungalow (sleeps up to three), and The Maples, a post-and-beam Cape that includes a king-bedded bedroom, an upstairs bedroom with twins, a loft with a sleep sofa, two baths, plus a living

room with fireplace, dining room, and full kitchen. Overall this place is great for families; pony-cart rides, berry picking, and helping with the horses and goats are encouraged. $95–250 per night, 2-night minimum; cheaper by the week and month.

✦ **The Oxbow** (413-625-6011; www.oxbowresortmotel.com), 1741 Mohawk Trail, Charlemont 01339. A one-story family-owned motel with 25 rooms (19 with two double beds), grouped around a swimming pool. All have air-conditioning and TV, and the property includes tennis courts and furnishes balls and racquets; there's also a six-hole golf course, horseshoes, and a basketball court. Stillwaters Restaurant (see *Dining Out*) is next door, and the Deerfield River is just across Rt. 2. Rooms in the front have river views, but those in the rear are quieter. In summer/fall $75–89 double; from $55 off-season. No charge for children under 16. Inquire about ski packages with Berkshire East.

CAMPGROUNDS

State Parks and Forests
See www.mass.gov/dcr. For camping reservations, call 877-422-6762 or reserve online through www.reserve america.com. For detailed fees, see *Camping* in "What's Where." For details on camping in the **Mohawk Trail State Forest** and **Savoy Mountain State Forest**, see "Along the Mohawk Trail."

Private
Zoar Outdoor (800-532-7483; www.zoaroutdoor.com), Rt. 2, Charlemont. Set in a wooded area surrounded by 80 acres of woods and offering 10 cabin tents, each with a wooden deck, four cots, a gas lantern, a gas grill, and

a porch; there are also several primitive tent sites. (See *White-Water Rafting.*)

Also see **Hawk Mountain Lodge** under *Other Lodging.*

✳ Where to Eat

DINING OUT

In Shelburne Falls
Café Martin (413-625-2795; www.cafemartin.wp.net), 24 Bridge St. Open for lunch Tue.–Sat. (11–3), dinner Tue.–Sat. (5–8:30), and Sunday brunch (11–1) and dinner. This gets top local reviews. It's an informal, atmospheric storefront restaurant with a varied menu and daily specials. Lunch on a salade Niçoise or black bean burger. Dinner ranges from a veggie burrito to a 12-oz. Delmonico steak topped with Gorgonzola butter. Dinner entrées $13.95–21.95. Full liquor license.

Tusk'n'Rattle (413-625-0200; www.tusknrattle.com), 10 Bridge St. Open Wed.–Sun. for dinner 5–9 (bar and appetizers until 11). Margaritas are a specialty, along with "Indian-Latin" cuisine. Step down into this lively, exotic space and dine on honey tamarind pork loin with caramelized plantains and grilled pineapple, or cilantro chicken breast with grilled gazpacho relish and salsa verde. Microbrews on tap. Entrées $9.95–18.95.

☺ The Warfield House (413-339-6600 or 888-339-VIEW), 200 Warfield Rd., off Rt. 2. Dinner Tue.–Sun., lunch Fri.–Sun. brunch. Set high on a hilltop with views across this steep-sided valley to Berkshire East ski area. Weddings are a specialty. Dinner might begin with pan-fried crabcakes. Entrées might range from

maple-glazed chicken, to filet mignon with roasted garlic mashed potatoes and fresh vegetables with thyme butter. The **Hawk's Nest Pub** offers less formal dining: fish-and-chips, chicken tenders, and burgers. Nightly specials such as roast turkey. $11.95–17.95. Check out the exotic animals in the neighboring barnyard.

♪ Stillwaters Restaurant (413-625-6200), 1745 Mohawk Trail (Rt. 2). Open for dinner nightly except Tue. Under ownership by Michael Phelps, this Mohawk Trail landmark has gained a solid reputation. It's a big old dining room set high above the road, with a view of the river across the way. The big menu ranges from a burger to blue cheese sirloin fillets or Caribbean chicken stir-fry with mango salsa; you can choose small or large portions of each entrée (with commensurate pricing). All entrées ($8.95–17.95) include homemade bread, starch, and veggie. Good children's menu. Full liquor license.

EATING OUT

Along Route 2
Gould's Sugar House (413-625-6170), Rt. 2, Shelburne. Open in sugaring season (Mar.–Apr.) and during foliage (Sep.–Oct.), daily 8:30–2. If it's open, be sure to stop at this great roadside eatery that's been in the family for generations; specialties include pancakes, waffles, and fritters laced with the family's maple syrup, also their homemade dill pickles. We last lunched on a memorable BLT.

♪ Charlemont Inn (413-339-5796; www.charlemontinn.com), Main St. Open daily 6 AM through dinner, best known for live entertainment on weekends. The Full Moon Tavern is the apt name of the inn's big, informal dining room with its friendly bar and pool table; dining is also available on the sunporch, and in summer there's a patio. Anything goes here, from burgers to vegetarian dishes; specialties include home fries, Zoar steak, and BBQ ribs, and may include roast duck. There's also a children's menu.

Charlemont Pizza (413-339-4472), Main St. Open at 11 daily, noon Sunday, until at least 9. Try the kielbasa pizza with extra cheese.

✪ **Pine Hill Orchards Restaurant** (413-624-3325), Greenfield Rd. Open weekdays 7–2, weekends 8–3. Closed Tue. Rebuilt better than ever after a fire, this country oasis serves home-baked items, as well as soups and sandwiches. The property also includes a petting zoo and picnic tables.

The Coffee Bean (413-339-4760), 90-2 Main St., Charlemont. Open daily 6–5. A particularly good breakfast menu, then hot and cold sandwiches, brownies.

In Shelburne Falls

McCusker's Market & Deli (413-625-9411; www.mccuskersmarket .com), 3 State St. Open Sun.–Thu. 7–7, weekends 7 AM–8 PM. Michael McCusker's brightly painted (in its original colors) former Odd Fellows Hall (built in 1877) is on the Buckland side of the two bridges. Since 1979 the market has specialized in natural foods, vitamins, local cheeses, organic produce, fresh-baked breads and cookies, and much more. The deli is good for a "vegiwich," "turkey-berry," or variety of roll-ups and wraps as well as an OatsCream soft-serve. There are booths in back with WiFi; also outdoor tables in-season. A favorite place to catch up on the

Christina Tree

MCCUSKER'S MARKET & DELI

news, especially if it's local.

The Village Restaurant (413-625-6300), 43 Bridge St. Open for lunch and dinner except Tue.; breakfast, too, on weekends. Don and Andrea McLaughlin—who used to operate the Warfield House Restaurant—have created an inviting place for burgers, chili, pasta, and full dinners.

Shelburne Falls Coffee Roasters (413-625-6474), Roasters Café, 35 Bridge St. Open 6–6 daily, this pleasant café is the original in a chain that's good enough to have sprouted an expanded version out on Rt. 2 and other offshoots in the Valley. Coffees and baked-from-scratch pastries are the draw, as well as blended frozen drinks.

Bridge Street Café (413-625-6345), 65 Bridge St. Open except Wed. at 7:30 for breakfast and Sunday brunch with a varied menu of eggs, pancakes, and baked goods; also for lunch basics (sandwiches and burgers, salads and melts). A pleasant space with seasonal backyard tables. Inquire about dinner on selected nights.

In Ashfield

✎ **Countrypie Pizza Company** (413-628-4488), 343 Main St. Open Mon.–Sat. 11:30–9. Good pizza with plenty of veggie varieties, including eggplant, broccoli, artichoke hearts, feta, and Garden Delight, featuring fresh spinach, mushrooms, and so forth. Also Sicilian wraps and grinders.

Elmer's Store (413-628-4003; www.elmersstore.com), Main St., Ashfield. This traditional heart of town was vacant for several years until Nan Palati arrived, a New Orleans transplant after Katrina. It's now open weekdays at 7 for breakfast till 10:30, weekends till noon. Breakfast features local eggs and Ashfield-made syrup; "sides" for eggs include black beans and salsa. All kinds of omelets, espressos, teas, smoothies. Drinks and pastries all day, groceries, papers, original art and crafts also sold. Check the web site for evening programs.

Ashfield Lake House (413-628-0158). Open Wed.–Sun. for lunch and dinner, Mon.–Tue. from 3 PM. Under new ownership, this local hangout (since 1925) is far more inviting. Just off Main Street, it offers a deck overlooking the small lake, good for burgers, sandwiches, pasta, dinner entrées like baked stuffed haddock, fish-and-chips, and grilled rib-eye steak.

✴ Entertainment

MUSIC **Mohawk Trail Concerts** (413-625-9511 or 800-MTC-MUSE; www.mohawktrailconcerts.org). Since 1969 the acoustically fine, 225-seat Federated Church on Rt. 2 in Charlemont has been the summer venue for chamber and choral music from many styles, periods, and places, performed by internationally known artists. Open rehearsals are Friday, 7:30 PM. Concerts are Saturday at 8, late June to mid-August.

Hilltown Folk Concerts (413-625-2580; www.hilltownfolk.com). A series of weekend performances held frequently in Memorial Hall, Shelburne Falls. At this writing the schedule includes Odetta, the Huun-Huur-Tu Tuvan Throat-Singers, country and rock musicians, and the Gyoto monks from Tibet. $20 advance, $25 at the door.

Shelburne Falls Military Band. Billed as the country's oldest military band. Concerts are held on Wednesdays from mid-June through August at various locations in Shelburne Falls.

The Charlemont Inn (www.charlemontinn.com). Saturday-night music ranges from bluegrass and folk through jazz.

Mocha Maya's Coffee Co. (413-828-1413), 47 Bridge St. A coffeehouse hung with exhibits of local art; live music weekends and at art openings.

FILM **Pothole Pictures** (413-625-2896), Memorial Hall Theater, Shelburne Falls. A series of independent, classic, and art films Fri. and Sat. throughout the year but not every week. The 425-seat restored Memorial Hall Theater is upstairs in the town hall. For the current schedule, check www.shelburnefallsmemorialhall.org.

Zoar Outdoor (800-532-7483; www.zoaroutdoor.com), Rt. 2 in Charlemont (see *White-Water Rafting*), schedules a summer series of Saturday-night films, free and usually depicting paddling adventures. A nominally priced barbecue usually precedes the films.

THEATER West County Players (413-625-9863), Community Theater. Worth seeing. For performances see www.shelburnefallsmemorialhall.org. Advance tickets are available from Boswell's Books (see *Selective Shopping*).

❋ Selective Shopping

ANTIQUES SHOPS The **Shelburne Falls Village Information Center** (see *Guidance*) publishes a list of local dealers. Our local favorite is Strawberry Fields (413-625-2039), 1204 Mohawk Trail (Rt. 2), on the corner of the road to Colrain.

CRAFTS SHOPS AND STUDIOS

In Shelburne Falls

Note: **Gallery Walks** promote village galleries and studios the third Friday of every month, 5–8 PM.

Salmon Falls Artisans Showroom (413-625-9833), 1 Ashfield St. Open Apr.–Dec., daily 10–5, Sun. noon–5; Jan.–Mar., Wed.–Sat. 10–5, Sun. noon–5. Housed in a former granary, this is an exceptional gallery showcasing some 190 local craftspeople and artists drawn from within a radius of 65 miles. It's a prime outlet for the widely acclaimed glass orbs by Shelburne-based Josh Simpson. The quality of work displayed—notably jewelry and woodwork—is outstanding. This is a hidden treasure; the entrance is through an unrelated ground-floor shop.

Shelburne Artisans Cooperative (413-625-9324), 26 Bridge St., closed

Tue., open Thu.–Sat. 11–7; otherwise noon–4. A shop filled with striking work by some 70 members, mostly local.

Bald Mountain Pottery (413-625-8110), 28 State St. Open except Tue. 11–5; also closed Mon. off-season. The distinctive, functional pottery by Sarah Hettinger and James Gleason includes striking vases and lamps made in this riverside studio overlooking the Bridge of Flowers.

Laurie Goddard Studios (413-625-0201; www.lauriegoddard.com), 9 Bridge St. Open year-round. Laurie Goddard is best known for her museum-quality translucent bowls, but more recently she has been creating striking abstract designs on gessoed Masonite panels, gilded with combinations of semiprecious leaf such as copper, Dutch metal, and metallic powders, then overpainted and finally varnished.

Stillwater Art and Design (413-625-8250; www.stillwaterart.com), 50 State St. Housed in a former Sunoco station and car wash, Pat Pyott's porcelain studio produces and sells professional porcelain works featuring nature designs in relief.

Väv Stuga Swedish Weaving and Folks Arts (413-625-8241; www.vavstuga.com), 16 Water St. A showcase for the neighboring center, with classes in Swedish weaving; also Swedish looms, equipment, and yarns.

Tregellys Weaving Room (413-625-6448; www.tregellysfibers.com), 44 State St., Shelburne Falls. Ed Cohey has moved his weaving room from Tregellys Fiber Farm to sit beside the river.

Ann Brauer Quilt Studio (413-625-8605), 2 Conway St. Open Wed.–Sat.

10–5, Sun. noon–5. This nationally known quilter is usually to be found in her small pink shop on the Buckland side of the river, frequently stitching away on stunning quilts, wall hangings, pot holders, shoulder bags, place mats, and other creations.

Dick Muller & Co. Leather (413-625-6205), 6 Bridge St. Open Thu.–Sat. 11–5:30, Sun. 11–5. Diane and Dick Muller have been working together for more than 36 years, crafting custom sandals and lovely wallets, one-of-a-kind handbags, and belts in their Shelburne studio.

Mole Hollow Candles (413-625-6337), Deerfield Ave. Open daily 10–5, later in summer. Overlooks the Potholes along the Deerfield River; candles are made on weekdays. The shop also sells gifts and cards.

Wandering Moon (413-625-9667; www.thewanderingmoon.com), 59 Bridge St. Open Wed.–Sat. 10:30–5, Sun. 11–4. Since 1991 Laura and David Roberson's shop has acquired an ever-widening reputation for unusual jewelry (some made by Laura) as well as an eclectic mix of handcrafted work and books relating to nature and pre-industrial history.

W. C. Lyones Gallery (413-625-2256), 20 State St. Open Thu.–Sun. 10–5ish. This riverside shop features hand-painted "spirit paintings" by owner Willie Lyons.

Young & Constantine Gallery (413-625-6866), 4 Deerfield Ave. Open daily in-season. Kathleen Young, owner of North River Glass—which was formerly blown on these premises —has revamped the former gallery here, doubling its size and now carrying jewelry, fine art, furnishings, and more.

Elsewhere
Moonshine Designs at Keldaby Farm (413-634-3090; www.keldaby .com), 12 Heath Rd. Cynthia Herbert is a weaver producing hand-dyed mohair yarns, throws, and wearables, both handwoven and knitted from her herd of Angora goats. Visitors are welcome at the sunflower-yellow house with its barn, fields, and shop/studio.

Mike Purington Wood Bowls (413-624-0036; www.naturalturnedwood bowls.com), 285 Thompson Rd., Colrain. Open Sun. 2–6 and by appointment. Purington turns bowls in his shop facing north toward the Green Mountains. Each piece of wood is turned to a shape that suits its character, then set to dry for several months before being finished with oils and beeswax.

SPECIAL SHOPS

In Shelburne Falls

McCusker's Market (413-625-9411), 3 State St. The hub of the Hilltowns, a combination health food store and deli/café with internet access (see *Eating Out*) in a picturesque 1877 former Odd Fellows Hall.

Boswell's Books (413-625-9362; www.boswellsbooks.com), 10 Bridge St. Closed Mondays. A full-service independent bookshop with new and used books. Rachel Popwich also offers audio and video rentals, games, notebooks, pens, puzzles, pleasant reading corners, and Boswell the cat.

Nancy L. Dole Books & Ephemera (413-625-9850; ndole@crocker.com), 32 Bridge St., second floor. Open Tue.–Fri. from 11, Sat.–Sun. no later than 1. This is a find, an upstairs cache of some 25,000 books plus old prints, photos, postcards.

The Shelburne Falls Wine Merchant (413-825-6506; www.hilltown winemerchant.com), 1 State St. (adjoining McCusker's). Open Mon.–Sat. 10–7, Sun. noon–6. A wine mecca with frequent tastings and special events.

Lamson & Goodnow Mfg. Co. (413-625-6331 or 800-872-6504), 45 Conway St. This venerable complex of classic, mostly 19th-century wood and brick mill buildings dates from 1837 and is, sadly at this writing, up for sale. The fate of its fabulous outlet is unclear.

Eddie's Wheels for Pets (413-625-0033 or 888-211-2700; www.eddies wheels.com), 140 State St., Shelburne Falls. This thriving business is dedicated to making custom carts for dogs who have lost mobility in their hind legs. They are sold throughout the world.

Christina Tree

J. H. Sherburne Fine Art (413-625-8306), 40 State St. A framery and gallery with changing exhibits, overlooking the Bridge of Flowers.

Elsewhere

Ashfield Hardware & Supply (413-628-3299), 343 Main St., Ashfield. A store that's housed many enterprises over the years, but none more varied and useful than at present under its female owners. An exceptional independent hardware store specializing in hard-to-find items and those with natural ingredients, plus soaps and toys, hand-forged items, plants, and 50-cent ice cream cones.

Curtis Country Store (413-339-4900), 159 Main St., Charlemont. Open Mon.–Sat. 7–6, Sun. 7–5. This store gets more interesting as you find yourself to the back, the area suffused with the smell of freshly baked breads and pies. It's here you can find and sample owner John Miller's Goat Rising and Jersey Maid farmstead cheeses, made with milk from his Nubian goats and Jersey cows on his nearby farm. Curtis is the 12th generation of his family to make maple syrup, also sold here.

Note: See "Along the Mohawk Trail" for more information on the trading posts and gift shops along Rt. 2.

✳ Farms

Tregellys Fiber Farm (413-625-6448; www.tregellysfibers.com), 15 Dodge Branch Rd., Hawley. Open Wed.–Sun. 10:30–5. Turn off Rt. 112 at the Ashfield–Buckland line onto Clesson Brook Rd., and follow the camels. Donation suggested. Spreading for some 138 acres across Hog Mountain in the Dodge Corner area of Hawley, this farm is well named. *Tregelly* means "hidden homestead" in

Cornish, whence Ed Cothey originally came. Ed and wife Jody envisioned a few animals and a garden when they moved here a decade or so back, but their passion for animals and fiber arts took on a life of its own. The animals now include unusual heritage breeds such as Galloway cattle, yaks, llamas, and Bactrian (two-humped) camels from Mongolia, not to mention peacocks and an assortment of birds. Many visitors come just for the raw fibers in an array of natural colors and a rainbow of processed fibers, also hand-dyed using only botanical dye extracts. The base for the yarns comes from the Angora goats, blended with wool and other fibers before spinning. Needless to say, this is a mecca for knitters and weavers—but it's also just a fascinating all-around place to visit. Look for the farm's weaving shop in Shelburne Falls.

Apex Orchards (413-625-2744), 153 Pecksville Rd., Shelburne. The retail store is open Mon.–Fri. 7–2, Sat.–Sun. 8–3. PYO apples in Sep. and Oct. Also available: peaches, honey, cider vinegar, and one of the region's more amazing views. This glorious orchard has been in Tim Smith's family since 1828.

Donovan Farm (413-339-4213), Forget Rd., Hawley. The state's largest organically certified farm, with sweeping views and five kinds of potatoes, produces its own hand-cooked, organic potato chips.

Hall Tavern Farm (413-625-9008; jayhealy6387@aol.com), Rt. 2, East Charlemont. The state's oldest privately owned tree farm produces timbers and lumber for its sawmill and offers a variety of kiln-dried wood products, including wide pine flooring, paneling, and wainscoting as well

as ash, cherry, maple, and oak flooring from its 500 acres. The property includes a 4-mile hiking and snowshoeing trail.

Burnt Hill Farm (413-337-4454), Burnt Hill, Heath. Pick-your-own blueberries in-season on top of a mountain with a 50-mile view.

The Benson Place (413-337-5340), 182 Flag Hill Rd., Heath. Unsprayed, wild, lowbush blueberries. PYO late July through late August; the farm stand is also open 9–5 daily.

Walnut Hill Farm (413-625-9002), 104 Ashfield Rd., Shelburne Falls. Open daily 7:30–7. A dairy farm and vegetable stand welcome visitors. The world's largest ox, weighing 4,700 pounds, was raised here at the turn of the 20th century.

Johnson Hill Farm (413-625-6423), 51 Hog Hollow Rd., Shelburne Falls. Guests are invited to walk the lavender labyrinth. Lavender is harvested and dried; lavender products sold. Inquire about the Lavender Festival.

SUGARHOUSES Sugaring season can begin as early as late February and extend well into April. A brochure detailing information about the sugaring process and each producer is available from the **Massachusetts Maple Producers Association** (www.massmaple.org), Watson–Spruce Corner Rd., Ashfield 01330. During sugaring season you can call the **Massachusetts Maple Phone** (413-628-3912) to get an overall view on whether the sap is flowing and producers are "boiling off." The following sugarhouses (a partial list) are geared toward visitors more than most, but it's still a good idea to call before coming. All also sell their syrup from their farms year-round.

In Ashfield
South Face Farm (413-628-3268; www.southfacefarm.com). Tom McCrumm and Judy Haupt offer a sit-down dining room during sugaring season, as well as exhibits of antique maple-sugaring equipment. This has been a working farm for 150 years, and some of the maples along the road are probably that old. The present sugarhouse dates back 50 years, recycled from a 19th-century barn. **Gray's Sugarhouse** (413-625-6559; www.grayssugarhouse.com) also has a long-established, visitor-geared sugarhouse in another corner of town.

In Charlemont
Blue Heron Farm (413-339-4045) welcomes visitors with rental units attached to its sugarhouse (see *Lodging*); the farm also features dairy goats, Norwegian Fjord horses, and organic produce.

Tom McCrumm

In Conway
Boyden Brothers, right on Rt. 116, is the big producer here, but a number of other producers using wood-burning evaporators are scattered through the hills.

In Hawley
Clarks Sugarhouse (413-337-5788). Call for directions. It's not far from Berkshire East.

In Heath
Girard's Sugarhouse (413-337-5788) has been operating for more than 100 years. **Maple Ledge Farm** (413-337-4705), 107 Branch Hill Rd., is just beyond the Heath Fairgrounds heading north toward Rt. 8A; **Berkshire Sweet Gold Maple Farm** (888-57-MAPLE) bottles single-batch high-grade syrups in imported glass.

In Shelburne
Gould's Sugar House (413-625-6170), right on Rt. 2, features locally made syrup on waffles; also home-made sausage and sugar-on-snow among its other items (see *Eating Out*). **Davenport Maple Farm** (413-625-2866), 111 Tower Rd., set high above the valley with a splendid view, operates a restaurant during sugaring season and sells syrup from the house year-round (a good excuse to drive up). **Graves Sugarhouse** (413-625-6174), 104 Wilson Graves Rd. on the Greenfield–Colrain Rd., is an old-fashioned wood-burning operation with an open barn.

✳ Special Events
Note: Check www.shelburnefalls.com for current Shelburne Falls–area events, and www.mafa.org for dates and details on agricultural fairs.

March: **Art on Sunday** (413-628-

4696), a major auction of work by juried artists and artisans, benefits the Franklin Land Trust.

May: **Indian Powwow** at Indian Plaza, Charlemont. **Memorial Day Parade**, Shelburne Falls.

June: **Riverfest** is a daylong festival along the street and river in Shelburne Falls.

July: July 4 **Indian Pow Wow**, Charlemont; **July 4 parade** in Shelburne Falls. **Rowe Old Home Day** (*first weekend*). **Franklin Land Trust Annual Farm and Garden Tour** (413-625-9151; www.franklin landtrust.org) is a great excuse to explore back roads leading to some amazing properties (*midmonth*). **Charlemont Yankee Doodle Days** at the Charlemont Fair Grounds offers 3 days of music and games, square dancing, fireworks, and BBQ (*third weekend*).

August: **Bridge of Flowers 10K road race** and **Bridge Dinner**, Shelburne Falls. **Heath Fair** (413-337-5716) is one of the state's most colorful country fairs (*midmonth*). **Shelburne Grange Fair** (*last weekend*).

September: **Annual Shelburne Falls Wine and Cheese Festival**. **Colrain Fair** (*midmonth*). The big September event is the **Conway Festival of the Hills** (413-369-4631), one of New England's most colorful foliage festivals, featuring arts and crafts, skillet toss, weaving, ox driving, and more (*last weekend*).

October: **Ashfield Fall Festival** on Columbus Day weekend is not to be missed—art and crafts exhibits, music, games, antiques sales, demonstrations, all kinds of food, farm products, and more.

November: **Cider Day** (www.cider day.com), on the first weekend of the month 10–5, includes tours of orchards, hard-cider-making demos, apple pie tasting, crafts fair, lunch and supper; there's also an open house and tasting at **West County Winery** (www.westcountycider.com). **Crafts of Colrain Studio Tour** (www.crafts ofcolrain.com) opens upward of 20 studios scattered through the hills (*second weekend, 10–5*). **Moonlight Madness** features tree lighting, caroling, and special sales in Shelburne Falls (*day after Thanksgiving*).

Sunday after Thanksgiving: **Tuba Christmas** concert in Shelburne Falls.

HAMPSHIRE HILLTOWNS

This 225-square-mile spread of rolling hill and woodland is so far off the tourist map that it's sometimes called "the Hidden Hills." It's been bypassed by the Massachusetts Turnpike—there are no exits in the 33 miles between Westfield and Lee—which suits most of its residents just fine. Along the meandering Westfield River and its branches, these fertile valleys between wooded hills remain profoundly Yankee.

During the decades before income taxes, when wealthy Americans were building themselves summer palaces in Stockbridge and Lenox, a number of farms around Worthington and Cummington were gentrified; the William Cullen

Bryant Homestead in Cummington is the most obvious surviving example. For much of the 20th century, however, this area was just a nameless region to pass through.

It was in 1982 that the Hilltown Community Development Corporation placed an ad in local papers asking people with spare rooms to consider the bed & breakfast business. A dozen or so households responded, forming the Hampshire Hills Bed & Breakfast Association and publishing a descriptive brochure. Their towns became known as the Hampshire Hills, a name that still applies generally to this area, despite the fact that some of the B&Bs as well as the swimming holes, craftspeople, fishing spots, waterfalls, and otherwise hard-to-find gems are actually in Hampden County to the south. This area offers few restaurants but many, many likely picnic spots and sources.

Jacob's Pillow Dance Festival in Becket, the Miniature Theatre of Chester, and the Sevenars concerts in South Worthington are all widely acclaimed, but most events—such as auctions, agricultural fairs, and town homecomings—are only promoted locally, usually with flyers tacked up on general store bulletin boards and other public places. March is the time to sample this region's true culinary specialty: maple syrup, served up on pancakes or snow, at the sugarhouses in which it's just been made. April brings fishing and one of the country's most famous white-water races. All summer is prime time, highlighted by August's old-fashioned agricultural fairs. September brings PYO apples and fresh cider throughout the area, and during foliage season its high, maple-lined roads rival any in Vermont.

AREA CODE 413.

GUIDANCE The Hills of Jacob's Ladder (www.jlba.org) has helpful material about towns on and off Jacob's Ladder, the 33 miles of Rt. 20 between Russell and Lee. Also see www.hidden-hills.com, www.hilltowns.com, and *Lodging*. Bear in mind that information on all these web sites represents advertising and may be dated.

THE GRANVILLE COUNTRY STORE IS FAMOUS FOR ITS CHEDDAR.
Christina Tree

GETTING THERE Part of the beauty of this area is in its approach. Few places in this region are much more than half an hour's drive from I-91 or the Mass Pike, but you are quickly on back roads. The principal east–west roads—Rts. 9, 20, and 23—follow the river valleys, while Rt. 57 to the south is a high old byway. The major north–south routes, Rts. 112 and 8, also follow rivers. If you are coming from the east via the Mass Pike, take exit 3 in Westfield.

MEDICAL EMERGENCY Dial **911**.

Chester (population: c. 1,200; www.chestermass.com) is a town with a split per-
sonality: Chester Village, down on Rt. 20, and Chester Center up on Chester
Hill. **Chester Village** boomed with the mining and grinding of emery (as in
emery boards and sandpaper) and with the advent of the railroad, which heads
northwest out of town, all uphill. It's still the way Amtrak goes from Boston to
Chicago, and it was a huge engineering feat to snake tracks up these ridges in
the 1840s. The **Chester Railroad Museum** (413-354-7778) in the vintage-1841
depot at the head of Main St. (off Rt. 20) was originally built as a place to eat
(dining cars had yet to be invented) midway between Springfield and Pittsfield.
The museum is open July–Sep., Sat. and Sun. 11–3. The **Chester Historical
Society Museum** (open the first Wed. of each month and by appointment: 413-
354-7829) is headquartered in the former small brick jailhouse on Rt. 20. The
town hall is seasonal home to the distinguished **Miniature Theatre of
Chester**. On Rt. 20 in the middle of the village a sign for Middlefield points the
way up to the Skyline Trail. Turn off onto Johnson Hill Road to find **Chester
Center**, the picturesque 18th-century heart of town with its church and grave-
yard. Signs steer you to **Chester Hill Winery**. Ask locally about how to find the
Keystone Arch Bridges off Rt. 20.

Chesterfield. A white-clapboard village with an 1835 Congregational church,
1848 town hall, and the **Edward Memorial** (historical) **Museum** near the
library. But the big attraction is **Chesterfield Gorge**. The town stages a rousing
July 4 parade. The **Bisbee Mill Museum** includes a working 19th-century gristmill as well as a rare collection of tools, equipment, and photographs of the
town's past industries.

Cummington. The classic village center is posted from Rt. 9 and worth a stop
to see the **Kingman Tavern** (open Sat. 2–5 in July and Aug.), a lovingly
restored combination tavern, fully stocked general store, and post office. There
are a dozen period rooms filled with town mementos like the palm-leaf hats and
cigars once made here. There is also a barn full of tools and a shed full of horse-
drawn vehicles. The big annual event is the **Hillside Agricultural Society
Fair**, the last weekend in August. Cummington has nurtured a number of poets
over the years and is the longtime home of America's former poet laureate
Richard Wilbur. The **William Cullen Bryant Homestead** offers one of the
best views of the town and its valley.

Middlefield (population: 542), a town in which the main road (one of the few
that's paved) is known as the Skyline Trail because it follows the edge of a 1,650-
foot-high plateau and offers long views west to the Berkshires. The only specific
site to visit here is **Glendale Falls**, but everywhere you walk or drive is rewarding. The **Middlefield Fair** (second week in August) is one of the oldest (since
1856) and most colorful (horse and oxen draws, a sheep show, country bands,
and plenty of food).

Plainfield. This beautiful old farming town has a population of 589, which
swells to 2,000 in summer. Roads are lined with stone walls and avenues of
maples, and the center has its mid-19th-century white Congregational church

and town hall. The **Shaw-Hudson House** was built in 1833 by Dr. Samuel Shaw, medical partner and brother-in-law of William Cullen Bryant. Note the post office in the back of the white house across Rt. 116.

Williamsburg. The easternmost of the Hilltowns, this village is something of a bedroom town for Northampton 8 miles to the east. The village center straddles the Mill River and invites you to stroll, munching something you've bought at the **Williamsburg General Store**, the source of a *Walking Guide* published by the **Williamsburg Historical Society**, which is housed in the 1841 town hall. Exhibits include photographs of the 1874 flood that burst a dam 3 miles above the village, killing 136 residents, collapsing buildings, and wiping out most of the mills. The museum also includes the Olde Grist Mill with its collection of farm tools and equipment and the one-room Nash Hill School (the buildings are open summer Sundays). **Snow Farm** (see *Arts and Crafts Programs*) attracts participants from around the country.

Worthington. The village at the heart of this town, known locally as Worthington Corners, is a classic, mid-19th-century crossroads with its general store and surrounding old homes along roads that radiate in every direction. Note the grocery, golf course (vintage 1904), B&Bs, cross-country ski center, and hot-air ballooning. Turn off Rt. 112 in South Worthington to see the 19th-century academy building that now houses the **Sevenars Music Festival**. Continue on Ireland Street to farms and orchards spread along a high ridge.

THE INTERIOR OF THE WILLIAM CULLEN BRYANT HOMESTEAD

✳ To See

HISTORIC HOMES ⅋ **William Cullen Bryant Homestead** (413-634-2244) in Cummington, south of Rt. 9 off Rt. 112. Open for guided tours from the last week in June through Labor Day, Fri., Sat., Sun., and holidays 1–5; until Columbus Day, weekends and holidays. $5 adults; $2.50 ages 6–12. This graceful mansion is filled with the spirit of an obviously tough-minded and original individual and with a sense of the era in which he was thoroughly involved. William Cullen Bryant was born in Cummington in 1794 and is remembered for his early nature poems—"Thanatopsis" and "To a Waterfowl," for example—and for his impact as editor and part owner for half a century (1829–78) of the *New York Evening Post*. Bryant successfully advocated causes ranging from abolitionism to free trade to the creation of Central Park. He returned to his boyhood home at age 72, buying back the family homestead, adding another floor, and totally transforming it into a 23-room Victorian summer manse set atop 195 acres of farmland. The land has since been reduced to 189 acres, but the expansive view remains. The house has been preserved (painted in its original chocolate browns) by the Trustees of Reservations to look as it did during Bryant's last summer here, in 1878. There's a visitor center and a museum shop, featuring Bryant's poetry as well as maple syrup from trees on the property. The 2.5 miles of footpaths are open to the public without charge.

SCENIC DRIVES In the Hilltowns, the drive that is *not* scenic is the exception. You almost can't lose, especially if you turn off the main roads in search of the waterfalls, swimming holes, crafts studios, and maple producers described in this chapter. Several drives, however, are particularly noteworthy.

The Skyline Trail, accessible from Rt. 143 in Hinsdale and from Rt. 20 in Chester, follows the edge of the Berkshire plateau through the middle of Middlefield. It's possible to make a loop from Chesterfield through Middlefield, stopping at Glendale Falls and the River Studio and returning via Chester Hill (another high point), but it's best to ask directions locally.

Ireland Street, Chesterfield, to South Worthington. A mile or so west of the village of Chesterfield, turn left off Rt. 143 at the bridge. This is Ireland Street and best known as the way to **Chesterfield Gorge** (0.8 mile from Rt. 143 at River Rd.). Be sure to stop. Then continue along Ireland, which is a straight, high ridge road. Stop at **Ireland Street Orchards** for the view, if for nothing else. Continue on to South Worthington. If you feel like a swim, **Gardner State Park** is just down Rt. 112.

Jacob's Ladder Trail Scenic Byway. The 33 miles of Rt. 20 between Russell and Becket are now promoted as "Jacob's Ladder," an early auto route (long since backroaded by the Mass Pike) that takes its name from the Becket farmer who is said to have hauled autos up the steepest pitch with oxen. This route actually predated the Mohawk Trail as a motorway between the Pioneer Valley and Berkshire County. The Ladder crests in Becket at a ridge billed variously as 1,781 and 2,100 feet high. Whichever it is, the view of the Berkshire Valley is splendid. Note "Jacob's Well," the spring used to cool the radiators of early cars, still in use beside a rest area.

General Knox Trail (Rt. 23) forks off from Rt. 20 in Blandford heading west through Otis. The Otis Reservoir, with swimming and boating, is just over the line. This route got its name (which actually applies to much of Rt. 20, too) because it was the path over which Boston book dealer Henry Knox mounted a successful winter effort to drag the cannons captured by Benedict Arnold and Ethan Allen at Fort Ticonderoga back to Boston, where they played a crucial role in liberating the city.

Route 57 from Westfield through Tolland and Granville. This route is well-known to South Berkshire residents as a shortcut to Bradley International Airport in Connecticut, but it's otherwise one of the most obscure and backroaded of the state's historic east–west highways. It's the most southerly and one of the highest, obviously the reason why the railroad chose to follow the Westfield River instead. These villages—which prospered in the late 18th and early 19th centuries, judging from the buildings along the road—were left to fade away. Tolland today is known chiefly for the Tolland State Forest, with some of the best campsites in the state. West Granville is worth pausing to note its early-18th-century meetinghouse; Granville is a must-stop to buy the cheese that's been sold at the general store here since the 1850s. The road then spirals down out of the Berkshire Hills into the Connecticut River Valley at Southwick, notable for its many tobacco sheds and farm stands. Coming from the east, take Mass Pike exit 6 to 291 to I-91 south, and I-91 exit 2 to Rt. 57.

Get lost. Seriously. This is high, largely open countryside that was far more populated a couple of hundred years ago than it is now. If we try to direct you from Plainfield to Buckland via the web of back roads that begin with Union Street north from the middle of Plainfield, you will have us to blame. So, bring a camera, a map, and a compass and explore.

✳ To Do

BALLOONING Worthington Hot Air Ballooning (413-238-5514), Buffington Hill Rd., Worthington. Paul Sena offers champagne flights year-round. He will pick up passengers almost anywhere in the Berkshires but prefers to fly from Worthington and neighboring Cummington, over the hills and down into the Connecticut River Valley. Request the multicolored "Thunderbuster" balloon: yellow, red, and orange on one side, blue and purple on the other.

BICYCLING Mountain bikers enthuse about the unpaved **River Road** south from Chesterfield Gorge in Worthington (see *Green Space*) to Knightville Dam. The *Rubel Western Massachusetts Bicycle and Road Map* is an excellent guide to biking throughout this area. See *Special Events* for the **Great River Ride** on the Columbus Day weekend.

CAMPING To reserve campsites in state forests, phone 877-422-6762 and check out what we say under *Camping* in "What's Where." The web site of the Department of Conservation and Recreation (formerly Department of Environmental Management) describes each park: www.mass.gov/dcr. **DAR State Forest** (413-268-7098), Goshen, provides 50 campsites, each with a table and fireplace. **Windsor State Forest** (413-663-8469), marked from Rt. 9 in West Cummington, offers 24 campsites. also see **Savoy Mountain State Forest** in "Along the Mohawk Trail." All three areas offer swimming.

ARTS AND CRAFTS PROGRAMS Snow Farm (413-268-3101; www.snowfarm .org), 5 Clary Rd., Williamsburg 01096. A full and varied program of weekend and weeklong workshops are taught by dozens of skilled craftspeople, most of whom already have a long association with this special place. Check out the web site or request a catalog for a sense of current courses, which typically include ceramics, glassblowing, silk screening, wood sculpture, basket making, and pho-

tography. The setting is a 50-acre farm with lodging in dormitories and doubles
(gender-specific shared baths), a common room, and a dining hall in which the
meals served are all made from scratch. A "Seconds Sale" featuring the work of
craftspeople from around the country is held three weekends in November.

Becket Arts Center (413-623-6635; becketartscenter.org). A former wooden
schoolhouse offers June–Aug. arts programs and workshops in writing and
music.

FISHING The **Little River** and all three branches of the **Westfield River** are
recognized throughout the country for the quality of their fishing.

GOLF The **Worthington Golf Club** (413-238-4464), founded in 1904, covers 88
acres and, at 1,700 feet in elevation, commands a view of surrunding hills and
valleys. Just nine holes, it's a destination course, with an attractive clubhouse and
restaurant. The **Beaver Brook Golf Club** (413-268-7229), 191 Haydenville Rd.
(Rt. 9), Williamsburg, and the Blandford Golf Club (tennis, too), 17 North St.,
Blandford, are both nine holes. **Whippernon Country Club** (413-862-3606),
490 Westfield Rd., Russell. A nine-hole course, challenging for beginners, with
nice views and terrain.

SWIMMING The **West Branch**, **Middle Branch**, and **Westfield River** proper
all weave their way through this area, offering countless swimming holes to
which B&B hosts can direct you. More formal, public swimming spots like Plainfield Pond tend to be restricted to residents.

DAR State Forest (413-268-7098; www.mass.gov/dcr), Goshen, maintains a
swimming area on Upper Highland Lake (see *Green Space*).

Windsor State Forest (413-684-9760; www.mass.gov/dcr), River Rd., West
Cummington, has a swimming area on a dammed portion of the river (see *Green
Space*).

🌢 **Gardner State Park** (www.mass.gov/dcr), Rt. 112, Huntington. Probably the
best-known swimming hole on the Westfield River, this is a great spot to bring
small children. There's an old-fashioned picnic pavilion in the pines.

✴ Winter Sports

CROSS-COUNTRY SKIING AND SNOWSHOEING **Notchview Reservation**
(413-684-0148; www.thetrustees.org), Rt. 9, Windsor. The highest cross-country
trails in Massachusetts are found on this 3,000-acre Trustees of Reservations
property. Admittedly, it takes a new snowfall to work your way up to the summit
of 2,297-foot-high Judges Hill, but frequently there is snow on the former lawns
of the General Budd Homesite. The panoramic view from this open area
includes the notch in the hills cut by the Westfield River, for which the preserve
is named. Adults $9, children $2.

Maple Corner Farm (413-357-8829; snow phone, 413-357-6697; www.xcski
mass.com/MapleCorner), Beech Hill Rd., Granville. This 500-acre working farm

at an elevation of 1,400 feet offers 20 km of groomed trail over varied terrain. There is a rental shop and a lodge with a fireplace and snack bar. Open 10–5 weekdays, 9–5 weekends.

Also see **Canterbury Farm** in the South County chapter and **Stump Sprouts** in West County.

DOWNHILL SKIING Blandford Ski Area (413-848-2860; snow phone, 413-568-4341; www.skiblandford.org), Blandford. Call for directions. A small ski area that's been owned and operated by the Springfield Ski Club since 1936: 26 trails and slopes, two chairlifts, a T-bar, and multilift. Snowmaking. Open late Dec. to mid-Mar.

✳ Green Space

STATE FORESTS *Note:* All state parks and forests are detailed at www.mass.gov/dcr.

DAR State Forest (413-268-7098), Goshen, provides 50 campsites, each with a table and fireplace. The swimming area at Upper Highland Lake, complete with bathhouses and lifeguards, also has a boat ramp (no motors allowed). Trails lead to Moore's Hill, just 1,697 feet high but with an extensive view.

Windsor State Forest (www.mass.gov/dcr). Marked from Rt. 9 in West Cummington. You can swim in the dammed section of the river; there are campsites, bathhouses, 80 picnic tables, and grills here. This stretch of the Westfield River is a popular spot for white-water canoeing. There are also many miles of hiking trails. **Windsor Jambs** is a 0.25-mile-long gorge with sheer cliffs, topped with hemlocks above the rushing water. A trail leads along the edge. Unfortunately, picnicking is not permitted at the edge of the gorge, but it's a beautiful walk (there's a railing).

East Branch State Forest (413-268-7098), River Rd., Chesterfield, offers some good fishing.

Chester-Blandford State Forest (413-354-6347), Rt. 20, Chester, offers camping, fishing, as well as extensive hiking trails and easy access (a 0.5-mile walk over a cement and then two steel-grate bridges) to the picnic site by 100-foot **Sanderson Brook Falls**.

HIKING AND WALKING Notchview Reservation (413-684-0148; www.the trustees.org). The **Budd Visitor Center** on Rt. 9 in Windsor (1 mile east of the junction with Rt. 8A) is open daily year-round. There are picnic tables and trail maps for the 25 miles of hiking and cross-country trails on this former 3,000-acre estate maintained by the Trustees of Reservations. This is a good place for birding.

Petticoat Hill Reservation (www.thetrustees.org) in Williamsburg (up Petticoat Hill Rd. from the village). A trail leads to the summit of Scott Hill. Stone walls and cellar holes hint that this spot was the most populated part of town in the 1700s, but it's now forested, a good spot for wildflowers.

Devil's Den Brook in Williamsburg is a rocky gorge off Old Goshen Rd. (turn right onto Hemenway Rd. at the western fringe of the center, then branch left onto Old Goshen). If you take the next left, up Brier Hill Rd., you come to 70 acres of wooded trails, good for cross-country skiing and hiking. Ask locally about **Rheena's Cave**.

WATERFALLS Glendale Falls, Middlefield (www.thetrustees.org). Turn off Skyline Trail Rd. onto Clark Wright Rd.—which is closed in winter—some 3.5 miles southeast of the village. Glendale Brook drops more than 150 feet over rocky ledges. There are 60 surrounding acres.

Chesterfield Gorge (www.thetrustees.org). Turn off Rt. 143 at the West Chesterfield Bridge; the gorge turnoff is marked 1 mile south on River Rd. Open daily 8 AM–sunset. $2 per adult, free under age 12. A deep canyon was carved by the Westfield River and walled by sheer granite cliffs topped with hemlock, ash, and yellow birch. Swimming is not allowed, but the Trustees of Reservations provide picnic tables.

Salmon Brook Falls. A drop of 50 feet in the Chester-Blandford State Forest, south of Chester, marked from Rt. 20; a good spot for a picnic.

Also see **Sanderson Brook Falls** and **Windsor Jambs** under *State Forests*.

✳ Lodging

BED & BREAKFASTS *Note:* The B&Bs described below are widely scattered. Some border Berkshire County on the west, while those on the east offer easy access to the Five-College Area. Most are pictured on the **Hampshire Hills Bed & Breakfast Association** (888-414-7664) web site: www.hhbba .com or at www.hidden-hills.com.

In the Cummington/Worthington area

⌾ ✑ ❀ **Upland Meadows Farm** (413-634-8884), 338 West Cummington Rd. (Rt. 112), Cummington 01026. This is a find! A beautifully restored 18th-century house on 200 acres, set at an elevation of 2,000 feet with a long view of hills and valley rolling away to the east. Owner Judy Bogart has given her B&B an uncluttered, modern feeling while respecting the character of the house. The three bedrooms with private bath are bright and cheerfully, comfortably furnished; located in a rear wing, each has a private entrance from the porch. No extra charge for dogs. Horses are $10. Animals in residence on the farm include sheep, goats, a horse—and a llama. $90 year-round with full breakfast.

⌾ ✑ **The Worthington Inn** (413-238-4441), at Four Corners Farm, Old North Rd. (Rt. 143), Worthington 01098. Debi and Joe Shaw's striking, 1780 house has wide floorboards, five fireplaces, and fine paneling, restored in 1942 by the architect responsible for much of the Old Deerfield restoration. There are horses in the horse barn and 60 surrounding acres on the edge of a picturesque village, really someplace special. The three bedrooms are sparely, tastefully furnished with antiques and down comforters; all have a private bath and wonderful light. Common space is elegant and comfortable, lived in by a real family. As appealing in winter as summer. Children and horses are welcome. The Shaws are hospitable, helpful hosts. $80–90.

♣ ✍ Cumworth Farm (413-634-5529), 472 West Cummington Rd. (Rt. 112), Cummington 01026. Open May–Nov. only. This is still a working farm growing berries, raising sheep, and producing maple syrup. Eileen McColgan continues the hospitable tradition of her parents, who were among the first B&B operators in the area. There are six guest rooms in the handsome 18th-century, hip-roofed farmhouse, all furnished with antiques. Shared baths, but a hot tub is also available. Full farm-style breakfast. $75–85.

✍ Old North Road Bed & Breakfast (413-238-7747; www.oldnorth road.com), 126 Old North Rd. (Rt. 143), Worthington 01098. A contemporary house but built and furnished along traditional lines with a sense of the outdoors brought inside in the practically glass-walled breakfast room. Dick Pulley is an enthusiastic golfer (Worthington's nine-hole course with its panoramic views is minutes away) and Mary is an avid gardener, creator of many flower beds. Set on 5 landscaped acres, the property abuts fields, woods, and a series of beaver ponds, the source of bird life around Mary's feeders. There are two guest rooms (shared bath), each with a double bed, and a "common room" with a queen, which folds out. Downstairs there's a living room and formal dining room; also a TV, videos, games, and books. The Pulleys are enthusiastic grandparents, and children are welcome.

The Hill Gallery (413-238-5914), 137 East Windsor Rd., Worthington 01098. In his multilevel country contemporary home, which he designed and built himself, Walter Korzec has been welcoming guests since 1982.

The Windsor Suite, on two levels apart from the rest of the house, has its own entrance, a rec room (with pool table, fridge, and phone), an exercise bike, a working fireplace, and plenty of space; the bedroom has a four-poster double bed, wide floorboards, mirrored closet doors, and a private bath. The Worthington Room, with a Palladian window overlooking the two ponds and hills beyond, also has a mini fridge and a phone. Guests are welcome to use the living room with its working fieldstone fireplace. $75 single, $90 double includes a full breakfast. Korzec is an artist whose paintings and often whimsical constructions decorate the house and are displayed in the barn (which he also designed and built) that functions as an art gallery. A cottage is available, too.

Brennan's Inn (413-634-5493), 21 West Main St., Cummington 01026. This is the former Remington's Lodge. Recently totally revamped, primarily as a restaurant (see *Dining Out*) but with three attractive upstairs guest rooms (shared bath) and a basement bunk room adjoining a game room with a Ping-Pong table and hot tub. $80 per guest room includes an expanded continental breakfast.

In the Chesterfield/Williamsburg area

Seven Hearths (413-296-4312; www.sevenhearths.com), 412 Main Rd., Chesterfield 01012. An 1890s Colonial Revival house, set in the middle of the village historic district. Doc and Denise LeDuc serve memorable multicourse breakfasts (maybe stuffed French toast prefaced by a fruit-stuffed melon) in the formal dining room. The common rooms and three of the four guest rooms have working fireplace; the larger guest room offers sitting and writing space and a private bath, while the fourth room is reserved for guests traveling together. Facilities include high-speed wireless and a hot tub. $80–130 double, $70–120 single.

🐚 **Twin Maples** (413-268-7925; www .twinmaplesbnb.com), 106 South St., Williamsburg 01096. This vintage-1806 house is set in its own 27 acres and surrounding farmland on a back road not far from the center of town. It's been home to Eleanor and Martin Hebert for more than 40 years. The three bedrooms and shared bath are clean and crisp (we like the blue room with the antique iron-and-brass bed), and the welcome is genuine. During March you can watch sap turn into syrup in the sugarhouse, and any season you can meet the farm animals, which at latest count included a dozen Hereford heifers, two calves, a flock of Rhode Island Red hens and roosters, a number of sheep, and two dogs. $75–85.

🌿 **Flower Hill Farm** (413-268-7481; www.caroldukeflowers.com), P.O. Box 454, Williamsburg 01096. Carol Duke has created 5 acres of flower gardens on the slope below her vintage-1790 home, which sits high on a back road. While she promotes herself primarily as a place to stay within easy striking distance of Northampton, the location and feel are very much up-in-the-hills and away-from-it-all. Carol offers two suites, both unusually large and attractive. Downstairs there's a bedroom with queen-sized bed, fireplace, and bath adjoining a beautiful sitting room with a large fireplace. Upstairs is a bright bedroom with a queen bed, bath, small sitting and dining area, kitchen facilities, and a balcony. Both suites enjoy a view across the gardens to the mountains. Furnishings are appropriate to the age of the house and include many antiques. The dining room doubles as an art gallery. Floors are all gleaming hardwood, and guests are asked to bring slippers. The 20-acre property includes blueberries as well as flowers. $150 double, $135 single depending on room and time; weekly and longer rates. Snow Farm is minutes away. Rates include an organic vegetarian/vegan breakfast (organic fruit salad, muffins, juice, tea, and coffee).

1886 House, Chesterfield. See "Five-College Area."

Elsewhere

🌿 **Baird Tavern** (413-848-2096; www .bairdtavern.com), 2 Old Chester Rd., Blandford 01008. This 1768 house retains its original wide paneling and floorboards and conveys a sense of comfort as well as history. Host Carolyn Taylor has carefully preserved the authentic look of the house, originally a tavern catering to travelers on the old Boston-to-Albany turnpike. (The Massachusetts Turnpike follows the same approximate route but is out of sight of the house.) A kettle sits next to the big old fireplace in the original kitchen, and the onetime taproom is now a comfortable but uncluttered sitting room. Guest rooms are up the stairs built around the central chimney; one room retains its original walls and has a spinning wheel and period decor, but again nothing is cluttered. In all there are three guest rooms, the largest with a Shaker-style pencil-post canopy bed. Rooms share one and a half baths. A cot and crib are available; Persian cats (which Carolyn raises) are usually in residence. There is a beautiful peren-

Christina Tree

TRANQUILLITY AT THE BAIRD TAVERN IN BLANDFORD

nial flower garden. Carolyn is a local caterer, and breakfasts can as easily be quiche or omelets as blueberry pancakes, although the berry-packed latter is the house specialty. $90–110 double, $15 per extra person.

✳ Where to Eat

DINING OUT & **Brennan's Inn** (413-634-5493), 21 W. Main St., Cummington. Open Tue.–Sun. for dinner 4–9. On both Friday and Saturday a five-course prix fixe ($25) menu might begin with lobster bisque, then move on to veal Oscar and chocolate truffle cake. On Friday night there's also live local music, frequently fiddling; on Sunday there's jazz to go with brunch, 10–1. A pub menu features homemade soups and salads. This rambling lodge by the Westfield River was formerly known as Remington's and geared to groups. Chef-owner Maureen Brennan, well-known locally as executive chef of the Wahconah Country Club in Dalton, has totally renovated this old place, adding a deck and landscaped garden. Big weekends are celebrated here with lobster bakes, pig roasts, and the like.

EATING OUT **The Creamery** (413-634-5560), corner of Rts. 9 and 112,

Cummington. Open daily 7 AM–7:30 PM weekdays, from 7:30 Sat., 9 on Sun. This expanded general store with its deli and hot food items, fabulous baked goods, crafts, and wine selection is an oasis in these hills. The tables are limited but round, and strangers share—although it's true that most patrons know one another. The blackboard menu features soups and sandwiches. Bread is freshly baked.

Spruce Corner Restaurant (413-268-3188), Rt. 9, Goshen. Jerry Bird is the chef-owner of this cheery way stop. Open for breakfast, lunch, and dinner. This is pickup truck and Harley-Davidson country, which doesn't mean the food isn't fine. Everyone feels welcome.

Otis Poultry Farm (413-269-4438; www.otispoultryfarm.com), 1570 N. Main Rd. (Rt. 8), North Otis. Home of "the custom laid egg." Still in the same family that established this as a working poultry farm in 1904, but there no longer seem to be resident chickens. The old chicken house is now a vast store selling Yankee Candles, wine and beer, souvenirs, and

THE OTIS POULTRY FARM SERVES BREAKFAST AND LUNCH.

Christina Tree

homemade pies, breads, and eggs. A café is open for breakfast and lunch.

✳ Entertainment

Jacob's Pillow Dance Festival (413-243-0745; www.jacobspillow.org), George Carter Rd., Becket (off Rt. 20, 8 miles east of Lee). America's oldest dance festival and still its most prestigious, Jacob's Pillow presents a 10-week summer program of classic and experimental dance. For more details, see "South Berkshire."

Miniature Theatre of Chester (413-354-7771; www.miniature theatre.org), P.O. Box 722, Chester 01011-0722. The season runs 5 nights a week from the last week of June to the first week in October. Vincent Dowling, a former artistic director at Dublin's famed Abbey Theatre, first came to Chester to fish and swim in the Westfield River and has since built himself a house while staging a summer program of plays—a mix of lesser-known classics and original works, performed in Chester's town hall (150 seats). Cast members are professional actors and generally outstanding. Tickets are $20 Wed.–Thu., $24 Fri.–Sun.

Sevenars Music Festival (413-238-5854; www.sevenars.org), the Academy, S. Ireland St. and Rt. 112, Worthington. Concerts are Friday evenings (at 7:30) and Sunday afternoons (at 5), early July–Labor Day. The *seven R's* are the seven Schrades, who include Robert (longtime soloist with orchestras and a member of the faculty at the Manhattan School of Music), his wife Rolande (a concert pianist in her own right and composer of more than 1,000 songs), Robelyn, Rorianne, and Randolf Schrade (all with impressive degrees and concert careers). The twins Rhonda-Lee and Rolisa don't perform, but Robelyn's husband, well-known New Zealand pianist David James, and their daughter, Lynelle, do. Concerts are staged in the tongue-and-groove paneled hall of a double-porched, 19th-century academy just off Rt. 112 by the South Worthington Cascade. Door donation $20 adults, $18 seniors and students.

Dream Away Lodge (413-623-8725) 1342 County Rd., Becket. An old roadhouse that once had a funky reputation; see "South Berkshire."

Bel Canto Opera Concerts (413-848-2052), at the Historic White Church, North St., Blandford. Arias and ensembles held in August.

Note: Tanglewood Music Festival and the many other Lenox- and Stockbridge-area summer music and theater events are an easy drive from most parts of this region. See "South Berkshire."

✳ Selective Shopping

AUCTIONS **Sena's Auctions** (413-238-5377), Buffington Hill Rd., Worthington. Since the 1950s, auctions have taken place on Tuesdays, but check to make sure.

CRAFTS **The Basket Shop** (413-296-4278), 513 Main Rd. (Rt. 143), Chesterfield. The shop itself is special, built by hand by Ben Higgins with an open basket-weave ceiling, woven cabinet doors, dovetailed drawers, and a variety of timeworn tools. Ben specialized in the rare art of weaving ash baskets, a skill his son-in-law Milton Lafond carries on using a variety of wooden molds, some of them 100 years old. The baskets are striking and unusually durable. Call before making a special trip; inquire about Open Days.

Stonepool Pottery (413-238-5362; www.stonepottery.com), 42 Conwell Rd., Worthington, just up Ireland Street from the old academy in South Worthington (take the next left). Open by chance or appointment year-round. Distinctive. Functional work by potter Mark Shapiro and his apprentices is displayed in a small gallery above Shapiro's home, an old homestead in which the Rev. Russell Conwell was born. Conwell later added an unusual "stone pool" and built the nearby academy, but he is better known as the founder of Philadelphia's Temple University.

River Studio (413-238-7755; www.andrewdevries.com), 36 East River Rd., Middlefield. Open Fri. and Sat. 11–3, by appointment at other times. The internationally acclaimed dancing statues of Andrew DeVries are a find in their own right—especially set as they are on a meadow stage in a particularly obscure and lovely corner of Middlefield.

Quilts by Jane (413-634-5703; www.quiltsbyjane.com), Rt. 116, Plainfield. Jane Neri's eye-catching quilts festoon her front porch; visitors are welcome. Neri enjoys coming out to escort you into her studio (alias garage), hung with dozens of bright quilts, all made from castoff materials friends and neighbors bring her. Quilts are priced reasonably.

Snow Farm (413-268-3101; www.snowfarm.org), 5 Clary Rd., Williamsburg 01096. Operated by the New England Craft Program, Snow Farm offers workshops and classes year-round in a variety of crafts including ceramics, glassblowing, silk screening, wood sculpture, basket making, and photography. A sale featuring the work of craftspeople from around the country is held all through November.

GENERAL STORES Granville Country Store (800-356-3141), Granville, just off Rt. 57. Open daily 7–7. A typical village store but with a difference: A store cheese called Granville Cellar Aged Cheddar has been sold here since 1851. Current owners Tina Deblois and Tracy Strniste still use the original recipe and aging method, producing a cheddar that's sharper and tastier than most. They'll ship anywhere. No deli, but there are picnic tables outside.

Huntington Country Store (413-667-3232; www.hcstore.com), Rt. 112 north of the village, Huntington. Known for its baked goods and candy; 20 flavors of ice cream and jams, mustards and herbs, also greeting cards, specialty foods, gifts, gadgets, and local crafts.

Williamsburg General Store (413-268-3036; www.wgstore.com), 3 Main St., Williamsburg. Local maple products, daily-made breads and pastries, candy, handcrafted jewelry and many local crafts, 32 flavors of real ice cream, coffees, teas, cheese, jams, jellies, mustards, herbs, spices, and more.

The Corners Grocery (413-238-5531), Worthington Center. A double-porched, extremely photogenic store in the middle of a matching village; good picnic makings.

Also see **The Creamery** in Cummington under *Eating Out*.

✳ Farms

Hanging Meadow Farm (413-527-0710), 188 North Rd., Westhampton. This farm, up a country road, has

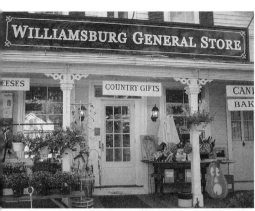

WILLIAMSBURG GENERAL STORE

CHEESES · COUNTRY GIFTS · CANDLES · BAKERY

Christina Tree

been in the Aloisi family since the 1940s. They've been known since then for their maple syrup and sit-down meals in maple season. In 2006 they opened the year-round **Straw-bale Café** (Wed.–Sun., 8–2) featuring straw walls—which we're assured are not flammable—also home-baked breads and syrup. From Northampton take Rt. 66 west.

High Meadow Farm (413-667-3640), 410 Skyline Trail, Chester. Pick-your-own apples and blueberries in-season. Call ahead. Children welcome. Maple syrup year-round.

Ireland Street Orchards (413-296-4024), Ireland St., Chesterfield. Apr.–Nov., open 10–6. Pick-your-own apples and flowers; a farm stand with local produce and crafts. Doughnuts and cider.

🍦 **Gran-Val Scoop** (413-357-6632; www.gran-valscoop.com), 233 Granby Rd. (Rt. 189), Granville. Open mid-Apr. to mid-Oct., 10:30–9. This century-old family farm has a large dairy herd (along with sheep, goats, chickens, and rabbits) and makes more than two dozen flavors of gourmet ice cream using locally produced maple syrup, wild blueberries, peaches, and other fruits.

Maple Corner Farm (413-357-8829), 794 Beech Hill Rd., Granville. A working farm since 1840, Maple Corner sells maple syrup and products along with jams and jellies year-round. Pick-your-own blueberries daily July through mid-September. A sugarhouse and pancake restaurant is open late February to early April; in winter the farm is a cross-country ski center with rental equipment and 20 km of groomed trails.

Mountain Orchard (413-357-8877), 668 Main Rd., Granville. Pick-your-own apples (eight varieties), nectarines, and peaches. Open Aug.–Nov., daily 8–8.

Waryjasz's Potato Farm (413-634-5336), 166 E. Main St. (Rt. 116), Plainfield. It's difficult to miss this hilltop barn with its painted people and many signs. Potato lovers can choose from white, red-skinned, table

CORNERS GROCERY, WORTHINGTON CENTER

Christina Tree

stock, and rye seed potatoes; browsers will find a flea market's worth of trash and treasure in the barn.

Outlook Farm (413-529-9388), Rt. 66, Westhampton. Open weekdays 6 AM–7 PM, weekends 6–6. You can pick your own apples and find seasonal fruit and produce here, but the real specialties of the roadside store are homemade sausage, smoked hams, bacon, and ribs (although the pigs are no longer raised here the way they used to be, the USDA-certified slaughterhouse and smokehouse continue to operate). Sandwiches and daily specials are served. Hayrides available.

WINERY Chester Hill Winery (413-354-2340; www.blueberrywine.com), 47 Lyon Hill Rd., Chester. Joe and Mary Ann Sullivan make three kinds of blueberry wine—semidry New Blue, full-bodied Best Blue, and the sweet, brandy-enhanced Bay Blue—using local blueberries from nearby Kelso Homestead. They also make a white wine with grapes from upstate New York. The winery, which has a gift shop and tasting room, is open June–Dec., Sat. and Sun. 1–5, or by appointment. A blueberry festival, "Blueberry Days of Summer," is held the second week of August.

SUGARHOUSES As already noted, the Hilltowns are the prime source of Massachusetts's maple sugar. Sugaring season can begin as early as late February and extend well into April. Locals and visitors alike are drawn to sugarhouses and pancake breakfasts featuring the new syrup. A brochure detailing the sugaring process and listing each producer is available from the **Massachusetts Maple Produc-**

ers Association (413-628-3912), Watson–Spruce Corner Rd., Ashfield 01330, to which most area producers belong. The association web site, www.massmaple.org, lists producers and sugarhouses open to the public and has a map showing where they are. It also has links to some 30 sites where you can learn just about all there is to know about maple syrup—including how to make it and cook with it. The following sugarhouses welcome visitors during sugaring-off, but call before coming. All also sell their syrup from their farms year-round.

In Chester
High Meadow Sugar Shack (413-667-3640) on the Skyline Trail offers spectacular views. **Roaring Brook Farm** (413-667-3692), 190 Skyline Trail, is a traditional operation that still uses a wood-fired evaporator to make syrup.

In Cummington
Tessiers Sugarhouse (413-634-5022), 60 Fairgrounds Rd., is 0.5 mile south of Rt. 9. **Maple Hollow Sugarhouse**, 337 Stage Rd., 0.4 mile east off Plainfield Rd.

In Granville
Maple Corner Farm (413-357-8829), 794 Beech Hill Rd. Maple museum, sugarhouse tours, and a restaurant open weekends March to mid-April.

In Heath
Girard's Sugarhouse (413-337-5788), 57 Number Nine Rd. An old-fashioned sugarhouse in operation for more than a century. **Berkshire Sweet Gold Maple Farm** (888-57-MAPLE; www.berkshiresweetgold .com) produces only single batch, unblended syrup from sap harvested

on this family farm. There's a self-serve farm stand on Rt. 8A, 4.5 miles north of Charlemont, just past mile marker 31. Call ahead for tours. **Maple Lane Farm** (413-337-8312), 292 Jackson Stage Rd. (Rt. 8A). The entrance to the farm is at mile marker 35. **Freeman Farm** (413-337-4766), 20 Town Farm Rd.

In Huntington
Norwich Lake Farm (413-667-8830), 87 Searle Rd. A traditional, wood-burning sugarhouse with eating facilities.

In Plainfield
Bob's Sugar House (413-634-5399), Rt. 16. A wood-burning sugar shack just a mile west of Plainfield Center. **Thatcher's Sugar House** (413-634-5582; www.thatcherssugarhouse.com), 12 Broom St. A traditional operation 0.5 mile south of Rt. 16 and 3.5 miles north of Rt. 9.

In Westhampton
See *Farms* for **Hanging Meadow Farm**. It has one of the area's oldest sugar shacks and offers sit-down meals year-round.

In Williamsburg
Paul's Sugar House (413-268-3544), Rt. 9, a mile west of Williamsburg Center. Antique equipment is on display, along with a maple-syrup-making video. Maple candies as well as apple, cherry, and blackberry syrups. **Lawton Family Sugar House** (413-268-3145), 47 Goshen Rd. A family tradition for six generations. **Dufresne Sugar House** (413-268-7509; www.berkshiremaple.com), 113 Goshen Rd., is a large-scale (4,000 maple trees) family operation. Most of the boiling is done in the late afternoon or at night. Call ahead.

In Worthington
High Hopes Sugarshack (413-238-5919; www.highhopesmaple.com) displays work by local artists and features an "all-you-can-eat" pancake buffet. **The Red Bucket Sugar Shack** (413-238-7710) features pancakes, French toast, wagon rides, and snowshoeing. **Windy Hill Farm** (413-238-5869), the oldest sugarhouse in town, offers a dining room with a full maple menu in-season.

Justamere Tree Farm (413-238-5306; www.justamerefarm.com), Patterson Rd. From Worthington Center go 2 miles south on Rt. 112, turn right onto Kinne Brook Rd., go 2.5 miles, turn right onto Adams Rd. and continue to the end. Then turn left onto Patterson Rd. and go 0.5 mile to the farm, the second house on your left.

✳ Special Events
March: **Chester Hill Maplefest** (413-354-6315), Chester Hill on Skyline Dr., features a pancake breakfast, tractor-pulled hayrides to a local sugar shack, music, and crafts (*third Saturday*).

April: **Westfield River Wildwater Canoe Races** (413-354-9684), Huntington, is billed as the oldest continuously run white-water race in America (*third weekend*).

Mid-May through Columbus Day weekend: **Hilltown Farmer's Market**, Huntington town common, Sat. 9–1.

May: **Chester on Track** (413-354-6570) commemorates that town's railroading history with a parade, live music, and antique car show and open house at the Railroad Museum.

July: **Independence Day** (413-296-4049), Chesterfield, with a parade, fireworks, and much more. **Bryant Homestead Craft Festival** (413-634-2244) is a superlative 2-day weekend (10–5) happening at the William Cullen Bryant Homestead in Cummington, with more than 100 juried artisans, live bands, food, pony rides and petting zoo, classic autos, and tea on the veranda (*midmonth*). **Scottish Festival** in Blandford (*third weekend*).

August: Some of the state's oldest and most colorful fairs are held in this area; visit www.mafa.org for exact dates. Check out the **Littleville Fair** (413-667-8738) at the Littleville Fairgrounds, Chester (*first weekend*); the **Middlefield Fair** (413-623-6423), Bell Road (*second weekend*); and the **Hillside Agricultural Society Fair** (Cummington Fair; 413-634-5091) in Cummington (*last weekend*).

September: **Blandford Fair** (www .theblandfordfair.com), held since 1867 on Labor Day weekend, is big. **The Williamsburg Grange Fair** is the following weekend.

Columbus Day weekend: The **Great River Ride** (413-562-5237; www.new horizonsbikes.com) is a 100-mile bicycle tour of the Hilltowns.

The Pioneer Valley

Kim Grant

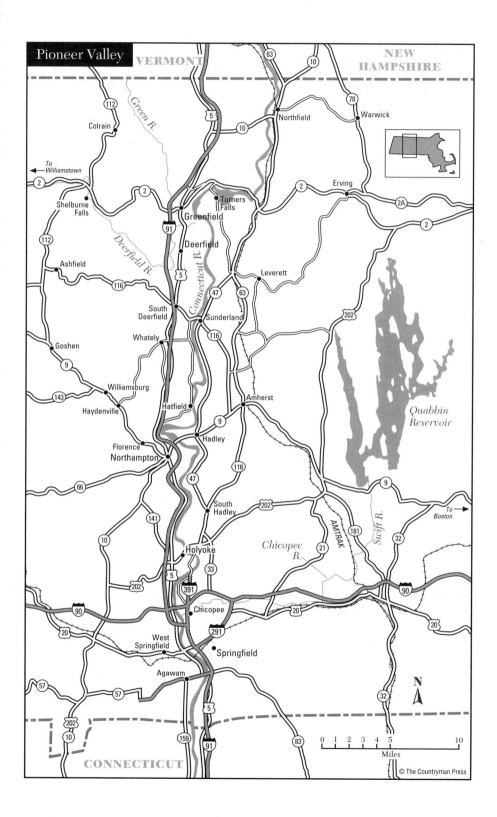

THE PIONEER VALLEY

The Valley seems to have been a Yankee version of the Garden of Eden: rich soil bordering a waterway to the ocean. It was farmed for thousands of years before the first English colonists arrived in the 17th century, "settling" here almost a full century before moving into the flanking hills.

Just 5 miles wide up around the Vermont–New Hampshire line, the Valley widens to 20 miles down around Springfield. It's divided by the Holyoke Range, an abrupt east–west chain of mountains, yielding views from ridge paths and from two peaks—Mount Tom and Mount Holyoke (both accessible by road)—on opposite sides of the Valley.

New England's longest river, the Connecticut plays a far more obvious role as the boundary between New Hampshire and Vermont and is commemorated in the name of another state. Still, in its 69-mile passage through Western Massachusetts, the Connecticut has created a region as distinctive as any. The problem has always been what to call it.

In 1939 the Western Massachusetts Visitors Association sponsored a contest for a name to promote the area. The winner was *King Philip's Realm*, a reference to the 17th-century Indian chief who unquestionably visited here but received a far-from-warm welcome. Instead the *Pioneer Valley* was adopted, and the name has come to apply to the three counties—Hampden, Hampshire, and Franklin—that flank as well as include the Valley. We like the name to the extent that it underscores its early settlement. What we don't like is the way it suggests that the entire area is a flat valley when, in fact, these counties include some of the hilliest country in the state. At any rate, *Pioneer Valley* is the only name that's stuck.

Perhaps the Valley's most striking feature is the way in which its many layers of history—from dinosaurs to diners—are visible, far more than in most places. The dinosaurs left tracks, lots of them. In 1839 Amherst College geologist Edward Hitchcock was the first to identify them; his collection, the largest in the world, is displayed in the stunning new Amherst College Museum of Natural

History. Many more tracks were unearthed during construction of I-91 in the 1960s and can be viewed in half a dozen places.

In the 18th and early 19th centuries Massachusetts's communities along the Connecticut—isolated from the state's coastal capital and population centers—developed their own distinctive, Valley-centered society, architecture, and religion. In the 1730s and 1740s the Northampton-based Rev. Jonathan Edwards challenged the theology of Boston-based Congregationalism, trumpeting instead the message that everyone (not just the "elect") could be saved. Edwards's emotionally charged revival meetings launched a "Great Awakening" that rippled throughout New England.

In the Valley itself this fire-and-brimstone brand of Calvinism lingered on well into the 19th century, long after Boston had forgotten its Puritan horror of sin and embraced a more permissive Unitarianism. Puzzling on the themes of death and eternity in Amherst in the 1850s through 1870s, the poet Emily Dickinson was more a part of her time and place than is generally understood.

The Valley's stern religion bred a concern for proper schooling. Deerfield Academy, founded in 1797, quickly attracted female as well as male students from throughout the area. Amherst College was founded in 1821 by town patriarchs, and in 1837 all-female Mount Holyoke College opened in South Hadley. Both contributed more than their share of Protestant missionaries.

Subtly but surely, education became a religion in its own right, and today it represents one of the Valley's leading industries. Its heart is the Five-College Area, home to Smith, Hampshire, Amherst, and Mount Holyoke Colleges and the University of Massachusetts at Amherst. It represents one of the country's largest rural concentrations of students and certainly one of its liveliest rural music, crafts, art, and dining scenes.

The Connecticut served as a highway on which new settlers continuously arrived and crops were exported. Flat-bottomed, square-rigged boats plied this thoroughfare, deftly negotiating half a dozen patches of "quick water." In 1794

VIEW FROM MOUNT HOLYOKE, BY WILLIAM HENRY BARTLETT, IS IN THE COLLECTION OF SPRINGFIELD'S CONNECTICUT VALLEY HISTORICAL MUSEUM.

Connecticut Valley Historical Museum

Springfield was chosen for the site of a federal armory. Skilled workmen flocked to the spot and began turning out muskets that went downriver, too.

Today it is difficult to grasp the former importance of this waterway. In the 1790s transportation canals were built around the falls at Holyoke and at Turners Falls. A number of vessels were built on West Springfield's common around 1800, and at the height of the subsequent canal-building craze, a canal system linked Northampton with New Haven.

With the dawn of the industrial revolution in the 1820s, the waterfalls that had been obstacles in the canal era were viewed as the Valley's biggest assets. In the 1820s Boston developers began to build textile mills at Chicopee Falls, and in the 1840s developed Holyoke from scratch—a planned, brick town, complete with factories, 4.5 miles of power canals, workers' housing, and mill owners' mansions. Meanwhile, Springfield was booming thanks to its own home-grown inventors and investors, a breed initially drawn to the area by the armory.

The 1890s through 1920s—the period to which most buildings in its towns and cities still date—was obviously the Valley's most colorful and exuberant era. In Springfield public buildings like the magnificent City Hall and Symphony Hall, the soaring Florentine-style campanile, and the Quadrangle of museums all conjure up this era. Trolley lines webbed the Valley, transporting mill workers to mountaintops and parks. Also during this period, volleyball was invented in Holyoke (look for exhibits in the Children's Museum complex), and basketball (the spectacular Hall of Fame tells the story) in Springfield.

The Valley today is distinguished by its number of extensive manicured parks, its elaborate stone and brick public buildings, and its private school and institutional buildings designed in every conceivable "Revival" style—all gifts of 19th-century philanthropists who refused to be forgotten (each bears the donor's name). Mount Holyoke itself now stands in vast Skinner Park, donated by a family that made its fortune producing satin in the country's largest silk mill. Northampton's 200-acre Look and 22-acre Childs Parks were both donated by the industrialists whose names they bear, and Stanley Park in Westfield was created by Stanley Home Products founder Frank Stanley Beveridge. Although Springfield's 795-acre Forest Park isn't named for its principal benefactor, it does harbor New England's most elaborate mausoleum, built by ice-skate tycoon Everett H. Barney.

Still linked both physically (by I-91, which superseded old north–south highways Rts. 5/10, which in turn had upstaged the railway, which had replaced the river) and culturally with Connecticut's cities and with Brattleboro, Vermont, more than with Boston, the Valley remains a place unto itself.

A case can be made that this Massachusetts stretch of the Connecticut Valley is the cultural heart of New England. The distance from Springfield's Quadrangle of art, science, and heritage museums on the south to Old Deerfield's house and town museums on the north is little more than 40 miles, a straight scenic shot up I-91. Midway between these destinations lies the Five-College Area, with its extraordinary art museums at Smith, Amherst, and Mount Holyoke Colleges; the illustrations to be seen at the Eric Carle Museum; two house museums devoted to Emily Dickinson; and the National Yiddish Book Center—all within an 11-mile radius.

These cultural attractions are unusually accessible, set in one of New England's most intensely cultivated agricultural pockets, a distinctive landscape in which paved roads climb to hilltop lookouts, hiking trails follow ridgelines, and bike paths trace old trolley and rail lines.

The Connecticut itself is recapturing some of its old status as the region's focal point. It has made a dramatic comeback since the federally mandated Clean Water Act began to take effect in the 1970s. Now swimmable and fishable, it has been further improved through the protection of more than 4,000 riparian acres, the 52-mile Riverway State Park.

On summer weekends hundreds of powerboats emerge from marinas sited on the deep lakelike stretches of the river above the power dams at Holyoke and Turners Falls, but the dozen miles below Turners Falls is too shallow for powerboating and particularly appealing to paddlers. The easiest way onto the river is aboard two snappy riverboats: The *Quinnetukut II* cruises back and forth through French King Gorge, while the *Lady Bea* is based in South Hadley. The sleepy old roads along both sides of the river are also becoming increasingly popular with bicyclists.

DEERFIELD/GREENFIELD AREA

Old Deerfield's single, mile-long street—lined with 18th- and early-19th-century buildings, canopied by old trees, and set against a thousand acres of cornfields—evokes the Valley's first prosperous era. It's one of those rare places in which you can virtually step back in time through Historic Deerfield's period houses and Memorial Hall's wonderfully eclectic exhibits.

With the industrial revolution and advent of the railroad, Greenfield replaced Deerfield as the area's commercial center. It's now a throwback to an entirely different era—the 1950s. Greenfield's century-old department store and vintage movie theater, its eateries, family-owned shops, and newspaper, and its fine community college all serve a lively community that extends west up into the surrounding hills, north up to the quietest reaches of the Valley. Neighboring Turners Falls is the smallest of the Valley's mill villages but has its most dramatic waterfalls and a major discovery center devoted to the region's natural history. Indeed, this area is all about discovery. Follow the winding road up Mount Sugarloaf (now state owned) to the summit to see the wide, shimmering ribbon of the Connecticut River far below, flanked by a baffle of trees and a broad patchwork of yellow and green fields, spotted with century-old wooden tobacco sheds and walled on the south by the magnificent east–west march of the Holyoke Range.

Bicycle or drive along river roads on either shore, through farmland in Whately, Sunderland, Montague. Find your way to the Bookmill in Montague Center and on up into Northfield along the river. Munch at farm stands selling fresh-picked produce: asparagus in May, strawberries in June, blueberries in July, apples and peaches in September, and pumpkins in October. And get out on the Connecticut. Above Turners Falls the river itself is accessible by excursion boat as well as by rental kayaks and canoes.

AREA CODE 413.

GUIDANCE **Franklin County Chamber of Commerce** (413-773-5463, www.franklincc.org), 395 Main St., Greenfield. This Regional Tourism Council covers a broad area, including the West County Hilltowns as well as the northern reaches of the Valley. Request a map and guide. The chamber operates the **Visitor**

Christina Tree

SUNDERLAND

Center in Greenfield (413-773-9393) off I-91 exit 26, behind Applebee's on Rt. 2A east, marked from the Rt. 2 rotary. Open daily 8:30–6, until 8 on Fri., closing at 5 PM off-season, it features a friendly, helpful staff, restrooms, and local products. Also check **www.masscountryroads.com**.

GETTING THERE *By bus:* **Peter Pan–Trailways** (800-343-9999; www .peterpanbus.com) connects Greenfield, Amherst, South Hadley, and Holyoke with Boston, Springfield, Bradley International Airport, and points beyond. The local departure point is town hall, Court Square, Greenfield. *By car:* Rt. 2 is the quickest as well as most scenic access from east or west, and I-91 is the way north and south.

PARKING *In Greenfield:* There's metered parallel and angled parking on Main St. and in the lot across from the chamber of commerce.

MEDICAL EMERGENCY Dial **911**. **Franklin Medical Center** (413-773-0211), 164 High St., Greenfield.

✳ Towns and Villages

Deerfield (population: 4,750). Founded on a lush plain between the Deerfield and Connecticut Rivers in 1669, Deerfield is best known for the mile-long street of 18th- and early-19th-century homes in **Old Deerfield**. The current town center with its shops and restaurants is 6 miles south in South Deerfield, also the site of **Mount Sugarloaf** and (on N. Main St.) of the obelisk marking the site on which most of the town's first male settlers were killed in 1675. This region was the homeland of the Pocumtuck tribe, which had farmed the land for many centuries. Deerfield's natural as well as human-made beauty is unusually accessible: Follow River Road north along the Connecticut from Rt. 116 to its terminus in East Deerfield, also great for bicycling. Or hike the **Pocumtuck Ridge Trail**, the **Channing Blake Meadow Walk**, and the **Mahican-Mohawk Trail**. **Yankee Candle** is found along Rts. 5/10.

Greenfield. This proud old town (population: 18,170) is sited at the confluence of the Green and Connecticut Rivers, and also at the junction of Rt. 2 and I-91. Main Street is distinguished by a number of interesting buildings in a wide variety of styles, several by native son Asher Benjamin, the unsung hero responsible for the architectural look of much of rural New England. In the 1790s, a period when much of Western Massachusetts and northern New England was quickly settled, Benjamin was keenly aware of the need for a "do-it-yourself" guide to the new architectural styles being introduced in Boston by Charles Bulfinch. In

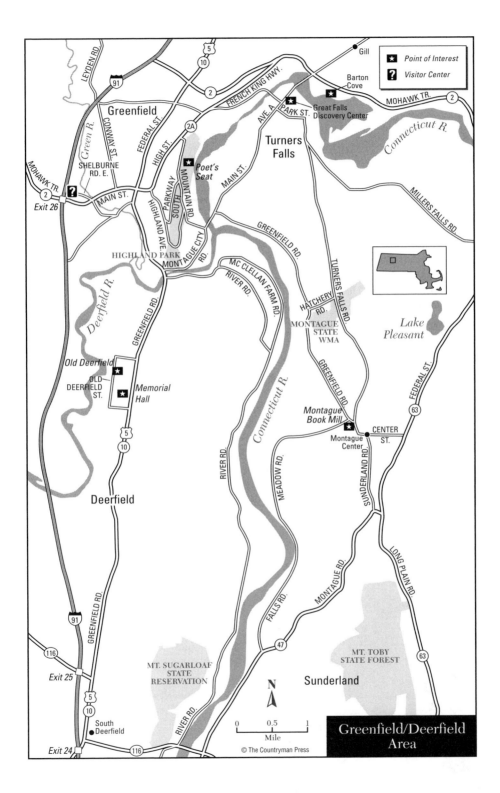

Greenfield/Deerfield
Area

© The Countryman Press

1796 Benjamin wrote *The Country Builder's Assistant*, followed by six more books that resulted in the construction of thousands of homes and hundreds of churches—the distinctive three-story houses and high-steepled churches that remain the pride of New England villages. The **Greenfield Public Library** (413-772-1544), 402 Main St., said to be the first building designed by Asher Benjamin, has an exceptional children's room and an interesting historical collection. Greenfield's entire Main Street is, moreover, remarkable because it has all the downtown essentials that most towns used to have but have lost since the 1950s. They're all here: the coffee shops, the movie theater and family-owned department store, the banks and bakeries, sporting goods shops and grocery store, plus people who all seem to know one another. **Energy Park** off Main Street (50 Miles St.) features sculptures, climbing structures, and exhibits demonstrating solar energy and transportation alternatives; it's the setting for frequent happenings. The **Poet's Seat Tower** up in the Highlands above town is also well worth finding, as is the quiet farmland along the Green and Deerfield Rivers. The **Greenfield Historical Society** (413-774-3663), 3 Church St. (open summer Sunday afternoons and by appointment), offers eight rooms filled with furnishings, portraits, early Greenfield artifacts, and photos. You learn that Greenfield's J. Russell Company, "America's first cutlery factory," was once known for its Green River buffalo skinning knife.

Montague. Few towns with a population of just 8,500 encompass as many contrasting villages. By far the biggest of these is **Turners Falls**, sited at the "Great Falls" (visible from Rt. 2), one of the first waterfalls in the country to be circumvented by a transportation canal (begun in 1794, completed in 1800, operating until 1856). Its sophisticated power canal system functioned from 1860 to 1940, attracting cotton, silk, and cutlery factories as well as three paper mills, collectively employing between 1,200 and 1,500 in their heyday. The original 1860s building of Montague Paper (once a 15-building complex covering 5 acres) now houses the **Great Falls Discovery Center**, with outstanding displays focusing on the natural history of the Connecticut River watershed. The **Shea Community Theater** stages frequent music and drama. Turners Falls sits at a bend in the Connecticut River, which surrounds it on three sides—wide and placid as it enters town at **Barton Cove** (which offers camping, paddling, and nesting eagles), then dividing into two strips, the narrow old power canal and the wide river, magnificently wild as it plunges over the dam beneath the bridge linking the town with Rt. 2. The brick commercial buildings and blocks of mill housing flanking the town's wide, grandly conceived Avenue A (down which trolleys once ran to Amherst and Northampton) are beginning to fill with studios and galleries. The **Hallmark Museum of Contemporary Photography** (413-

THE NIGHT KITCHEN AND BOOK MILL AT THE MONTAGUE MILL

Christina Tree

863-0009; www.hmcp.org; open Thu.–Sun. 1–5), 84 Ave. A, displays work by well-known photographers and members of the 250-member student body at the nearby **Hallmark Institute of Photography** (www.hallmark-institute.com). **Unity Park** overlooking Barton Cove is a great picnic site; a fish ladder at the dam is staffed by naturalists late May to mid-June, when the fish are running upstream (call 800-859-2960). Art Walks and other village events are listed at **www.turnersfallsriverculture.org**. The town's many churches served German, French Canadian, Italian, Lithuanian, Bohemian, Irish, and Polish immigrants. In **Our Lady of Czestochowa Catholic Church** (413-863-4748), 84 K St. (turn off Ave. A onto 7th and then left up K; open Sat. 7–4 and otherwise 3–6:30), the painting of the Black Madonna, the famous Polish icon, is an object of special veneration, a 1920s copy of the original embellished with the jewelry of parishioners. The village is named for Captain William Turner, whose company massacred virtually all the local Indians (the Pocumtucks) near the falls in 1617. This brick mill town was, however, designed and built in the 1860s by Colonel Alvah Crocker.

Montague Center, south of Turners Falls (best accessed from Rt. 2 via Rt. 63 south) has a classic New England green, the site of Montague Old Home Days and the town's Independence Day activities. Nearby **Montague Mill** is an early-19th-century gristmill on the Sawmill River, now housing crafts studios, a large antiquarian bookshop, and a café. The town's other hidden gem is **Lake Pleasant**, off Rt. 63 north of Montague Center, a pristine lake (the town's drinking supply) rimmed by 19th-century gingerbread cottages built as a spiritualist camp in the late 19th century. It's still the site of frequent "psychic fairs" (call 413-774-4705). North and west of Lake Pleasant lies one of the state's most extensive pine barrens. The town also includes **Millers Falls**, another small mill town just off Rt. 2, bisected by the Millers Falls River.

Northfield (population: c. 3,000). A Connecticut River town bounded on the north by both Vermont and New Hampshire, Northfield has an unusually wide and long Main Street lined with many houses built during the heyday of river traffic and sheep farming. The college-sized campus of Northfield Mount Hermon school is closed at this writing and up for sale. The distinguished prep school, founded by the evangelist minister Dwight Moody in the late 19th century, has consolidated on its campus in nearby Gill. The attraction here is **Northfield Mountain**, an unusual hydroelectric facility hidden inside the mountain, webbed with hiking trails maintained for snowshoeing and cross-country skiing in winter. In-season it also offers river cruises on excursion boat *Quinnetukut II*, as well as a visitor center with historical displays and nature-geared programs.

Sunderland (population: 3,777). Settled as "Swampfield" at the turn of the 18th century, this riverside town represents some of the richest and best-protected farmland in the state, much of it still planted in shade-grown tobacco. Early industries included covered buttons, and the big sight-to-see in town is the **Buttonwood Tree**, said to be the largest of its kind (a variety of sycamore) east of the Mississippi and dating to the 18th century. It's on Main Street (Rt. 47), which is lined with handsome old homes. The brick town hall here, built in 1867 to double as the school, is the new home to the **Blue Heron**, the area's most

OLD DEERFIELD

Marked from Rt. 5; 6 miles north of exit 24 off I-91, or 3.5 miles south of Greenfield (I-91 exit 26). Also see the shortcut from Rt. 2 to Old Deerfield under *Scenic Drives.*

Old Deerfield's serene good looks belie its ups and downs during the 19th and 20th, as well as the 17th and 18th, centuries. Founded in 1669, the first settlement here was deserted in 1675 after King Philip's Native Americans burned the town and killed most of its young men in an ambush that's remembered as the Bloody Brook Massacre. Seven years later, however, the settlers were back, harvesting crops and listening to Sunday sermons in the square, tower-topped meetinghouse (reconstructed on a smaller scale as the present village post office). In all there were 30 attacks in the community's first 50 years, the most famous one on a blustery February night in 1704, when more than 100 villagers were carried off to Montreal. Today visitors are amazed by the richness and sophistication of life as it was lived here during and after the Revolution—as judged from the quality of the architectural detailing, furniture, silver, and furnishings on view. Ironically, after all those early struggles, Old Deerfield survives today as a unique sampling of life in the late 18th and early 19th centuries.

By the 1820s, however, Deerfield had been upstaged by Greenfield as the local commercial center. Already it had become a place to come to school (Deerfield Academy was founded in 1797) and to visit "historic" sites. In 1830 an elaborate granite obelisk replaced the vintage-1720s wooden marker at the site of the Bloody Brook Massacre in South Deerfield; it's believed to be the first historic monument in what became the United States. In 1848 a campaign was mounted to save the Indian House, which still bore the mark of the hatchet implanted in its door during the 1704 raid. Though the campaign failed, it is now cited as the first effort in this country to save a historic house. The door was acquired by a Boston antiquarian, which so outraged local residents that he had to return it. For some time it was displayed in the Pocumtuck House, a hotel that stood on the village common.

Deerfield's zeal for self-preservation was fanned in the 19th century by George Sheldon, a self-appointed town historian given to raiding his neighbors' attics. Sheldon organized the **Pocumtuck Valley Memorial Association** in 1870 and a decade later acquired a striking, three-story brick building designed by Asher Benjamin (it had been the original Deerfield Academy building). The society filled this Memorial Hall with local relics ranging from the Indian House door to colonial-era cooking utensils, displayed in what is now recognized as the first "period room" to be seen in any American museum.

Sheldon also enticed his cousin C. Alice Baker back to town. Born in Deerfield, Baker had become a teacher and noted preservationist in the Boston area (she was involved in the campaign to preserve the Old South Meeting House) and was familiar with the then-current attempts to restore colonial buildings in and around the village of York, Maine. Back in Deerfield, Alice Baker acquired the Frary House and restored it. At this time two societies were also founded to revive colonial-era crafts such as weaving, hearth cookery, pottery, and basketry. Visitors came. They came by rail and later by rural trolley, stayed in local farms and several now vanished hotels (including Jewitt House atop Mount Sugarloaf), and shopped for arts and crafts in local homes and studios.

By the 1930s Deerfield was again forgotten. The 1937 *WPA Guide to Massachusetts* described it as "the ghost of a town, its dimness almost transparent, its quiet almost a cessation, but it is essential to add that it is probably quite the most beautiful ghost of its kind, and with the deepest poetic and historic significance to be found in America."

Following World War II, Deerfield Academy headmaster Frank Boyden came to the rescue of the old houses, persuading Deerfield Academy alumnus and parent Henry Flynt and his wife, Helen, to buy a number of decaying Old Deerfield buildings. The Flynts subsequently restored many of these buildings, incorporating them as the nonprofit Heritage Foundation (now **Historic Deerfield**) in 1952. The entire town of Deerfield has been remarkably lucky in preserving some 5,900 acres of cultivated land. Although tract housing sprouted in several fields in the late 1980s, a Deerfield Land Trust was subsequently established and is now dedicated to preserving local farmland.

The largest property holder in Old Deerfield is Deerfield Academy, and there are two more private schools—Eaglebrook up on a hill and Bement School—in the village. Also in Old Deerfield is the Brick Church, built in 1824, which has arched doorways and a closed wooden cupola. It's the scene of frequent special events as well as regular services. The Old Burying Ground (walk along Albany Road) has many 18th-century stones and the mass grave of the English colonists killed in 1704. The big attraction here is Historic Deerfield; see the accompanying sidebar.

prestigious restaurant. Rts. 47 and 116 meet in the middle of town and then diverge again, both heading south through farmland. Follow Rt. 47 north and fork onto Falls Road for a scenic route along the river to Greenfield, or follow it northeast, turning down Reservation Road to find the access to trails up **Mount Toby** (1,269 feet), which offers an observation tower and fine view across the Valley. Also look for access to trout-stocked **Cranberry Pond**. The Division of Fisheries and Wildlife maintains a trout hatchery on Rt. 116 south, and the **Cronin National Salmon Station** (413-548-9010) is also open to the public, theoretically 8–4.

Whately (population: 1,771). Motorists from Canada to Florida know Whately's "Fillin' Station," a 24-hour diner just off I-91, but the town itself is blessedly little touristed, from the farm stands salted along River Road by the Connecticut River in "East Whately" to the steep hillside and ridgetop roads radiating from the tiny village of West Whately. Whately Center is just off Rt. 5, a classic old town center with two general stores, an old town hall, library, post office, church, and inn.

✳ To See

FOR FAMILIES ✐ **Great Falls Discovery Center at the Silvio O. Conte National Fish and Wildlife Refuge** (413-863-5221; www.greatfallsma.org), 52 Ave. A, Turners Falls. Open June–Columbus Day weekend, Tue.–Sun. 10–4; otherwise weekends 10–4. A free, publicly funded must-see showcase for the entire Connecticut River watershed, featuring superbly painted and constructed displays of local environmental history and current flora and fauna of the Valley and upland habitats as well as an aquarium of indigenous fish. A full schedule of nature-geared programs is offered. Nearby **Unity Park** offers picnicking facilities and a playground.

✐ **Magic Wings** (413-665-2805; www.magicwings.com), 281 Greenfield Rd. (Rts. 5/10), South Deerfield. Open spring and summer 9–6, fall and winter 9–5. $8 adults, $7 seniors, $5 ages 3–17. Some 4,000 butterflies flit though this vast glass conservatory filled with bright flowers and lush vegetation. A glassed display also reveals the evolution of butterflies. There's the bright **Monarch's Restaurant** (closed Mon.–Tue.) and, of course, an extensive gift shop.

✐ **Northfield Mountain Recreational and Environmental Center** (413-659-3714 or 800-859-2960; www.neenergyinc.com/Northfield), Rt. 63 in Northfield. Trails are open except during mud season; the visitor center is open Wed.–Sun. 9–5. A film about the construction and operation of the plant can be viewed in the visitor center. The project draws water from the Connecticut River up into an artificially created lake on top of the mountain, using it to generate power during high-use periods. The powerhouse itself is hidden in a cavern as high as a 10-story building, as wide as a four-lane highway, and longer than a football field. The center also houses superb displays dramatizing the story of the river's 18th- and early-19th-century flat-bottomed sailing barges for which canals were constructed in the 1790s. The story of steamboating and the advent of the railroad is also told, along with subsequent industrialization, logging, and the present hydro uses of the river's "white gold." See *To Do* for late-June through mid-October cruises on the Connecticut aboard the *Quinnetukut II* as well as snowshoeing and cross-country skiing opportunities. The web site has information on current programs.

✒ **Yankee Candle Company** (413-665-2929; www.yankeecandle.com), Rts. 5/10, 0.25 mile north of I-91, exit 24, South Deerfield. Open daily 9:30–6, except Thanksgiving and Christmas. In 1969 Michael Kittredge used his mother's kitchen to make his first candles. Now billed as "the world's largest candle store," Yankee Candle is a huge complex that includes a Bavarian Village complete with year-round falling snow, a make-your-own-country-candles kitchen, and Santa's Enchanted Toy Shop, complete with animatronic elves and a countdown-to-Christmas clock. Attractions also include a castle courtyard and waterfall, nutcracker castle, a Candle Making Museum, Yankee Candle Home with home furnishings for the bath, kitchen, and garden, and Chandler's Restaurant (see *Dining Out*).

✒ **Old Greenfield Village** (413-774-7138), Rt. 2 west from Greenfield. Open mid-May to mid-Oct., Sat. and holidays 10–4, Sun. noon–4; weekdays by appointment. $5 adult, $4 seniors, $3 ages 6–16; free under age 6. This is a genuine, Yankee kind of phenomenon displaying the basics found in stores, in dental offices, churches, barbershops, and tool shops around the turn of the 20th century. All were collected over 30 years by retired schoolteacher Waine Morse—not a man with a lot of money, but someone with a sense of where to find what, when. Morse also constructed the buildings himself. Raising the church steeple alone, he admits, was a bit tricky.

Also see Historic Deerfield on page 228.

SCENIC DRIVES

River Roads
Along the western shore of the Connecticut all the way from Hatfield north to the confluence with the Deerfield, **River Road** is lined with farms, tobacco sheds, and fields. It's flat except for the monadnock, Mount Sugarloaf, which thrusts up all alone; be sure to drive to the top. Note the old headstones in **Pine Nook Cemetery** some 4 miles north of Rt. 116. Also see *Views* and *Farms and Farm Stands*.

Along the eastern side of the Connecticut, follow **Falls Road** forking left off Rt. 47 a short way beyond the Buttonwood Tree. This becomes Meadow Street, shadowing the river and threading its way through farm country. At the junction with Ferry Road turn right onto Meadow Road, right again on Bridge Street, and into the **Montague Mill** (see below).

Route 2 to Montague Center to either Greenfield or Deerfield. Turn off Rt. 2 at Rt. 63 south to Swamp Road (a right). Stop at the **Montague Mill** with its crafts, bookstore, shops, and restaurants. You might also want to detour less than a mile south to Montague Center, a classic village with a Congregational church designed by Asher Benjamin and a brick town hall on its common. Otherwise continue west (Swamp changes at the mill to Ferry Road) and turn north

HISTORIC DEERFIELD

(413-774-5581; www.historic-deerfield.org). In Old Deerfield, marked from Rts. 5/10; 6 miles north of exit 24 off I-91 or 3.5 miles south of Greenfield, I-91 exit 26 and Rt. 2. Open daily Apr.–Dec., 9:30–4:30. Closed Thanksgiving, Christmas Eve, and Christmas Day. $14 adults, $5 ages 6–21 includes admission to Memorial Hall; $7

HISTORIC DEERFIELD

Kim Grant

adult buys admission to one house. Tickets (good for 2 consecutive days) are sold in the **Hall Tavern** (be sure to see the upstairs ballroom). Guided tours (on the hour) are presently offered through 13 buildings displaying a total of some 25,000 objects made or used in America between 1650 and 1850. **The Flynt Center of Early New England Life** (open, in addition to the usual museum season, weekends Jan.–Mar., except Christmas Eve and Day) houses objects not on display and a "visible storage gallery" featuring some 2,500 historic household furnishings and an outstanding collection of colonial-era powderhorns. Also inquire about special exhibitions, antiques forums, and frequent programs on traditional crafts and the decorative arts.

Historic Deerfield Houses Open to the Public

The **Wells-Thorn House** (sections built in 1717 and 1751) shows the dramatic changes in the lifestyles in Deerfield through two centuries. The **Ashley House** (1733), with its elegantly carved cupboards and furnishings, depicts the lifestyle of the village's Tory minister (note his 1730s Yale diploma). The **Asa Stebbins House** (1799/1810) is the first brick home in town, grandly furnished with French wallpaper, Chinese porcelain, and Federal-era pieces (self-guided). The **Wright House** (1824), another brick mansion, is a mini museum of high-style furniture and ceramics. The **Sheldon-Hawks House** (1743), a self-guided tour, is still filled with the spirit of George Sheldon, the town's colorful first historian. The **Frary House/Barnard Tavern** (1740/1795) has a classic tavern look, ballroom, and 1890s restoration by C. Alice Baker. The **Hinsdale and Anna Williams House** (1750s, rebuilt 1816–20), furnished from an 1838 inventory, is surprisingly airy and modern, with touches like the light-toned rag stair rug, "glass curtains," venetian blinds, and exceptionally beautiful patterned wallpapers and floorcloths. **Children's workshops** are offered weekend afternoons in July. Inquire about walking tours.

✒ ♿ **Memorial Hall** (413-774-7476; www.old-deerfield.org), Memorial St., Old Deerfield. Open May–Oct., daily 11–5. $6 adults, $3 ages 6–21; a combination ticket with Historic Deerfield is $14 or $5. In addition to the "Indian House door" and the country's first period room (see the *Old Deerfield* sidebar), this beautiful old building houses the Pocumtuck Valley Memorial Association's wonderfully eclectic collection. You learn about the Pocomtuck

Penny Leveritt

THIS ENGLISH BARBER'S BOWL, CIRCA 1700–20, IS ONE OF MANY COLONIAL ARTIFACTS AT HISTORIC DEERFIELD.

tribe, caught between the English who had settled in the lower Valley and the Mohawks to the west. In 1675, you learn, the Pocumtucks reclaimed the lands they had been tilling for centuries, replanting their cornfields until they were again dislodged by settlers, from whom they again attempted to wrest their ancestral homeland in 1704. Among "The Many Stories of 1704" you hear the Rev. John Williams describe the massacre in which his wife and children were murdered and a son and daughter kidnapped; the son was ransomed but the daughter refused to return, visiting 40 years later but remaining in a Mohawk community near Montreal until her death at age 81. There is also an exhibit on the history of African Americans in this village. Old Deerfield's 1890s–1920s era as an artistic center is illustrated in paintings by the Fuller family, among others, and by an extensive collection of work by the Deerfield Society of Blue and White Needlework. **The Old Indian House** (open daily Aug.–Labor Day, then weekends through Columbus Day, 11–5), a 1929 reproduction of the Sheldon House (demolished in 1848) houses activities geared to young visitors. Also see *Special Events*.

MEMORIAL HALL

Christina Tree

(right) onto Greenfield Road; take a left onto Montague City Road and cross the river. To reach the **Poet's Seat**, turn right onto Mountain Road. For Old Deerfield, continue to Rts. 5/10 and turn left; Old Deerfield is a mile or so south, on your right.

Route 2 to Turners Falls to Old Deerfield. This is a shortcut rather than a scenic drive, but it's handy to know since it lops off several tedious highway miles. Leave Rt. 2 at Turners Falls and cross the high bridge onto Avenue A, the main drag of this classic, late-19th-century mill town. Stop in at the **Great Falls Discovery Center**, then continue south on Avenue A—which turns into the Montague City Road—cross the iron bridge, bear left to Rts. 5/10, and watch for an OLD DEERFIELD sign.

River Road in Northfield runs south from the landing (off Rt. 63) at Northfield Mountain to Rt. 2. It's beautiful.

Mohawk Trail. The stretch of Rt. 2 designated in 1914 as the Mohawk Trail, New England's first official tourist trail, begins in Greenfield and heads west, abruptly uphill. Shelburne Falls, the hub of the Mohawk Trail, is just 8 miles west of downtown Greenfield. (See "Along the Mohawk Trail.")

Deerfield to Greenfield, the scenic route. From "The Street" in Old Deerfield, head south, continuing as the village ends and it becomes Mill Village Road, flanked by farmland. Turn right onto Stillwater Road and follow it along the Deerfield River. Turn right on the bridge across the river (this section of the Deerfield is popular with tubers) and follow the West Deerfield Upper Road through more beautiful farmland. Note Clarkdale Fruit Farms (303 Upper Rd.), a fourth-generation family farm offering pick-your-own apples, peaches, pears, and pumpkins; great plums and cider, too.

Route 116 west from South Deerfield climbs steeply and quickly out of the Valley and up into Conway. (See "Hampshire Hilltowns.")

Route 47 north from Sunderland runs through farmlands, past the turnoff (Reservation Rd.) for Mount Toby, farm stands, and sugarhouses.

✳ To Do

BICYCLING The river roads described under *Scenic Drives* are all suited to bicycle touring. River Road in Northfield, dating to the 1600s, passes under the French King Bridge (on a bicycle bridge) leading to Cabot Camp, a glorious spot for a picnic at the confluence of the Connecticut and Millers Rivers. The 3.5-mile **Canalside Rail Trail** will run from the Great Falls Discovery Center in Turners Falls south along the river. Mountain biking is also popular in summer on the 40 miles of trails at **Northfield Mountain**.

Basically Bicycles (413-863-3556) in Turners Falls and both **Bicycle World** (413-774-3701) and **Bicycles Unlimited** (413-772-2700) in Greenfield are knowledgeable about local routes.

BOATING EXCURSIONS The *Quinnetukut II* (413-659-3714 or 800-859-2960) offers seasonal cruises (Wed.–Sun., conditions permitting) on the Connecticut from the Riverview picnic area at the **Northfield Mountain Recreation and Environmental Center**, Rt. 63 in Northfield. The narrated cruise (12 miles round trip) is through French King Gorge downstream to Barton Cove, home to nesting eagles. Departures are three times per day from late June to mid-Oct. Call for reservations. $10 adults, $9 seniors, $5 ages 14 and under.

CANOEING AND KAYAKING **Northfield Mountain's Barton Cove** facility (413-863-9300), on Rt. 2 in Gill, offers rental kayaks and canoes and shuttle service as far north along the Connecticut as Vernon Dam (20 miles). This is also a source for information about canoeing sites that Northfield Mountain maintains for public access: **Munn's Ferry Campground** (with Adirondack shelters and tent sites, accessible only by boat), and **River View**, a float dock, picnic tables, and sanitary facilities on the river across from the entrance to Northfield Mountain. Also note **Bennett Meadow Wildlife Management Area** with parking and river access at the Rt. 10 bridge in Northfield.

FISHING **The Connecticut River** offers outstanding fishing for bass, shad, yellow perch, all kinds of sunfish, carp, walleye, and trout (check out the mouths of feeder streams). Cranberry Pond in Sunderland is known locally for trout. The most user-friendly put-in place for visitors is Barton Cove.

Pipione's Sport Shop (413-863-4246), 101 Ave. A (the main drag), Turners Falls, open daily from 7 AM, is a source of advice, as well as equipment and licenses.

Note: The nearby **Quabbin Reservoir** is the state's premier fishing hole, and the **Deerfield**, **West**, and **Millers rivers** are nationally famed among anglers for fly-fishing.

GOLF **Crumpin-Fox Golf Club** (413-648-9101), Rt. 10, Bernardston. 18 holes. The front nine were designed by Robert Trent Jones himself, and the back nine by his firm.

Northfield Golf Club (413-498-2432), 31 Holton St., Northfield. A nine-hole, par-36 course.

Oak Ridge Golf Club (413-863-9693), 231 West Gill Rd., Gill. Nine holes, par 36.

Thomas Memorial Golf Club & Country Club (413-863-8003), 29 Country Club Lane, Turners Falls. Nine holes, par 35.

HIKING AND WALKING **Barton Cove Nature and Camping Area** (413-863-9300; off-season, 800-859-2960), Rt. 2, just east of Turners Falls in Gill. An interpretive nature trail meanders along a rocky ridge overlooking the Connecticut River, and there's a picnic area in addition to tent sites. During nesting season, eagles are usually in residence. Canoe and kayak rentals available.

Along Route 2, Millers Falls, Gill, and Erving
French King Bridge (Rt. 2 west of Millers Falls) spans a dramatically steep, banked, narrow stretch of the Connecticut, 140 feet above the water. Park at the

THE FRENCH KING BRIDGE

Christina Tree

rest area and walk back onto the bridge (there's a pedestrian walk) for the view. Note the mouth of the Millers River just downstream. The bridge is named for French King Rock, 0.5 mile upriver. No one knows why the rock was so named.

Erving Castle/Hermit Cave. In Erving, turn at the sign onto Mountain Road, which climbs steadily for 1.8 miles. The trail sign is on your left before a gated access road. Park here (don't block the gate) and follow the blazes into the woods. After about 1.5 miles, turn left, following blue blazes or a sign down a steep pitch to the crevice cave in an impressive cliff. Hermit John Smith lived here for 30 years in a shack near the cave. Allow more than an hour for the hike.

In Deerfield

Channing Blake Meadow Walk in Old Deerfield. A 0.5-mile path through the village's north meadows and a working 700-acre farm begins at the northern end of Deerfield Street; inquire at Historic Deerfield about special family tours and nature activities.

Pocumtuck Ridge Trail, South Deerfield. Take North Main Street to Hillside Drive (across from Hardigg Industries) to Stage Road. Turn left at the top of the hill onto Ridge Road for the trailhead for paths through Deerfield Land Trust's 120-acre preserve.

Mahican-Mohawk Trail. The first 1.5 miles of this 7.5-mile trail, said to be the actual 10,000-year-old route along the Lower Deerfield, is accessible from Deerfield. Drive south on Deerfield Street but, instead of turning back onto Rt. 5, jog right and then south along Mill Village Road. Turn right at the small stone building at the corner of Stillwater Road; at 0.9 mile take Hoosac Road, and you will see the trailhead at 0.2 mile. The trail follows an abandoned railbed to the South River. For a description of the rest of the trail, see "Along the Mohawk Trail."

ON TOP OF MOUNT SUGARLOAF

Christina Tree

VIEWS Mount Sugarloaf State Reservation, off Rt. 116, South Deerfield. A road winds up this red sandstone mountain (said to resemble the old loaves into which sugar was shaped) to a modern observation tower on the summit, supposedly the site from which King Philip surveyed his prey before the mid-17th-century Bloody Brook Massacre. There are picnic tables, restrooms, and great views down the Valley.

Poet's Seat Tower and Rocky Mountain Trails, off High St. in Greenfield (or see *Scenic Drives* from Turners Falls). This medieval-looking sandstone tower on Rocky Mountain honors local 19th-century poet Frederick Goddard Tuckerman, who liked to sit near this spot. You can understand why. The Ridge Trail (blue blazes) loops along the top of the hill.

Mount Toby, at 1,269 feet offers great views plus caves and waterfalls. As is the case with Mount Holyoke and Mount Sugarloaf, a hotel once capped its summit, but now there is just a fire tower. Access is off Rt. 47, 4 miles south of Sunderland Center. It's a 3-hour round-trip hike, but you can go just as far as the cascades. From Rt. 47 in North Sunderland, turn right onto Reservation Road; the parking area is in 0.5 mile.

Crag Mountain, off Rt. 63, Northfield. This 1,500-foot summit offers sweeping views east, south, and west. Ask directions at the Northfield Mountain Environmental and Recreation Center.

CROSS-COUNTRY SKIING/SNOWSHOEING **Northfield Mountain Ski Touring Center** (413-583-9073 or 800-959-2960), Rt. 63, Northfield, open Dec.–Mar., Wed.–Sun., offers cross-country and snowshoe rentals for use on its 40 km of doubletrack trail.

✳ Lodging

INNS ✿ ♿ **Deerfield Inn** (413-774-5587 or 800-926-3865; www.deerfieldinn.com), 81 Old Main St., Deerfield 01342. Open year-round, except Christmas. A newcomer by Old Deerfield standards (it opened in 1884), the antiques-filled inn is dignified but not stiff. It is the place to stay when visiting Historic Deerfield, enabling you to steep and sleep in the full atmosphere of the village after other visitors have gone. There are 23 rooms, all with private bath, 12 in an annex added since the 1979 fire (from which townspeople and Deerfield Academy students heroically rescued most of the antiques). Rooms feature wallpaper and fabric from the Historic Deerfield collection, and furnishings are either antiques or reproduction antiques; some canopy

THE DEERFIELD INN

Christina Tree

beds. Attention to details, phones. Some annex rooms are quite spacious. $173–206 includes breakfast. Rates vary with the season, not the room, which strikes us as strange since rooms vary in size and feel, and come with and without ghosts. Small pets accepted by prior arrangement.

BED & BREAKFASTS 🐾 🏠 **Centennial House** (413-498-5921 or 877-977-5950; www.thecentennialhouse .com), 94 Main St., Northfield 01360. Built handsomely in 1811 for a local magistrate who heard cases in the parlor—explaining why Calvin Stearns (the town's premier builder) included so many Greek and Roman motifs on the mantels and woodwork in the front two rooms. Later it was home to the headmaster of the Northfield Seminary for Girls. There are six guest rooms, including a third-floor (air-conditioned) suite with skylights, a kitchen, dining and sitting areas, and both an antique sleigh bed and a twin. All guest rooms are furnished in antiques; three have a fireplace. Common space includes a pine-paneled living room with a hearth, a gracious parlor, and, best of all, a glassed sunporch overlooking the 2-acre "back meadow" with its sunset views. The house sits on Northfield's long, wide Main Street, which invites strolling. $99–209 (for the king suite with an electric fireplace and whirlpool tub) includes breakfast. Innkeepers Joan and Steve Stoia offer numerous "specials" including tickets to local museums and attractions. Inquire about midweek "learning vacations" in conjunction with local experts in art, antiques, food, and agriculture.

🏠 🏨 **The Brandt House** (413-774-3329 or 800-235-3329; www.brandt house.com), 29 Highland Ave., Greenfield 01301. This expansive, 16-room Georgian Revival house is set on more than 3 acres and offers seven guest rooms, all with private bath. Common rooms include a tastefully comfortable, plant-filled living room, a dining room with large sash windows overlooking the garden, a game room with a full-sized pool table, a wicker-furnished porch and patio, and an upstairs sunroom stocked with local menus, a microwave, and TV; there's also a clay tennis court. Guest rooms are all relatively small but tastefully furnished, two with working fireplace, and the top floor harbors a two-room suite. $110–295 includes a full breakfast. There's also a lower "corporate rate" weekdays (single occupancy). Extra guests, children, or well-behaved dogs are all $25 extra.

The Ashley Graves House (413-665-6656; www.ashleygraveshouse .com), 121 N. Main St., Sunderland 01375. One of the finest houses around, proudly built in 1830 and lovingly preserved but centrally air-conditioned by Carole and Mike Skibiski. Guests enter through the Barn Room, a large comfortably furnished common space with guest fridge and adjoining dining and breakfast rooms. The King Philip Suite is a beauty with skylights in a post-and-beam ceiling and a "Vermont crazy window" in the wall. It's huge, with a king-sized bed, private entrance, and private bath with whirlpool tub ($175). There is also a room with twins, another with a lovely antique double bed and a balcony, and a second-floor suite with a queen bed and a pullout sofa in the adjoining sitting room. All rooms have private bath and are tastefully furnished with antiques, as is a front parlor with a brick fireplace. From $150, including a full breakfast.

☞ **Poetry Ridge Bed & Breakfast** (413-773-5143), 55 Stone Ridge Lane, Greenfield 01310. One of the showplaces of Greenfield, a town with many imposing houses. Built in 1910 as a summer home for a New York doctor, it sits high on the wooded ridge above town that's now primarily parkland, webbed with walking trails leading to the Poet's Seat Tower (see *Views*). Errol and Mary Sorensen came from California to buy this gem with seven working fireplaces and long views. All rooms have private bath and wireless DSL access; all are furnished with a mix of reproduction and genuine antiques. The two high-end rooms both have a large deck as well as a fireplace and a king bed. Children are welcome (there's a two-room family suite). Breakfast is served in the formal dining room. Allow time here to hike or at least take advantage of the game room. $125–295 includes a full breakfast.

☞ **House on the Hill B&B** (413-774-2070; www.thehouseonthehillbnb .com), 330 Leyden Rd., Greenfield 01301. Donna and Alain Mollard's big old white 1920s farmhouse is minutes from Rt. 2 and downtown Greenfield but high on a quiet green shoulder of the Valley, overlooking (literally) a wide spread of green fields. There are three second-floor air-conditioned guest rooms (two queens, one king), all with private bath and TV and DVD player; wireless access is available throughout the house. Shared space includes an attractive living/ dining area with a large fireplace and a big, comfortable front porch. Anoth-

er ground-level guest room with private bath is available on request. $100–130 double, from $80 single, includes a full breakfast.

Hillside House (413-665-5515; www.hillsidehousebb.com), P.O. Box 183, 60 Masterson Rd., Whately 01093. Julia and Ed Berman searched the country before picking this hillside home as their B&B. A modern home wasn't what they had in mind, but when you step into its airy, glass-walled spaces and out onto the deck, you understand why anyone would like to spend much of their life here. Furnishings are comfortable and tasteful with some exceptional pieces, art and mementos from their far-flung travels. The Pink Guest Room is what you want here, spacious and bright with a Valley view—but the Yellow Guest Room also has its charm, and both have a private bath. There is also a Spa Room, and a swimming pool is set below the house in landscaped gardens. The Bermans dine out around the Valley and share with guests their critiques of local restaurants. Children over age 12 are welcome. $95–145 includes a generous breakfast.

Old Tavern Farm Bed & Breakfast (413-772-0474; www.oldtavern farm.com), 817 Colrain Rd., Greenfield 01301. A quiet byway today in the lush Green River part of town, this was a main road between Boston and Albany when the tavern was first licensed in 1746. Present hosts Gary and Joanne Sanderson are devoted to preserving the feel of this very special place, which retains its classic old ballroom (still a great place for a dance). Common space includes the sunny, low-ceilinged dining room, warmed by a soapstone woodstove, and a pleasant former "ladies' parlor," as well as the old taproom with fireplaces and attractive but authentic antiques, some rather rare and special. The master bedroom is warmed by a Rumford fireplace and features a vintage-1814 Sheridan bird's-eye maple four-poster. There is also a smaller upstairs bedroom and a downstairs suite with a genuine feather bed. Bathrooms are shared, and breakfast is full. Gary is a local sportscaster and also a licensed fishing and hunting guide. $135 May–Oct., $110 off-season. The house and ballroom can be rented for small weddings.

West Winds (413-774-4025; www.westwindsinn.com), 151 Smead Hill Rd., Greenfield 01301. Sandy Richardson designed this contemporary dream house with cathedral ceilings and great spaces, and her husband, Tim, built it. There are now nine guest rooms, all with private bath. Several feature a patio or balcony overlooking a sweep of valley and hills beyond, and some are fitted with Jacuzzi. Breakfast is served in the light-filled dining area with a fieldstone fireplace off the open kitchen. $105–195 includes a continental breakfast weekdays, full on weekends.

Yellow Gabled House (413-665-4922 or 866-665-4922; www.yellowgabledhouse.com), 111 N. Main St., South Deerfield 01373. Minutes from Historic Deerfield, overlooking Bloody Brook (now tamed to a small stream) and the obelisk-shaped memorial to the 1675 massacre on the site, this Gothic Revival house is both snug and elegant. There are three carefully furnished upstairs guest rooms, all with fan and air-conditioning. Two rooms (one with queen-sized beds and matching tailored spreads and window treatments; the other has a canopy bed) share a bath, and a suite has a tall posted bed, adjoining sitting room with TV, and private bath. Host Edna Julia Stahelek is a cartographer and local historian who feels so strongly that her guests should visit Historic Deerfield that she offers complimentary tickets. $110–160 includes a full breakfast.

Deerfield Guest House Bed&Breakfast (413-665-0922), 108 N. Hillside Rd., P.O. Box 404, Deerfield 01242. Squirreled away on a side road near Magic Wings and Yankee Candle, this is an 1840s house with three upstairs guest rooms, all fairly basic but with private bath. There's also a small, shared upstairs TV room as well as the downstairs dining room/parlor. Midweek $90, weekends $100–185, depending on the season.

❧ **Sunnyside Farm** (413-665-3113), River Rd., Whately 01093. Mary Lou Green welcomes visitors to her big yellow turn-of-the-20th-century farmhouse, 5 miles south of Deerfield. It's been in their family since it was built and stands on 50 acres of farmland that grew tobacco and is now leased in part to the neighboring berry farm. All three guest rooms overlook fields. Two spacious front rooms with small TVs face River Road. There's a small but appealing corner double, and a back room has a king-sized bed; baths are shared. Guests have full access to the downstairs rooms, which include a comfortable living room and a dining room in which everyone gathers around a long table for breakfast. Don't miss the porch swing. $75–100.

Also see "West County." Shelburne and Conway are but minutes from this end of the Valley.

MOTELS ☎ ✎ 🐾 **Fox Inn** (413-648-9101 or 800-436-9466; www.sandri.com), Rt. 10, Bernardston 01337. An unusually attractive motel just off I-91, exit 28, but with an out-in-the-country feel. Rooms all overlook greenery; request one with peaked ceilings. $55–76 double. Handy to golf.

✎ **French King Motor Lodge** (413-423-3328), Rt. 2, Erving 01344. A good bet for families, 18 units with a swimming pool and restaurant near the French King Bridge. $65–95.

OTHER **Barton Cove Nature and Camping Area** (for reservations prior to the season, phone 413-659-3714; otherwise, 413-863-9300), Rt. 2, Gill. This is an unusual facility maintained by Northfield Mountain on a peninsula that juts into the Connecticut River. Wooded tent sites are available.

✳ Where to Eat

DINING OUT **Blue Heron Restaurant** (413-665-2102; www.blueheron dining.com), 112 N. Main St., Sunderland. Open year-round Tue.–Sun. from 5 PM. Reservations advised. The dimly lit, melon-colored rooms of a handsome former town hall are a country-elegant setting for one of the Valley's top restaurants. The produce is local, but chef and co-owner Deborah Snow's preparation certainly isn't. We dined on local greens followed by tender, tangy seared skirt steak in a blackberry BBQ sauce, served with caramelized corn and red potato hash, creamed Swiss chard, and smoked paprika onion strings. Entrées ($11–26) may range from a portobello panini to dim sum, and from chiles rellenos with spicy Creole sauce to grilled shrimp with red lentil dal, basmati rice, cucumber raita, and chutney.

Night Kitchen (413-367-9580; http://montaguenightkitchen.com), 440 Greenfield Rd., Montague. Open most of the year Wed.–Sun. 5:30–9. Reservations a must. Housed in picturesque Montague Mill (also the incubator for the Blue Heron), this is a small gem with a chef-owner named Max, the son of a cookbook author who has trained in kitchens in Italy and Asia. On a hot summer night there's no better place to dine than on the terrace here with the brook racing down below. It's an ambitious menu with starters that might include sake ginger cured salmon in rice paper with wasabi crème fraîche and cilantro oil, and such entrées as roast quail with corn bread and chorizo stuffing with maple-bourbon glaze. Entrées $20–22.

Ristorante DiPaolo (413-863-4441; www.ristorantedipaolo.com), 166 Ave. A, Turners Falls. Open except Tue. for dinner. Reservations advised. Steps from the Shea Community Theater, this attractive place is worth seeking out in its own right. Denise DiPaolo's menu features all the Italian classics but with style: A calamari appetizer is lightly floured and flash-fried, served with sweet potato, leeks, and a citrus crème fraîche sauce; Rollatini de Pollo is a chicken breast wrapped around asparagus, spinach, prosciutto, and smoked Gouda, drizzled with a sun-dried tomato and Dijon mustard sauce, served with fettuccine. Pasta sauces are all house made. Entrées $15–21.

Deerfield Inn (413-774-2359), The Street, Old Deerfield. Open daily for lunch, dinner nightly. Reservations advised. This is a formal dining room with white tablecloths, Chippendale chairs, and a moderately expensive lunch menu. At dinner you might begin with escargots in puff pastry with Brie and garlic butter ($7.25), then dine on roasted half duck with poached pear in cider ($27), or fresh salmon steamed in orange juice, ginger broth, and vegetable pot-au-feu ($23). Wine is available by the glass, and the wine list itself is extensive. Inquire about late-afternoon carriage rides as part of the dinner package.

Sienna (413-665-0215), 6 Elm St., South Deerfield. Dinner from 5:30 Wed.–Sun.; reservations recommended. An unpretentious storefront is the setting for this restaurant that's ranked among the best in the Valley. Richard Labonte's menu changes frequently and always features local produce. You might begin with a baby artichoke tart, then feast on pan-seared Atlantic cod with crabmeat mashed potato and crispy hearts of palm with lobster demiglaze; other options might range from forest mushroom potpie to grilled beef tenderloin. Leave room for dessert— perhaps a strawberry napoleon, or a Chardonnay-poached pear with mascarpone-pistachio filling and ginger-champagne sabayon. The one complaint we hear is that the wine list is overpriced. Entrées $21–26.

✣ **Goten of Japan** (413-665-3628), 104 Old Amherst Rd. (Rt. 116), Sunderland. Open for dinner, also lunch on Sat. Closed Mon. Set back from the road in its own grounds, this long-established Valley favorite offers a varied menu of traditional teriyaki, hibachi, and sukiyaki dishes ($13.95–21.50 including soup, salad, green tea, and dessert). A special

"Delight Dinner Menu" features lobster and seafood ($26.95–37.95); there's also a kids' menu.

Chandler's Restaurant at Yankee Candle (413-665-5089). Open for lunch and dinner. The decor is both rustic and romantic, with dinner lit by candles (some 200 of them). Lunch on tomato, basil, mushroom, and onion quiche, and dine on carrot ginger soup followed by veal roulade or crispy roast duck. Entrées $18–24.

Bella Notte (413-648-9107), Huckle Hill Rd., Bernardston. Open nightly for dinner; Nov. to early Apr., closed Mon.–Tue. Reservations please. A glass-faced, hilltop building with the best views of any restaurant in the Valley. The huge menu features northern Italian dishes: many appetizers, pastas, veal, chicken, and seafood dishes. Entrées $10.95–28.95.

EATING OUT

In and around Greenfield
The People's Pint (413-773-0333), 24 Federal St. From 4 PM. A first-rate brew pub that's also a great people place; good food, too. Specialties include soups, breads, and "the ploughman classic" (crusty sourdough topped with sharp cheddar, a pickle, and mustard). Reasonably priced entrées like New Orleans red beans and rice, and grilled chicken salad. Chess, board games, and darts weekday evenings, live music Saturday night, Celtic music Sunday.

China Gourmet (413-774-2299), 78 Mohawk Trail (Rt. 2A). Open for lunch and dinner, until 10 most nights and to 11 Fri. and Sat. A local favorite, light on the MSG, a reasonably priced menu and new sushi bar. Szechuan and Hunan specialties include hot-and-sour seafood soup, General Tso's chicken, and "Hot Lovers Triple Treat."

✐ **Bill's Restaurant** (413-773-8331), 30 Federal St. Open daily at 4, Sun. 11–8. This friendly, traditional restaurant remains a local favorite; liquor served. Plenty of pasta and fried dishes. Lobster pie is a specialty, and there are "Lite Dinners" for kids and seniors.

Brad's Place (413-773-9567), 353 Main St. Open 6–3, Sat. 6–2. "Serving downtown for 30 years," this is the kind of place where everyone knows everybody—but visitors are also served quickly and well. Daily specials, burgers, soups, and sandwiches, a long counter and booths.

Green Fields Market (413-773-9567), 144 Main St. This natural foods cooperative occupies a former JCPenney and includes a tempting deli and "from scratch" bakery with attractive seating space near the windows.

Thai Blue Ginger (413-772-0921), 298 Main St. Classic Thai dishes get good reviews for flavor and freshness.

Manna House (413-774-5955), 205 Main St. Open except Sun. for lunch and dinner. Not much from the outside but bright and inviting within, this Korean restaurant offers tantalizing vegetarian dishes as well as noodle soups, rice, and meat dishes.

Rose-ann's Bakery (413-772-6333), 10 Miles St. (between Energy Park and World Eye Bookstore). Doug and Rose-ann Harder run a small tea shop, always good for soup and sandwich, or tea and baked goods.

Elsewhere

Wolfie's (413-665-7068), 52 S. Main St., South Deerfield. Open 11–10 Mon.–Sat. This is our kind of place: wooden booths, fast friendly service, an appealing family restaurant. The menu features a blackened Wolfie-burger (a Cajun charbroiled 5-oz. ground round with melted cheddar, etc.), a "big bad wolfburger" (8 oz. ground round with melted cheese, etc.), many sandwiches, grinders, and salads as well as dinner specials starting at $8.95, draft beer, mixed drinks, and wine.

Lady Killigrew Café (413-367-9666; www.theladykillegrew.com), 440 Greenfield Rd., Montague Center. Open Wed.–Sat. for lunch and dinner, until midnight on weekends when there is usually live music. This is an attractive space with windows overlooking the brook and a feel and menu that's a cross between a café and pub. The "Bill of Fare" includes a warm brown rice salad and unusual sandwiches such as Brie with apricot jam and marinated apples. Tea, coffee, wine, and beer are also served.

Bub's Bar BQ (413-548-9630; www.bubsbbq.com), Rt. 116, Sunderland. Open at 4 weekdays, noon Sat.–Sun. Rated "best barbecue joint in New England" by *Yankee*, this place offers great variety: kielbasa and blackened fish, "spicy dirty rice" and "orange-glazed sweet potatoes," as well as pulled-pork back ribs.

Smiarowski Farm Stand and Creamy (413-665-3880), 320 River Rd. (Rt. 47), Sunderland. Open May–Nov., 8–6. The thing to order here is Karen Smiarowski's "Polish Power Plate": a *golabki*, a "lazy cabbage pierogi," and a chunk of kielbasa, plus homemade potato salad, baked beans, and rye bread. Desserts change with what's in season, beginning in June with rhubarb pie, then strawberry shortcake, then crisps—

blueberry, peach, and finally apple in September and October. Fruit toppings for the Snow's ice cream are also homemade. The self-serve snack bar (picnic tables) is attached to the family's post-and-beam farm stand. Also see The Smokin Hippo, below.

ROAD FOOD

Along Route 2
♫ **The Smokin' Hippo** (413-423-3220; www.thesmokinghippo.com), 20 French King Hwy., Erving. Open Tue.–Thu. 11–9, Fri.–Sat. 11–10, Sun. noon–8. Tucked into one of Rt. 2's upwardly spiraling curves, this landmark restaurant acquired a new identity and instant following when it opened in 2006. Owner Gary Weiss is a well-known local executive chef whose dual passions are BBQ and hippos (there's a story there). House-smoked ribs, chicken, and salmon are the specialties, but there are also seafood and Italian dishes, burgers and pygmy hippo burgers (for kids). Berkshire Brewery beers are on tap (including a house blend); full liquor license.

Skip's Italian and Polish Food, Rt. 2, Gill. A classic, seasonal take-out lunch wagon at the bridge to Turners Falls with picnic tables. The kielbasa and pierogi are worth a stop.

Wagon Wheel Restaurant (413-863-8210), 39 French King Hwy., Gill. Open seasonally for all three meals. Home-style cooking.

&. **Shady Glen Restaurant** (413-863-9636), 7 Ave. A, Turners Falls. Open Mon.–Sat. 5 AM–9 PM. No credit cards. A step back to the 1950s, this diner with its L-shaped counter and eight cozy booths is just off Rt. 2—

over the bridge across the Great Falls. Not the deal it was under previous longtime owners, but still a pleasant place with decent food—and now there's no wait.

Countree Living Restaurant (413-423-3624), 63 French King Hwy. (Rt. 2), Erving. Open Wed.–Sun. for dinner (4:30–8), Sat. for breakfast, too (11–2). Basic American fare with dinner specials, entrées $10–18. Full liquor license.

French King Restaurant (413-659-3328), handy to Rt. 2, Millers Falls. A family restaurant, open (except Mon.) for lunch and dinner.

Off I-91
Tom's Hot Dog, Rts. 5/10 south of I-91 exit 23 in North Hatfield. Legendary steamed hot dogs.

Fillin' Station (413-665-3696), Rts. 5/10 just off I-91, exit 24. The best we can say is that this classic chrome diner is open 24 hours, adjacent to a gas station–truck stop. The flashy decor is great, but on a recent visit the service was slow, food below par.

The Four Leaf Clover Restaurant (413-648-9514), Rt. 5, Bernardston. Open daily for lunch and dinner, until 9 Fri. and Sat. Just off I-91 exit 28, a family restaurant that's a local favorite, good for chicken potpie, baked haddock, and liver and onions as well as homemade soups and bread pudding.

7 South Bakery (413-648-0070), 7 South St. (Rt. 5), Bernardston. Open 6:30 AM–5 PM, closed Sun. The moment you walk into Kay and Mike Dougherty's small shop, you know you've struck gold. There's an irresistible aroma of freshly baked breads and coffee; pastries, too.

✱ Entertainment

Shea Community Theater (413-863-2281; www.theshea.org), 71 Ave. A, Turners Falls. Call Tue.–Fri. noon–3 to inquire about year-round plays and musicals staged by three local community theater organizations. This is also home to the Shea Young Stage Company for actors ages 11–18.

Music in Deerfield (413-774-4200; www.musicindeerfield.org). A fall-through-spring series of performances by nationally known musicians, presented by Mohawk Trail Concerts at the Brick Church Meeting House in Old Deerfield.

1794 New Salem Meetinghouse (978-544-5200), off Rt. 202, New Salem. A beautiful setting for music—choral, folk, and jazz—also an assortment of live performances.

Full Moon Coffee House (978-544-2086), Wendell. Monthly concerts held in the town hall on the Saturday night closest to the full moon.

Pioneer Valley Symphony and Chorus (413-773-3664) based in Greenfield. One of the oldest symphony orchestras in the country.

FILM Northfield Drive-In (603-239-4054), Rt. 63 north of Northfield. Half in New Hampshire and half in Massachusetts, an old-fashioned drive-in showing new releases, open seasonally.

Greenfield Garden Cinemas (413-774-4881), 361 Main St., Greenfield. No longer the movie palace it once was but still a place to see first-run films.

✱ Selective Shopping

ANTIQUES AND AUCTIONS This is a particularly rich antiquing area. Auc-tion houses include **Douglas** (413-665-2877; www.douglasauctioneeers .com), Rt. 5, Deerfield (Fri. night); and **Northfield Auctions** (413-498-4420; www.northfieldauctions.com), 105 Main St., Northfield.

Yesterdays Antique Center (413-665-7226), Rts. 5/10 in Deerfield. Open Tue. and Thu.–Sun. 10–4; some two dozen dealers, displaying everything from books to major furniture pieces.

ART AND CRAFTS GALLERIES At the **Montague Mill** (www.montague bookmill.com), 440 Greenfield Rd., Montague. **Mill Music** (413-367-2062) displays local crafts and **Millworks Studio** (413-367-2885; www .louiseminks.com) features Louise Minks's outstanding paintings, prints, and cards depicting mostly local landscapes.

Artspace Gallery (413-772-6811), Mill St., Greenfield. Changing crafts shows represent area artists and artisans.

Hallmark Museum of Contemporary Photography (413-863-0009; www.hmcp.org); open Thu.–Sun. 1–5), 84 Ave. A, displays work by well-known photographers and students at the nearby **Hallmark Institute of Photography**.

Pure Light Gallery (413-863-9652; www.purelightgallery.com), 37 3rd St., Turners Falls. Open Thu. and Fri. 10–2, Sat. 10–3, or by appointment.

Tim de Christopher (413-586-7496; www.ohmysoul.org), Williams Garage (147 2nd St.), Turners Falls. The sculptor has converted a classic 1940s garage into a studio for his garden and other creations.

Green Trees Gallery (413-498-0283), 105 Main St., Northfield. A

THE PURE LIGHT GALLERY

very attractive consignment gallery featuring handmade pottery, weaving, paintings, sculpture, and the **Media Arts Café**, showing art movies on Fri. and Sat.

Tom White Pottery (413-498-2175), 205 Winchester Rd., Northfield. Sited at the corner of Pierson and Winchester Roads, this studio is a source of wheel-thrown, porcelain production work that's obviously been influenced by traditional Chinese forms and glazes. Call ahead.

11 South Gallery/Workshop, Rts. 5/10, Bernardston. Open Wed.–Sat. 11–5. On the southern fringe of the village, this is a magical space, featuring painted local and Maine landscapes by Elice Davis Pieropan and pottery by her daugher Pamela. There are also exceptional woodcarvings and decorative weavings from the Pacific atoll of Kapingamarangi, where the family lived for many years.

BOOKSTORES Meetinghouse Books (413-665-0500; www.meetinghouse books.com), 70 N. Main St., South Deerfield. Open Wed.–Fri. 10–6, weekends noon–6. A destination for browsers for more than 20 years: Judith Tingley and Ken Haverly have

filled an old wooden church with their eclectic selection of thousands of used and out-of-print books, literature, history, the arts, children's books, and much more, "priced to every budget."

Books & More (413-863-9417), 74 Ave. A, Turners Falls. A genuine full-service independent bookstore just down from the discovery center, another great addition to downtown Turners Falls.

World Eye Bookshop (413-772-2186; www.worldeyebookshop.com), 156 Main St., Greenfield. Open daily. This well-stocked book- and gift store serves a wide upcountry area.

Book Mill (413-367-9206; www.montaguebookmill.com) in the Montague Mill, Greenfield, and on Depot Rd., Montague. Open daily 10–6. True to its slogan, "Books you don't need in a place you can't find," this bookworm's mecca offers thousands

MEETINGHOUSE BOOKS IN SOUTH DEERFIELD

of used and discounted books with plenty of reading corners and frequent concerts and readings. It's housed in a picturesque old mill by a rushing stream, along with Lady Killigrew Café (see *Eating Out*) and the Night Kitchen (see *Dining Out*).

Whately Antiquarian Book Center (413-247-3272), Rts. 5/10, Whately. Open 10–5:30, Sun. noon–5; closed Wed., Sep.–June. A group shop with 40 dealers and 30,000 good used and rare books.

SPECIAL STORES **Wilson's Department Store** (413-774-4326), 258 Main St., Greenfield. Open Mon.–Sat. from 9:30, most nights until 6 PM; to 8 Thu. and 9 Fri. In business since 1882, one of New England's few surviving independently owned downtown department stores: four floors with everything from appliances and bedspreads, through cosmetics, to toys, cards, and clothing.

Magical Child (413-773-5721), 134 Main St., Greenfield. A first-rate toy and children's clothing store.

Pekarski's Sausage (413-665-4537), Rt. 116, South Deerfield. Homemade Polish kielbasa, breakfast sausage, smoked ham, and bacon.

Millstone's (413-665-0543), 24 S. Main St. (Rt. 47), Sunderland. The store's name and design, both featuring genuine millstones, date to 1929. Known for its meat, this is an exceptionally friendly store featuring local produce.

Richardson's Candy Kitchen (413-772-0443 or 800-817-9338; www .richardsonscandy.com), Rts. 5/10, Deerfield. Open daily 10–5:30. Handmade chocolates and specialty candies with a wide and enthusiastic following.

Also see **Yankee Candle** under *For Families*.

The Textile Co., Inc. (413-773-7516), 21 Power Square, Greenfield. Open Mon.–Sat. 9–5:20, Fri. until 8:20. Closed Mon. in June, July, August. Customers come from far and wide to this old-fashioned, quality fabric store good for cottons, silks, polysters, vinyls, linen, acetate, calicos, notions, and patterns.

✳ Farms and Farm Stands

Also see **Smiarowski Farm Stand and Creamy** under *Eating Out*.

Hamilton Orchards (978-544-6867), 22 West St. (just off Rt. 202), New Salem. Open July–Aug., daily 9–5; Sep.–Oct., weekends 9–5. Bill and Barb Hamilton have been welcoming visitors to their 100-acre hilltop farm since 1943. In fall, with four kinds of apples to pick and tables piled with apple pies and dumplings, the place is hopping and the snack bar is open. In summer there are PYO raspberries and blueberries. Picnic tables overlook the hills.

Upinngil (413-863-2297), 411 Main Rd., Gill. Open June–Oct. Organically grown asparagus, melons, sweet corn, potatoes (many varieties), pumpkins, winter squash, honey, hay, maple products. Strawberries picked and U-pick.

Riverland Farm (413-665-2041; www.riverlandfarm.com), 197 River Rd. (Rt. 47), Sunderland. Open early June–late Oct., daily. A large selection of farm-grown organic vegetables, plus other local milk, cheese, eggs, goat cheese, fruit, and maple syrup.

Warner Farm (413-665-8331), 159 Old Amherst Rd., Sunderland. Open May–Oct., 10–6. Farm-grown produce: asparagus, strawberries, peas, beans, peppers, sweet corn, pumpkins, and squash. Pick-your-own strawberries in June. Sep.–Oct. visit "Mike's Amazing Maze" (www.mikes maze.com), the area's first and only corn maze, 9–5 at 23 S. Main St. (Rt. 47).

Golonka Farm (413-247-3256), 6 State Rd., Whately. Open June 15 through Oct., daily 9–6. Specializing in sweet corn, but has a variety of other home-grown vegetables.

Long Plain Farm (413-665-1210), 149 Christian Lane, Whately. Open May–Dec., 9–5. Onions, potatoes, cabbage, eggplant, summer and winter squash, pickle and salad cucumbers, sweet corn, Halloween and sugar pumpkins.

Songline Emu Farm (413-863-2700; www.allaboutemu.com), 66 French King Hwy. (Rt. 2), Gill. Open Apr.–Sep. 15, Thu.–Sat. noon–6. A working emu farm offering tours, selling lean emu burgers and steak. Admission: $3 adults, $2 ages 12 and under.

Chee Chee Mamook Farm (413-498-2160), 341 Caldwell Rd., Northfield. Open year-round. Hours by appointment. This is a visitor-geared alpaca farm with a store selling homespun alpaca-fleece yarn and clothing.

FLOWERS **Baystate Perennial Farm** (413-665-3525), 36 State Rd. (Rts. 5/10), Whately. Open mid-Apr. through Sep., daily 9–6. New and unusual as well as proven classic perennials, shrubs, and vines. Free gardening workshops and informal garden walks/talks.

Mill River Farm (413-665-3034), corner of Rts. 5 and 116, South Deerfield, across from the fire station. Open Apr.–late June, Sep.–Oct., and Thanksgiving weekend–Christmas. Annuals, herbs, hanging baskets, mums, asters, pumpkins, Christmas trees, perennials.

PICK-YOUR-OWN **Clarkdale Fruit Farms** (413-772-6797), 303 Upper Rd., Deerfield, a fourth-generation farm, has PYO apples, pumpkins, peaches, pears, and great cider, including pear if you're lucky.

Nourse Farm (413-665-2650; www .noursefarms.com), 41 River Rd., South Deerfield. This 400-acre riverside farm ships some 15 million "virus-free plants" throughout the world. While most business is through its catalog and web site, it also welcomes PYO customers June–Oct. daily (8–4) for whatever is in-season: strawberries (24 varieties) and several kinds and colors of raspberries.

Quonquont Farm (413-575-4680), 9 North St., Whately. Open mid-July through early Nov., 10–6. Closed Mon. and holidays. Pick-your-own blueberries, peaches, and apples. Farm stand with fruit, cider, and preserves. A blueberry maze.

SUGARHOUSES Maple producers who welcome visitors include **Williams Farm Sugar House** (413-773-5186; www.williamsfarm.com),

Christina Tree

Rts. 5/10 in Deerfield, open mid-Feb. to mid-Apr., 8:30–5, with pancake breakfasts served daily and sugarhouse tours; products available year-round; **Brookledge Sugarhouse** (413-665-3837; www.brookledgesugar house.com), 159 Haydenville Rd. (2 miles fom Whately Center), Whately; **River Maple Farm** (413-648-9767), Rt. 5, Bernardston; and **Ripley's Sugarhouse** (413-367-2031), 195 Chestnut Hill Rd., Montague.

✳ Special Events

February: **Greenfield Winter Carnival** (413-772-1553) at Highland Pond, Beacon Field, and all around town, includes an ice sculpture contest, ice skating, cross-country skiing, and sledding (*first weekend*).

March: **Sugaring**—local sugarhouses invite the public; check the listings above or visit www.massmaple.org.

May: **Gas and Steam Engine Show**, Rt. 10, Bernardston.

Mid-May–June: The **Fish Ladder** behind town hall in Turners Falls, operated by Northfield Mountain (800-859-2960), offers views through a window behind the falls of shad and occasional Atlantic salmon finding their way up the Connecticut River.

Spring–fall: **Farmer's markets** are held in Greenfield, Sat. 8–12:30; in Northfield Thu. 4–7; and in Turners Falls Wed. 3–6.

June: **Old Deerfield Summer Crafts Fair at Memorial Hall** (413-774-7476; www.deerfield-craft.org) includes more than 200 exhibitors (*last weekend*). **Old Deerfield Sun-**day **Afternoon Concert Series** (413-774-3768) celebrates chamber music. **Western Massachusetts Highland Games and Celtic Festival** (413-586-9182).

July: **Old-Fashioned Independence Day** (413-774-3768) in Old Deerfield. The **Green River Festival** (413-773-5463) features nationally known musicians, a crafts fair, and hot-air balloon launches.

Late August: **Montague Old Home Days** (413-367-9467) has games, an auction, food, music, and a footrace in Montague Village and Montague Center.

September: **Franklin County Fair**, held at the fairgrounds in Greenfield, includes livestock, crafts, music, a midway, and food (*first weekend after Labor Day*). **Old Deerfield Fall Craft Fair** (413-774-3768) boasts more than 200 juried exhibitors from throughout the country, featuring traditional crafts. **Garlic and Arts Festival**, New Salem.

October: **Arts and Leaves Studio Tour in Turners Falls**. **Antique Dealers of America Historic Deerfield Antiques Show** (*early in the month*; www.adadealers.com). **Gill Craft Fair** (413-863-9708) has crafts and music (*second weekend*). **Fiber Twist** (413-773-5463) features open farms and a marketplace for fiber farmers, weavers, and spinners throughout Franklin County (*last Saturday*).

November: **Annual Franklin County Cider Day** (413-773-5463), with open farms, studios, and winery, a marketplace, and more.

FIVE-COLLEGE AREA

The "Five Colleges" are the University of Massachusetts as well as four small, prestigious private colleges: Amherst, Mount Holyoke, Hampshire, and Smith. Together these very different campuses are home to a total of 30,000 students within an 11-mile radius.

In cities, such academic concentrations are less noticeable. Here, against a backdrop of cornfields, apple orchards, and small towns, the visible and cultural impact of academia is dramatic. Art collections in seven college museums are exceptional. For families, the dinosaur tracks and remains in the Amherst College Museum of Natural History and the exhibits in the Eric Carle Museum of Picture Book Art are worth the trip. The area's galleries, shops, and restaurants are numerous and appealing.

Still, the Five-College Area is one of the state's better-kept secrets. This stretch of the Connecticut River was better known as a destination more than a century ago. As early as the 1820s, sophisticated visitors came to view the Valley's peculiar mix of factory and farmscape, bottomland and abrupt mountains. In 1836 Thomas Cole, one of America's most celebrated landscape artists, painted the mammoth work *The Oxbow: View from Mt. Holyoke, Northampton, Massachusetts, after a Thunderstorm*, now owned by New York's Metropolitan Museum. The Oxbow subsequently became the "motif number one" of Western Massachusetts, and the small Mountain House on the summit of Mount Holyoke was soon replaced with a more elaborate hotel (a portion of which survives), accessed from riverboats and a riverside train station by a perpendicular cog-and-cable-driven railway. There was also a hotel on Mount Tom and a mineral spa in Northampton. During the academic year, buses circulate among the five campuses (residents and visitors welcome). Thousands of students annually take courses at the other institutions, and all share a lively "Five-College" calendar of plays, concerts, and lectures. Many graduates have opted to stay on in the Valley, establishing the crafts and art galleries, restaurants, shops, and coffeehouses for which the area is now known.

Northampton, the Valley's focal point both for students and visitors, is known for the quantity and quality of its restaurants, galleries, and evening music venues. It's an architecturally interesting old county seat, with an outstanding art museum at Smith College and the country's oldest municipal theater, the Academy of Music.

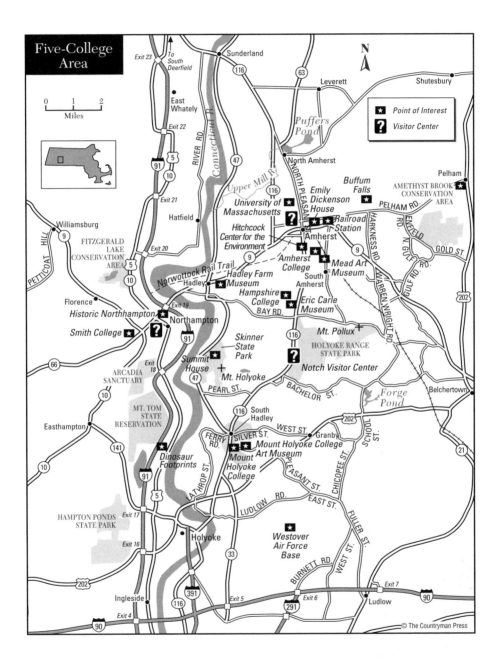

Five-College Area

Exit 23
To South Deerfield

0   1   2
Miles

N

★ Point of Interest
? Visitor Center

Sunderland
116
63
Leverett
Shutesbury

East Whately

Exit 22

Puffers Pond

North Amherst

Pelham

Exit 21

Upper Mill R.

Emily Dickenson House
Buffum Falls
AMETHYST BROOK CONSERVATION AREA

PELHAM RD.

Williamsburg
9

Hatfield

University of Massachusetts ★
?
Hitchcock Center for the Environment

Railroad Station
Amherst
9

GOLD ST.

PETTICOAT HILL

FITZGERALD LAKE CONSERVATION AREA

Exit 20

Norwottock Rail Trail

Hadley Farm Museum ★
Hadley

Amherst College
South Amherst

Mead Art Museum ★

202

Connecticut R.

RIVER RD.

NORTH PLEASANT

HARKNESS RD.
N. GULF RD.
GULF RD.
WARREN WRIGHT RD.

Florence

Historic Northhampton ★
Northampton

Smith College ★
?

Hampshire College
BAY RD.

Eric Carle Museum ★

Mt. Pollux +

66

Exit 19

Exit 18
Summit House +
Mt. Holyoke
47

Skinner State Park ★

116
?
HOLYOKE RANGE STATE PARK

Notch Visitor Center

Forge Pond
Belchertown

ARCADIA SANCTUARY

10

PEARL ST.

BACHELOR ST.

Easthampton

MT. TOM STATE RESERVATION

116
South Hadley

WEST ST.
Granby
202

21

141

FERRY RD.
SILVER ST.
Mount Holyoke College Art Museum

SCHOOL ST.
CHICOPEE ST.
PLEASANT ST.
EAST ST.

10

Dinosaur Footprints ★

Mount Holyoke College

LATHROP ST.
91
5

LUDLOW RD.

EAST ST.

FULLER ST.

HAMPTON PONDS STATE PARK

Exit 17

Exit 16
Holyoke

33

Westover Air Force Base ★

BURNETT RD.
WEST ST.

202

391
116

Ingleside

Exit 5
291

Exit 6
Ludlow

Exit 7
90

Exit 4
90

© The Countryman Press

Amherst is a classic, increasingly lively college town. The large, shaded common, framed by the Amherst College campus and 19th-century shops, remains its centerpiece, connected to the UMass campus (curiously invisible, despite its high-rise dormitories and library, unless you go looking for it) by one long street of shops and restaurants. The evolving new Cinema Arts Center just off the common will complement the wide choice of good, inexpensive places to eat or simply sit and sip while working on your computer (the downtown is virtually all WiFi).

Innovative Hampshire College is a few minutes' drive south of downtown Amherst. Mount Holyoke, a few more miles south in the village of South Hadley, is the country's oldest women's college and arguably the most beautiful of the five campuses, an 800-acre spread designed by the firm of Frederick Law Olmsted with two lakes and majestic trees.

The fact that each of the five is so different contributes to the beauty of their mix—a phenomenon that can be experienced year-round. Entertainment options include concerts in such venues as the Summit House atop Mount Holyoke and the garden at Forty Acres in Hadley, as well as several theaters. Hiking trails run east–west across the Valley, along the ridge of the Holyoke Range and through many miles of conservation land.

We include the small brick-mill city of Holyoke in the Five-College Area. Designed from scratch by Boston developers in the 1840s and '50s, it's a sharp contrast with the nearby ivy-covered communities. Industrial-architecture buffs will be intrigued by canal-side mill buildings, and families will appreciate the attractions conveniently grouped around the Holyoke Heritage State Park—the Children's Museum and a working antique merry-go-round. Mount Tom offers great views.

Thanks to Amtrak from New York City and frequent buses from Boston and among the campuses, the Five-College Area is almost accessible without a car, especially if you bring your bicycle.

GUIDANCE **Amherst Area Chamber of Commerce** (413-253-0700; fax, 413-256-0771; www.amherstarea.com), 28 Amity St., open Mon.–Fri. 8:30–4:30. This friendly, well-stocked storefront in the new Cinema Arts Center Building is worth a stop. A volunteer-dependent information booth on the common is also open summer weekends.

IVY-COVERED MOUNT HOLYOKE COLLEGE IN SOUTH HADLEY
Kim Grant

Greater Northampton Chamber of Commerce (413-584-1900; www.explorenorthampton.com), 99 Pleasant St. (Rt. 5 south), Northampton 01060. Open Mon.–Fri. 9–5, also weekends June–Oct., 10–2.

For area museums, visit www.museums10.org.

By air: **Bradley International Airport**; see "Springfield."

By bus: **Peter Pan–Trailways** (800-343-9999; www.peterpanbus.com) connects Greenfield, Amherst, South Hadley, and Holyoke with Boston, Springfield, Bradley International Airport, and points beyond. The departure point in Amherst is 79 S. Pleasant St. (but buy tickets in Amherst Books); the Northampton terminal is at 1 Round House Place (413-586-1030) behind City Hall. From New York City, **Greyhound** (800-231-2222; www.greyhound.com) and **Vermont Transit** (800-552-8737; www.vttransit.com) serve Greenfield on north–south routes.

By train: **Amtrak** (800-872-7245; www.Amtrak.com), Amherst.

By car: The Mass Pike and Rt. 2 offer east–west access, and I-91 runs north–south. From Rt. 2, the quickest and most scenic way to the Amherst area is via Rt. 202 (exit 16), the Daniel Shays Highway, running down along the Quabbin Reservoir; turn west at the Pelham Town Hall.

For Northampton the quickest access is via I-91.

GETTING AROUND **The Pioneer Valley Transit Authority**, or PVTA (413-586-5806), connecting Northampton, Amherst, and South Hadley, is free and frequent. It circles among the five campuses from 6:45 AM until 11:35 PM weekdays during the academic year, less frequently on weekends and in summer.

PARKING *In Northampton:* The parking garage (Hampton Ave. behind Thornes Market) does require prepayment; the first hour is free. Scattered through town, lots are heavily patrolled. Some streets and lots have a 2-hour limit. Meters are free after 6 PM.

In Amherst: In addition to metered street parking, there are four downtown lots. The Boltwood lot (access from Main St.) is the handiest, with access to N. Pleasant St. shops. Behind the CVS on N. Pleasant St. is another lot, and there are also small lots on Spring St. (adjacent to the common) and Amity St. (across from the Jones Library). All are closely monitored. Note: Parking on side streets is by permit during the academic year.

In Holyoke: The downtown parking garage is on Dwight St., one block from the Heritage State Park.

MEDICAL EMERGENCY Dial **911**.

Cooley Dickinson Hospital (413-582-2000), 30 Locust St. (Rt. 9), Northampton.

Providence Hospital (413-536-5111), 1233 Main St., Holyoke.

✳ Villages, Towns, and Cities

Amherst. With significantly more students than Northampton (the town's population of some 35,000 includes a percentage of the 24,000 undergraduates and 5,500 graduate students at UMass, 1,600 at Amherst, and 1,200 at Hampshire

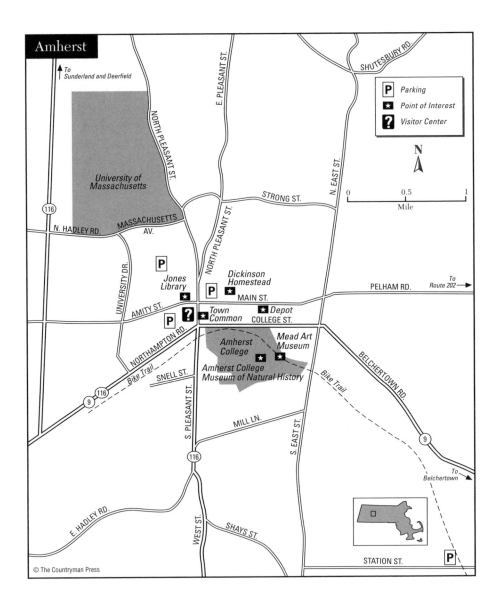

College), Amherst is a lively college town. It's also walkable, with intriguing shops and restaurants lining two sides of its common as well as North Pleasant Street. More restaurants cluster around Boltwood Walk, squirreled away between North Pleasant and Main. As noted in the introduction, the vast and high-rise UMass campus, north of downtown Amherst, is curiously invisible. The far smaller Amherst College campus, just off the common, also eludes visitors but is well worth finding, both for the treasures in its **Mead Art Museum** and the dinosaurs in its newly revamped **Amherst College Museum of Natural History**. Emily Dickinson buffs should visit not only her home but also the

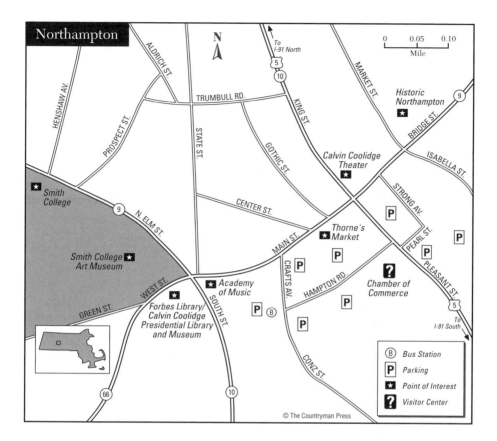

exhibits devoted to the poet's life in the **Jones Library**, just off the common. The Special Collections here form the literary heart of town, with exhibits and material devoted to Emily Dickinson but also an 11,000-item collection relating to poet Robert Frost. Portraits depict Frost not as the shaggy poet laureate we usually see but as the strikingly handsome young man who lived in Amherst from 1931 to 1938 and returned in the 1940s to teach at Amherst College. As noted in the introduction, Amherst enjoys direct train service to Manhattan and a direct bus from Boston, as well as excellent local public transport and a bike trail to Northampton. It also offers a surprising amount of very accessible natural beauty, if you know where to look.

Northampton. Despite a population of less than 30,000, this is a city, one with more art and music, film and drama, shopping and dining than most urban centers a dozen times its size. Thanks to Round Hill, an 1840s–1860 mineral water spa, Northampton loomed large on New England's pre–Civil War tourist map. In 1852 Jenny Lind, the Swedish Nightingale, spent a 3-month honeymoon at Round Hill and called Northampton "Paradise City," a name that's stuck (current local listings include Paradise City Travel, Paradise Copies, etc.). The brick hotel

Kim Grant

DOWNTOWN NORTHAMPTON

itself survives as part of the **Clarke School for the Deaf** (established 1867) on Round Hill Road, off Elm Street. Northampton is home to **Smith College** as well as to historical figures as different as the fiery 18th-century preacher Jonathan Edwards, the 19th-century former slave and advocate for justice Sojourner Truth, food faddist Sylvester Graham (as in *graham cracker*), and the 1920s Northampton mayor and U.S. president Calvin Coolidge. The city's unusual history is nicely depicted in the **Historic Northampton** museum.

Northampton has reinvented itself several times over the centuries; the present Main Street lineup of restaurants, art galleries, and boutiques is relatively recent. Now known as Noho, Northampton continues to evolve, having a long tradition of tolerating people with dissenting religious and political views and nontraditional lifestyles. The town has a vibrant gay and lesbian community, the latter especially active in local cultural life. Civic pride runs as high as it did during the years the city's former mayor was sitting in the Oval Office (1923–29), a brief era in which the Hotel Northampton (which opened with a mini museum village attached, to serve as an auto touring destination) and several handsome art deco buildings appeared. These include a jewel box of a building featuring a stained-glass skylight that now appropriately houses Silverscape Designs; another splendid former bank is the setting for sculpture and prints (R. Michelson Galleries), and the fabulously restored Calvin Theatre serves regularly as a venue for stellar live performances.

Northampton these days has a synergy all its own. It's not unusual to find the city's internationally famed Young at Heart Chorus of senior citizens sharing a stage with the Northampton Gay Men's Chorus, or for visitors to view a Matisse or Picasso in the Smith College Museum of Art and then stroll down the street to see a concert or a locally produced film at the municipally owned (since 1890) Academy of Music. Live music is a nightly given in several venues. Restaurants are so plentiful that patrons know they can always find a table within a block or two.

Don't overlook the village of **Florence**, still in Northampton, west on Rt. 9. Once known for silk mills, today its landmarks are the Miss Florence Diner and Look Park. Florence was also home to Sojourner Truth; her statue stands in a triangular park on Pine Street.

Hadley. Sandwiched between Northampton and Amherst, Hadley is easy to
miss because it's still predominantly tobacco, onion, and asparagus fields—
beyond the Rt. 9 shops, greenhouses (the Hadley rose, the Talisman rose, and
the Hadley gardenia were all developed here), and the many malls. Settled in
1659, it is the mother town of Amherst, South Hadley, Sunderland, Granby, and
Hatfield and was originally known as Norwottuck, a name resurrected for the
bike path that threads its fields. In 1675 a white-bearded recluse, reputedly
William Goffe (a Charles I regicide), saved the town from an Indian attack and
has ever since been known as the Angel of Hadley. Turn off Rt. 9 at Middle
Street to see the pillared town hall (1841), the **Hadley Farm Museum**, and the
First Congregational Church (1808). The **Porter-Phelps-Huntington House**
(1742) hidden away on the river (Rt. 47, north from Rt. 9) is a jewel.

Holyoke (www.holyoke.org). In 1847 Boston investors formed the Hadley Falls
Company, buying 1,000 acres with the idea of utilizing the waterpower from the
magnificent falls here. The company—and its dam—went bust but was soon
replaced by the Holyoke Water Power Company, until recently the city's major
political and economic force. Holyoke is a classic planned mill city. Its 4.5 miles
of canals rise in tiers past dozens of mills; the commercial area is set in a neat
grid above the mills. Housing changes with the altitude—from 1840s brick workers' housing on "The Flats" near the river, through hundreds of hastily built late-
19th- and early-20th-century tenements, to the mill owners' mansions above, and
above that the parkland on **Mount Tom**. In the visitor center at **Holyoke Heritage State Park** (413-534-1723; 221 Appleton St.; open Tue.–Sun. noon–4:30;
follow the signs for downtown), a short film conveys a sense of the city's late-
19th-century vitality, of the era in which immigrants turned neighborhoods into
"Little" Ireland, Poland, France, and half a dozen more ethnic bastions. If the
film were remade today, it would note the last two decades' influx of Puerto
Ricans, a group first drawn in the 1960s to work in the nearby tobacco fields.
Specialty papers, from college bluebooks to hospital johnnies, remain Holyoke's
most notable product. Inquire about guided and leaflet walking tours and frequent special events. Mill-architecture buffs will appreciate the beauty of the
canal-side Graham Mill (Second Level Canal near the Rt. 116 bridge).

✳ To See

HISTORIC HOUSES AND MUSEUMS **The Amherst History Museum at the
Strong House** (413-256-0678; www.amhersthistory.org), 67 Amity St., Amherst.
Open mid-May through Oct., Wed. and Sat. 12:30–3:30, or by appointment. $4
adults, $3 seniors and students, free under age 6. This circa-1750 gambrel-
roofed house largely reflects several periods, including one in which it was a
home and a "Young Ladies School." In addition to period rooms there are pictures and products (like palm-leaf hats) of Amherst past, also changing exhibits.
The garden is 18th century. In 1899 it was the Amherst Historical Society's colorful founder, Mabel Loomis Todd, who secured this property. A room dedicated
to her includes her paintings and souvenirs from world travels. Todd was Austin
Dickinson's mistress and was responsible for editing and publishing early volumes
of Emily Dickinson's poetry (see *Voice of the Valley*). Inquire about special events.

Porter-Phelps-Huntington Historic House Museum (413-584-4699), 130 River Dr. (Rt. 47, 2 miles north of the junction of Rts. 9 and 47), Hadley. Open May 15–Oct. 15 for hour-long guided tours, Sat.–Wed. 1–4:30. $4 per adult, $1 per child. **Wednesday Folk Traditions** (ethnic folk music) at 7 PM in June and July are staged in the garden, weather permitting ($8, $7 seniors, $2 children; picnickers welcome before concerts). **A Perfect Spot of Tea**, Saturdays in July and August (pastries and music at 2:30 and 3:30, $8). Also known as Forty Acres, this aristocratic old farm was built near the banks of the Connecticut River in 1752, and there have been no structural changes since 1799. The furnishings have accumulated over six generations of one extended family.

The Hadley Farm Museum (413-586-1160), Rts. 9 and 47, Hadley. Open May–Oct., Wed.–Sat. 11–4, Sun. 1–4. Free. The 1782 barn from Forty Acres (see above) was moved in 1930 to its present site near the First Congregational Church and white-pillared town hall. It houses old broom-making machines (broom corn was once the town's chief crop) and other old farm implements, pottery, an old stagecoach from Hardwick, and other assorted mementos of life in the Valley.

In Holyoke

⊙ **Wistariahurst Museum** (413-332-5660; www.wistariahurst.org), 238 Cabot St. Open Sat.–Mon. noon–4. Admission by donation. An opulent 19th-century, 26-room mansion with leather wall coverings, elaborate woodwork, and etched glass, built for the Skinner family, owners of the world's largest silk mill. It evokes the expansive spirit of Belle Skinner, the socialite who added a marble lobby, grand staircase, and great hall. Inquire about changing exhibits, concerts, and other events. The 3 acres of landscaped grounds include dinosaur footprints and fossil marks. Check the web site for a lively program of art exhibits, concerts, and lectures. This is also a popular venue for weddings.

THE PORTER-PHELPS-HUNTINGTON HISTORIC HOUSE MUSEUM IN HADLEY

Christina Tree

Also see **Holyoke Heritage State Park** under *Villages, Towns, and Cities* and the **Volleyball Hall of Fame** under *For Families*.

In Northampton

Historic Northampton (413-584-6011; www.historic-northampton.org), 46 Bridge St. (Rt. 9 between I-91 and downtown). Open year-round, Tue.–Fri. 10–4; Sat.–Sun. noon–4, when house tours are offered. The Museum and Education Center features *A Place Called Paradise*, a permanent exhibit dramatizing the city's history. Displays range from extensive Indian artifacts to Jonathan Edwards, industrial products to Coolidge years.

There are also changing special exhibits. Three historic houses—the **Parsons House** (1719), the **Damon House** (1813, home of architect Isaac Damon), and the **Shepherd House** (1796) reflecting lifestyles over three generations—are on their original sites, set in landscaped grounds. Inquire about special programs and events.

Christina Tree

THE HADLEY FARM MUSEUM

ART MUSEUMS Smith College Museum of Art (413-585-2760; www.smith.edu/artmuseum), Elm St. (Rt. 9, just beyond College Hall), Northampton. Open Tue.–Sat. 10–4, Sun. noon–5, until 9 Wed. Free. On the second Fri. it's open until 8 (free after 4). $5 adults; less for students, seniors, children. This world-class art collection is second in Western Massachusetts only to the Clark Art Institute in Williamstown. The third-floor, naturally lit gallery is hung with works by Picasso, Degas, Winslow Homer, Rockwell Kent, Marsden Hartley, Seurat, and Whistler, and sculpture by Rodin and Leonard Baskin, also American primitives and impressionists such as the starkly realistic oils by Edwin Romanzo Elmer evoking 19th-century scenes from the nearby Hilltowns. From its 1870s beginnings, the college's art collecting focused on "contemporary American art" and by the 1920s included European "Modern Art." Curator Jere Abbott, who had served on the founding staff of New York's Museum of Modern Art, was instrumental in acquiring works like Picasso's cubist piece *La Table.* The museum's second floor houses its European collection and a remarkable print room; the first floor is devoted to special exhibits and includes a gift store and what are undoubtedly the most artistic restrooms in any museum.

Mead Art Museum (413-542-2335; www.amherst.edu/mead), on the campus of Amherst College, Amherst. Open Tue.–Sun. 10–4:30, until 9 Thu. The building, designed by McKim, Mead & White, has been totally revamped within the past few years. The well-rounded permanent collection includes paintings by Thomas Eakins, Winslow Homer, Marsden Hartley, and Childe Hassam. The stunning *Salome* by Robert Henri and *Morning on the Seine* by Claude Monet are usually on display; special exhibits are frequently contemporary

MOURNING PICTURE BY EDWIN ROMANZO ELMER IS SET IN BUCKLAND.

Smith College Museum of Art

MAN WALKING BY VINCENT VAN GOGH

works by William Glackens, Robert Henri, and Milton Avery. Special exhibits.

⚓ **The Eric Carle Museum of Picture Book Art** (413-658-1100; www .picturebookart.org), 125 West Bay Rd. (off Rt. 116), Amherst. Open Tue.–Fri. 10–4, Sat. 10–5, Sun. noon–5. $7 adults; $5 seniors, children, and students. Opened in 2003 adjacent to the Hampshire College campus, this independently funded museum showcases the work of world-acclaimed illustrators and is aimed at "children of all ages." Local artist Eric Carle, author of *The Very Hungry Caterpillar* among many other books, contributed a founding gift and is frequently but not necessarily represented in the frequently changing exhibits—which are

and provocative. Totally unexpected is the Rotherwas Room, an ornately paneled, vintage-1611 English hall, a setting for furniture, portraits, and silver.

Mount Holyoke College Art Museum (413-538-2245; www.mtholyoke .edu/go/artmuseum), Lower Lake Rd., South Hadley. Open Tue.–Fri. 11–5, weekends 1–5. Free. One of the oldest collegiate art collections in the country, but housed in a modern building with 10 spacious galleries. Permanent holdings number 14,000 objects ranging from ancient Asian and Egyptian works and Pompeiian frescoes, through Roman and medieval statuary, to some outstanding 19th-century landscapes by Albert Bierstadt and George Inness; also

SALOME BY ROBERT HENRY (1909)

Mount Holyoke College Art Museum

A CHILD ADMIRES *FAUSTINA*, A SCULP-
TURE OF EMPRESS FAUSTINA THE ELDER.

hung at child's-eye level. Facilities include a library of children's books, a hands-on painting room, a family-friendly café, and a big museum store.

Note: Art lovers should also visit Northampton's major art galleries (see *Selective Shopping*), which represent current artists whose works hang in many of the world's major museums.

Calvin Coolidge Presidential Library and Museum at the Forbes Library (413-587-1014 or 413-587-1012; www.forbeslibrary.org), 20 West St. Open Mon. and Wed. 3–8, Tue. and Thu. 1–5, Sat. 9–noon. The only presidential library in a public library, this recently renovated area contains all of Calvin Coolidge's papers from his years as governor, vice president, and president. The Amherst College graduate (1895) studied law and first hung out his shingle in Northampton. He became city solicitor, met his wife (Grace Goodhue was teaching at the Clarke School for the Deaf in Northampton when she met fellow Vermonter Cal), was elected a state representative, then mayor of Northampton (two terms). He became state senator, then governor, then vice president, and, when Harding died suddenly (August 3, 1923), president (for six years). The Coolidges had remained Northampton residents, and they returned to their Northampton house from Washington; Calvin died here in 1933. Personal belongings on display range from a replica of Coolidge's Northampton office, fitted with all its original furnishings, to an elaborate headdress presented by the Sioux nation, to an electric horse.

In South Hadley
Skinner Museum (413-538-2085), Rt. 116. Open mid-May through Oct., Wed. and Sun. 2–5. Housed in the 1821 First Congregational Church that once stood in the town of Prescott (flooded by Quabbin Reservoir), this is a classic "cabinet of curiosities," some 4,000 items collected by Joseph Allen Skinner (1862–1946). The Skinner family owned major silk mills in Holyoke (see Wistariahurst Museum, above) and built The Orchards, a summer "cottage" across Rt. 116. Skinner's wealth permitted him to indulge his passion for collecting, which he did in his own world travels as well as those of his friends. To preserve it all, he acquired the once famous resort atop

A CAT AND A GIRL FROM ERIC CARLE'S FAMOUS *HEAD TO TOE*

© 1997 Eric Carle

Mount Holyoke in 1916, and in 1930 he rescued this church and its surrounding buildings (a school and carriage house) with the idea of creating his own small museum village. Exhibits in the basement re-create a colonial hearth and early crafts, but the real wonder of this place is the eclectic mix of the collection, much of it displayed in high, old-fashioned glass cabinets—with and without labels: shells and fossils, scrimshaw, glass and china, here a huge old key to the Northampton jail, there two medieval sets of armor (one real and one fake—see if you can guess which is which).

MORE MUSEUMS National Yiddish Book Center (413-256-4900; www.yiddish bookcenter.org), 1021 West St., adjacent to the Hampshire College campus, off Rt. 116. Visitor center open Sun.–Fri. 10–3:30; closed Shabbat and Jewish and legal holidays. A cultural center, this handsome wooden complex of work, exhibition, and performance spaces is designed to resemble an Eastern European shtetl. Credit for the very idea of rescuing Yiddish literature (roughly a century's worth of works in the Yiddish language, beginning in the 1860s) goes to the center's director, Hampshire College graduate Aaron Lansky. This is a clearinghouse for books of a genre presumed almost dead when the center was founded in 1980; at the opening of the current facility in 1997 it had collected 1.3 million works, with an average 1,000 arriving weekly. Volumes are distributed to shops and libraries throughout the world. Exhibits change, but the quality of the artwork on display alone would have been worth our trip; also inquire about frequent lectures and performances.

The Emily Dickinson Museum: The Homestead and The Evergreens (413-542-8161; www.emilydickinsonmuseum.org), 280 Main St., Amherst. Open June–Aug., Wed.–Sat. 10–5, Sun. 1–5; Sep.–Oct. and Apr.–May, Wed.–Sat. 1–5; Mar., Nov., and early Dec., Wed. *and* Sat. 1–5; closed mid-Dec. through Feb. Call to reserve a place. Two tours are offered: "Emily Dickinson's World," an in-depth tour of the Homestead and The Evergreens ($8 adults, $7 seniors and students, $5 ages 6–18); and "This Was a Poet," an introduction to Dickinson and her poetry ($6 adults, $5 seniors and students).

The Jones Library (413-256-4090), 43 Amity St., Amherst. Open Mon.–Sat. 9–8:30, Tue. and Thu. until 9:30. The Special Collections rooms are open Mon. 1–5, Tue.–Fri. 10–5, Sat. 2–5, but call to check.

AT THE AMHERST COLLEGE MUSEUM OF NATURAL HISTORY

Christina Tree

❧ **Amherst College Museum of Natural History** (413-542-2165; www.amherst.edu/museumofnatural history). Open Tue.–Sun. 11–4 (from noon in summer). Reopened in a stunning new museum in 2006, this is one of the country's outstanding collections of paleontology (dinosaurs), minerals and other geological specimens, and anthropological material. While the mammoth dinosaur skeletons aren't themselves native to the Valley, the fact that Amherst scholars were collecting them from the ends of the earth in the 19th century is directly related to Amherst College geologist Edward Hitchcock's identification of a local dinosaur track in 1836. Hitchcok's famous collection of 21,000 dinosaur tracks (on 1,200 slabs) is beautifully displayed. The story of the evolution of the Valley over the past 200 million years is dramatized in numerous and fascinating exhibits.

THE COLLEGES For an overview and current programs, see www.fivecolleges.edu.

Amherst College (413-542-2000; www.amherst.edu), Amherst. Founded in 1821 to educate "promising but needy youths who wished to enter the ministry," Amherst is today one of the country's most selective colleges. The campus is handsome and nicely sited, its oldest buildings grouped around a common over-looking the Valley to the south and the Holyoke Range beyond. The **Mead Art Museum** is well worth a look.

Hampshire College (413-549-4600; www.hampshirecollege.edu), 893 West St. (Rt. 116), Amherst. Opened in 1970, this liberal arts college is predicated on cooperative programming with the other four colleges. Its 1,200 students design their own programs of study. Inquire about current exhibits at the College Art Gallery in the Johnson Library Center and events at the Performing Arts Center. A "cultural village" has evolved in the former apple orchard adjacent to the campus. To date it includes the **National Yiddish Book Center** and the **Eric Carle Museum**.

Mount Holyoke College (413-538-2000; www.mtholyoke.edu), Rt. 116, South Hadley. Founded in 1837, Mount Holyoke is the country's oldest women's college. The 800-acre campus, with its Upper and Lower Ponds and ivied buildings in a number of Revival styles, is home to some 2,000 women drawn from throughout the country and the world. The adjacent Village Commons, a complex of restaurants, shops, and a theater, was designed by Graham Gund. Spend some time in the **Talcott Arboretum** (413-538-2116), open weekdays 9–4, weekends 1–4. This exquisite little Victorian-style greenhouse is filled with a jungle of exotic flora, featuring special late-winter and spring flower shows. *Note:* Prospective students, parents, and others with an MHC affiliation are welcome to stay at the attractive, on-campus **Willits-Hallowell Center** (413-538-2217). Be sure to see the **Mount Holyoke College Art Museum**, marked from the South Hadley common.

Smith College (413-584-2700), Northampton. Founded in 1875 for "the education of the intelligent gentlewoman," the 125-acre campus now includes 97 buildings, an eclectic mix of ages and styles. Don't miss **Paradise Pond**. The newly renovated **Lyman Plant House** (413-585-2740), open daily 8:30–4, is known for its spring and fall flower shows; adjacent are an arboretum and gardens. Definitely don't miss the **Smith College Museum of Art**.

University of Massachusetts (413-545-0111; www.umass.edu), Amherst 01003. Founded in the mid-19th century as the state's agricultural college, "UMass" now includes 10 undergraduate schools and colleges, also graduate schools, in more than 150 buildings on a 1,200-acre campus. Some 5,500 courses are

VOICE OF THE VALLEY: EMILY DICKINSON

Emily Dickinson (1830–86) was born in the staid, 1813 Dickinson Homestead not far from Amherst College. After attending Mount Holyoke Female Seminary for one year, she returned to her father's house, leaving rarely between 1855 and 1886, consumed with writing her honest puzzlings on the grand themes of love and nature, God and death, ragged-edged lines like:

Amherst College Archives and Special Collections
DAGUERREOTYPE PORTRAIT OF EMILY DICKINSON

"Hope" is the thing with feathers,
That perches in the soul,
And sings the tune without the words
And never stops—at all.

One of the most phenomenal aspects of Dickinson's story is that only 10 of these poems were published during her lifetime. The poet's work did not achieve widespread fame until well after her death.

The quality of the tour at the Emily Dickinson Museum is excellent. Dickinson's own room in the Homestead looks much as she knew it. The house itself was sold out of the family in 1916, but by 1965, when Dickinson's work was known worldwide, the house was purchased by Amherst College and opened to the public.

Though changes were made to the house, luckily the small world in which Emily Dickinson moved so intensely has been uncannily well preserved. The garden she tended remains a pleasant place to sit, and a path still leads next door to The Evergreens, an Italianate villa built in 1856 on the occasion of her brother Austin's marriage.

Emily and Austin's wife, Susan, were close friends, and Emily was a frequent visitor and present at social events with intimate friends and family. She was very much a part of this family, attached to their children, first a son and daughter and then, 10 years later, another little boy. When "Gib," the much-loved third child, died from typhoid fever, Emily grieved so deeply that she is said to have never fully recovered; she died herself two years later. Austin began an affair that is still the talk of the town, and many of his meetings with Mabel Loomis Todd, the lively wife of an Amherst College professor (she also founded the Amherst History Museum), were at the Dickinson Homestead, where his two sisters Emily and Lavinia still lived.

After Emily's death Lavinia first approached her sister-in-law Susan to edit Emily's poetry, but Lavinia later turned to Mabel Todd. Austin Dickinson died in 1895, and subsequent bitterness between the Todd and Dickinson families clouded publication of Dickinson's poetry for many decades after her death as competing versions of her verses appeared.

After Susan Dickinson died in 1913, her daughter, Martha Dickinson Bianchi, dedicated herself to publishing the Emily Dickinson poems she had inherited from her mother, and to writing about her memories of her aunt Emily. After the Homestead was sold out of the family in 1916, Bianchi began to establish The Evergreens as a destination for admirers of the poet's work, and she set up a room with her aunt's belongings that people could visit. Although some of these artifacts were subsequently transferred to the Houghton Library at Harvard University, The Evergreens retains its own original furnishings and interiors as well the feel of the house that Emily Dickinson knew so well. The quality of this experience is due in large part to Bianchi's heirs and to the work of the Martha Dickinson Bianchi Trust, established in 1988 to ensure the preservation of the house.

The Homestead and The Evergreens recently joined forces as the Emily Dickinson Museum. Both houses are now owned by Amherst College. The Dickinson Homestead—with its formal displays about Emily Dickinson and her second-floor bedroom—and the magic of The Evergreens next door complement each other nicely.

For more about Emily Dickinson, visit the Special Collections rooms upstairs in the nearby Jones Library. Here panels depict the poet's life in Amherst. Several of her handwritten poems are among the collection of 8,000 items related to the history of Amherst.

Dickinson buffs might want to continue on to West Cemetery on Triangle Street. It's not diffcult to find the Dickinson family plot, which is bounded by an ornate black iron fence. Here Emily lies surrounded by her grandparents, parents, and sister Lavinia. Note that on the Saturday nearest May 15 (the anniversary of her death), visitors are invited to meet at the Emily Dickinson Museum and walk to the cemetery. The museum offers other special events throughout the year. Also note the profile sculptures of Dickinson and Robert Frost in the small neighboring park across from the puzzlingly grandiose Amherst Police Station (site of an apartment in which Frost wrote "Fire and Ice").

THE EVERGREENS

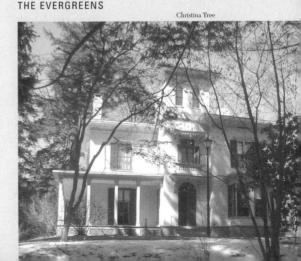

Christina Tree

offered by 1,000 faculty to 24,000 undergraduates and 5,500 graduate students. Sights to see at UMass: **Fine Arts Center and Gallery** (413-545-3670), changing exhibits. **William Smith Clark Memorial**, a 0.5-acre memorial at the eastern entrance to the campus (off N. Pleasant St.) dedicated to the first president of the university and his work in Japan, where he founded Sapporo Agricultural College, now the University of Hokkaido. The unusual memorial encompasses two circles linked by a spiral walk and twin steel walls depicting Clark's Amherst home and the Agricultural Hall at Hokkaido. Clark is widely revered in Japan, and many youth clubs are still dedicated to his memory. The memorial garden is sited on a hill with views extending across the campus to the river and hills. **Durfee Gardens and Durfee Conservatory** (413-545-5234), open weekdays 8:30–4:30. The conservatory dates from 1867 and houses tropical plants such as banana, coffee, and papaya divided by a 40-foot pool with an ornamental bridge and fountain. Five interlocking garden spaces offer benches, paths, and trellised wisteria and morning glories.

FOR FAMILIES ✍ **Dinosaurs**. The Pioneer Valley is a rich trove of dinosaur prints, said to range in age from 200,000 to 65,000 years old. The Valley's dramatic topographic and climatic history is told in the **Amherst College Museum of Natural History**, the **Springfield Science Museum**, and **Nash Dinosaur Track Quarry** (413-467-9566), off Rt. 116 north of the village of South Hadley. The sign on "Dino Land's" door reads PLEASE SOUND HORN. That fetches Kornell Nash from his house to this shop, which has been in the Nash family for more than 60 years. Billed as the "world's largest dinosaur footprint quarry," Dino Land is the source of more than 3,000 dinosaur tracks sold ($50–500 apiece) over the years, clearly embedded in shale. Admission is $2.50 per adult, $1.50 per child. **Dinosaur Footprints** is in Smith's Ferry on Rt. 5, near Mount Tom, Holyoke. Look for a well-marked turnout on the river side of the road. A path leads down to smooth rocks in which you can look for three-toed tracks, each 15 inches long and belonging to a 20-foot-long dinosaur (*Eubrontes giganteus*) that lumbered by 200 million years ago. Smaller tracks and other fossils have also been preserved. Also note the dinosaur footprints in the garden at **Wistariahurst Museum** in Holyoke.

✍ **Merry-Go-Round** (413-538-9838), next to the Holyoke Heritage State Park Visitor Center. Sep.–June, weekends noon–4; July–Labor Day, Tue.–Sun. 10:30–4. This vintage-1929 carousel with 48 hand-carved steeds, two chariots, and 800 lights was built for Mountain Park, an old-fashioned amusement park that closed in 1987. It was restored and moved to this handsome pavilion at a total cost of $2 million. Rides are $1; there's popcorn and a snack bar. Also available for private parties.

✍ **Children's Museum** (413-536-KIDS; www.childrensmuseumholyoke.org), 444 Dwight St. (across from the Heritage State Park Visitor Center), Holyoke. Hours vary. $6 adults and children, $3 seniors; children under 12 months free. A stimulating space with a Main Street that simulates downtown Holyoke's shops and enterprises (the favorite is a working TV station), also a kids' TV studio and "body of water" exhibit.

✎ **Robert Barrett Fishway**, Holyoke Dam, Holyoke, just off Rt. 116 at the South Hadley Falls Bridge. Open May and June only. For details contact Northfield Mountain (800-859-2960). Viewing windows and an observation platform overlook American shad and Atlantic salmon as elevators help them bypass the falls on their trip upriver to spawn.

✎ **Volleyball Hall of Fame** (413-536-0926; www.volleyhall.org), 444 Dwight St., Holyoke. Housed in the Children's Museum complex (see above). Open Tue.–Sun. noon–4:30. Invented in Holyoke in 1895, volleyball is commemorated here in a series of interpretive panels, an interactive video presentation, and a model half court.

Christina Tree

THE MERRY-GO-ROUND AT HOLYOKE HERITAGE STATE PARK

✎ **McCray Farm** (413-533-3714), 55 Alvord St., South Hadley. Open daily except Nov. and Mar., with a dairy selling many delectable flavors of homemade ice cream (open spring through fall). A petting zoo, mini golf, wagon rides, and PYO pumpkins.

✎ **Flayvors of Cook Farm** (413-584-2224), 129 S. Maple St., Hadley. Open weekdays 8–7, 10–8 on weekends. Great ice cream (see *Snacks*) made from the cows in residence.

✎ **Look Memorial Park** (413-584-5457; www.lookpark.org), 300 N. Main St. (Rt. 9), Florence. Open Memorial Day–Labor Day. The many attractions of this 150-acre park include swimming and wading pools; pedal boating and canoeing on **Willow Lake**; bumper boats around "the lagoon"; a playground; the small **Christenson Zoo**, with native deer, peacocks, pheasants, and raccoons; the **Pines Outdoor Theater** (summer concerts and children's entertainment); and a miniature replica of an 1863 train that circles the zoo, as well as fishing in the **Mill River** (perch and small trout), an 18-hole miniature golf course, six all-weather tennis courts, a Picnic Store at which you can rent horseshoes, volleyballs, and other sports equipment, and plenty of places to picnic. Admission is free on foot or bike, but cars are $4 on weekends, $3 midweek, and there are charges for rides and rentals—though not for the zoo.

FLAYVORS OF COOK FARM PATRONS THANK THE COWS THAT MADE THE MILK THAT MADE THEIR ICE CREAM.

Christina Tree

✍ **Western Massachusetts Family Golf Center Practice Range and Miniature Golf** (413-586-2311), Rt. 9 in Hadley. Open daily in-season 8 AM–10:30 PM.

SCENIC DRIVES **Route 47, South Hadley to Hadley**. This beautiful road runs along the Connecticut River and through its floodplain, below Mount Holyoke. Be sure to turn in and follow the road through Skinner State Park to the summit.

Route 47, Hadley to Sunderland. The 9 miles from Rt. 9 in Hadley to the village of Sunderland shadow the river, passing through cultivated fields spotted with distinctive long tobacco sheds and some of the best farm stands in the Valley.

Bay Road. For a quick sense of the beautiful farm country still surviving in Hadley at the heart of the Valley, cut across Bay Rd. from Rt. 47 to Rt. 116. It runs along the southern foot of the Holyoke Range.

Also see *Views*.

✳ To Do

BALLOONING **Pioneer Valley Balloons** (413-586-3009; www.pioneervalley balloons.com). Hot-air balloon flights, daily, year-round weather permitting. Inquire about special events and flight instruction. $225 for a 1-hour ride.

BICYCLING Given the number of young and young-in-spirit residents of this Valley, combined with relatively level, quiet, unusually scenic rural roads, it's not surprising that bicycle touring is big here. At this writing it's possible to arrive on the Amtrak Vermonter in Amherst, unload your bike, and take off along the **Norwottuck Rail Trail**, a 10-mile bike path linking Northampton, Hadley, and Amherst along the former Boston & Maine Railroad right-of-way. You could also find a room within walking distance of the station and rent a bike (including a limited number of hand-cycles for handicapped cyclists) from **Valley Bicycles** (413-256-0880), 319 Main St., Amherst, or from its annex right on the trail: **Trailside Bicycles** at 8 Railroad St., Hadley (413-584-4466). See also **Laughing Dog Bicycles** (413-253-7722), 63 S. Pleasant St., Amherst.

Other access points to the rail-trail are at Mountain Farms Mall on Rt. 9 in Hadley and at **Elwell Recreation Area** on Damon Rd. (just north of the Rt. 9 bridge) in Northampton. The trail crosses the Connecticut on an old rail bridge and passes through open farmland, with views to the Holyoke Range to the south and to Mount Toby and Mount Sugarloaf to the north. Unfortunately a congested mile-plus gap presently exists between the western terminus of the Norwottuck Trail at Elwell Recreation Area and the eastern end of the **Northampton Bikeway**, which runs from State Street west 2.6 miles to Look Park. *Note:* The bikeway begins in a residential neighborhood without parking. Your best access option is the bike path entrance behind Stop & Shop on King Street. It's a great ride to do with kids; bring a picnic and explore Look Park (see *For Families*).

Bicycling the Pioneer Valley . . . and Beyond by Marion Gorham (New England Cartographics) is a valuable resource for touring this area by bike.

All the scenic drives outlined in this book lend themselves to bike touring, but there are many more loops. Inquire at local bike shops. For mountain biking trails, see **Northfield Mountain** in "Deerfield/Greenfield Area."

BIRDING **Arcadia Wildlife Sanctuary** in Easthampton (see *Hiking and Walking*) is the area's most obvious birding center, but there are others. The Valley represents a major migratory flyway and is known especially for its many soaring hawks in fall. Prime watching spots include Goat Peak on Mount Tom and Prospect House on Mount Holyoke. **The Hitchcock Center for the Environment** (see *Hiking and Walking*) offers some birding workshops and is the base for the Hampshire Bird Club. An excellent guide, *Birding Western Massachusetts: The Central Connecticut River Valley*, edited by Peter Westover for the Kestrel Trust and Hampshire Bird Club, is available in local bookstores. *Birding in Massachusetts* by Robert Tougias (New England Cartographics) describes 26 prime birding sites.

BOATING & **Elwell Recreation Area**, just north of Rt. 9 at the Northampton end of the Coolidge Bridge, is a handicapped-accessible state-of-the-art boat dock.

River information. The **Connecticut River Watershed Council** (413-529-9500), 1 Ferry St., Easthampton, publishes a canoe guide to the entire river and offers periodic guided canoe trips. The **Great Falls Discovery Center** (413-863-3221), Ave. A, Turners Falls, is also a source of river information. At **Barton Cove** (413-863-9300 or 800-859-2960), Northfield Mountain maintains tent sites, rents canoes and rowboats, and offers shuttle service to put-in places in Northfield. Also see "Greenfield/Deerfield Area."

BOAT RENTALS **Sportsman's Marina** (413-586-2426), Rt. 9 at the Coolidge Bridge, Hadley, rents boats Apr.–Oct. (weather permitting): canoes, aluminum outboards, and pontoon boats. Bring a picnic and head for an island. **Brunelle's Marina** (413-536-3132) in South Hadley has a restaurant and launch area. There is also a state access ramp almost 1.5 miles north of Hatfield Center, and another off Rt. 5 at the Oxbow in Easthampton. The 16-mile stretch of the Connecticut River above the Holyoke Dam is heavily used on summer weekends by water-skiers, fishermen, and powerboat owners as well as canoeists.

Oxbow Marina (413-584-2775), Island Road off Rt. 5 south of I-91, Northampton. The largest marina in the area offers a boat launch, rentals, instruction, a picnic area, and a beach.

BOAT EXCURSIONS *Lady Bea* (413-315-6342), an excursion boat based at Brunelle's Landing in South Hadley,

AT BRUNELLE'S MARINA IN SOUTH HADLEY
Christina Tree

offers seasonal 75-minute narrated tours up and down the Connecticut River, daily (weather permitting) at noon, 2, and 4; inquire about special evening cruises. See also *Quinnektikut II* in "Deerfield/Greenfield Area."

CANOEING AND KAYAKING **Arcadia Nature Center and Wildlife Sanctuary** (see *Hiking and Walking*), marked from Rt. 5, Easthampton, but on the Northampton–Easthampton line in Northampton is a great place for novice canoeists to explore quiet waters. Inquire about guided canoe trips.

&. **The Connecticut River Greenway State Park** (see "Greenfield/Deerfield Area") includes a 12-mile Connecticut River Water Trail that runs from the Turners Falls Dam in Montague to the Hatfield state boat ramp. The water along this trail is too shallow for powerboating, so the area is limited to small boats and canoes and to low-impact recreation. A detailed brochure guide to the trail is available from the Department of Conservation and Recreation (DCR; 413-586-8706), 136 Damon Rd. near the Elwell Recreation Area (access for paddlers only) on the river in Northampton.

Fitzgerald Lake off North Farms Rd. (in Florence, turn off Rt. 9 onto Maple), Northampton. An oasis of quiet roughly 1 mile long and 0.25 mile wide; look for a wooden dock about 100 yards off North Farms Road.

Puffers Pond, North Amherst (see *Swimming*). No powerboats allowed.

Adventure Oufitters (413-586-2323), Rt. 9, Hadley, rents canoes and kayaks.

FISHING For licensing, see "What's Where."

Quabbin Reservoir is open for fishing mid-Apr. to mid-Oct., 6 AM to 1 hour before sunset. To rent a boat you must be 16 years or older and have a Massachusetts fishing license; licenses and bait are available from such local shops as Bill and Cathy Martel's **Bait Shop** (413-323-7117) at Gate 8 in Pelham. Much of the reservoir is off-limits, but Gate 8 (Rt. 202 in Pelham) accesses cold salmon- and trout-filled water. For detailed information, contact the **Quabbin Visitor Center** (413-323-7221). The **Charles L. McGloughlin Trout Hatchery** (413-323-7671) in Belchertown (open daily 9–3:45) adjoins the **Swift River Wildlife Management Area**, which offers good fishing in the Swift River, as well as fields and woodlands webbed with trails.

Christina Tree

The Connecticut River

The Pioneer Sporting Center (413-584-9944), 137E Damon Rd. (next door to the DCR offices), Northampton, is a source of advice as well as equipment. During migrating shad and salmon season in mid-June, the **Robert E. Barrett Fishway** at the Holyoke Dam, just off Rt. 116 at the South Hadley Falls Bridge, is staffed by naturalists from Northfield Mountain (800-859-2960); viewing windows and an observation platform overlook the two elevators that hoist more than a million migrating fish over the falls. Open Wed.–Sun. 9–5.

GOLF **Hickory Ridge Country Club** (413-256-6638), W. Pomeroy Lane, Amherst, is an 18-hole championship course with a clubhouse and (snack bar) restaurant. **Orchards Golf Course** (413-534-3806), Silverwood Terrace, South Hadley. 18 holes. **Pine Grove Golf Course** (413-584-4570), Highland Ave., Northampton. 18 holes. **Ledges Golf Course** (413-532-2307), 18 Mulligan Dr., South Hadley. 18 holes. **Beaver Brook Golf Club** (413-568-1636), Williamsburg. Nine holes.

HIKING AND WALKING

In Amherst and Pelham
The Amherst Conservation Department (413-256-4045) maintains some 1,450 acres scattered in 45 distinct holdings, with 60 miles of trails for walking, birding, and ski touring. It's worth stopping by the town hall or local bookstores to pick up printed maps or guides.

& The most popular (and most heavily used) areas include **Upper Mill River** and **Puffers Pond**, State St. off Pine, in North Amherst, good for swimming and picnicking. Trails—including one designed for handicapped access and blind walkers—lead upstream from the pond along the Cushman Brook's cascades.

Hitchcock Center for the Environment (413-256-6006; www.hitchcock center.org) at the Larch Hill Conservation Area, 1 mile south of Amherst Center on Rt. 116. The 25 acres include hiking trails, formal gardens, and ponds. The center offers a variety of lectures and workshops; it also exhibits local artwork.

Mount Pollux, Amherst, is a favorite spot from which to watch the sunset, a gentle slope to climb through old apple orchards to a summit with a 365-degree view. The entrance is just off South East Street in South Amherst (turn left heading south). It's a very small sign and then a short way to the parking area, plus a brief walk to the top of a hill with the memorable view.

Amethyst Brook Conservation Area, Pelham Road, Pelham, is a great spot to walk or ski through woods and fields.

Buffum Falls, Amherst Rd., Pelham. Heading east, turn left onto North Valley Road (almost a mile west of Amethyst Brook); look for a parking area on your left. Not particularly well marked but well used, an unusually beautiful spot. A 1-hour hike.

Between Amherst and South Hadley
Holyoke Range State Park (413-253-2883), Rt. 116. Trail maps are available at the Notch Visitor Center (staffed and with restrooms), which is open daily 9–4 except Tue. and Wed. in winter. Inquire about guided hikes. This dramatic east–west range rises from the Valley's floor. It is the most striking feature of the area, visible everywhere from Belchertown to Northampton. Mount Holyoke at its western tip (see Skinner State Park under *Views*) is the only summit accessible

by road, but a trail traverses the entire 9-mile-long ridgeline. From the visitor center, a trail leads east to Mount Norwottuck (connecting with trails to Mount Toby in Sunderland and Mount Monadnock in New Hampshire). Ask about the Horse Caves below Mount Norwottuck in which Daniel Shays and his men supposedly sheltered after raiding the Springfield Armory (the caves are actually so shallow that two Boy Scouts and a pony would have trouble fitting in).

In Northampton
Fitzgerald Lake, in the Broad Brook Conservation Area, North Farms Rd. A 550-acre town-owned preserve with 5 miles of well-marked trails, including a self-guided nature trail geared to kids. Much of the trail is right along the lake, under tall pines. Allow 2 hours. Maps are at the trailhead. No restrooms. From Rt. 9 in Florence, take Maple St., which turns into North Farms Rd.

In Easthampton
& **Arcadia Wildlife Sanctuary** (413-584-3009; www.massaudubon.org), 127 Combs Rd., on the Northampton–Easthampton line. Trails and restrooms open Tue.–Sun. and Mon. holidays, dawn to dusk. Nature Center open Mon.–Fri. 1–3, closed holidays. $4 adults, $3 children and seniors. Five miles of trail meander through meadows, marsh, and wetlands. Inquire about the many programs, including canoe trips.

Also see *Green Space*.

SWIMMING In Amherst the swimming hole is **Puffers Pond** (413-256-4045), off Pine St. in North Amherst. Open June–Sep., dawn to dusk. It's a beauty, with a small beach and woods area, no lifeguards.

Carroll A. Holmes Recreation Area (413-367-0317) in Shutesbury, better known as Lake Wyola, is a sandy public beach with changing rooms on a wooded lake, maintained by the Department of Recreation and Conservation ($5 parking fee).

Musante Beach (413-587-1040), off Reservation Rd., Leeds, Northampton. Open June 30 until Labor Day, 10–7. Nominal admission. Lifeguards and bathrooms.

ICE SKATING **Mullins Center** (413-545-0505), UMass campus, Amherst. Olympic-sized skating rink open to the public. Rentals; call for hours.

✳ Green Space

VIEWS What sets off this Massachusetts stretch from the rest of the Connecticut River Valley is the number of abrupt mountains thrusting from its floor and the fact that so many old carriage roads, built to serve long-vanished 19th-century hotels, access their summits. Only by taking advantage of these amazing vantage points can you appreciate the Valley's unusual mix of farmland and villages, cities and woods—a mix that has not altered essentially since Thomas Cole painted the Oxbow from the top of Mount Holyoke in 1836.

Mount Tom State Reservation (413-527-4805; off-season, 413-534-1186), access from Rt. 5 in Holyoke or from Rt. 141, Easthampton. This 1,800-acre mountaintop woodland contains 20 miles of trails, picnic tables, lookout towers, and a visitor center (May–late Oct.). Inquire about programs. Midweek, even in midsummer, the road out to **Goat Peak** is eerily empty; chances are you will be alone with the spectacular view north to Easthampton and off across the Valley. This is one of the outstanding places in the state for hawk-watching from mid-August through late October. In winter the road isn't plowed, but you can ski or snowshoe in. Lake Bray near the Rt. 5 entrance offers fishing.

∞ **Skinner State Park** (413-586-0350), Rt. 47, Hadley. Summit Road is open mid-Apr. through mid-Nov.; the Summit House on weekends mid-May through mid-Oct. "The Paradise of America" is the way Swedish singer Jenny Lind described the view from the top of Mount Holyoke in 1850—the same view of the Connecticut River Oxbow, surrounding towns, and distant hills that Thomas Cole popularized in his 1836 painting. One of the first mountaintop inns to be built in New England (the first inn opened in 1821) and the only one preserved in any shape today, the surviving part of the Summit House (also known as Prospect House) is nicely restored, accessible by an auto road and hiking trails. In 1938 Joseph Skinner donated the Summit House and the surrounding 390 acres to the state. It's the setting for sunset concerts on summer Thursdays, along with lectures and other events sponsored by the Friends of Mount Holyoke. The badly marked access is just south of Mitch's Marina. This is a popular wedding venue; information packets are available on request. The park is webbed with hiking trails, one of which—the Seven Sisters Trail—leads back along the ridgeline of the Holyoke Range to the Notch Visitor Center (see **Holyoke Range State Park** under *Hiking and Walking*).

✳ Lodging

Note: "High" and "low" season rates tend to be pinned to the academic season. There are crunch periods in late May and early June during graduation, for instance; midweek in summer is relatively low season, while fall is high.

HOTELS AND INNS ∞ 🐾 ♿ **Lord Jeffery Inn** (413-253-2576 or 800-742-0358; www.lordjefferyinn.com), 30 Boltwood Ave., Amherst 01002. Built in 1926 by the same architect who designed the matching Colonial Revival Jones Library across the common, this Amherst College–owned and –geared inn is a comfortable place to rendezvous. You can picture Robert Frost rocking on the porch. The 48 rooms include 8 suites, all with private bath, phone, and cable TV; a number also have a balcony overlooking the garden. All rooms are periodically refurbished, and there's

PROSPECT HOUSE ON TOP OF MOUNT HOLYOKE

Christina Tree

now wireless Internet throughout the inn. Dining options include informal **Elijah Boltwood's Tavern** and **The Windowed Hearth**. Groups meet here all week, and on weekends there are frequently wedding receptions in the brick courtyard. From $99 (for an economy double, low season) to $259 for the King Suite in high season. There's an elevator and handicapped access. Pets are accepted for a $15 fee.

∞ ♂ ⛭ **Hotel Northampton** (413-584-3100 or 800-547-3529; www.hotel northampton.com), 36 King St., Northampton 01060. Built in 1927, this is a proud five-story, redbrick downtown hotel with guest cottages, handy to all the town's shops and restaurants. The lobby has a hearth, wing chairs, and a soaring ceiling. There are 106 rooms including 13 suites, recently renovated and taste-fully furnished with reproduction antiques, all with wireless Internet access. The glass-fronted **Coolidge Park Café** serves breakfast, lunch, and dinner. Note also the vintage-1786 **Wiggins Tavern** restaurant, a Valley landmark that was moved here from Hopkinton, New Hampshire, and incorporated into the hotel as part of a mini museum village. It once enhanced the hotel's appeal as a "motoring objec-tive" in an era when auto touring was largely restricted to the wealthy. Unfortunately the tavern now occu-pies a dark, airless corner. Hotel rates include continental breakfast, parking, and use of the exercise room. $165–195 per couple; "deluxe" rooms and suites are $210–350. Packages avail-able. Amenities include valet and full room service. Four handicapped-accessible suites; children free under age 18.

BED & BREAKFASTS *Note:* The **Five College Area Bed & Breakfast Association** (www.fivecollegebb.com) details a number of area B&Bs, and the **Hampshire Hills B&B Assoca-tion** (www.hhbba.com) offers more listings within easy striking distance of Northampton. What follows is our selection.

In Amherst/Hadley
♂ 🐾 ⛭ **Ivory Creek Bed & Break-fast Inn** (413-587-3115 or 866-331-3115; www.ivorycreek.com), 31 Chmura Rd., Hadley 01035. Judy Loebel grew up on a farm in Hadley and graduated from Mount Holyoke College ('65), then went on to live in many places before returning with her husband, Tod, to build this gra-cious retreat on 24 acres beside Skin-ner State Park. At first glance you assume the house is vintage 1890s, but the comforts include central air-conditioning, luxurious baths, gas fire-places, and WiFi in all the unusually spacious guest rooms. An attractive, totally handicapped-accessible first-floor room features a private deck. Each room is different, but furnish-ings throughout are tasteful. There's comfortable common space, a guest pantry, and an aviary with finches, parakeets, and parrots. Judy and Tod have nine (grown) children and 18 grandchildren, and kids—dogs, too—are welcome in a garden-level room. $135–225 includes a full breakfast with yogurt, granola, and perhaps lemon soufflé pancakes or Tod's "Red Pepper Surprise."

Wilbur Homestead (413-253-2281; www.wilburhomestead.com; craked limb@yahoo.com), 126 Northampton Rd. (Rt. 9), Amherst 01002. Within walking distance of the Amherst Col-lege campus and downtown, this is a big, gracious, exquisitely crafted 1880s house that Al and Barbara Wilbur purchased in the 1970s but have only recently restored as a B&B. A retired state trooper, Al is an enthusiastic host. He presides over the state-of-the-art country kitchen in which the cookie and muffin jar is always full. The three upstairs rooms (private baths) are all nicely furnished, and the two-room Shannon Suite (comfortably sleeping three or four) is definitely worth the top dollar. There's a pleasant garden to sit in and a small but elaborate fishpond. A full breakfast—maybe apple cinnamon pancakes or an asparagus and feta cheese omelet—is included in $95–160.

Amherst Inn (413-253-5000; www .allenhouse.com), 257 Main St., Amherst 01002. This is one of two houses lovingly restored by Ann and Alan Zieminski and it's the one we recommend, both because of its better location (across from the Emily Dickinson homes) and because it's the lighter, airier, and more comfortable of the two. It's a genuine Victorian "painted lady," furnished with Eastlake chairs and mantels with a pleasant garden behind. There are eight rooms, all with private bath, phone, central air-conditioning, and WiFi, some papered in hand-silk-screened William Morris paper and hand-stenciled by Ann. Breakfast is full. There's a sense of caring here: hot water and munchies on the sideboards, genuine attention to guests' needs. Well-behaved children over age 8 are welcome. From $75 in low season to $175 on graduation weekends.

Kellogg Homestead (413-253-4988; www.hkhbb.com), 459 S. Pleasant St., Amherst 01002. On the southern edge of town but still an easy walk from the Amherst College campus, this is an 1828 clapboard house. Steve and Sue Mallett offer two attractive but very different guest rooms (one with a formal four-poster, the second with a queen and single) with in-room cable, DVD/VCR, shared bath. $85 includes a full breakfast, served in the dining room off a pleasant, wicker-furnished screened porch.

✍ **Stone House Farm Bed & Breakfast** (413-549-4455; www .stonehousefarmbb.com), 695 E. Pleasant St., Amherst 01002. On the northern edge of town just beyond the UMass campus, this is a great spot for families: an upstairs suite in a pretty clapboard house. There's an inviting central dining/eating area with microwave and fridge and two country-fresh bedrooms sharing a bath. Innkeeper Candace Tulley maintains an extensive, commercial flower garden in the rear of the house and the barn, in which she also offers children's crafts programs. Resident animals include ducks, chickens, and goats. $150–200 includes a breakfast featuring granola, fruit, and fresh-baked scones.

✍ **Garden of Delights** (413-584-8970; www.gardenofdelights-bb.com), 20 Rocky Hill Rd., Hadley 01035. The 19th-century farmhouse is still surrounded by pesticide-free fields, and its barn is a farm stand. Guests enjoy their own entrance and a small parlor. Two rooms (one queen and one with twins) share a bathroom and also have access to a lovely swimming pool. $100 for one room, $175 for both, including continental breakfast.

In Northampton/Easthampton
Park Street Bed and Breakfast (413-527-7861; www.parkstreetbb

.com), 238 Park St., Easthampton 01207. A bit out of the way but worth it, this striking 19th-century brick home has been nicely renovated. The three guest rooms are furnished with antiques and an eye to comfort, each with a TV/VCR and small fridge. There's plenty of common space, inside and out; $80 (shared bath) and $120 (private) includes a very full breakfast on weekends, continental on weekdays. Innkeeper Sue Lehman is knowledgeable and helpful with local sights and dining.

Sugar Maple Trailside B&B (413-585-8559; www.sugar-maple-inn.com), 62 Chestnut St., Florence 01062. Kathy and Craig Della Penna's 1860s bicyclist-geared house is sited beside the Northampton Bikeway, no coincidence since Craig is a rail-trail activist who has written three books on rail-trails. The two guest rooms with private bath are $75–120 per night with breakfast. High-speed wireless available. Common space is attractive; the library features a large collection of antique rail maps and information. Amenities include a couple of retro cruiser bikes.

The Knoll (413-584-8164), 230 N. Main St., Florence 01020. An English Tudor–style home set well back from Rt. 9 on 17 acres 3 miles west of downtown Northampton, handy to the Northampton Bikeway and adjacent to Look Memorial Park. This has been Lee and Ed Lesko's home since 1963, when their former home by the Connecticut River was moved to make way for I-91. The house itself is quite grand, but decor is homey. The three guest rooms (two with double and one with twin beds) are furnished simply and comfortably, sharing two baths. Breakfast is included

in $80. No smokers, and no children under 12.

Mount Tom River Bed & Breakfast (413-584-4884), 4 Symansky Ave., Mount Tom 01207. Open May until early Nov., weekends only during spring and fall. Sited 2 miles south of Northampton, just off Rt. 5, this big Victorian house was built as a lodging place in 1902. Beverly Wodick, the fourth generation of her family to live here, is a graphic-design professor, and rooms are tasteful, minimally decorated (nice prints, no fluff). The Yellow Room, a two-room suite with a sleep sofa, and the Rose Room (with a double sleigh bed) share a bath. The small, sunny White Room has its own. A full breakfast is served in the big, old-fashioned dining room. Common space includes a wraparound porch with a view of the Connecticut River as well as an attractive, antiques-furnished living room. $75–90.

Elsewhere
1886 House (413-296-0223 or 800-893-2425, ext. 44; www.1886house.com), 202 East St., Chesterfield 01012. This farmhouse isn't far west of the Northampton line, but it has a way-out-in-the-country feel. The three second-floor rooms all have central air. The Rose Room and the spacious Chelsea Room (TV/VCR) both have queen beds and private bath. There's a general air of hospitality here. $85–130 with full breakfast; no minimum-stay requirement.

MOTELS AND MOTOR INNS Autumn Inn (413-584-7660), 259 Elm St., Northampton 01060. This is a splendidly built and maintained two-story, 31-unit motel, geared to the parents of Smith students. The 29 rooms are large with varied bed arrangements, TV, phone, WiFi, and private bath; a couple of one-bedroom suites have cooking facilities, and a third has a microwave. Breakfast and lunch are served in the coffee shop with a hearth, and there's a landscaped pool. $110–120 weekdays, $130–180 weekends, $30 more for efficiencies or suites and more than two guests.

Note: We don't pretend to have checked the following chain motels, but to omit them would be wrong, too. Rates vary with the day at the following:

Country Inn and Suites by Carlson (413-533-2100), 1 Country Club Rd. (Rt. 3 at Smith's Ferry), Holyoke 01040. Sited between I-91 and the Connecticut River, this 61-room "inn" features luxurious rooms and suites with gas fireplace, two phones, and dataport. Facilities include a pool and exercise room. The Delaney House restaurant (see *Dining Out*) is next door.

✎ **Clarion Hotel & Conference Center** (413-586-1211), junction of Rt. 5 and I-91, Northampton 01060. A good bet if you have children along: 124 rooms, an indoor and an outdoor pool, sauna, game room, and lighted tennis court; also a restaurant and lounge.

✎ **Holiday Inn** (413-534-3311 or 800-465-4329), Holidrome and Conference Center, junction of I-91 and the Mass Pike at Ingleside, Holyoke 01040. A 219-room, four-story complex featuring a tropical recreational area with 18-foot-high palm trees, a pool, a full spa, and, of course, a volleyball court.

✎ **Holiday Inn Express Hotel & Suites** (413-582-0002; www.HI

Express.com/Amherst-Hadley), Rt. 9, Hadley 01035, offers 78 rooms, 22 suites, and an indoor pool.

✎ **Econo Lodge** (413-582-7707; www.hampshirehospitality.com), 329 Russell St. (Rt. 9), Hadley 01035, offers 63 rooms and an indoor pool.

✎ 🐾 **Howard Johnson** (413-586-0014; www.thhg.com), 401 Russell St. (Rt. 9), Hadley 01035. 100 rooms, outdoor pool.

✎ 🐾 **Quality Inn** (413-584-9816; qualityinnhadley@charter.net), 237 Russell St. (Rt. 9), Hadley 01035. 70 rooms, indoor pool.

✎ **Best Western** (413-586-1500), 117 Conz St., Northampton 01060. 65 rooms, outdoor pool.

✎ ♿ **Hampton Inn** (413-586-4851; www.hamptoninn.com), 24 Bay Rd., Hadley 01035, offers 73 rooms and suites and an indoor pool.

✳ Where to Eat

DINING OUT This is recognized as one of the liveliest dining areas in New England. Because the largely academic clientele is unusually sophisticated but not particularly flush, many of the top restaurants aren't that expensive.

In Amherst

Chez Albert (413-253-3811; www.chezalbert.net), 27 S. Pleasant St. Open for lunch Wed.–Fri., dinner Tue.–Sat., Sunday brunch 11:30–2:30. Reservations a must. An intimate (less than 30 seats), warmly painted, dimly lit bistro ambience complements a menu featuring "tartines" and tuna Niçoise salad for a summer lunch. Dinner hors d'oeuvres include a vegetable napoleon, escargots, and duck confit. For an entrée, you might select sweet corn risotto, or bouillabaisse. Chef-owner Paul Hathaway has worked closely with several of the country's top chefs and in many places. There's a sense of caring here, and a good wine list.

& **Judie's** (413-253-3491; www.judies restaurant.com), 51 N. Pleasant St. Closed Mon. Open Sun.–Thu. 11:30–10, until 11 weekends. This cheerful, glass-fronted restaurant seems to be everyone's favorite: casual, friendly, and specializing in oversized, overstuffed popovers; we recommend the gumbo and basil chicken. The menu is extensive, with many salads and veggie dishes at lunch. Dinner entrées ($17.25–19.25) include a salad and popover or bread. Full bar.

DEL RAYE BAR & GRILL IN NORTHAMPTON
Kim Grant

Bistro 63 at The Monkey Bar (413-259-1600; www.mymonkeybar.com), 63 N. Pleasant St. Open daily 11:30–10. This sleek bistro offers a menu as hip as its decor. Lunch on coconut-breaded shrimp, blackened scallops, or a salade Niçoise. Dine on sesame charred tuna, jambalaya, or iron steak Gorgonzola. Outdoor seating in-season. Dinner entrées $12.95–19.95.

In Northampton

& **Del Raye Bar & Grill** (413-586-2664; www.fundining.com), 1 Bridge St. Open nightly for dinner; the lounge closes at 11 PM, 1 AM Fri. and Sat. You can reserve—a plus on busy nights in Northampton, where most of the popular places are first come, first served—and the food is outstanding. The à la carte menu may include cumin- and oregano-dusted duck breast with roasted corn and duck confit hash, or cashew- and mint-encrusted lamb rack with plums and mace. Entrées $18–29, but you can get a bistro burger for $15. Free parking in the rear of the building.

Green Street Café (413-586-5650), 62 Green St. Open for lunch weekdays, dinner nightly from 5, brunch on Sunday. Owner-chef John Sielski is a Valley native who operated a restaurant in Brooklyn before opening this elegant storefront bistro. The plum-colored rooms are hung with original art, and the menu is handwritten. You might start with mussels stewed in white wine, or homemade green ravioli with butter sauce. Entrées ($18–24) might include chicken with apples and hazelnuts. The restaurant grows its own vegetables and herbs. Liquor is served.

❦ **Mulino's Trattoria** (413-586-8900; www.mulinos.com), 41 Strong Ave. Open nightly for dinner. Anthony

Bishop's popular trattoria remains as popular as ever. Antipasti are large, as is the choice of freshly made pasta dishes like ziti zuccala (julienned chicken sautéed with prosciutto, zucchini, onions, garlic, and tomatoes, tossed with ziti and ricotta cheese). Pastas $13.95–16.95; entrées $16.95–26.95. *Warning:* Portions are large. Try the veal balsamico (scaloppine sautéed with olive oil in a balsamic vinegar, butter, and wine sauce). There's music nightly in the third-floor **Bishop's Lounge**.

Spoleto (413-586-6313; www.fund ining.com), 50 Main St. Open for dinner nightly. Featuring Spoleto Festival posters and creative "Fine Italian" dishes like eggplant terrine (layers of eggplant, roasted red peppers, spinach, ricotta, mozzarella, and mascarpone cheese), or hazelnut-crusted veal. Entrées run $15.95–26.95.

& **Eastside Grill** (413-586-3347), 19 Strong Ave. Open for dinner weekdays from 5, weekends from 4. A popular place with a pleasant, multilevel dining room (try for a booth), as well as a big, reasonably priced menu with something for everyone. No reservations, so come early if you don't want to wait at dinner. A raw bar features shrimp and oysters. Start with gumbo of the day, then maybe try a blackened steak salad or sesame scallops with lobster and sake. Dinner entrées $11.95–19.95.

Circa (413-586-2622), 57 Center St. We've never heard a less-than-enthusiastic word about this popular restaurant. The menu might include snow crab stuffed prawns as a starter and such entrées as pistachio-crusted Alaskan halibut and artichokes braised in white wine with pepper and corn risotto and oven-dried tomatoes. Entrées $17–23.50.

India House (413-586-6344; www .indiahousenorthampton.com), 45 State St. Open nightly for dinner. Decorated with Indian prints and featuring background sitar music, tandoori cooking, many vegetarian dishes; the Valley's original Indian restaurant, the real stuff. Try the shrimp masala in a sauce of curried tomatoes and ginger with onions ($14.95), or coconut shrimp and chicken ($16.95).

Osaka Japanese Sushi and Steakhouse (413-587-9548; www.osaka northampton.com), 7 Old South St. Open for lunch and dinner (until 11 most nights, and midnight Fri. and Sat.). The menu is large with a wide choice of hibachi dinners as well as sushi and chef's specials such as tuna steak, grilled eel, and grilled chicken rolled with avocado. Dinner entrées $10.95–25.95. Lunch specials.

Elsewhere
Apollo Grill (413-517-0031), Eastworks Building, 116 Pleasant St., Easthampton. Open Tue.–Fri. for lunch 11:30–2, dinner Tue.–Sat. Chef-owner Casey Douglas has created a hip dining spot in the Valley. The decor is zany, the locale offbeat (the ground floor of a vast mill, with tenants ranging from the registry of motor vehicles to several galleries). The reasonable menu is varied and the food, fabulous. Lunch on a hummus plate with eggplant, caviar, sun-dried tomato puree, grilled onion, and red pepper in a fried tortilla; dine on fried catfish with smoked shrimp cream sauce, sautéed greens, and polenta fries. Dinner entrées $13–22.

Tavern on The Hill (413-493-1700), 100 Mountain Rd. (Rt. 41), Easthampton. Open nightly for dinner. Across from the entrance to the

Mount Tom Reservation, this restaurant has been through many incarnations and for all the big draw has been the view. We hear good things about the food this time. The menu might include smoked Gouda stuffed chicken breast wrapped in bacon with spinach, blackened beef tips, and a fresh herb crêpe. Entrées come with salad: $13.95–23.95.

Yankee Pedlar Inn (413-532-9494; www.yankeepedlar.com), 1866 Northampton St. (Rt. 5 near I-91, exit 16), Holyoke. Open for lunch Tue.–Fri., dinner Tue.–Sat., champagne brunch Sun. 10–2. A landmark with a number of function rooms and a small, richly paneled dining room. The chef specialties are honest and local—chicken potpie, Yankee pot roast, New England baked scrod, and turkey dinner—but it's a vast and varied menu, and you can dine on Pedlar crab and lobster cakes or grilled filet mignon. Entrées $15.95–23.95.

✍ **Delaney House** (413-532-1800; www.delaneyhouse.com), Rt. 5 at Smith's Ferry, Holyoke. Open nightly for dinner and for Sunday brunch. Now a franchise but still the same chef who has made this a local special-occasion place for many years. American cuisine specializing in fresh fish and game. An à la carte menu, with entrées $21–36. Children's menu.

EATING OUT

All located in Amherst unless otherwise specified
✍ **Esselon Café** (413-585-1515), 99 Russell St. (Rt. 9), Hadley. Open Mon.–Fri. 11–3 for lunch and weekends 8–3 for brunch, also open 7–6 weekdays and 8–5 weekends for coffee and munchies. A former auto parts store has been transformed into an open-sided (weather permitting) café with terrace seating overlooking a garden and a large round table for singles who simply want to sit with their laptops (it's WiFi). Patrons order at the deli counter from a menu and blackboard daily specials. We lunched on a Mediterranean salad that included hummus, roasted red pepper, eggplant, feta, tomatoes, and more. Many people just come for the coffee, reputedly the best in the Valley. There's also wine.

✍ **Crazy Noodles Café** (413-253-3287), 36 Main St. Open daily lunch through dinner. This is an attractive, casual Asian café with wine and WiFi, good for some interesting salads (like peanut noodle and crispy wonton), noodle soups. Free ice cream for kids.

Fresh Side (413-256-0296), 61 Main St. Open daily 11–10. A delightful eatery and teahouse serving healthy wraps filled with warm sea vegetables, spicy bean concoctions, ginger tofu, and the like, plus a similar selection of salads, noodle soups, rice and pasta dishes.

Baku's African Restaurant (413-253-7202), 197 N. Pleasant St. Open Mon.–Sat. for lunch and dinner, Sun. from 4 PM. Colorful, authentic, and

ESSELON CAFÉ

Christina Tree

reasonably priced, this inviting eatery offers a gluten- and lactose-free menu. House specialties include black-eyed pea fritters, roasted plantain with peanut sauce, pounded yams, and a choice of vegetarian or meat-based West African melon seed soup.

Antonio's (413-253-0808), 31 N. Pleasant St. Ask any student around. This is simply the best pizza.

Amherst Brewing Company, 36 N. Pleasant St. Open daily for lunch and dinner; live entertainment Thu.–Sat. 10 PM–1 AM. The town's first microbrewery, with a reasonably priced menu that includes traditional pub food like Irish stew, shepherd's pie, and cock-a-leekie pie. Tell us what you think of the brew.

Amherst Chinese (413-253-7835), 62 Main St. Open daily for lunch and dinner. A mural in the dining room depicts the restaurant's nearby farm, source of the vegetables in its dishes. Known fondly as AmChin, this is a local favorite. Note the daily specials; no MSG.

La Veracruzana (413-253-6900), 63 S. Pleasant St. Reasonably priced Mexican specialties.

Pasta e Basta (413-256-3550), 26 Main St. Open 11–11, until midnight Thu.–Sun. An unusually attractive little trattoria with a wide selection of homemade pastas. Specialties include penne chicken, and broccoli cream and spinach linguine. The reasonably priced menu also includes grilled and skewered seafood and chicken.

Panda East Restaurant (413-256-8923), 103 N. Pleasant St. Open 11:30–10 daily, until 11 Fri. and Sat. This is part of an excellent local chain specializing in traditional Hunan-style Chinese food, also Japanese staples (sushi, tempura, and teriyaki). Full bar.

Black Sheep Deli and Bakery (413-253-3442; www.blacksheepdeli .com), 79 Main St. A genuine coffeehouse-deli since 1986, with exceptional pastries made daily with natural ingredients and real butter, deli sandwiches, and a deli with pasta and salads; good picnic makings, also now hot entrées Mon.–Sat. 5–9.

Bueno y Sano (413-253-4000; www .buenoysano.com), 1 Boltwood Walk. Open daily lunch through dinner. An old-timer in a new location with reasonably priced, authentic Mexican food.

Atkins Farms Fruit Bowl (413-253-9528), corner of Rt. 116 and Bay Rd., South Amherst. Open daily; hours vary. Probably the fanciest farm stand in New England, this handsome redwood building sits amid thousands of fruit trees on the 190 acres that have been farmed for generations. There is a first-rate deli, but for some reason it's on the opposite side of the building from the bakery, where there's seating.

Cushman Market and Café (413-549-0100), 491 Pine St., North Amherst. Open Mon.–Sat. 7–7, Sun. 8–4. This is a neighborhood crossroads store that's so good it's become a local icon and added tables in the rear. Baked breads and pastry, local produce and products are the attraction. There are plenty of breakfast rolls, sandwiches, burgers, and panini.

In Northampton
🍴 ✦ ♿ **Sylvester's Restaurant, Cafe & Bakery** (413-586-5343), 111 Pleasant St. Open for breakfast and lunch. Named for and housed in the onetime

home of pioneer vegetarian and whole-wheat advocate Dr. Sylvester Graham of graham cracker fame. The long, well-lit dining room and adjoining café are cheery, perfect for breakfast (try the Lox-Ness omelet); there's also a large choice of soups, salads, sandwiches, wraps, burgers, and hot entrées at lunch, from a Mango Tango Salada, to a "West of Woostah" (sliced avocado and veggies on homemade toast), to shrimp sautéed with spinach, garlic butter, white wine, artichoke hearts, and mushrooms, served over grilled polenta. Tea isn't from a bag, and coffees are from the café. The food is so good here, in fact, that we lament the fact dinner is no longer served. Come early for lunch. There's a specials menu and trivia cards for kids. Beer and wine served.

Amanouz Café (413-585-9128; www.amanouz-casablanca.com), 44 Main St. Open for breakfast, lunch, and dinner. A narrow but deep and rewarding Moroccan oasis to which we keep returning. Specialties include tabbouleh salad, great falafel, salads, kebabs, a selection of couscous dishes (including chicken or lamb), and both vegetarian and meat sandwiches, like *shawerma* (marinated lamb and beef, vegetables, and tahini). Wine and beer.

Paul & Elizabeth's (413-584-4832; www.paulandelizabeths.com), entrances from Thornes Market (150 Main St.) and Old South St. Open Sun.–Thu. 11:30–9:15, Fri. and Sat. 11:30–9:45. The town's oldest natural foods restaurant, a great space with big old second-story plate-glass windows overhung with fanciful stained glass and a high tin ceiling, plenty of plants and wood. The extensive menu specializes in but is not limited to vegetarian dishes, soups and salads, tem-

pura and noodle dishes; also seafood, home-baked breads and pastries. Sides of baked brown rice, deep-fried tofu, sea vegetables, and more. Daily specials. Dinner entrées average $10.25–14.50. Beer and wine.

Spoleto Express (413-586-8646), 225 King St. Open daily from 11 AM, until 9:30 Sun.–Wed. and until 10:30 Thu.–Sat. This offshoot of the popular Main Street dining spot (see *Dining Out*) is good for wraps in a tomato-basil tortilla or on grilled rosemary focaccia; also soups, pizzas, salads, and pastas. Eat in or take out.

Fitzwilly's (413-584-8666), 23 Main St. Open daily 11:30 AM–midnight. One of New England's first fern bars: brick walls, plenty of copper, antiques, hanging plants. It all works, including the immense menu with blue plate luncheon specials like chicken potpie and sandwiches; burgers are a specialty, along with "lotsa pasta."

La Cazuela (413-586-0400), 271 Main St. Open daily, closed Mon. off-season. One of the most popular places in town, specializing in spicy Mexican and southwestern fare, including plenty of vegetarian dishes. Try the spinach enchiladas or *pollo verde*. Full bar.

Northampton Brewery (413-584-9903), 11 Brewer Court. Open Mon.–Sat. 11:30–1 AM, Sun. noon–1 AM. Housed in a 19th-century livery stable, this is a pleasant, multilevel space with a popular roof deck, serving sandwiches, pizza, burgers, steaks, seafood, and stir-fries. Beer changes daily.

Pizzeria Paradiso (413-586-1468; www.fundining.com), 12 Crafts St. Open nightly. This is all about wood-fired, brick-oven, very-thin-crust pizza, both white and red, in unusual varieties such as Chèvre Delight—goat cheese, sun-dried tomatoes, and roasted garlic cloves with mozzarella and Parmesan. Beer is served, along with kids-only pizza, finger food, and salads.

Bela Vegetarian Restaurant (413-586-8011), 68 Masonic St. Open Tue.–Sat. noon–8:45. A small, bright eatery with a full vegetarian menu: soups, pasta and tofu entrées, polenta. Try the butternut bisque and tempeh with zucchini in red wine rosemary butter, served with salad and brown rice.

Viva Fresh Pasta Co. (413-586-5875), 249 Main St. A cheerful corner storefront with white brick walls and a varied menu, including focaccia, pizza, pasta, and chicken specialties. Try the grilled eggplant with fresh basil and goat cheese. Wine and beer served.

Teapot (413-585-0880 or 413-585-9308), 116 Main St. Open from lunch through 11 PM, until midnight on weekends. Said by many to be the Valley's best Asian restaurant with a wide selection of reasonably priced meat and vegetarian dishes. Specialties include tea-smoked duck and chicken, shrimp and eggplant with scallions and garlic.

Smokin Lils BBQ (413-587-0400), 7 Strong Ave. Open daily for lunch and dinner. This popular transplant from Easthampton gets rave reviews. The menu features hush puppies, marinated and smoked ribs, mounds of pulled chicken and pork, brisket, jambalaya with crawfish, and, because this is Northampton, lunch salads.

Side Street Café (413-587-8900), 42 Maple St., Florence. Open for lunch through dinner except Sunday. A pleasant new café, good for some imaginative sandwiches and salads plus a serious dinner menu ranging from grilled vegetable risotto to honey bourbon glazed flatiron steak. At this writing BYOB, but wine and beer are coming.

In Holyoke
Black Sheep Deli (413-532-9535; www.blacksheepdeli.com), 1 Open Square Way. Open 7–5 weekdays. Off Dwight St., with parking by the canal. Open Square is a huge old rehabbed mill building housing a number of enterprises, with this the easiest to find. The café features warm colors and brick walls, casual seating, and all the freshly baked goods, sandwiches, and salads of the mother café in Amherst. Seasonal outdoor seating. WiFi.

VIVA FRESH PASTA ON NORTHAMPTON'S MAIN STREET

Kim Grant

HOLYOKE'S VERSION OF THE BLACK SHEEP DELI IS AT 1 OPEN SQUARE WAY.

Gramps Restaurant (413-534-1996), 216 Lyman St. Open for breakfast and lunch. An attractive, easy-to-find Polish restaurant that's as genuine as they come, operated by Danuta and Krzysztof Wojick, longtime owners of the neighboring Polish deli. Pierogi and blintzes are made fresh each day. It's definitely the place for *golabki* (stuffed cabbage).

Fernandez Family Restaurant (413-532-1139), 161 High St. Open Mon.–Fri. 10–5:30. A Puerto Rican eatery with some 20 dishes on display so that you can point rather than having to pronounce *surullitos* (sweet cornmeal with cheese), *boquito* (crabmeat fritter), or *mofongo* (plantains, garlic, and bacon).

Mi Plaza Restaurant (413-532-2700), 325 Main St. (corner of Cabot). Open 8–6 except Sat. This is a bright, inviting, and authentic Puerto Rican eatery with a menu that includes sandwiches and fish-and-chips as well as *rellenos de carne*, soups, and rice dishes.

Elsewhere

🌸 **Woodbridge's** (413-536-7341), 3 Hadley St., South Hadley. Open daily for all three meals. Early-bird specials 4–6. This big, friendly old tavern (booths on the bar side, tables on the other) on the common is known up and down the Valley for its clam chowder, but the menu is large and reasonably priced, including veal piccata and London broil as well as veggie melts, salads, and butcher-style deli sandwiches. Daily specials.

Dockside at Brunelle's (413-536-2342), 1 Alvord St., South Hadley. Open daily for lunch and dinner (until 9); the lounge is open until midnight. A local favorite with a large, reasonably priced menu, nightly specials, down on a scenic stretch of the river. This is the departure point for the *Lady Bea.*

Zoe's Fish & Chop House (413-527-0313), 238 Northampton St. (Rt. 10), Easthampton. Open for lunch weekdays, dinner nightly. A big, bright standby with booths and function rooms, basic American restaurant featuring shellfish and fried fish. Vegetarians can opt for beer-battered artichoke with a sour cream dill dip. Not a place for calorie counters. It's a big menu, and there are plenty of meat dishes, including "pork mignon." Dinner entrées $12.95–22.95.

DINERING OUT Miss Florence Diner (413-584-3179), 99 Main St., Florence (Northampton). Open for early breakfast through late dinner, 3 miles west of downtown Northampton. Known locally as Miss Flo's, this is the most famous diner in Western Massachusetts, in the same family since the 1940s. Forget the banquet addition and stick to the stools or booths. Unexpected specialties like clam and oyster stew and baked stuffed lobster casserole, a soup and salad bar, and full liquor license. Good beef barley soup and coconut and macaroon cream pudding.

Bluebonnet Diner (413-584-3333), 324 King St., Northampton. Open Mon.–Fri. 5:30 AM–midnight, Sat. 6 AM–midnight. A classic diner with "home cooking." Full bar, smoking section. Dinners average $6.95.

Look Restaurant (413-584-9850), 410 N. Main St., Leeds (Northampton). A landmark with a 1950s look and menu, "homestyle cooking," breakfast available all day. Fresh-made breads, muffins, and pies.

Easthampton Diner (413-527-0855), 117 Union St., Easthampton. Open 24 hours on weekends, otherwise from 6:30 AM until 9:30 PM (closing Sun. at 7). This is the real deal with a huge menu, seafood and Italian specialties, home fries with bacon or gravy. Beer and wine. Early-bird specials.

Pleasant St., Amherst. Open Sun.–Thu. until 11, Fri. and Sat. until midnight. Since 1976, milk from local cows has been used for great ice cream in 100 flavors including mud pie, blueberry cheesecake, and orange Dutch chocolate.

La Fiorentina Pastry Shop (413-586-7693), 25 Armory St., Northampton. Facing the parking lot, a hidden jewel of a coffee shop with delectable desserts like sfogliatelle and tiramisu as well as coffees, Italian soft drinks and juices, gelati, and memorable biscotti. For the story of the original Fiorentina, see "Springfield Area."

✧ Flayvors of Cook Farm (413-584-2224; www.cookfarm.com), 129 S. Maple St., Hadley. Open year-round,

Kim Grant

daily, seasonal hours. Milk from the resident cows is used to make outstanding ice cream (try the ginger!). Also available: turkey pie, chili, soups, and salads. The setting is one of the most beautiful in the Valley, surrounded by fields at the foot of the Holyoke Range. Plenty of outdoor tables and plenty of cows, both behind the fence and in the neighboring meadow. Sunday music 2–5, the kind to please both kids and cows.

Amherst Coffee (413-256-8987), 28 Amity St. This has quickly become the center of town. It's a casual café with espresso, loose-leaf tea, wine, spirits, and WiFi. The Noho version is **Northampton Coffee**, 269 Pleasant St.

⚓ **McCray Farm** (413-533-3714), 55 Alvord St., South Hadley. The dairy bar, open spring through fall, features homemade ice cream. This working dairy farm is near the river, with a small petting zoo; maple breakfasts during sugaring season.

Bakery Normand (413-584-0717), 192 Main St., Northampton. Open Tue.–Sat. 7:30–5:30. Tempting German tortes and other pastries, also breads plus cookies for the stroll.

The Moan and Dove (413-256-1710; www.themoananddove.com), 460 West St. (Rt. 116 south), Amherst. A serious pub with 20 beers on tap, several casks, and some 125 bottled brands to choose from. It's been so successful that owner Daniel Lanigan has opened a similar watering hole, **The Dirty Truth** (413-585-5999; www.dirtytruthbeerhall.com), 29 Main St., in Northampton.

Paper City Brewery (413-535-1588; www.papercity.com), 108 Cabot St., Holyoke, offers Friday-evening "tastings" 6–8. A microbrewery: amber ale, Cabot Street wheat, and Irish stout.

✳ Entertainment

For the academic year consult the *Five College Calendar of Events*, published monthly and available at all campuses as well as at http://calendar.fivecolleges.edu. A typical month lists more than 27 films, 30 lectures, 19 concerts, and 32 theatrical performances. Visitors welcome.

The Valley Advocate, with weekly arts listings, is published Thursday. It's free and everywhere in Northampton/Amherst, also online: www.valleyadvocate.com.

Academy of Music (413-584-9032; www.academyofmusictheatre.com), 274 Main St., Northampton. This Renaissance-style, century-old, municipally owned, 300-seat theater features a balcony and a baby grand in the women's lounge. It schedules live entertainment as well as films.

The Calvin Theatre (413-584-1444), 19 King St. First opened in 1924 as a 1,300-seat vaudeville house, it's now the splendidly restored venue for stellar live performances 3 to 6 nights a week during the academic season, less frequently in summer. Check out **Bar 19** after the show.

Mullins Center (413-545-0505), UMass campus, Amherst. A 10,500-seat sports and entertainment arena with a year-round schedule of theater and concerts as well as sports.

Fine Arts Center (413-545-2511; www.fineartscenter.com), UMass campus, Amherst. Performing arts series of theater, music, dance.

The Commonwealth Opera (413-586-5026; www.commonwealth

opera.org), with offices at 140 Pine St., Florence, stages a fall opera, a December *Messiah*, a March Broadway musical, and other performances at local venues.

Center for the Arts (413-584-7327; www.nohoarts.org), 17 New South St., Northampton. Theater, dance, art exhibits.

MUSIC Northampton Box Office (413-586-8686 or 800-THE-TICK) serves the Calvin Theater, the Iron Horse, and Pearl Street.

The Iron Horse (413-584-0610), 20 Center St., Northampton. This is only open when there's a performance, but that tends to be nightly. Live folk, jazz, and comedy, plus 50 brands of imported beer; dinner served. According to *Billboard* magazine, the Iron Horse "boasts one of the richest musical traditions in the country."

Pearl Street (413-584-7771), 10 Pearl St., Northampton. Dancing on Fri. and Sat., live music several nights a week. DJ.

Jazz in July at UMass (413-545-3530) in Amherst, a series of summer concerts and workshops celebrating jazz music.

The Mount Holyoke Summit House (413-586-8686) is the scene of a sunset concert series (folk, jazz, barbershop), 7:30 Thursdays.

Look Memorial Park Sunday Concerts are held Sundays at 4 PM, late June to mid-August, in Look Park, Rt. 9, Northampton.

Pioneer Arts Center of Easthampton (PACE; 413-527-3700; www.pioneerarts.org), 41 Union St., downtown Easthampton. A coffeehouse with a lively calendar of music, stand-up comedy, and more.

THEATER *Note:* For on-campus performances during the academic year, check www.fivecolleges.edu/theater.

✆ **Pioneer Valley Summer Theatre** (413-529-3434; www.summertheatre .net) at Williston Northampton School (P.O. Box 53), Easthampton 01027. The theater is in Scott Hall on Payson Avenue. Performances late June to mid-August. Inquire about **Theater for Young Audiences**, Wed.–Sat. at 10 AM during the company's season.

New Century Theatre (413-585-3220; www.smith.edu/theatre/nct). Over the past decade this regional company has developed a reputation for quality performances, staged late June to mid-August at the air-conditioned Hallie Flanagan Studio Theatre within the Mendenhall Center for Performing Arts at Smith College on Green Street, Northampton.

Hampshire Shakespeare Company (413-548-8118; wwww.hamsphire shakespeare.org). Summer Shakespeare plays and varied performances in other months—but no permanent home, so check the web site or call.

New World Theater (413-545-1972; www.newworldtheater.org), based at UMass, presents works by people of color.

FILM Amherst Cinema (413-253-CLIP; www.amherstcinema.org), 28 Amity St., Amherst. Opened in the winter of 2006, this new, nonprofit, three-screen theater offers nightly showings of independent, art, and foreign films. It replaces the old Amity Cinema, which occupied the front of this complex from 1926 until 1999. A community group bought the property, intending to turn it into a performing arts center, but failed to raise enough money. The new theater has been built at the rear of this historic building, which now also houses the Amherst Chamber of Commerce Visitor Center.

Academy of Music (413-584-8435), 274 Main St., Northampton. Art films and general releases alternate with live performances (see above).

Cinemark at Hampshire Mall (for movie times, 413-587-4237), Café Square, Hampshire Mall, Rt. 9, has 12 theaters.

Pleasant Street Theatre (413-586-0935), 27 Pleasant St., Northampton. First-run and art films, one theater upstairs and the well-named Little Theater in the basement.

Tower Theaters (413-533-2663), 19 College St., South Hadley. First-run and art films; seats may be reserved.

✳ Selective Shopping

ANTIQUES Northampton antiques shops are just east of its big higher-rent shops. Check out the **Antique Center of Northampton** (413-584-3600), 91/2 Market St. Open 5 days 10–5; closed Wed.; Sun. noon–5. A multidealer shop on three levels. **American Decorative Arts** (413-584-6804), 3 Olive St., has become something of a mecca for collectors of early-20th-century furniture. **Collector Galleries** (413-584-6734), 11 Bridge St. Open daily 11–5, Sun. noon–5. This is one of the oldest and biggest shops around, a good bet for furniture.

ART GALLERIES *Note:* In recent years Northampton has become an arts center in its own right as aspiring artists gather to study with established names. Many restaurants and coffeehouses also mount constantly chang-

ing work (for sale) by local artists. There's even a distinctive Northampton school of realism. Amherst, too, has its share of galleries; an **Amherst (Gallery) Art Walk** is held the first Thursday of each month, when many nongallery businesses also open their space to artists. In **Northampton** it's the first Friday of each month.

R. Michelson Galleries (413-586-3964; www.rmichelson.com), 132 Main St., Northampton, and 25 S. Pleasant St., Amherst. Open Mon.–Wed. 10–6, Thu.–Sat. 10–9, Sun. noon–5. Since 1976 Richard Michelson has maintained galleries at various locations, in 1995 moving into the huge and handsome two-story-high space designed in 1913 for the Northampton Savings Bank. The

RICHARD MICHELSON, OWNER OF R. MICHELSON GALLERIES

Christina Tree

gallery showcases work by 50 local artists, including Leonard Baskin, one of America's most respected sculptors, painters, and printmakers, with works selling here from $100 to $100,000. Other well-known artists whose work is usually on view include Barry Moser, Gregory Gillespie, Linda Post, and Lewis Bryden. Note the special gallery devoted to original children's book illustrations, featuring work by nationally known local illustrators.

Leverett Crafts and Arts Center (413-548-9070), 13 Montague Rd., Leverett. Open Wed.–Fri. 2–5, Sat. 1–4. Off the beaten track, a long-established nonprofit gallery with changing exhibits, talks, classes, and workshops.

CRAFTS Some 1,500 craftspeople work in the Valley and nearby Hill-towns, and Northampton is their major showcase, known particularly for handcrafted jewelry, pottery, and furniture. One Cottage Street in East-hampton, the Cutlery Building in Northampton, and the Pro-Brush Building in Florence all house artisans. For periodic tours and open houses, check with the Greater Northampton Chamber of Commerce (see *Guidance*).

The Valley is also the venue for several major crafts and fine arts happenings: **The Paradise City Arts Festivals** (413-527-8994; www.paradisecityarts .com)—held Memorial Day weekend and Columbus Day weekend at North-ampton's Tri-Country Fairgrounds—are rated as the state's premier showcases for fine, contemporary juried crafts and art. **Arts Easthampton** (www.artseasthampton.com) sees dozens of open studios once in early June and again the first weekend in

December at **One Cottage Street** and **Eastworks**, two large former mill buildings now each honeycombed with studios. Also see **Snow Farm** in "Hampshire Hilltowns."

In Northampton
Pinch (413-586-4509; www.epinch .com), 179 Main St. A variety of artistic, functional pottery and decorative accessories.

Skera (413-586-4563; www.skera .com), 221 Main St. Open daily, Sun. from noon, Thu. until 9. Longtime owners Harriet and Steve Rogers specialize more and more in stunning handcrafted clothing, "wearable art."

Silverscape Designs (413-586-3324; www.silverscapedesigns.com), 1 King St., Northampton; also 264 N. Pleasant St., Amherst (413-253-3324). The Northampton store (open weekdays 10–6, Sat. until 9, Sun. noon–5) is a beauty, the Tiffany's of the Valley—a former bank building with art deco detailing and a glorious stained-glass skylight. The old tellers' windows are still in place; there's also a cascading fountain. A wide variety of jewelry and accessories, also Tiffany-style lamps.

Don Muller Gallery (413-586-1119), 40 Main St. An outstanding store displaying a wide variety of crafted items, specializing in art glass, always exhibiting the deeply colored signature orbs hand blown by locally based Josh Simpson.

Artisan Gallery (413-586-1942; www .theartisangallery.com), Thornes Market, 150 Main St. A quality selection of jewelry, pottery, woodwork, and glass; kaleidoscopes are a specialty.

Alfredo's Gallery, Fine Art Photography (413-253-1707), 6 Crafts Ave. A serious gallery with changing exhibits as well as work by photographer Alfredo DiLascia.

Bill Brough Jewelry Designs (413-586-8985), 104 Main St. Original jewelry designs in gold, diamonds, pearls, and special stones.

Ten Thousand Villages (413-582-9338), 82 Main St. Open Mon.–Wed. 10–6, Thu.–Sat. until 8. Fairly traded handicrafts from around the world.

In Amherst
Fiber Art Center (413-256-1818; www.fiberartcenter.com), 79 S. Pleasant St. Open Tue.–Sat. 10–6. Changing exhibits plus a permanent tapestry collection and a retail gallery specializing in woven, quilted, and other quality fiber arts; also crafted jewelry, fiber supplies, and more.

Gallery A3 (413-253-4171), 28 Amity St. at the Amherst Cinema Center. Open Wed.–Sun. noon–6. The Amherst Art Alliance mounts changing exhibits, frequently first rate.

BOOKSTORES Book browsing is a major pastime in this area.

In South Hadley
Odyssey Bookshop (413-534-7307 or 800-540-7307; www.odysseybks .com), Village Commons, 9 College St. Open Mon.–Sat. 10–8, Sun. noon–5. An independent bookstore across from Mount Holyoke College. Large children's books and poetry sections, author readings, and other special events.

In Northampton
Broadside Bookshop (413-586-4235), 247 Main St. A general trade bookstore with a strong emphasis on fiction and literature as well as personal advice.

Booklink (413-585-9955), 150 Main St., in Thornes Market. Specialties include travel and local books.

Bookends (413-585-8667), 80 Maple St., Florence. Nine rooms of quality used books. **Raven Used Books** (413-584-9868), 4 Old South St., specializes in scholarly titles, women's studies, and philosophy.

In Amherst
Jeffery Amherst Bookstore (413-253-3381), 55 S. Pleasant St. A full-service bookstore with a strong children's book section, specializing in Emily Dickinson.

Amherst Books (413-256-1547), 8 Main St., has a wide selection of new books, specializing in poetry, literature, and philosophy. Frequent author readings.

Book Marks (413-549-6136), 1 E. Pleasant St. (Carriage Shops). A wide selection of used books specializing in art, poetry, photography, and Emily Dickinson.

Food for Thought Books (413-253-5432), 106 N. Pleasant St., featuring gay and lesbian, progressive political, and African American titles.

Laos Religious Book Center (413-548-3909), 867 N. Pleasant St., an ecumenical bookstore with both Christian and Jewish titles.

CLOTHING

In Amherst
Rural chic is the look at **Zanna** (413-253-2563), 187 N. Pleasant St., and **Clay's** (413-256-4200), 32 Main St.

In Northampton
Zanna (413-584-8866; www.zanna .com) is at 126 Main St. here. **Talbots** (413-858-5985) is at 34 Bridge St.; **Cathy Cross** (413-596-9398), 151 Main St.; **Country Comfort, Ltd.** (413-584-0042), 153 Main St.; and

Eileen Fisher Store, 24 Pleasant St. Also: **J Rich Clothing for Men** (413-586-6336), 22 Masonic St.

OTHER SPECIAL STORES AND ENTERPRISES **Northampton Wools** (413-586-4331), 11 Pleasant St., Northampton. Linda Daniels's small shop just off Main Street is crammed with bright wools and knitting gear; workshops offered.

Webs (413-584-2225; www.yarn.com), 75 Service Center Rd., Northampton. A warehouse-sized, family-owned yarn store.

Faces (413-584-4081), 175 Main St., Northampton. Open daily. A hip, student-geared department store with toys, clothing, furniture and furnishings, cards, and much more.

The Mountain Goat (413-586-0803), 177 Main St., Northampton. The area's premier outdoor "funfitters"; mostly clothing, some hiking and camping equipment, a great selection of shoes.

Table & Vine (413-584-7775 or 800-474-2449; www.tableandvine.com), 122 N. King St., Northampton. Open Mon.–Sat. 9–9. Featuring more than 5,000 wines, 400 beers, over 100 cheeses, dozens of kinds of olives, pastas, and thousands of other delicacies plus glassware, books, and kitchen accessories. Inquire about wine tastings.

SHOPPING CENTERS **Thornes Marketplace**, 150 Main St., Northampton. An incubator for many Northampton stores: a five-story, 30-shop complex with high ceilings, wood floors.

The Village Commons in South Hadley. A whimsical, white-clapboard complex of shops designed by Boston architect Graham Gund to house shops, restaurants, and a movie theater (two screens).

Holyoke Mall (413-536-1440) at Ingleside (I-91 exit 15, and Mass Pike exit 4), open Mon.–Sat. 10–9:30 and Sun. 11–6. The single biggest mall in Western Massachusetts, second largest in all of New England, with Filene's and JCPenney anchors.

✴ Farm Stands

In Amherst
Atkins Farms Country Market (413-253-9528), 1150 West St. (Rt. 116 south). Open daily 8–6 except holidays, later in summer. The Valley's largest and fanciest farm stand, a vast redwood market with a huge selection of quality produce, much it from the family's 290 acres and 25,000 fruit trees; the complex includes a popular deli café and is surrounded by apple orchards.

Delta Organic Farm (413-253-1893; www.deltaorganicfarm.com), 352 East Hadley St., sells herbs, syrup, and organic produce; also soup and salads to go.

J&J Farms (413-549-1877), 324 Meadow St., North Amherst. Open June to Nov., daily 9–7. Fourth-generation farm open for seasonal produce specializing in sweet corn, tomatoes, peppers, squash, strawberries, and six varieties of potatoes.

In Granby
Red Fire Farm (413-467-SOIL), 7 Carver St. Open May to Nov. daily. Over 30 types of certified organic vegetables grown and over 50 varieties of tomatoes test-tasted at the August Tomato Festival. Fruit and berries from other local farms also sold.

In Hadley

Mapleline Farm (413-549-6174; www.maplelinefarm.com), 78 Comins Rd. Farm-bottled milk and other products.

North Hadley Sugar Shack (413-585-8820; www.northhadleysugarshack.com), 181 River Dr. Open mid-Feb. until Christmas week. Maple syrup, maple candy, and maple ice cream; sugaring breakfasts February into April. Then strawberries, asparagus, pumpkins, squash, Harvest Moon Pumpkin Festival in late October.

Szwawlowski Potato Farm (413-247-9240), 103 Main St. Open (except Sun.) May–Nov. 7–5, weekdays off-season. Potatoes—all varieties!

FLOWERS **Andrew's Greenhouse** (413-253-2937), 1178 South East St., Amherst. Open daily Apr.–June, and except for Tue. in July and August. A favorite source of perennials, herbs, bedding plants, and cut-your-own flowers.

Hadley Garden Center (413-584-1423), 285 Russell St. (Rt. 9), Hadley. Open daily, year-round. Herbs, orchids, bulbs, bird food, indoor plants, firewood, and gardening workshops.

Twenty Acre Farm and Greenhouses (413-549-5708), 351 River Dr. (Rt. 47). A wide variety of flowering annuals starting in March; also hanging baskets, vegetable plants, 20 shades of geraniums. It hosts the Rt. 47 Flea Market Sale on weekends in September, October (plants).

Wanczyk Evergreen Nursery (413-584-3709), 166 Russell St. (Rt. 9), Hadley. Open daily April 10 to Nov. A great source of perennials and nursery plants.

PICK-YOUR-OWN **Atkins Farms** (413-253-9528), 1150 West St. (Rt. 116 south), Amherst. Pick-your-own apples in fall.

Lakeside U-Pick Strawberries (413-549-0805), 281 River Dr., Hadley. Open daily in-season, 7:30–7.

Sapowsky Farms (413-467-7952), 436 East St., Granby. Pick-your-own strawberries. They also sell milk, cheese, eggs, syrups, honey, jams, and firewood.

Teddy C. Smiarowski Farm (413-247-5181), 487 Main St., Hatfield. Asparagus.

❋ **Special Events**

Year-round: **Arts Night Out**, Northampton, a gallery walk with openings and lectures in many galleries, is the first Friday of the month. In Amherst, **Art Walk** is held the first Thursday of each month; many non-gallery businesses also open their space to artists.

See the town web sites listed under *Guidance* for these and all the following events. Also see *The Valley Advocate*, published Thursdays, for current entertainment and events.

Spring–fall: **Farmer's markets** are held on Saturday in Northampton (on Gothic St.) and Amherst (on the common); in Holyoke on Thursday afternoons (2:30–5:30, Hampden Park off Dwight St.).

March: **Annual Bulb Show**, Smith College (*first 2 weeks*). **St. Patrick's Day Parade**, Holyoke (*Sunday after St. Patrick's Day*).

May: **Emily Dickinson's World Weekend. Western Massachusetts Appaloosa Horse Show**, Three-County Fairgrounds, Northampton.

Memorial Day weekend: **Paradise City Arts Festivals** (www.paradise cityarts.com).

July: **Fireworks**, Amherst (*July 4*). **Amherst Crafts Fair** (*weekend after Indpendence Day*). **Morgan Horse Show**, Northampton.

August: **Amherst Teddy Bear Rally** (*first weekend*). **Taste of Northampton**, with more than 40 participating restaurants (*second weekend*). **Three-County Fair** at the Three-County Fairgrounds, Northampton. **Celebrate Holyoke** at Heritage State Park is a 4-day, multicultural music festival with food and dancing (*weekend before Labor Day*).

October, every other year: **Book and Plow Festival**, Amherst, features 3 days honoring local writers and farmers.

November: **Northampton Independent Film Festival** (www.niff.org).

December: **Open crafts studios** (www.artseasthampton.com) at East-works in Easthampton (*first weekend*). **First Night**, Northampton (*New Year's Eve*).

SPRINGFIELD AREA

One of the oldest cities in the country—it was founded in 1636 on the east bank of the Connecticut River between two waterfalls—Springfield has known booms and busts over three centuries. Unlike many other old New England industrial communities, it has tried hard to adapt creatively to change, although with mixed success. Today a city that once based its prosperity on manufacturing firearms is a tourist destination thanks to its central location, the worldwide craze for basketball, and the endearing characters created by local boy Theodor Geisel, better known as Dr. Seuss.

With a population of 156,000, Springfield is the third largest city in Massachusetts and the metropolis of the Pioneer Valley. Although 33 square miles in area, most of its attractions—shops, restaurants, stately Courthouse Square (a monument to the city's glory days), the Springfield Museums at the Quadrangle, the Dr. Seuss Memorial Sculpture Garden, and the MassMutual Center (the renovated Springfield Civic Center arena and attached convention center)—are within a few blocks of one another in the compact downtown area known as Springfield Center. The Basketball Hall of Fame, the city's most popular attraction, is just a few minutes' drive away, as is the Springfield Armory National Historic Site.

Both Springfield Center and the Basketball Hall of Fame are well marked from Interstates 91 and 391. Within Greater Springfield all you have to do to find downtown is follow signs with the impish image of Dr. Seuss's Cat in the Hat, about as engaging a guide as you could ask for.

The Springfield you see today is largely the result of the young federal government's decision in 1794 to establish a national armory to manufacture muskets for the U.S. Army in the then-small riverside village. The armory attracted skilled workers and developed machinery and manufacturing techniques that made Springfield one of the engines of the industrial revolution in America. Machine shops and factories utilizing tools and methods developed at the armory were established up and down the Connecticut Valley, which in time became known as Precision Valley.

With the War of 1812 Springfield became an overnight boomtown, but it was the Civil War that really transformed the city, which doubled in population as it became the chief arsenal of the Union army. The armory produced more than

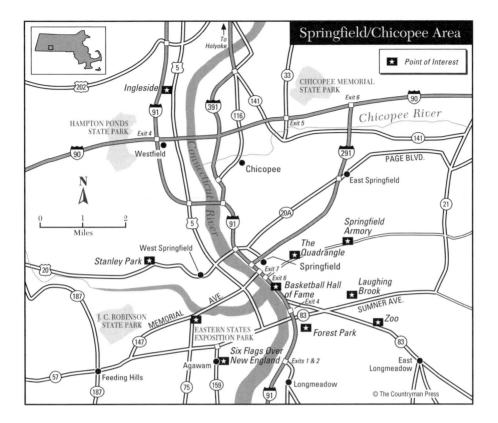

Springfield/Chicopee Area

★ Point of Interest

half the rifled muskets used by northern troops, while nearby Smith and Wesson turned out 110,000 revolvers and the Ames Sword Company in neighboring Chicopee made 150,000 cavalry sabers.

After the Civil War, Springfield evolved into a prosperous diversified manufacturing city known for an impressive variety of inventions including the first gas-powered car and the first motorcycle, along with pioneering versions of airplanes and vacuum cleaners. The city was also the home to manufacturers of household-word products such as Breck Shampoo and Milton Bradley board games.

Most workers were well-paid craftsmen who could afford to buy their own houses, rather than live in rented tenement flats as in most New England cities, and Springfield boasted that it was "the City of Homes." Wealthy industrialists built themselves grand mansions, of course, but also supported the arts, endowing the Springfield Museums at the Quadrangle—an extraordinary civic amenity— and creating grand public spaces like Forest Park with its delightful zoo.

Theodor Geisel, born in Springfield in 1904, spent his childhood following his father, the city's superintendent of parks, around Forest Park. The zoo provided the inspiration for Dr. Seuss's whimsical creatures, his father was the model for the kindly zookeeper, and the park was the setting for many of his stories. A visit

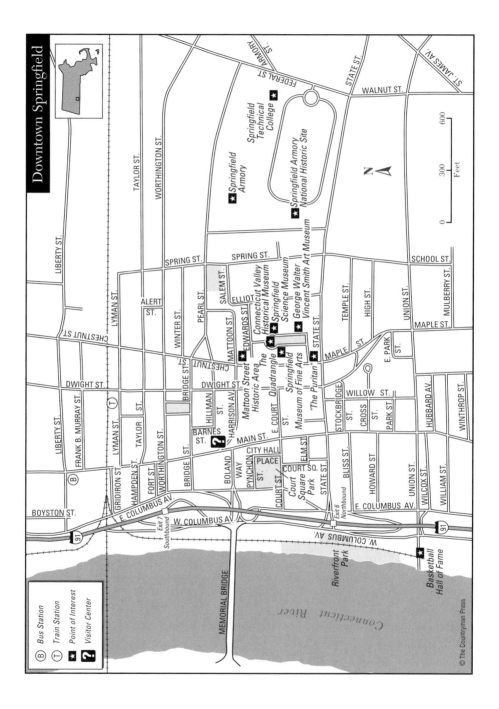

Downtown Springfield

to Forest Park is particularly rewarding after seeing the sculptures in the Dr. Seuss Memorial in the Quadrangle and viewing the exhibit on Geisel's life in Springfield at the nearby Connecticut Valley Historical Museum.

Well-to-do local businessmen were also major supporters of self-improvement organizations such as the Young Men's Christian Association. It was at a YMCA training school for physical education instructors in Springfield in 1891 that Dr. James Naismith took a soccer ball and two peach baskets and created the game of "basket ball." His students, and other graduates of the school, took the game around the world.

The closure of the Springfield Armory in 1968 marked the end of an era for the already economically troubled city, which saw its industrial base continue to shrink and the population decline. Many formerly pleasant neighborhoods deteriorated into near slums, and once-busy downtown department stores, hotels, theaters, and restaurants were forced to close.

Impressive but rather sterile urban renewal projects such as the MassMutual Center and the Tower Square complex (a 29-story office tower and hotel with a shopping arcade and large parking garage) have brought life back to downtown, particularly after dark. However, many handsome 19th- and early-20th-century buildings that gave the city its distinctive character were bulldozed away to create them. Efforts are now being made to preserve landmark buildings, restore historic older neighborhoods, and revitalize downtown, which these days has more entertainment options and is much livelier at night.

More recent projects, such as Riverfront Park between I-91 and the Connecticut River, have a more human dimension than their predecessors. The park includes a 3.5-mile-long bicycle path and is also home to the new Naismith Basketball Hall of Fame.

Built at a cost of $45 million, the Hall of Fame is an architecturally striking building shaped like a basketball and with a 15-story spire topped by one 14 feet in circumference. At night, when it's illuminated in changing colors, the Hall of Fame looks like something from outer space and definitely brightens the Springfield skyline.

One local institution that has endured through Springfield's vicissitudes is the Eastern States Exposition—always referred to locally as "the Big E"—founded in 1917 and still going strong. Held for 17 days starting in mid-September in its vast fairgrounds in West Springfield, the Big E is the only annual event of its kind encompassing all six New England states. A huge and still basically agricultural fair, it also includes big-name entertainment and the Avenue of States, with replicas of the various New England state capitol buildings, each housing exhibits.

Also a survivor is the large amusement park just across the river in Agawam. Now called Six Flags New England and operated by the giant Six Flags national theme park corporation, it was originally Riverside Park and founded at the turn of the 20th century to provide inexpensive entertainment for Springfield factory workers and their families. The park was famous for its roller coaster and other scary rides back then—and still is.

GUIDANCE Greater Springfield Convention and Visitors Bureau (413-787-1548 or 800-723-1548; www.valleyvisitor.com), 1441 Main St., Springfield 01103. The well-stocked and -staffed visitor center is open 9–5 weekdays. **William C. Sullivan Visitor Information Center** (413-750-2980), 1200 W. Columbus Ave., Springfield 01103. Open year-round, daily 8–6. An attractive walk-in, staffed visitor center in the riverfront development area near the Basketball Hall of Fame, it offers information about the Pioneer Valley as well as Springfield.

GETTING THERE *By air:* **Bradley International Airport** (860-292-2000; www.bradleyairport.com). Eighteen miles south of Springfield in Windsor Locks, CT, served by most national and regional carriers and major car rentals. See *Getting Around* for taxis.

By train: **Amtrak** (800-USA-RAIL), 66 Lyman St., connects Springfield with Hartford, New Haven, New York City, Philadelphia, Baltimore, Washington, DC, and Chicago. There is frequent service from New York (change in New Haven). The bus depot is right around the corner from the train station.

By bus: **Peter Pan** (413-781-2900 or 800-237- 8747; www.peterpanbus.com), based in Springfield with its own terminal at 1776 Main St., connects with the airport, Boston, Hartford, Cape Cod, Albany, and New York City. **Vermont Transit** (800-552-8737) stops en route from New York and Albany to Vermont, New Hampshire, and Montreal.

By car: From points north take I-91 to exit 7, and from points south to exit 6. From Boston, take the Mass Pike to exit 6 to I-291 to I-91 north to exit 2B (Dwight St.), which parallels Main; take it to State St. and turn left for the Quadrangle complex; from Holyoke, I-391 is another connector.

GETTING AROUND Pioneer Valley Transit Authority (413-781-7882) serves the Springfield/Holyoke area.

By taxi: **City Cab** (413-734-8294), and **Yellow Cab** (413-739-9999).

PARKING The Quadrangle museums, Springfield Armory National Historic Site, and Basketball Hall of Fame all offer parking (see map), and downtown parking lots are reasonably priced.

MEDICAL EMERGENCY Dial 911.

Baystate Medical Center (413-794-0000), Chestnut at Spring St.

✳ To See

MUSEUMS Naismith Memorial Basketball Hall of Fame (413-781-6500; www.hoophall.com), 1000 W. Columbus Ave. (Just off I-91 and well marked: Look for the 15-story-high spire with the basketball on top.) Open 9–5 mid-June to mid-Sep.; 10–4 mid-Sep. to mid-June. Admission $16.99 adults, $13.99 seniors (65-plus), $11.99 ages 5–15. Dr. James Naismith invented basketball at a YMCA college in Springfield in 1891, and the Hall of Fame has been at various locations around the city since 1968. The present $45 million museum is Springfield's pride, its most visible landmark (it's shaped like a giant basketball and illuminated in different colors at night), and its biggest tourist attraction. A combination history museum, shrine, computer game arcade, and gymnasium—there's nothing else quite like it.

Basketball is anything but static and neither is the Hall of Fame, which has 41 interactive computer stations where visitors can, among other things, get answers to basketball trivia questions and play virtual reality basketball games. Some 70 TV screens are going all the time, showing interviews with players and coaches and highlights of championship games. There are also plenty of opportunities to toss basketballs around. The Hall of Fame gallery, the game's Valhalla, displays photos and mementos of basketball's greatest players, coaches, managers, and teams. Among the museum artifacts on display are Milwaukee Buck Bob Lanier's size 22 sneakers, a pair of gym bloomers worn by a member of the first women's basketball team (Smith College), and Naismith's not-very-well-typed 13 original rules of the game. The heart of the building is a regulation basketball court—pickup games are encouraged—directly under the 90-foot-high basketball-shaped dome.

Springfield Museums at the Quadrangle (413-263-6800, www.springfield museums.org), 220 State St. (The main entrance to the complex is on the Edwards St. side.) At this unique cultural common, four museums—a science and a history museum and two art museums—and the city's main library are all assembled around a grassy green. The Quadrangle green is now the site of a sculpture garden memorializing the work of children's book author and illustrator Dr. Seuss, nom de plume of native son Theodor Geisel. The museums are open Tue.–Sun. 11–4. A ticket good for admission to all four museums is $10 adults, $7 seniors and college students, $5 ages 3–17; under 3 free. Inquire about frequent special events. The **Quadrangle Welcome Center** adjacent to the Science Museum contains the ticket office, a large gift shop, and a café.

Dr. Seuss National Memorial (413-263-6800; www.catinthehat.org), the Quadrangle. Open daily 9–8 spring and summer, 9–5 fall and winter. Free. This imaginative sculpture garden is the kind of humorous, fantasti-

SAM-I-AM, ONE OF THE CHARACTERS IN HORTON COURT, AT THE DR. SEUSS NATIONAL MEMORIAL
Springfield Library & Museum Association

HISTORICAL MONUMENT OF THE AMERICAN REPUBLIC.

HISTORICAL MONUMENT OF THE AMERICAN REPUBLIC BY ERASTUS SALISBURY (1876)

cal tribute Theodor Geisel would have appreciated. The 22 bronze figures range in size from a tiny Lorax (a gnome with a walrus mustache) to a 14-foot-high trunk-waving Horton the Elephant, depicted stepping out of a giant book with Thidwick the Big Hearted Moose, Sam I Am, and other beloved Dr. Seuss characters. All the sculptures are the work of Lark Grey Diamond-Cates, Geisel's stepdaughter. The man himself is depicted sitting at his drawing board—and standing beside him, grinning mischievously, is Dr. Seuss's muse: the Cat in the Hat. As you might imagine, this sculpture garden is kid-friendly: Sculptures can be climbed on, and there is even a bronze "storyteller chair" where parents can sit and read a favorite Dr. Seuss story to their child.

The Museum of Fine Arts (413-263-6800; www.springfieldmuseums.org), the Quadrangle. A 1930s art deco building with a central court, the museum houses a surprisingly superb collection. You might expect the 18th- and 19th-century portraits and Hudson River landscapes (be sure to locate *New England Scenery* by Frederic Church), some memorable Winslow Homers and Frederick Remingtons, but what you don't expect is the wealth of early-20th-century paintings by Georgia O'Keeffe, Charles Sheeler, Charles Demuth, Reginald Marsh, and others. Paul Sample's *Church Supper* alone is worth a trip. The modern art collection is also far more than token. The museum's 20th-century as well as earlier paintings and sculpture are complemented in an interesting way by period furnishings and decorative art. Another surprise: Erastus Field's *Historical Monument of the American Republic*, a huge, absorbing fantasy depicting 300 scenes on 10 elaborate towers, a visual saga culminating with the triumph over slavery (note Abraham Lincoln rising to heaven in a fiery chariot near the top of the central tower). *The Newsboy*, a moment in 1889 captured by George Newhall, Springfield's leading late-19th-century artist, is also worth noting. The museum has the country's only permanent gallery devoted to Currier & Ives prints. There are frequent changing exhibits.

George Walter Vincent Smith Art Museum (413-263-6800; www.springfield museums.org), the Quadrangle. The first museum on the Quadrangle (1896), this is a one-man collection housed in a magnificent palazzo. G. W. V. Smith (always called by his full name locally) amassed a fortune in New York and married Springfield's Belle Townsley, retiring here at age 35. The couple devoted the next five decades to collecting ancient Japanese swords, armor, and art; Islamic rugs; the largest Western collection of cloisonné; and 19th-century landscape paintings. A recent addition to the museum is the Art Discovery Center, an interactive, colorfully decorated gallery designed to introduce children and fami-

lies to the museum's collection. Like Boston's Isabella Stewart Gardner, the
Smiths stipulated that the collection not be altered after their deaths, and their
ashes are interred in the museum. The couple's portraits are just off the entry
hall, surrounded by those of stern past captains of Valley industry.

Connecticut Valley Historical Museum (413-263-6800; www.springfield
museums.org), the Quadrangle. A Colonial Revival mansion built in 1927 (note
the replicated Connecticut Valley front door) houses an excellent genealogical
library and interesting exhibits on Springfield inventions, personalities, and institutions. An imaginative permanent exhibit on Theodor Geisel called *Seuss on the
Loose in Springfield* matches the sites of the author and artist's boyhood in
Springfield with the landscape of his books (a turreted old National Guard
armory became a castle, for example). There is plenty here for children to relate
to and with, and the special exhibits are usually outstanding.

Science Museum (413-263-6800; www.springfieldmuseums.org), the Quadrangle. Dinosaur buffs will find a 20-foot-high model of *Tyrannosaurus rex* and the
tracks of much smaller dinosaurs. Exhibits also include a vintage-1937 Gee Bee
monoplane made in Springfield, a hands-on Exploration Center, an impressive
African Hall full of animals, some great old-fashioned dioramas, Native American artifacts, and a new Eco-Center featuring live animals in realistic habitats—
lifelike vegetation, fish that walk on land, turtles that look like leaves, and an
Amazon rain forest. Planetarium shows daily. $3 adults, $2 children.

Springfield Armory National Historic Site (413-734-8551; www.nps.gov/spar).
Open early Sep.–May, Tue.–Sat. 10–5; rest of the year Tue.–Sun. 10–5. Armory
Square (1 mile east on State St. from the Quadrangle; enter from Federal St.
near the corner of State). Free. It was the presence of this federal armory, estab-
lished in 1794 to manufacture muskets for the U.S. Army, that transformed
Springfield from a sleepy village into a vibrant industrial city. The museum in the
Main Arsenal Building, which dates to 1847, contains one of the world's largest
and most comprehensive collections of firearms.

Exhibits include an array of weapons,
from flintlock muskets to M16 rifles,
used in every American war since the
Revolution. There are also film presentations, displays of innovative
machinery invented at the armory,
special exhibits on firearms development, and weapons firing demonstrations. Only about 20 percent of the
armory's vast firearms collection is on
view in the public galleries, but hour-
long guided tours of the second-floor
storage area, where the bulk of the
collection is kept, are given one day
each week. (Tours are limited to a
maximum of 10 people. Call ahead to
confirm dates and times. There is a

ANIMAL EXHIBITS IN THE R. E. PHELON
AFRICAN HALL AT SPRINGFIELD'S SCIENCE
MUSEUM

Springfield Library & Museum Association

$12 charge.) The imposing brick armory complex, which occupies more than 15 acres along a bluff above the city, was deactivated by the Defense Department in 1968, and most of the buildings are now used by Springfield Technical Community College.

Titanic Historical Society Museum (413-543-4770; www.titanichistorical society.org), rear of Henry's Jewelry Store, 208 Main St., Indian Orchard. Open weekdays 10–4, Sat. 10–3. A large collection of thousands of objects recovered from the RMS *Titanic*, the world's most famous shipwreck (April 15, 1912, with a loss of 1,600 lives). The society's founder and president, Edward Kamuda, was inspired to begin the collection after seeing the 1953 film *A Night to Remember*.

Storrowton Village Museum (413-205-5051; www.thebige.com/village/storrow ton_village.html), 1305 Memorial Ave., West Springfield, at the Eastern States Exposition grounds (Rt. 147). Open mid-June to late Aug., Tue.–Sat. 11–3. $5 adults, $4 children. The gift shop is open year-round (closed Sun.). Donated to the exposition in 1929 by Mrs. James Storrow of Boston (the same family for whom Storrow Drive is named), this grouping of restored 18th- and early-19th-century buildings makes up one of the first museum villages in the country. The buildings, all of which were moved here from their original locations, include a vintage-1834 meetinghouse, an 1810 brick school, a smith, a huge and handsome vintage-1776 mansion, and a genuine 1789 tavern that would now be deep in Quabbin Reservoir if it hadn't been rescued.

HISTORIC HOMES AND SITES Court Square, bounded by Court and Elm Sts. Springfield's "Municipal Group" recalls the city's golden era. Completed in 1913, the monumental, many-columned, Greek Revival City Hall and Symphony Hall buildings are separated by a soaring, 300-foot Italianate campanile. The **City Hall** interior is graced by 27 kinds of marble and fine wood paneling and includes a Municipal Auditorium seating 3,000. **Symphony Hall** is equally elegant and known for its acoustics. In the columned **Old First Church** (413-737-1411), check out the art gallery (open Mon.–Fri. 9:30–2:30 or by appointment), topped with a rooster shipped from England in 1749. The park here, created in 1812 to complement the first Hampden County Courthouse, is the scene of frequent events. Note the Victorian-era courthouse designed by Henry Hobson Richardson.

Historic Springfield neighborhoods. In the late 19th century Springfield became known as the City of Homes, reflecting the quality of the thousands of wooden homes—single- and two-family houses instead of the usual tenements and triple-deckers for the working class, and truly splendid houses for the middle and upper classes. Unfortunately, with the flight of families to the suburbs, several once-proud neighborhoods are now shabby, but still well worth driving through. **Forest Park**, developed almost entirely between the 1890s and 1920, is filled with turreted, shingled Victorian homes, many built by the McKnight brothers (for whom the **McKnight District**, boasting some 900 of these homes, is named). Some of the city's stateliest houses, a number on the National Register of Historic Places, are found in the **Maple Hill District**. Right downtown the **Mattoon Street Historic District** is a street of 19th-century brick row houses, leading to the 1870s Grace Baptist Church designed by Henry Hobson Richardson.

FOR FAMILIES ✐ **Six Flags New England** (413-786-9300 or 877-4-SIXFLAGS; www.sixflags.com/parks/newengland), 1623 Main St. (Rt. 159), Agawam. Open weekends mid-April through May, daily June through Labor Day, weekends in Sep.; call for hours. Largest theme and water park in New England with over 160 rides (including eight roller coasters) and an 8-acre water park; also midway, arcades, food, and live entertainment. $49.99 adults ($39.99 if bought online), $29.99 kids; $15 parking.

✐ **The Zoo in Forest Park** (413-733-2251; www.forestparkzoo.org). Off Summer Ave./Rt. 83 (I-91 north, exit 2; I-91 south, exit 4). Open Apr. 15–Nov. 15, weekends through Dec. and Feb.–Apr. 15. Admission: $4.50 adults, $3.50 seniors and children 5–12, $2 under 5. A small wild-animal zoo (deer, bears, woodland and exotic animals) and a petting zoo.

✐ **Eastern States Exposition**. See *Special Events*.

✳ Green Space

Forest Park (413-787-6434). Three miles south of the center of Springfield (see directions to the zoo under *For Families*). Open year-round. Free for walk-ins, nominal charge for cars. The 735 acres include two small zoos. The park also offers paddleboats, 21 miles of nature trails, tennis courts, picnic groves, swimming pools, and summer concerts at the **Barney Amphitheater**. A magnificent, columned mausoleum built by ice-skate tycoon Everett H. Barney (his mansion was destroyed to make way for I-91) commands a great view of the Connecticut.

Riverfront Park, foot of State St., Springfield. This 6-acre riverfront park offers a 3.5-mile-long bicycle path and a view of the Connecticut River, which is otherwise walled from the city by railroad tracks and interstate highway.

Stanley Park (413-568-9312), Westfield, open mid-May to mid-Oct., 8 AM–dusk. Endowed by the founder of Stanley Home Products, the 300-acre park is known for its extensive rose garden (more than 50 varieties), mini New England village, 96-foot-high carillon tower, Japanese garden with teahouse, arboretum, and large fountain. Sunday-evening concerts range from singing groups to the Springfield Symphony Pops.

Laughing Brook Education Center & Wildlife Sanctuary (413-566-8034), 789 Main St., Hampden. From I-91 in Springfield, take exit 4 (Rt. 83) to Sumner Ave., then go 3.6

FOREST PARK OFFERS TWO SMALL ZOOS FOR CHILDREN.

Kim Grant

miles. The nature center open Tue.–Fri. 10–noon, Sat. 2–4, Sun. 10–4, Mon. and holidays 12:30–4. $3 adults, $2 children. Off any main route to anywhere, this is a popular destination for families drawn by the onetime home of storyteller Thornton Burgess. The house is now part of a 356-acre preserve owned by the Massachusetts Audubon Society; it includes hiking trails, fields, streams, a pond, caged animals, a picnic pavilion, and a "touch-and-see" trail.

✳ Lodging

The downtown convention hotels include the 265-room high-rise **Springfield-Marriott Hotel** (413-781-7111) and the 325-room **Sheraton Springfield Monarch Place** (413-781-1010), both right at the downtown I-91 exit, both with indoor heated pools and full health clubs. Marriott rates are $129–179 per couple, and Sheraton's are $99–159. A 12-story, 245-room **Holiday Inn** (413-781-0900), 711 Dwight St. (I-291, exit 2A), has an indoor pool and rooftop restaurant. $79–159 double, but inquire about specials. The **Hilton Garden Inn** (413-886-8000 or 800-234-3744; www.springfield gardeninn.com) is an attractive 143-room hotel adjacent to the Basketball Hall of Fame (they share a parking lot) with a large indoor pool. $89–159.

Berkshire Folkstone Bed & Breakfast Homes (413-731-8785), 37 George St. This reservation service offers bed & breakfast in homes in Springfield and around Western Massachusetts. We were delighted with the one we stayed at; our host, a lifelong Springfield resident and enthusiast, insisted on giving us a tour of Forest Park. $75–350.

✳ Where to Eat

DINING OUT **Student Prince & Fort Restaurant** (413-788-6628; www.studentprince.com), 8 Fort St. (off Main). Open 11–11; Sun. noon–10. A downtown Springfield institution, the Student Prince was founded in 1935 by German immigrants, and its decor and menu are still thoroughly Germanic. The place is festooned with decorative beer steins—one of the largest collections of them in the country—and the extensive menu offers diners a choice of hearty Middle European dishes such as sauerbraten, Wiener schnitzel, Hungarian goulash, bratwurst, and chicken paprika. Specials change with the seasons. Lunch runs $5.95–19.95, dinner $10–25.

Zaffino's (413-781-0900), Holiday Inn, 711 Dwight St. At the top of a high-rise hotel, Zaffino's glass-walled dining room has a great panoramic view over the city and the Valley. The food—mainstream American with some Italian dishes—is pretty good, too. Entrées $11.50–23.95.

Storrowton Tavern & Carriage House (413-732-4188; www.storrow ton.com), 1305 Memorial Ave., West Springfield. Located in Storrowton Village Museum on the grounds of the Eastern States Exposition, the tavern occupies two antique buildings that were moved to the site. It serves traditional New England fare such as Yankee pot roast and baked Boston scrod, along with some Italian specialties, year-round. Open Tue.–Sun. for lunch and dinner (daily 10–10 during the 17-day Eastern States Exposition in mid-Sep.). Reservations recommended. Luncheon entrées $8.95–12.95; dinner $14.95–24.95.

Cara Mia Ristorante (413-739-0101), 1011 E. Columbus Ave. Open Tue.–Sat. 4–10. An upstairs place in "Little Italy" with red-velvet decor, but delightfully nonstuffy. Jackets not mandatory, but the food is elegant and the wine list, extensive. The veal and lamb dishes are particularly good. Live Italian popular and classical music Fri.–Sat. nights. Entrées run $12.95–23.95.

Hofbrauhaus (413-737-4905; www .hofbrauhaus.org), 1105 Main St., West Springfield. The dining room features murals of German landscapes, and the atmosphere is quite formal but fun. Try deep-fried sauerkraut balls or goulash soup, a selection of good veal dishes, and a sparkling German wine among a choice of 300 vintages. Be sure to leave room for a torte. Dinner entrées are $14–26.

Red Rose Pizzeria (413-739-8519), 1060 Main St. Open Tue.–Sun. for lunch and dinner. A full-service restaurant despite the name, Red Rose is one of Springfield's most popular dining spots. The cavernous dining room seats 400 but there is often a line to get in, particularly on weekends. (Reservations are taken only for parties of 10 or more.) The food is authentically Italian and the portions, including the pizzas, are famously outsized. Entrées $9.50–16.99.

L'uVA (413-734-1010; www.luva.us), 1676 Main St. Open only for dinner. Specializes in eclectic dishes such as iron-charred swordfish with mangoes, honey and maple basted rack of lamb, or spinach-stuffed tilapia. There are some 500 different vintages on the wine list, more than 50 of which are available by the glass. Dinner entrées $16–30.

EATING OUT **Gus & Paul's** (413-781-2253), Tower Square, 1500 Main St. A popular breakfast and lunch spot in downtown Springfield. Freshly baked bagels and deli sandwiches are the specialty; also egg dishes like egg and pastrami scramble, knishes, gefilte fish, blintzes, and chopped liver, not to mention knockwurst on a bagel with mustard and kraut. There is also always a choice of freshly made soups, sandwiches, and salads; beverages include Dr. Brown's Soda, including celery flavor (our favorite and seldom seen.)

Cafe Lebanon (413-737-7373; www .cafelebanon.com), 1390 Main St. Traditional Middle Eastern cuisine at its flavorful best. Full liquor license. Live belly dancing every Fri. and Sat.

Blue Eagle (413-737-6135), 930 Worthington St. Open from 11:30 daily, until 9 Sun.–Thu., until 10 on weekends. Diner fans should drive—this is not a walking neighborhood—

GUS & PAUL'S DELI

Christina Tree

up Worthington Street to this popular place with a loyal local following. The menu is large and better than basic, ranging from a BLT to surf and turf, including lamb shish kebab and fried seafood dinners.

Mom & Rico's Market (413-732-8941), 899 Main St. Open Mon.–Fri. 8–5:30. A great Italian deli and grocery with a self-service buffet that usually includes lasagna, sausage and peppers, and eggplant parmigiana (better than your mother's). Pay by the pound or order from the large choice of grinders. This is headquarters for local bocci fans. For cappuccino and a cannoli, step next door to the La Fiorentina Pastry Shop (883 Main St.; see *Snacks*).

Frigo's (413-731-7797), 1244 Main St. Open Mon.–Fri. 8–5, until 6 in summer. The blackboard menu features take-out specialties like pizza rustica, veal parmigiana, large and interesting sandwich combinations; a favorite with the downtown lunch crowd. If you have time, step around to **Frigo's Market** at 90 Williams St., a cheese lover's mecca, also Italian cold cuts and takeout.

Lido (413-736-9433), 555 Worthington. Open Mon.–Sat. 11–11. Drive (don't walk) to this Italian favorite, good for the basics like lasagna and eggplant parmigiana and hot or sweet sausage. Best garlic bread in town.

Sitar (413-732-8011), 1688 Main St. Open Mon.–Sat. for lunch and dinner, Sun. for dinner 5–10. Sampler platters and luncheon specials help the uninitiated choose from a large menu of Indian and Pakistani dishes.

Uno's Chicago Bar & Grill (413-733-1300), 820 W. Columbus Ave. Open daily for lunch and dinner. A large, moderately priced family restaurant next to the Basketball Hall of Fame. Deep-dish pizza is the specialty, but there is a full menu. Live music nightly in the garden courtyard.

SNACKS La Fiorentina Pastry Shop (413-732-3151), 883 Main St. Open Mon.–Sat. 8–6, Sun. 8–2. The real thing. Mauro and Clara Daniele first opened La Fiorentina in 1947, using recipes for which Mauro's father Giuseppe had won awards for baking in Florence. Try the tiramisu (espresso, liqueur, mascarpone cheese, and cocoa powder layered between ladyfingers). Gelati, coffees, biscotti, many pastries, and known for rum cake soaked with rum and layered with custard and chocolate.

✳ Entertainment

City Stage (413-788-7033), 1 Columbus Center. Professional theater, Sep.–May.

MassMutual Center (413-787-6600; www.massmutualcenter.com), Main at E. Court St. Contains a 6,677-seat arena and hosts concerts, conventions, trade shows, and sporting events, including home games of the Springfield Falcons hockey team.

Symphony Hall (413-787-6600 or 413-788-7033). The classic, columned music hall on Court Square is the home of the Springfield Symphony Orchestra. It also stages top-name performers, Broadway shows, and children's theater.

The Hippodrome (413-787-0600), 1700 Main St. A former 1920s movie palace, now the largest nightclub in Western Massachusetts, featuring live (frequently Latin) entertainment.

Showcase Cinemas (413-733-5131), 864 Riverdale Rd., West Springfield; a multiplex showing first-run films.

✳ Selective Shopping

Tower Square (413-733-2171; www .visittowersquare.com), 1500 Main St., Springfield. This indoor mall has some 30 shops and restaurants selling clothing, books, antiques, and more.

Springfield Museums Gift Shop (413-263-6800; www.springfield museums.org), 220 State St., Spring-field. Located in the welcome center of the four-museum complex (adja-cent to the Science Museum), besides the usual museum store items this attractive shop has all the Dr. Seuss books and a wide assortment of Dr. Seuss–themed toys, stuffed animals, lunch boxes, and other gifts.

Holyoke Mall (413-536-1440; www .holyokemall.com) in the Ingleside section of Holyoke (I-91 exit 15, and Mass Pike exit 4). Open Mon.–Sat. 10–9:30, Sun. 11–6. The biggest mall in Western Massachusetts and one of the largest in New England. There are nearly 200 stores, with Macy's, JCPenney, and Sears among the anchors. Also a dozen food outlets.

✳ Farms

Bluebird Acres (413-525-6012), 747 Parker St., East Longmeadow. Open Apr.–Dec., daily 9–6. Some 80 differ-ent varieties of apples are grown and sold at this farm complex, which includes a grocery store and bakery.

Fini's Plant Farm (800-342-2205; www.finiplants.com), 217 James St., Feeding Hills. Open May–Oct., Mon.–Fri 8–6, weekends 9–5. A large selection of perennials, annuals, and herbs. There are wagon rides, corn

and hay mazes, and a perennial garden.

Bird Haven Blueberry Farm (413-527-4671; www.birdhavenblueberry .com), 55 Gunn Rd., Southampton. Open year-round, Tue.–Fri. 9–6, weekends 9–5. Homemade pies, jams, and jellies sold at the farm store. Pick-your-own flowers, blueberries, and raspberries in-season.

Calabrese Farms (413-569-6417), 257 Feeding Hills Rd. (Rt. 57), Southwick. Open Apr.–Sep., daily 8:30–7. Has bedding plants, hangers, geraniums, and perennials in spring, its own corn, tomatoes, melons, and other produce in summer.

Coward Farms (413-569-6724), Col-lege Hwy. (Rt. 202), Southwick. Open from the day after Thanksgiving through the Christmas season. Cut-your-own Christmas trees (four kinds of fir trees and blue spruce) as well as

Kim Grant

wreaths, swags, and kissing balls.

Ray's Family Farm (413-569-3366), 723 College Hwy. (Rts. 202 and 10), Southwick. Open mid-Apr. through Dec., daily 8–8. Annual bedding plants and farm-grown produce.

Kosinski Farms/North Country Harvest (413-562-4643; www .kosinskifarms.com), 420 Russellville Rd., Westfield. Open Jan.–Mar., Tue.– Sun. 8–5; Apr.–Dec., daily 6–8. Plants, flowers, apples, berries, also sweet corn, pumpkins, and other produce. The farm store sells bread, muffins, mulled cider, and fresh fruit sundaes. There is a corn maze. Special events include blueberry, apple, and pumpkin fests; Santa visits the month before Christmas. Daily hayrides Sep.–Nov., with "haunted hayrides" on weekends around Halloween.

Pomeroy Farm (413-568-0049 or 413-568-3484), Russellville Rd., Westfield. Sugarhouse open mid-Feb. through first week in Apr.; farm stand open seasonally selling fresh produce. Maple syrup, candy, and gift baskets are available year-round. B&B accommodation is available (413-568-3783).

✳ Special Events

Note: For event information, call 413-787-1548 or visit www.valleyvisitor .com.

May: **World's Largest Pancake Breakfast** (413-733-3800), Eastfield Mall, Boston Road, Springfield.

June: **WestSide's Taste on the Common** (413-734-1118), Town Common, West Springfield. More than 25 restaurants participate.

July: **Star Spangled Springfield** (413-733-3800) is a Fourth of July celebration with live music, food, an arts festival, and fireworks in Court Square.

July–August: Sunday performances by **Springfield Pops** in Stanley Park, Westfield. Theatrical and musical performances in Forest Park, Sunday evenings.

July–September: Free concerts in **Stearns Square** Thursday evenings.

September: **Harambee Festival of Black Culture**, Winchester Square, Springfield. **Eastern States Exposition** (413-737-2443), West Springfield. "The Big E" is the biggest annual fair in the East with livestock shows, horse shows, a giant midway, and entertainment. Always runs 17 days, including the third week in September.

Quadrangle Weekend (413-737-1750) features outdoor festivities, films, lectures, and crafts demonstrations.

Mattoon Arts Festival is an outdoor fair on a downtown Springfield street lined with brownstones and gaslights.

October: **FrightFest** (413-786-9300), Six Flags New England, Agawam.

November: **Parade of the Big Balloons** (413-733-3800), downtown Springfield (*day after Thanksgiving*).

Late November–mid-January: **Bright Nights at Forest Park** (413-733-3800) is New England's largest Christmas light display, with themes like Seuss Land, Victorian Village, and North Pole Village. Evenings from six o'clock.

INDEX